PAKI

THE FORMA

1857–1948

PAKISTAN

THE FORMATIVE PHASE

1857–1948

KHALID B. SAYEED

with a foreword by
GEORGE CUNNINGHAM

Second Edition

OXFORD
UNIVERSITY PRESS

OXFORD
UNIVERSITY PRESS

Oxford University Press is a department of the University of Oxford.
It furthers the University's objective of excellence in research, scholarship,
and education by publishing worldwide. Oxford is a registered trade mark of
Oxford University Press in the UK and in certain other countries

Published in Pakistan by
Oxford University Press
No. 38, Sector 15, Korangi Industrial Area,
PO Box 8214, Karachi-74900, Pakistan

© Oxford University Press 1968

The moral rights of the author have been asserted

First Edition published in Pakistan by Pakistan Publishing House, Karachi, 1960
Second edition published by Oxford University Press, London, 1968
Reprinted in Pakistan 1969

This edition in Oxford Pakistan Paperbacks 1998

ISBN 978-0-19-577114-5

Twenty-fifth Impression 2019

Typeset in Baskerville
Printed on 55gsm Book Paper

Printed by The Times Press Pvt. Ltd., Karachi

PREFACE

The first edition of *Pakistan—The Formative Phase* consisted of five parts and the period it dealt with was 1857–1960. The present edition, as the title suggests, deals with a shorter period, that is, 1857 to 1948. The present edition also has an additional chapter, Chapter 10, 'The Viceregal System and the Muslim Nationalist Movement'.

I have tried to trace the growth of the Muslim separatist movement from the year 1857. This does not mean that a full assessment of Muslim participation in the Mutiny of 1857 has been attempted. The year 1857 has been treated as a turning point. An influential section of Muslims led by Sir Sayyid Ahmad Khan impressed upon the Muslims that the failure of the Mutiny clearly meant that the old order could not be resuscitated. Instead of withdrawing themselves into an attitude of gloom and despair, Muslims could save Islam and at the same time build a prosperous future for their community by adopting a modern outlook and taking full advantage of Western education. Instead of ending the formative phase of Pakistan on 14 August 1947, when Pakistan was established, I have carried the analysis forward to 1948, when Jinnah died. This has been done in order to show that the foundations on which the future political structure of Pakistan was built were shaped both by a whole set of events preceeding the year 1947 as well as by the unique role that Jinnah played both as the President of the All-India Muslim League and, after 14 August 1947, as the Governor General of Pakistan. Thus, it is in this sense that the author has suggested that the period 1857 to 1948 represents the formative phase in Pakistan's political development.

This book is not a mere historical narrative, but an attempt by a Political Scientist to evaluate the strength and weaknesses of the Muslim separatist movement that eventually culminated in the creation of Pakistan. There has been a tendency among Muslim writers and intellectuals to attribute the creation of Pakistan to Hindu short-sightedness and exclusiveness, whereas Indian intellectuals and writers have explained the establishment of Pakistan as a result of certain wrong tactical moves that the Congress Party made in its dealings both with the British and the Muslim League. Neither of these views seems to do full justice to the depth and intensity of the Muslim separatist movement. In addition to the basic theme of the Muslim nationalist movement, the author has also kept in focus the working and development of the British Viceregal system. If it can be said that the Muslim separatist movement was perhaps the most creative force behind the establishment of Pakistan, it may also be said that the Viceregal system that Pakistan has inherited from the British has sustained the State of Pakistan as an on-going political entity despite the political and cultural tensions it has faced ever since its establishment.

Sir Francis Mudie (Governor of Sind, 1946–7, and Governor of West Punjab, 1947–9) and the late Sir George Cunningham (Governor of the NWFP, 1937–45 and 1947–8) have placed me in enormous debt by letting me read their diaries and papers. In addition, both Sir Francis Mudie and Sir George Cunningham were kind enough to read the earlier drafts of some of the chapters. I profited immensely from their comments and suggestions. A list of persons interviewed appears towards the end of the book. To each one of these I am deeply grateful, for without the insights gained from these interviews the analysis that emerges in the book would not have been possible. I should also like to record my thanks to Mr Neal Burton and Mr Jon Stallworthy of the Oxford University Press. The help that I received from my wife at every stage of the writing of this book has been indispensable.

Queen's University,   K. B. S.
Kingston, Ontario.
12 June 1967

FOREWORD

Even if this admirably written book is not the last word in the history of Pakistan up to the present day—for some sources are probably not yet revealed to us—it is a book of enormous value. It collects in a scholarly and impartial survey a mass of material which no historian of the future can neglect.

There is, to begin with, a fair and well-balanced account of the diverse factors which periodically heightened or lowered the tension between Hindus and Muslims from the early days of political consciousness. The more spectacular incidents in this long story are familiar—Sir Sayyid Ahmad's missionary achievements, the emergence of the Indian National Congress and later of the Muslim League, the partition of Bengal, the coming of separate electorates, the Khilafat movement, and then the more recent manoeuvres of both sides as the prospect of eventual Dominion Status or Independence grew nearer. All this is excellently told. And the impact of the British Government's policy on this varying temperature chart is described without prejudice. The idea that Britain looked on as a *tertius gaudens* is scouted.

It is when we come to the last four or five convulsive years before the great Partition that I feel we are not yet in full possession of all the historical sources that may one day be available. Of exceptional interest I find the writer's account of what Jinnah thought about the Cabinet Mission's proposals in 1946. It was briefly this; that if Pakistan were not conceded, Jinnah would not be averse to the idea of a Super Centre entrusted by both sides to look after certain common subjects. There is too the illuminating comment of Maulana Abul Kalam Azad that, if the Congress had shown sufficient patience and far-sightedness and followed Lord Wavell's advice on the matter, Pakistan would not have been inevitable. This kind of speculation is no doubt academic. In 1947 Pakistan became, and is today, a reality of which there can be no question. But the historical problem is still one of intense interest—at what exact point (and there must have been at one particular moment a knife-edge decision) did Jinnah discard this quasi-federal idea and make up his mind that complete severance was the only solution?

It is possible, I think, that if Lord Wavell's private papers were made available, much light might be shed on the vitally important discussions which took place, both after and before the Cabinet Mission, during the two or three years preceding Partition. The silences of Lord Wavell have become almost legendary, but in reading this book one continually feels the extent of the power which the Viceroy still wielded in negotiating a long-term decision between the two major parties during 1946–7. In the last three or four months of his office the pace of the controversy, of which the Cabinet Mission's plan formed the main basis, accelerated at terrifying speed. I think justice has yet to be done to the part Lord Wavell played in these years of destiny.

The latter part of the book gives a clear and penetrating account of the development of Pakistan since Partition and of the difficulties she has had to face. The survey is in places critical but on the whole wisely optimistic, and the estimate the author has made of the leading personalities is not likely to be seriously challenged by future historians. I think he is right in holding that Jinnah was the only possible choice for the Governor Generalship. The criticism voiced by the *Economist* among others that as an active party politician Jinnah should have been ruled out is blind to the fact that in August 1947 the Muslim League was not merely a political party; it was in reality the 'successor authority' and its leader naturally took on the mantle of the Viceroy of India. I know without a doubt, having worked directly under him for nine months thereafter, that the Quaid-i-Azam never let party spirit influence his conduct of his high office.

Khalid bin Sayeed has deserved well of Pakistan in giving us this history, so well written and so thorough in its scope.

George Cunningham

Mavishaugh,
St. Andrews, Scotland.
4 October 1960

CONTENTS

PART ONE
ORIGINS OF PAKISTAN

1 Conflicting Views About the Origin of Pakistan   3

2 Anglo-Muslim Conciliation and the Beginnings of Hindu-Muslim Tension in India, 1857–1914   13

3 Attempts at Hindu-Muslim Unity, 1916–40   34

4 The Emergence of Pakistan—I   102

5 The Emergence of Pakistan—II   134

6 The Muslim League. Its Role and Organization   176

PART TWO
CONTINUATION OF THE VICEREGAL SYSTEM IN PAKISTAN, 1947–8

7 Jinnah's Appointment as Governor General of Pakistan   223

8 Constitutional and Political Powers of the Governor General   233

9 The Centre and the Provinces, 1947–8   258

10 The Viceregal System and the Muslim Nationalist Movement   279

Appendix I   301

Appendix II   306

Select Bibliography   308

Select List of Persons Interviewed   317

Index   321

PART ONE

ORIGINS OF PAKISTAN

'One lesson I have learnt from the history of Muslims. At critical moments in their history it is Islam that has saved Muslims and not *vice versa*.'

Sir Muhammad Iqbal

Presidential address, All-India Muslim League, Allahabad, 29 December 1930

'The politician in me has never dominated a single decision of mine, and if I take part in politics, it is only because politics encircle us today like the coil of a snake, from which one cannot go out, no matter how much one tries. In order to wrestle with this snake, I have been experimenting with myself and my friends in politics by introducing religion into politics.'

Mahatma Gandhi

Young India, 12 May 1920

1 CONFLICTING VIEWS ABOUT THE ORIGIN OF PAKISTAN

How does one explain the origin of Pakistan? Is Pakistan the final fulfilment of a clear, uninterrupted, and separate stream of Muslim political consciousness in Indian history? Or is it the crown and consummation of the British policy of 'divide and rule' in India? Mahatma Gandhi, whilst speaking in the second session of the Round Table Conference in London in 1931, said that the quarrel between Hindus and Muslims was 'coeval with the British advent' in India. It would be difficult to maintain such a position historically because the conflict between Hindus and Muslims had started long before the emergence of the British power in India. Perhaps Emperor Aurangzeb (1658–1707) was responsible for increasing Hindu-Muslim tension by trying to Islamicize the Moghal government. Several Muslim historians have actually glorified Aurangzeb for making Muslims conscious of their separate religious and ideological identity. It is also true that Maratha and Sikh leaders raised their banner of revolt against Aurangzeb because in trying to organize his government on Islamic lines, the Emperor was acting against their interests. Sir Jadunath Sarkar's observation on the role of Shivaji, the Maratha leader, is revealing:

> Shivaji has shown that the tree of Hinduism is not really dead, that it can rise from beneath the seemingly crushing load of centuries of political bondage, exclusion from the administration, and legal repression; it can put forth new leaves and branches; it can again lift its head up to the skies.[1]

After Aurangzeb's death, Muslim power started disintegrating. Muslims were so alarmed by the growing power of the Hindus under Maratha leadership that even a Sufi scholar like Shah Waliullah (1703–81), who would have normally passed his life

---

[1] Sir Jadunath Sarkar, *Shivaji and His Times*, Calcutta: Sarkar, 1952, p. 390.

either in meditation or teaching Islamic theology, was moved into writing a letter to Ahmad Shah Abdali to implore India to protect the Muslim position. In his letter to the Afghan King, Shah Waliullah wrote:

> In short, the Muslim community is in a pitiable condition. All control of the machinery of government is in the hands of Hindus, because they are the only people who are capable and industrious. Wealth and prosperity are concentrated in their hands, while the share of Muslims is nothing but poverty and misery.... At this time you are the only King who is powerful, far-sighted, and capable of defeating the enemy forces. Certainly it is incumbent upon you to march to India, destroy Maratha domination and rescue weak and old Muslims from the clutches of non-Muslims. If, God forbid, domination by infidels continues, Muslims will forget Islam and within a short time become such a nation that there will be nothing left to distinguish them from non-Muslims.[2]

It has also been argued that Muslim separatism really started after the British conceded separate electorates to Muslims in 1909. This decision has often been described as a deliberate attempt on the part of the British to divide the electorate and thus disrupt the growing Indian Nationalist movement. I examine these arguments in the following chapter, but the point which merits some consideration is whether separate electorates created a new political gulf between Hindus and Muslims, or whether the decision to grant separate electorates was no more than a recognition of the cultural and religious differences that already existed between Hindus and Muslims. Prior to 1909, when separate electorates were granted, no two books were more representative of Muslim and Hindu ways of thinking than Altaf Husain Hali's *Musaddas* (*The Ebb and Flow of Islam,* 1879) and Bankim Chandra Chatterjee's *Anandamath* (*The Abbey of Bliss,* 1882). Hali, in a lucid and flowing verse, described the rise and fall of Islam as a political and cultural force in the world. 'With my unskilful hands,' he wrote in the preface, 'I have constructed a house of mirrors, in which Muslims will find their face and stature reflected and can see what they were and what they have become.'[3] The entire burden of Hali's *Musaddas* was to

---

[2] Khaliq Ahmad Nizami, ed., *Shah Waliullah Ke Siyasi Maktuba* (*Political Letters of Shah Waliullah*), Aligarh: 1951, p. 106.

[3] Altaf Husain Hali, *Musaddas-i-Hali* (*The Ebb and Flow of Islam*), Lahore & Karachi: Taj. n.d., p. 5.

appeal to Indian Muslims to discard their ignorance, indolence, and selfishness and forge ahead as a disciplined, industrious, and united nation. *Anandamath,* portraying the rise of Hindu nationalism during the decline of Muslim power in Bengal, sounded a clarion call to Hindus to arise from their languor and take up arms against the degenerate and oppressive Muslim rule. Hindu leaders in the novel made it clear that their struggle was not against the British, who had really come to India as liberators, but against Muslim tyranny and misrule. Though the plot of *Anandamath* dealt with the themes of a bygone age, it left a clear impression on the minds of its readers that Hindus were still bitter towards Muslims.

However, one can argue that even if it were admitted that the Hindu-Muslim conflict existed both before the emergence of British power in India and the introduction of separate electorates in 1909, the British could have used their imperial power to compose these differences and help the two communities to evolve a common nationality. The British not only failed to do this but actually widened the gap that existed between the two communities through the concession of separate electorates to Muslims. These are very formidable arguments. But it may be pointed out that no imperial power in history has been so benevolent and farsighted as to bring about a *rapprochement* between two rival communities. The traditional British approach in the matter of racial or tribal conflict in the colonies has been very largely that of *laissez faire.* Furthermore, there was no guarantee that joint electorates would have necessarily helped Hindus and Muslims to develop a national outlook in political matters. On the contrary, it was possible that joint electorates, in the short run, when Muslim political leaders were thinking primarily in communal terms, might have worsened the relations between the two communities. At every election in those constituencies where Muslims were in substantial numbers, communal riots might have flared up. Joint electorates might have helped in the long run, but as it turned out Congress leaders were simply not prepared to wait long enough under British tutelage for parliamentary institutions to strike deep roots in the Indian soil.

Even if one were to concede some of the harmful consequences of separate electorates, it could still be argued that a generous attitude on the part of the majority community might have more than neutralized most of these harmful consequences. For example, if the Indian National Congress had agreed to include representatives of the Muslim League in the Provincial Congress Cabinets in 1937, much communal rancour and bitterness might have been avoided. Thus, if the British had planned to divide Hindus and Muslims, it seems that the Congress and Muslim League leaders did very little to frustrate British designs. It may also be stated in passing that some writers in their keenness to prove the 'divide and rule' thesis, tend to ignore the unifying influences of British rule in India—namely, modernization of Indian life through education, commerce, and industry, and the establishment of centripetal institutions like the Civil Service, the Army, and the Judiciary.

The British were caught in a vicious circle, which was not entirely of their own making, and from which there was probably no easy way out. The problem of administering justice between Hindus and Muslims was not merely a matter of holding balance between two equal communities. Muslims were not only a minority community, but also a politically backward community in the sense that they lagged behind the Hindus in education, in commerce, in political organization and leadership. To start with, when the British established their power in India, Muslims were sulky and resisted what they regarded as the imposition of British education and political system in India. The British impact on Hindu areas was not only earlier but was received with greater enthusiasm. The Hindus, unlike the Muslims, took to the learning of English with great eagerness and proficiency and soon supplanted the Muslims in most of the important offices of administration. When the Muslims found that they were being reduced to an inferior economic and social status, they tried to acquire English education and assure the British that they also would be loyal to their rule. The British, on the other hand, felt that they had probably been unfair to Muslims and, impressed by their pledges of loyalty, tried to help them. This created resentment among the Hindu intelligentsia and, particularly when Lord Curzon inaugurated his scheme of the partition of Bengal in 1905, there was a hue and cry among the Hindus in India. The British yielded to Hindu agitation, and revoked partition. In the wake of this, there followed a series of events in the Middle East which confirmed Muslim fears and suspicions regarding the

British policy towards Muslims in general and Muslim powers like Turkey in particular. A barometer of Muslim anger was the Khilafat Movement (1920–2) which was perhaps the first and the last occasion when Hindus and Muslims on an all-India and massive scale cooperated with each other in a political movement. The Hindu-Muslim conflict was further heightened when more and more political power was placed on the counter by the British after 1919, and Hindu and Muslim leaders appeared as rival contenders to grab as much of it as possible for their respective communities. Unfortunately, progressive realization of responsible government turned out to be progressive aggravation of the Hindu-Muslim conflict. The struggle for power between Hindus and Muslims, which the British policy of transferring more and more power to Indian hands generated, had its economic dimensions as well. Muslims and Hindus not only competed against each other for Government posts but also for jobs and opportunities created in the wake of industrialization and urbanization in India. Muslim middle-classes, starting from a backward position in this competitive struggle, found the idea of Pakistan extremely attractive because this would mean that Muslim banks, Muslim industries, and Muslim commercial houses would be established in Muslim Pakistan with the fear of Hindu competition removed permanently from their state. It was significant that Muslim commercial communities like the Memons and the Khojas in Bombay and Calcutta gave considerable financial support to the Muslim League during the elections of 1945–6. It may also be noted that Jinnah, who was a Khoja by origin and a successful lawyer in Bombay, enjoyed this support from the commercial communities more than any other Muslim leader, and this gave him a distinct advantage over leaders from areas like the Punjab and Bengal. Thus, it would not be fair or accurate to think that Muslim separatism was a product entirely of British machinations. It was Maulana Muhammad Ali, at one time an ardent Indian Nationalist and the famous leader of the Khilafat Movement, who told the British Government in the Round Table Conference in 1930 'We divide and you rule.'

The pendulum of British policy continued to oscillate between the two points—concession of Hindu demands and support of Muslim interests. In 1937, Congress governments were installed in office in seven provinces and Muslims became resentful and

suspicious once again. In August 1940, when the Congress refused
to cooperate with the British war effort, the Muslims were given
a solemn assurance by the British that no constitutional advance
in India would be contemplated without their assent and approval.
It would indeed be a daring historian who would single out the
British for all blame, because they were not complete masters of
the circumstances in which they were placed. They occupied the
apex, but the other two points of the triangle were held by Hindus
and Muslims.

For the Congress, the establishment of Pakistan was a cruel
blow to their claim of being a Nationalist organization. It meant
that Muslims did not trust the Hindus as a majority community
to be just and generous towards Muslim interests and culture. This
explains why Congress leaders have often tended to attribute the
creation of Pakistan almost entirely to the British policy of 'divide
and rule'. Obviously, Muslim leaders cannot accept this view, for
it not only belittles the tenacity and brilliant strategy of Jinnah
and the Muslim League, but also questions their claim that the
most potent force behind the Pakistan movement was the
consciousness of Muslims of being a separate nation. Truth
should lie somewhere between these two positions. The creation
of Pakistan was probably helped by British unwillingness, matched
by their inability to compose the differences between Hindus and
Muslims. But in the main, Pakistan was the end product of
Muslim anxiety at first to establish cultural and political autonomy
within the framework of a federal India, and later of their bold
assertion that Muslims, being a separate nation, must have a
sovereign state.

Muslims often claim that Pakistan came into being not only
because the Muslims in India were intensely conscious of their
national and cultural identity, but also because the Hindu
community in India was intolerant and exclusive. They do not
seem to be aware that this argument suggests that a genuine
secular attitude and magnanimity on the part of the majority
Hindu community might have overcome Muslim separatism and
thus avoided the partition of the subcontinent. Muslims argue that
just as Caste Hindus have maintained caste segregation against
Hindu inferior castes, the Hindu community, dominated by
Brahmins, has also regarded Muslims, who ate beef and brought
with them an alien culture as *Melechas* (unclean). Hindus, on

the other hand, have remembered the indignities and the occasional religious persecution that they suffered under Muslim rule in India. Even Jawaharlal Nehru admitted that many a Congressman was a communalist under a national cloak.[4] Similarly, a bitter opponent of the Muslim League, Maulana Abul Kalam Azad, pointed out that Jinnah could not be blamed entirely for the turn of events that brought about the establishment of Pakistan. It was Sardar Patel who had been communal-minded from the beginning and later, as a result of the obstructive attitude of the Muslim League in the Interim Government, became convinced that Muslims and Hindus were separate nations and that partition was the only solution. According to Azad, if the Congress had shown sufficient patience and far-sightedness and had followed Lord Wavell's advice on the matter, Pakistan would not have been inevitable.[5]

It would not be fair to think that Hindu short-sightedness or exclusiveness was the sole factor which created Pakistan. There were several Hindu leaders like Gandhi, the two Nehrus (Motilal Nehru and Jawaharlal Nehru), Sir Tej Bahadur Sapru, and C. Rajagopalachari who tried their best to be fair and sympathetic towards the Muslim demands. But after 1940 the charismatic leadership of Jinnah and the organization of the Muslim League had given Muslims a sense of power, and they were no longer interested in constitutional safeguards and assurances. It seemed that prior to 1940 the Muslims often regarded themselves as an aggrieved minority. They did not realize that at least in part the alleged Hindu hostility to their religion and culture was a product of Muslim ethnocentricity and a thinly concealed contempt for some of the practices of the Hindu religion. However, after the Pakistan Resolution of March 1940 was passed, the dominant theme in Muslim politics was not complaint against Hindu injustice but a demand for a separate political existence. Thus, it may be argued that Muslim separatism rather than Hindu exclusiveness was the principal cause behind the creation of Pakistan.

It is well known that Islam stresses the religious uniqueness and

---

[4] Jawaharlal Nehru, *An Autobiography*, London: The Bodley Head, 1958, p. 136.

[5] Maulana Abul Kalam Azad, *India Wins Freedom*, Calcutta: Orient Longmans, 1959, pp. 15, 177–8, 185.

cohesiveness of the Muslim community. This theme is also constantly preached in the sermons that are delivered in mosques every Friday. Muslim masses enthusiastically embraced the two-nation theory of the Muslim League, not because it was a revolutionary doctrine but because it confirmed the basic theme of the Qur'an and the sermons they had heard in the mosques. In addition, memories of Muslim rule in India not only remained alive, particularly among the upper-class Muslims, but were constantly used by them to impress upon the Muslim masses that having ruled India, Muslims should not allow themselves to be ruled by the Hindu majority. It was because of such separatist tendencies and memories of former Muslim rule in India that there was little deep-seated love for India as their motherland on the part of the Muslim élite.

Congress leaders tried to challenge the two-nation theory by pointing out that a large number of Muslims in India were descendants of Hindu forebears who had been converted to Islam. They also argued that there was hardly any cultural difference between Hindus and Muslims in the rural areas where the vast majority of both communities lived. But these arguments could not alter the fact that a change in religion from Hinduism to Islam in the Indian context not merely implied a change in one's religion, but also a significant change in the man's social and cultural status. The new convert became a member of an egalitarian social order as compared to the rigid caste distinctions of the Hindu community. In addition, it should be remembered that for at least seven hundred years Islam was a decisive cultural and social force in large parts of India. Particularly in the North Western part of India, which constitutes West Pakistan today, the dominant culture that emerged was clearly Islamic. As Sir Denzil Ibbetson observed: 'Where the tone and feeling is that of the country beyond the Indus, as it is on the Punjab Frontier, the Hindu even is almost as the Mussalman.'[6] It was true that as one moved away from the Indus basin, the Islamic cultural stream lost some of its vigour and identity, except at Muslim cultural centres like those in the United Provinces and Hyderabad. But it must be noted that ever since the disintegration of the Muslim empire, Muslim religious reformers tried to purify Muslims of

[6] Sir Denzil Ibbetson, *Punjab Castes*, Lahore: Government Printing, 1916, p. 14.

Hindu idolatrous customs and superstitions because they were against the spirit of Islam. The *Faraiziyah* movement[7] among the Muslims of Bengal was an outstanding example of this reformist movement.

Another popular view regards Pakistan as no more than a personal triumph of the brilliant strategy and will-power of Quaid-i-Azam Mohammad Ali Jinnah. Some have even gone so far as to suggest that had Jinnah died earlier, there would not have been Pakistan.[8] It is true that Jinnah's great role was a highly important contributory factor, but without intense religious fervour and zeal for an Islamic state on the part of Muslim masses, Jinnah could not have achieved Pakistan. Khilafat leaders like Maulana Muhammad Ali and Maulana Abul Kalam Azad and poets like Hali, Akbar Allahabadi, and Iqbal were mainly responsible for making Muslims conscious of their separate national and cultural identity. Thus, when the message of Pakistan was presented to the masses, it fell on fertile soil. Jinnah, who did not know Urdu, could not have achieved Pakistan without able and zealous lieutenants and without the vision of an Islamic state as an inspiring stimulant. One may even go so far as to say that the Muslim League, led largely by middle-class Muslim leaders, would have probably come to some sort of compromise on the issue of Pakistan had they not been swept off their feet by the intense Islamic fervour of the masses and the astounding success that the Muslim League achieved during the elections of 1945–6.[9] It has been reported that the Quaid-i-Azam himself never expected to see Pakistan in his lifetime.[10]

Each view taken by itself is a highly exaggerated account of the origin of Pakistan. Each, perhaps, contributed its share and Pakistan was brought about by a multiplicity of factors. But

---

[7] This was a puritanical movement, the aim of which was to take the Muslims back to the essentials of their faith and purify Islam as practised in India of Hindu idolatrous practices.

[8] Michael Brecher, *Jawaharlal Nehru: A Political Biography*, London: Oxford University Press, 1959, p. 353.

[9] The Muslim League did accept the Cabinet Mission Plan of 1946 which rejected the Pakistan scheme. It withdrew its acceptance when the Congress acceptance of the Cabinet Mission Plan turned out to be a conditional acceptance with its own interpretations of the Cabinet Mission proposals.

[10] Hector Bolitho, *Jinnah: Creator of Pakistan*, London: John Murray, 1954, p. 195.

perhaps a dominant or decisive cause of Pakistan is that there has never taken place a confluence of the two civilizations in India— the Hindu and the Muslim. They may have meandered towards each other here and there, but on the whole the two have flowed their separate courses—sometimes parallel and sometimes contrary to one another.

The significance and reality of Pakistan has not been fully understood in the West. To the West, nationality based on religion is an alien and often incomprehensible phenomenon. This is because religion in the West has come to play such a restricted role. In the West, Germany and France are accepted as two separate nations. But the fact of Hindus and Muslims in India representing two separate cultural entities is seldom appreciated. A young French student may visit a family in Germany, share their meals, may attend the same church and even marry a girl in the family without creating a scandal or surprise. But such instances of intermarriage have been extremely rare in the Indian subcontinent. Even some of the most ardent Indian Nationalists have found the idea totally unacceptable. As Sir Abdur Rahim observed:

> Any of us Indian Muslims travelling for instance in Afghanistan, Persia, and Central Asia, among Chinese Muslims, Arabs, and Turks, would at once be made at home and would not find anything to which we are not accustomed. On the contrary, in India we find ourselves in all social matters total aliens when we cross the street and enter that part of the town where our Hindu fellow townsmen live.[11]

---

[11] Cited in Sir John Cumming, ed., *Political India* 1832–1932, London: Oxford University Press, 1932, p. 104.

2 ANGLO-MUSLIM CONCILIATION AND THE BEGINNINGS OF HINDU-MUSLIM TENSION IN INDIA, 1857–1914

It has been suggested in the first chapter that the roots of Pakistan can be found in the pre-British period, but its full germination took place on the eve of the British departure from India. Since this part of the book is an attempt to portray the major contours of the modern Muslim separatist movement in India, it will be quite appropriate and useful to begin the story after the Mutiny of 1857.

No historian has as yet made a definitive assessment of the exact Muslim role in the Mutiny. But all versions agree on two points. The British, being struck by the intense hostility of Muslims to British rule in Delhi and Oudh, were determined to enfeeble Muslims in such a way that they would not rise again. Secondly, the political future in such a context looked extremely bleak to Muslim leaders in India. The fiscal measure known as the 'resumptions', whereby all land-holders had to show their tide deeds, had deprived many Muslim land-holders of their estates. Next to land, military service had been their best source of income. Their alleged role in the Mutiny had dealt the final blow to this source as well. 'A hundred years ago, the Musalmans', wrote Sir William Hunter, 'monopolized all the important offices of state. The Hindus accepted with thanks such crumbs as their former conquerors dropped from the table....'[1] But Persian had ceased to be the official language under Lord William Bentinck (1828–35) and the result was that Muslims had lost their forte in administration. In 1871, in Bengal, of the 773 Indians holding responsible government jobs, the Muslims, even though their numbers were approximately equal to Hindus in the province,

---

[1] W. W. Hunter, *The Indian Musalmans*, Calcutta: The Comrade Publishers, 1945, p. 161

occupied only ninety-two positions as compared with 68I held by the Hindus.

I. SIR SAYYID STRIKES A NEW PATH

It was in such a sombre setting that Sir Sayyid Ahmad Khan (1817–98) emerged to guide the Muslims. Sir Sayyid had to wrestle against two forces. Muslims were not only defeatists in their outlook, but also sulky. Long before the Mutiny the Moghul princes had abdicated their political leadership to religious leaders. It was Sayyid Ahmad Barelawi (1786–1831) who had waged a *jihad* against the Sikhs in the Punjab and the Frontier. It was Shah Abd-ul-Aziz (1746–1824), the son of Shah Waliullah, who had issued the famous *fatwa* declaring that India had virtually come under Christian domination and therefore become a *dar-ul-harb* (zone of war).[2] Similarly, in East Bengal around 1831 there emerged the famous *Faraiziyah* movement, which was designed to rid Muslims of idolatrous and superstitious practices which they had imbibed from the Hindus. It was because of this that Sir William Hunter had described Muslim hostility to the British as a movement led by the *Wahhabis* and extending from the North-West Frontier to the remote and riverine East Bengal. And in a woeful vein he pointed out: 'It has always seemed to me an inexpressibly painful incident of our position in India that the best men are not on our side.'[3]

In earlier times Sir Sayyid was deeply impressed by the piety and yeoman services rendered by religious leaders to the cause of Muslims. His sentiments in this regard were expressed clearly in his *Asar-al-Sanadid*.[4]

Thus, political and religious leadership had gravitated towards religious reformers, and orthodox religious leaders, who having been worsted in their struggle against the British, were preaching against the encroachment of Western culture and the learning of

---

[2] The *fatwa* is cited in *A History of the Freedom Movement*, Vol. I, 1707–1831, Karachi: Pakistan Historical Society, 1957, p. 576.

[3] W. W. Hunter, op. cit., p. 136.

[4] Chapter IV of *Asar-al-Sanadid*, which had Sir Sayyid's biographical sketches and comments on religious leaders like Sayyid Ahmad Barelawi and Shah Abd-ul-Aziz, was deleted from subsequent editions of the book, which was first published in 1846. This chapter has now been republished in the recent edition brought out by Anjuman-i-Taraqqi Urdu of Pakistan.

Western languages and sciences. Sir Sayyid had, on one hand, to wrest political and intellectual leadership from this group and persuade Muslims to learn English and Western sciences and, on the other, convince the British Government that in spite of the apparent Muslim resentment and hostility, Muslims were genuinely loyal to the British Government. His main purpose in doing the latter was to induce the British to change their policy of hostility towards the Muslims.

The technique and strategy that Sir Sayyid adopted in driving home some of these lessons to the Muslims were significant. He urged the Muslims to learn English not only because it was in their worldly interests to do so, but also because it was the best way of defending their religion against Western attacks. He pointed out that Jews and Christians had ably and adroitly defended their sacred writings against the apparent discrepancies that had arisen between their religious doctrines and principles of science. Therefore, he pleaded, 'Whilst other nations are so watchful and diligent, shall we not be equally so.'[5] It must also be said to the credit of Sir Sayyid that he tried to understand the spirit and philosophy that lay behind English education. He made it clear that he was not merely interested in making Muslims good and efficient clerks or even administrative officers. For him, the real value of modern education lay in the fact that it was designed to improve character and social morals and make its recipients better citizens. Equipped with education, Muslims would thus be able to discharge their social obligations and work for the progress and welfare of their country.[6]

The problem which constantly engaged his attention was that of infusing a sense of profound loyalty to the British in the minds of Muslims. Again and again he pleaded with the Muslims that they should remain loyal to the British. He made it quite clear that Muslims owed their primary loyalty to the British Government, which had ensured peace and religious freedom in India. Muslims were not subjects of Sultan Abdul Hamid of Turkey. He was only a Muslim king and not their *Khalifa.*[7] He also pointed

---

[5] A speech in Persian with translation into English on *Patriotism and Necessity of Promoting Knowledge in India,* Ghazeepore: The Mohamedan Literary Society, 1863, p. 13.

[6] Sir Sayyid Ahmad Khan, *Akhree Mazameen,* Lahore; n.d., p. 28.

[7] Ibid., pp. 32–33.

out that Islam was tolerant and respectful towards Christians and Christian doctrines. Differences between Muslims and Christians were almost like differences between Unitarians and Orthodox Christians. The Crusades had been basically political and international wars and since they had been fought with Muslims, who professed a different faith, religious fervour had been injected into them.[8] These were all shrewd attempts on the part of Sir Sayyid to achieve two things. Firstly, he wanted to minimize all grounds of animosity which the Muslims were likely to harbour against the British. And secondly, he wanted to remove all doubts from the British mind that Muslims were not likely to be loyal to the British because their religion did not permit them to adopt such an attitude.

Another great service of Sir Sayyid which has not been sufficiently stressed by many historians and scholars was his attempt to initiate a religious reformation of Islam. He was sincerely convinced that unless Islam could satisfy its young educated followers that it was basically a rational religion it would not continue to evoke their loyalty. It is certainly true to say that Sir Sayyid was too much impressed by Western rationalism and wanted to show that every doctrine of Islam could measure up to all principles of science, reason and common sense. In doing this he was trying to be both a rationalist and a good Muslim. Thus he tried to explain Qur'anic references to Satan's revolt against God's command as regards paying his respect to Adam as a simile deliberately used to drive home certain moral lessons. There was no evidence in the Qur'an to support the usually accepted beliefs about the existence of *Jinns*. He pointed out that there was no reference to any miracles being performed by Muhammad in the Qur'an. Similarly, there was nothing in the Qur'an to suggest that Jesus was bodily lifted alive to the heavens. According to Sir Sayyid, it was usury which was forbidden in the Qur'an and not interest in the modern sense of the term.[9]

The Anglo-Oriental College which Sir Sayyid established in 1875 became the main vehicle of Muslim education and not of Islamic religious reformation. It was not only the orthodox *ulama* who vehemently disagreed with his religious views but also some

---

[8] Ibid., p. 56.

[9] Altaf Husain Hali, *Hayat-i-Jawid,* Lahore: Punjab Academy Trust, 1957, pp. 604–9.

of his own trusted lieutenants who were staunch in support of his educational policy. As Mr A. Yusuf Ali has pointed out:

> Either English education was to be jeopardized by the preaching of religious views obnoxious to the community, or orthodox religious views were to be taught inconsistent with the promoter's views. The latter course was chosen, without bringing the matter to a definite issue.[10]

Many tributes have been paid to Sir Sayyid, particularly by modern educated Muslims for being daring enough to put forward such views in an age which was by no means liberal or tolerant. But what has not been stressed is the fact that Sir Sayyid in trying to marry reason with religion was not being influenced only by Western ideas. His was also a Moghul mind which at its best was catholic and eclectic. Moghuls had not only left behind brilliant architecture but also liberal scholarship. W.H. Sleeman, talking about Muslim education, wrote:

> After his seven years of study, the young Mahomedan binds his turban upon a head almost as well filled with the things which appertain to these three branches of knowledge, as the young man raw from Oxford—he will talk as fluently about Socrates and Aristotle, Plato and Hippocrates, Galen and Avicenna.[11]

II. SIR SAYYID AND THE INDIAN NATIONAL CONGRESS

It has been alleged by a number of Indian scholars that Sir Sayyid's opposition to Muslims joining the Indian National Congress was largely inspired by British influence. In his pamphlet, *Causes of the Indian Revolt*, he had pleaded for the admission of Indians to Legislative Councils. How was it that he was totally against Muslims joining an organization, one of whose principal objectives was to work for an increasing measure of representative government?

It cannot be said that he was anti-Hindu. His views on Hindu-Muslim unity have been frequently quoted. He often described India as a beautiful bride whose two eyes were Hindu and Muslim. But what is often forgotten is the fact that to this picturesque description Sir Sayyid added the proviso that the beauty of India

---

[10] L.S.S. O'Malley, ed., *Modern India and the West*, London: Oxford University Press, 1941, p. 401.

[11] W. H. Sleeman, *Rambles of An Indian Official*, London: J. Hatchard, 1844, Vol. II, p. 283.

depended upon the fact that the two eyes shone with equal lustre.[12] As regards cow sacrifice, he went so far as to say that for the sake of unity Muslims should be quite willing to give up slaughtering cows.[13]

Altaf Husain Hali in his biography of Sir Sayyid suggests that Sir Sayyid became suspicious about Hindu intentions after 1867 when they started campaigning in Benares for the substitution of Hindi with its Devnagri script for Urdu with its Persian script as a court language. But in his writings Hali sees no inconsistencies in Sir Sayyid's attitude towards the Congress. He was friendly towards the Hindus but opposed to the objectives of the Congress. His reasoning was simple and familiar. He pointed out that the Congress objective of representative government meant that Muslims would be swamped by the Hindu majority. He was also vehement in his opposition to Muslims joining the Congress because he feared, as he made clear in his letter to Budruddin Tyabji, the first Muslim President of the Congress, that the logical outcome of Congress agitation would be violence in which Muslims, as in the Mutiny, would bear the brunt of the consequences.[14]

However, the reasoning that Sir Sayyid used against wholesale extension of representative government to India was prophetic. He pointed out that majority government was possible only where voters belonged to a homogeneous nation. Where they were not, as in the case of India which was a continent and not a country, this would spell nothing but disaster to the Muslim minority.[15] In his speech in 1883 in the Governor General's Council he pleaded: 'The larger community would totally override the interest, of the smaller community,' adding at the same time the shrewd observation, 'and the ignorant public would hold government responsible for introducing measures which might make the differences of race and creed more violent than ever.'[16] It was significant that the dispatch from the Government of India in 1892 also described Indian society as 'essentially a congeries of widely separated classes, races and communities with divergences

---

[12] Sir Sayyid Ahmad Khan, op. cit., p. 70.
[13] Ibid., p. 71.
[14] Altaf Husain Hali, op. cit., p. 323.
[15] Sir Sayyid Ahmad Khan, op. cit., p. 46.
[16] Cited in R. Coupland, *The Indian Problem*, New York: Oxford University Press, 1944, Part I, p. 156.

of interests and hereditary sentiment,' and suggested that such sectional opinions could be adequately represented only by the representatives of these groups.[17] It may also be noted that Sir Sayyid before the close of the nineteenth century was advancing the same views that came to be associated with Jinnah in his advocacy of Pakistan and the two-nation theory after 1940.

III. RESULTS OF SIR SAYYID'S EFFORTS TO PROMOTE ANGLO-MUSLIM FRIENDSHIP.

There is no doubt that Sir Sayyid was successful in persuading the Muslims to stay aloof from the Congress. Professor W.C. Smith disagrees with this view and quoting Budruddin Tyabji's Presidential Address at the Congress of 1887 suggests that Sir Sayyid was not successful in preventing large numbers of Muslims from attending Congress sessions.[18] However, there is no convincing evidence to support this view. In the Congress session of 1886 there were only 33 Muslim delegates out of 431.[19] Sir Surendranath Banerjee also takes the view that the Congress in those days was not successful in attracting many Muslims to its sessions.

> Our critics regarded the National Congress as a Hindu Congress, and the opposition papers described it as such. We were straining every nerve to secure the cooperation of our Mohamedan fellowcountrymen in this great national work. We sometimes paid the fares of Mohamedan delegates and offered them other facilities.[20]

Another attraction that was offered to the Muslims was the rule that no resolution affecting a particular community would be considered by the Congress if the delegates representing that community, even if they were in a minority, objected to it. In this way, a resolution urging the prohibition of cow slaughter suggested by a Hindu landlord of Bengal was disallowed at the Congress session of 1887.

---

[17] Ibid., p. 24.

[18] W. C. Smith, *Modern Islam in India*, Lahore: Ripon Press, 1954, pp. 22–23. For a full text of Budruddin Tyabji's speech at the Congress session of 1887, see *The Indian Nation Builders*, Madras: Ganesh, n.d, Part II, pp. 129–43.

[19] Haridas Mukherjee and Uma Mukherjee, *The Growth of Nationalism in India (1857–1905)*, Calcutta: Presidency Library, 1957, p. 164.

[20] Sir Surendranath Banerjee, *A Nation in the Making*, Madras: Oxford University Press, 1925, p. 108.

It is very difficult to say at what precise point there took place a change in British policy towards Muslims in India. But it was clear that sometime in the seventies and eighties of the nineteenth century the British Government realized that their policy towards the Muslims had been unduly hostile. It was in 1872 that Sir William Hunter published his famous book, *The Indian Musalmans.* In the concluding paragraph Hunter made it clear that the British Government would hold no parley with the conspirators. This was clearly a reference to those Muslims in the Frontier, Bihar and Bengal who were still thinking of defying the British *raj*. But at the same time, Hunter pointed out that the Government was determined to see that no legitimate grievances went unattended. 'This, however, it can do only by removing the chronic sense of wrong which has grown in the hearts of the Musalmans under British rule.'[21] Thus, in this sense Sir William Hunter could claim that his book might have brought about a significant change in British policy.

There was another Englishman, Wilfrid Scawen Blunt, who visited India in 1883-4 and wrote a book, *India Under Ripon: A Private Diary*, who also took credit for having 'contributed something towards the cause I have made specially my own, that of the Indian Mohammedans'. On his return to England, he persuaded Lord Randolph Churchill that Indian Muslims had not been justly treated. He thought that Churchill's visit as Secretary of State for India in 1885 marked a turning point in the official policy towards the Indian Muslims.[22]

How radical a change had taken place in British policy towards the Muslims in the eighties of the nineteenth century may be seen from the following statements. In 1843 Lord Ellenborough, writing to Lord Wellington, said, 'I cannot close my eyes to the belief that that race [the Muslims] is fundamentally hostile to us and our true policy is to reconcile the Hindus.'[23] On the other hand, Lord Dufferin, replying to a farewell address from the Mohammedan National Association of Calcutta of 1888, observed:

---

[21] W. W. Hunter, op. cit., p. 140.

[22] W. S. Blunt, *India Under Ripon: A Private Diary*, London: T. Fisher Unwin, 1909, pp. 230-1.

[23] Cited by A. R. Mallick, 'The Muslims and the Mutiny', *The Listener*, 30 May 1957, p. 876.

In any event, be assured, Gentlemen, that I highly value those marks of sympathy and approbation which you have been pleased to express in regard to the general administration of the country. Descended as you are from those who formerly occupied such a commanding position in India, you are exceptionally able to understand the responsibility attaching to those who rule.[24]

IV. HINDU REVIVALIST MOVEMENT

The British gained their first foothold in the coastal areas of the Provinces of Madras, Bombay, and Bengal. Therefore, these coastal areas of Southern and Eastern India, where Hindus were in a majority, were exposed first to the impact of British ideas and culture. Universities of Calcutta, Madras and Bombay were established in 1857. Hindus had learnt Persian under the Moghuls and become proficient in it to handle various administrative posts. They applied themselves with the same diligence to learning English, the language of their new masters. It was not only intellectual penetration but also religious. The Christian missionaries produced no tangible impression on the Muslims. It was the Hindu mind which came directly and indirectly under their spell. This explains why there were such progressive reform movements as that of Raja Ram Mohan Roy among the Hindus whereas Muslim religious movements were mainly products of Shah Waliullah and the *Wahhabi* influence from Arabia. In addition Muslims were slow in reconciling themselves to the unpleasant fact that with the disappearance of the Moghul Empire their system of education with Persian as its medium of instruction could not be of any help to them in obtaining administrative posts under the British Government. This educational and intellectual imbalance created in the early stages persisted for a long time and was very largely responsible for the conflict and tension that took place between the two communities.

Towards the end of the nineteenth century one notices the emergence of a Hindu revivalist movement. It was perhaps more anti-Muslim than anti-British. But there is no doubt that it had substantial anti-British strains in it. One of the first and outstanding spokesmen of this movement was Swami Vivekananda (1863–1902). The great Swami's doctrine in substance was that Hindus should go back to the Vedas and that Hinduism was superior to

---

[24] Cited in *The Indian Annual Register,* Calcutta, 1937, Vol. I, p. 34.

the materialism of the West. This was militant nationalism couched in religious terms. In his famous lectures in Chicago in 1893, he observed, 'I have gone to the world to preach a religion of which Buddhism is a rebel child and Christianity a distant echo...'[25]

In 1877 the Arya Samaj was established by Dayanand Saraswati (1827–1883) and its strongholds were mainly in Western and Northern India. It was a reformist movement whose aim was to purify Hinduism of some of its gross idolatrous practices. The founder thought that this would enable him to reconvert those Hindus who had been converted to Islam and Christianity. Like other reform movements, it glorified the Hinduism of the Vedas for 'everything worth knowing, even in the most recent inventions of modern science, was alluded to in the Vedas. Steam-engines, railways and steam-boats—all were shown to have been known, at least in their germs, to the poets of the Vedas.'[26]

Bankim Chandra Chatterjee, perhaps the most famous and popular of the novelists of Bengal, published *Anandamath* (The Abbey of Bliss) in 1882. The whole tenor of the novel was bluntly anti-Muslim. In the novel one comes across the community of children (children of Kali) who believed in no caste distinctions and whose sole purpose was to destroy every vestige of Muslim rule in India. One also sees Jivananda with sword in hand at the gate of the temple exhorting the children in the following words:

> We have often thought to break up this bird's nest of Moslem rule, to pull down the city of the renegades and throw it into the river—to turn this pig-sty to ashes and make mother earth free from evil again. Friends, that day has come.[27]

The community of children in the novel went about burning Muslim villages, plundering Muslim property and killing Muslims in a wholesale fashion. What was interesting to note was that Hindu leaders in this novel made it quite clear that they were not fighting against the British, who had come to India to free the country from Muslim clutches. Towards the end, when the children had won against the Muslims, the holy man who was

---

[25] Haridas Mukherjee and Uma Mukherjee, op. cit., p. 114.

[26] Edward Thompson and G. T. Garratt, *Rise and Fulfilment of British Rule in India*, Allahabad: Central Book Depot, 1958, p. 489.

[27] Bankim Chandra Chatterjee, *Anandamath*, translated by Nares Chandra Sen-Gupta, Calcutta: Padmini Mohan Neogi, n.d., p. 78.

guiding and inspiring the movement appeared and instructed the leader of the children to abandon fighting and cooperate with the British. The British in God's good time would purify the country and hand it over to the Hindus to rule it. It was in this novel that the famous song, *Bande Mataram* (Hail Mother), appeared. One can understand why the Muslims later (during 1937–9) objected vehemently to the Congress Governments adopting it as a national song.

Another revivalist movement with a strong political tinge was started in Maharashtra by Bal Gangadhar Tilak, a Chitpavan Brahmin. It was under a Chitpavan dynasty that the Maratha empire had reached its apex. Tilak's ideas were based on the teachings of the great Indian philosophical poem, the *Bhagavad Gita* or Song Celestial, and inspired by the cult of the Maharashtra leader, Shivaji. Tilak borrowed the idea from the Gita that killing one's enemy in the cause of duty was no crime. This idea had been put into practice by Shivaji, who ambushed and killed the Muslim general, Afzal Khan, by deception. According to Tilak, Shivaji had committed no crime in killing Afzal Khan and his methods should be employed to purge the country of *melechas* (unclean). In his newspaper, the *Kesari*, he wrote a remarkable article in which he portrayed Shivaji as returning to his native land and being horrified at what he saw. Tilak also opposed bitterly the passing in 1891 of the Age of Consent Act which prohibited cohabitation before a wife reached the age of twelve. The inevitable consequence was the formation of a 'society for the removal of obstacles to the Hindu religion'. Two Brahmin members of this society murdered two British officers engaged on plague duty in Poona. Two informers were also assassinated and Tilak was sent to jail for a short period.[28]

It may be pertinent to ask as to how Muslims could be expected to participate in the activities of the Indian National Congress which was very largely in the hands of Hindus of Bengal and Maharashtra. Whatever charges of divide and rule may be laid at the doors of the British Government, it has to be borne in mind that Hindus were displaying anti-Muslim sentiments towards the

---

[28] H. H. Dodwell, ed., *The Cambridge History of the British Empire*, Vol. V., London: Cambridge University Press, 1932, pp. 549–50. Also, H. G. Rawlinson, *The British Achievement in India*, London: William Hodge, 1948, pp. 185–6.

end of the nineteenth century. It cannot be said that the British had encouraged the Hindus to start a Hindu revivalist movement. The author is not suggesting that the Muslims were free from all blame. Prior to the Mutiny, both Barelawi's and the *Faraiziyah* movements were intended to purify Islam as practised in India of Hindu superstitions and ideas. They continued, but they did not possess the vigour of the Hindu revivalist movements towards the end of the nineteenth century. Again, the British could not be charged with having started a Muslim puritanical movement. It was obvious that Muslim and Hindu religions were not religions in the Western sense of the term for the social and political lives of their followers were intertwined with their religious practices. It was not easy for such cultures to coalesce to produce a united Indian nation.

V. THE PARTITION OF BENGAL

Speaking in the House of Lords in February 1912, Lord Curzon disclosed that he was not the author of the partition of Bengal for it had been discussed for twenty years before his day. The scheme as it took shape gave the impression that it was the old game of divide and rule. But the author has found no conclusive evidence which indicates that it was deliberately designed to disrupt growing Indian nationalism. First of all, Muslims in Bengal were too disorganized and backward to take an active part in Indian nationalism which was predominantly Hindu. Therefore, in this sense the British could not be accused of disrupting a united Hindu-Muslim nationalism when it did not exist. Quite understandably Hindu lawyers, merchants, and landlords were opposed to it because the partition was a blow at Calcutta's commercial and professional supremacy in Bengal. Creation of the new East Bengal province meant that some of the trade then coming to Calcutta would gravitate towards Chittagong, and Calcutta lawyers would also lose their clientele to Dacca which would become the capital and the legal centre of the new province.

In April 1902, Lord Curzon wrote to the Secretary of State regarding the question of provincial boundaries. In his opinion Bengal, with an area of nearly 200,000 square miles and with a population of 78½ million, was too large a charge for any single man. He also pointed out that the districts of East Bengal had been neglected and the neighbouring province of Assam was too small for efficient administration. But the administrators were fully acquainted with this problem and a discussion had been going on in their files for many months without the Viceroy knowing anything about it. When the departmental file reached the Viceroy's table a few days after his letter to the Secretary of State, it produced a typical Curzonian and caustic comment on departmentalism:

> For fourteen months it never occurred to a single human being in the Departments to mention the matter or to suggest that it should be mentioned. Round and round like the diurnal revolution of the earth went the file, stately, solemn, sure and slow; and now in due season it has completed its orbit and I am invited to register the concluding stage.[29]

One does not get an impression either from Sir Bampfylde Fuller or Sir Andrew Fraser, both of whom were principal architects of the partition scheme, that partition was anything other than an administrative device to tackle the administrative problem of a province which had become far too unwieldy.[30] It was at a later stage that Lord Curzon, confronted with implacable opposition from the Hindu press and politicians, went down to Dacca to mobilize Muslim support for the scheme. In Dacca, the Viceroy declared that the city would become:

> the centre and possibly the capital of a new and self-sufficing administration which must give to the people of these districts by reason of their numerical strength and their superior culture the preponderating voice in the province so created, which would invest the Mahomedans in Eastern Bengal with a unity which they have not enjoyed since the days of the old Mussulman Viceroys and Kings.[31]

The partition scheme was announced on 1 September 1905. The new province, called Eastern Bengal and Assam, consisted of Assam and Eastern and Northern Bengal—an area of 106,650

---

[29] Lord Ronaldshay, *The Life of Lord Curzon*, Vol. II, London: Ernest Benn, 1928, p. 321.

[30] Sir Bampfylde Fuller, *Some Personal Experiences*, London: John Murray, 1930, pp. 123–5, and Sir Andrew H. L. Fraser, *Among Indian Rajahs and Ryots*, Philadelphia: J. B. Lippincott, 1912, pp. 317–24.

[31] Cited in Haridas Mukherjee and Uma Mukherjee, *India's Fight for Freedom*. Calcutta: Firma K. L. Mukhopadhyay, 1958, p. 20.

square miles with a population of 31 million out of which 18 million were Muslims and 12 million were Hindus.

The Nationalists thought that this was a deliberate blow aimed at the growing solidarity and self-consciousness of the Bengali-speaking population. Taking a cue from the Chinese boycott of American goods, the Bengalis launched the *Swadeshi* movement whose sole purpose was to organize a boycott of British goods. The aim was to bring pressure on important textile interests in Britain who, the agitators thought, would in their turn pressure the home government into abandoning the partition scheme. Hundreds of meetings were held and students took an active part in these demonstrations.

The fiery editorials that appeared in the local press indicate the kind of nationalism that had grown in Bengal. India was represented as *Kali,* the grim goddess, dark and naked, bearing a garland of human heads around her neck-heads from which blood was dripping. This was the state of India under the foreigners—first the Muslims and then the British. A Calcutta paper *Yugantar* (New Era) of 30 May 1908 wrote:

> The Mother is thirsty, and is pointing out to her sons the only thing that can quench that thirst. Nothing less than human blood and decapitated human heads will satisfy her. Let her sons, therefore, worship her with these offerings, and let them not shrink even from sacrificing their lives to procure them. On the day on which the Mother is worshipped in this way in every village, on that day will the people of India be inspired with a divine spirit and a crown of independence will fall into their hands.[32]

All this resulted in no pitched battles between the British and the Bengali Hindus. The whole movement degenerated into political murders. Four attempts to assassinate the Lieutenant Governor of Bengal were made. Lord Minto escaped assassination at Ahmedabad, but the Political Secretary of Lord Morley, Secretary of State, was shot and killed in London. A bomb intended for a District Magistrate in Bengal killed two English ladies. The perpetrator of the outrage was hailed as a hero. A Bengali public prosecutor was shot dead.

The movement took a clear anti-Muslim turn and was run and organized on Hindu lines. Hindu goddesses and gods were

---

[32] Cited in H. G. Rawlinson, op. cit., p. 186.

appealed to and oaths were taken in the temple of Kali. It was well-known that partition would benefit Muslims of East Bengal. Sir Bampfylde Fuller, who became Governor, referred in his book to the tremendous Muslim enthusiasm in favour of partition. Muslims attended Thanksgiving prayers to celebrate the establishment of the new province.[33]

If Hindu leaders thought that this was a deliberate move on the part of the British Government to sow the seeds of conflict between Hindus and Muslims, it was not too much to expect that they would put forward an alternative scheme whereby the legitimate grievances of Muslims in Bengal could be satisfied. Nothing of this kind was ever attempted. The movement from the beginning took a Hindu turn and the agitators appealed to Hindu sympathies. Even a highly educated and responsible editor like Aurobindo Ghose in an editorial in *Bande Mataram* wrote:

> The ground work of what may well be called the composite culture of India is undoubtedly Hindu. Though the present Indian nationality is composed of many races, and the present Indian culture of more than one world civilization, yet it must be admitted that the Hindu forms its base and centre.... And the type of spirituality that it seeks to develop, is essentially Hindu.[84]

A highly sensitive Hindu writer, recording his impressions of those days, has pointed out that Hindus always carried bitter memories of Muslim rule for its intolerance and oppression. But under the British administration there had emerged some friendly contacts between upper-class Hindus and Muslims, though the contempt for Muslim peasants continued unabated. After partition, all friendly contacts were torn asunder by the bitterness generated by the new political movement.

> A cold dislike for the Muslim settled down in our hearts, putting an end to all real intimacy of relationship. Curiously enough, with us, the boys of Kishorganj, it found visible expression in the division of our class into two sections, one composed purely of Hindus and the other of Muslims. We never came to know all the circumstances of this division. Whether or not the Muslim boys had also expressed unwillingness to sit with us, for some time past we, the Hindu boys,

---

[33] Sir Bampfylde Fuller, op. cit., pp. 125–6.

[34] Haridas Mukherjee and Uma Mukherjee, '*Bande Mataram' and Indian Nationalism (1906-1908)*, Calcutta: Firma K. L. Mukhopadhyay, 1957, pp. 93–94.

had been clamouring that we did not want to sit with the Muslim boys because they smelt of onions.... Compartmentalization by communities came into our education before it was introduced into our politics.[35]

VI. SEPARATE ELECTORATES, ALL-INDIA MUSLIM LEAGUE, AND THE ANNULMENT OF PARTITION

It was on 1 October 1906 that a delegation of about seventy Muslims led by the Aga Khan was received in the ballroom of the Viceroy's house at Simla by Lord Minto. The delegation had brought with it an address signed by 'nobles, ministers of various states, great landowners, lawyers, merchants, and of many other of His Majesty's Mahommedan subjects'. They asked for separate representation of Muslims in all levels of government—District Boards, Municipalities, and Legislative Councils. They drew the attention of the Viceroy to the fact that in the United Provinces, where Muslims constituted fourteen per cent of the population, they had not secured a single seat by joint franchise.[36] And if by chance they were to win any seats, Muslim candidates would have to pander to the views of the Hindu majority and thus go against the interests of their own community. Lord Minto assured the delegation that he was entirely in accord with their case. Muslims had won separate representation for themselves.[37]

A fierce controversy has raged in India ever since the time that this concession was granted to Muslims. Maulana Muhammad Ali is reported to have characterized the delegation as a command performance, though it is well-known that later he put forward the view that separate electorates diminished communal bitterness.[38] Rajendra Prasad has taken great pains to prove that the delegation was engineered by Mr Archbold, the British Principal of Aligarh College.[39] This was quite understandable. Sir Sayyid had tried to promote understanding between Muslims and

[35] Nirad C. Chaudhuri, *The Autobiography of an Unknown Indian*, New York: Macmillan, 1951, p. 232.

[36] Cited in H. G. Rawlinson, op. cit., p. 188.

[37] Mary Countess of Minto, *India Minto and Morley 1905–1910*, London: Macmillan, 1934, p. 47.

[38] Afzal Iqbal, ed., *Select Writings and Speeches of Maulana Mohamed Ali*, Lahore: Ashraf, 1944, p. 255.

[39] Rajendra Prasad, *India Divided*, Bombay: Hind Kitabs, 1947, pp. 112–3.

the British Government and Mr Archbold was, after all, a Principal of a Muslim college. Like his predecessors, he was extremely well-disposed towards Muslim interests. To show that the delegation was engineered by the British Government or officials is probably to suggest that Muslims were being supported by the British. This was quite true. But so was the establishment of the Indian National Congress largely inspired by British influence. And no less a person than the British Viceroy, Lord Dufferin, was behind the idea of the Congress being established on political lines, rather than it restricting its activities to purely social reforms. The latter was the idea of Mr A.O. Hume, the founder of the Indian National Congress and a former Home Secretary of the Government of India. It was because of Lord Dufferin's influence that he abandoned it.[40] When Lord Dufferin was encouraging the formation of the Indian National Congress, he knew that the Congress would largely be a Hindu organization for after all Muslims were nowhere in the political picture at that time. Thus, if the British could encourage the formation of a predominantly Hindu organization, why could they not help the Muslims to embark on a similar political career? As it has been suggested above, the British Government probably felt guilty about the fact that they had been unduly hostile to Muslims and that the time had come to bring about some kind of a balance in the growth of the two communities—Hindu and Muslim.

Probably where the Nationalists' case against British concession of separate electorates to the Muslims was at its strongest was that it was a deliberate attempt to sow the seeds of conflict between Hindus and Muslims. A British official is reported to have remarked at the time the Viceroy assured the Muslim delegation that they would get separate electorates, 'It is nothing less than the pulling back of sixty-two millions of people from joining the ranks of the seditious opposition.'[41] In order to establish this charge conclusively, one would have to prove two things. First, that the British foresaw the political development of India on British parliamentary lines whereby there would come into being in course of time a homogeneous electorate, mature enough to elect a government from two or three political parties. Secondly,

---

[40] B. Pattabhi Sitaramayya, *The History of the Indian National Congress*, Vol. I (1805–1935), Bombay: Padma Publications, 1946, p. 15.

[41] Mary Countess of Minto, op. cit., pp. 47–48.

that the British, having foreseen all this, were indulging in a game of dividing the electorate in order to postpone for as long as possible the transfer of political power. But all the evidence goes to suggest that the British Government at that time was firmly convinced that British parliamentary institutions could not be transplanted in India. And what was more, they did not regard India as a homogeneous nation, but a subcontinent inhabited by a number of nations. Lord Morley wrote to Lord Minto: 'Not one whit more than you do I think it desirable or possible, or even conceivable, to adapt English political institutions *to the nations who inhabit India*' (author's italics).[42] Thus, in conceding separate electorates to Muslims it could be said that the British were not dividing a united nation, but were recognizing the existing multi-national character of India.

It was on 30 December 1906 that the All-India Muslim League was established. Leaders who played a prominent part in creating this organization at Dacca were Nawab Viqar-ul-Mulk, Nawab Salimullah of Dacca, and Mazhar-ul-Huq. Maulana Muhammad Ali was also present and was one of the principal draftsmen of the League Constitution. The first resolution stated that the following were the three objectives of the League: firstly, to foster a sense of loyalty to the British Government among the Muslims of India; secondly, to look after the political interests of Indian Muslims; and thirdly, to bring about better understanding between Muslims and other communities.[43] Dacca was chosen as the first meeting place because it was capital of the new province in which Muslims were in a considerable majority and also because Muslims at that time were concerned about the future of this new province in view of the persistent Hindu agitation against it.

Separate electorates were given constitutional recognition in the Indian Councils Act of 1909. Muslims were accorded not only the right to elect their representatives by separate electorates, but also the right to vote in the general constituencies. In addition, they were also given weightage in representation. In spite of these concessions, one could see how politically weak they were

---

[42] John Viscount Morley, *Recollections*, Vol. II, London: Macmillan, 1918, p. 172.

[43] A. B. Rajput, *Muslim League Yesterday and Today*, Lahore: Ashraf, 1948, pp. 19–20.

in the composition of Legislative Councils under the Act of 1909. In Bengal, where they were in a majority, there were only five Muslim representatives out of twenty-eight elected members. In the United Provinces, where they were in a minority, but where their position was politically stronger than it was in Bengal, they had four representatives out of twenty-one elected members. The great irony was Punjab where Muslims were supposed to be in a majority and therefore not given any special protection under the Act. There were eight elected members out of whom there was not a single Muslim.[44]

What was significant was that it was becoming increasingly apparent that Sir Sayyid had been much too over-cautious in advising the Muslims to stay aloof from political activities. W.S. Blunt, who had visited India, and besides being a friend of the Muslims, was also politically shrewd, had advised Muslims on many occasions in 1883–4 that they should show their teeth in order to be feared and respected by the British.

> I told them, if the Mohammedans only knew their power they would not be neglected and ill-treated by the Government as they now were. In England we were perpetually scared at the idea of a Mohammedan rising in India, and any word uttered by a Mohammedan was paid more attention to than that of twenty Hindus. But, if they sat still, thanking Providence for the favours which were denied them, the English public would be only too happy to leave them as they were.[45]

When, in the Delhi Durbar of December 1911, it was announced in the name of the King Emperor that the partition of Bengal would be annulled, it became clear to the Muslims that the British Government, pressured by Hindu agitation, would not even leave the Muslim community 'as they were'. Disestablishment of the province of East Bengal meant that the Muslims would lose their strong majority position and be once again dominated by the more advanced Hindu community.

Lord Minto spoke of the repeated assurances that had been given to Muslims regarding the inviolability of partition in his speech in the House of Lords in February 1912:

---

[44] These figures are given in B. R. Ambedkar, *Pakistan or the Partition of India*, Bombay: Thacker, 1946, p. 242.

[45] W. S. Blunt, op. cit., pp. 103–4.

We told the Musalmans that the Partition was a settled fact and we over and over again asserted that it must continue to be so. We assured the Musalman population of Eastern Bengal of our appreciation of their loyalty and our determination to safeguard their interests. I should think there could have been scarcely a Civil Servant in India who had not declared that it would be impossible for the British Government to reverse the decision it had come to as regards the maintenance of the Partition of Bengal.

A bitter jest which became popular among the Muslims of Delhi was 'no bombs, no boons'.[46] The years following the abolition of partition of Bengal were a turning point in the history of Indian Muslims. They began to wonder whether they had gone too far in both profession and practice of loyalty to the British Government. But, instead of coolly examining their position and future prospects, they tried to swing from one extreme to the other—from cooperation with the British to an emotional cooperation with the Hindus. Muslim suspicions, aroused by the revocation of partition of Bengal, were further strengthened after the outbreak of the First World War when they found that the British Government was fighting against Turkey, which was the leading Muslim power. As early as 1913 the Muslim League formally adopted the Congress objective of self-government for India within the Empire. The culminating point was the Congress-League Lucknow Pact of 1916.

There is no denying the fact that no Muslim leader in the modern history of India has excelled Sir Sayyid in the great services that he rendered to his people. 'Other men have written books and founded colleges; but to arrest as with a wall the degeneration of a whole people, that is the work of the prophet.'[47] But in trying to build Aligarh Muslim College on the lines of an English university and in imparting an unadulterated English education to Muslim students, he not only made them less fanatical but also less sincere Muslims. W. S. Blunt, an admirer of Sir Sayyid, wrote:

I myself feel rather constrained with them, for one does not know whether to treat them as pious Mohammedans, or latter-day disciples of Jowett. Not that they are not extremely amiable, but there

---

[46] H. H. Dodwell, op. cit., p. 576.

[47] Sir John Cumming, ed., *Political India* 1832–1932, London: Oxford University Press, 1932, p. 88.

is a tone of apology in their talk to me, as much as to say 'we are not such infidels as you suppose'.[48]

But no one can better the satire on Sir Sayyid by Nazir Ahmad in his *Ibn ul Waqt* (The Opportunist) where the difficulties of a Muslim who was eager to adopt Western ways of living were vividly described. No translation can convey the subtlety with which Nazir Ahmad portrayed the characteristics of such a man and the qualms and contradictions that his conscience was plagued with. Nazir Ahmad pointed out that many Muslims who found the requirements of their religion too rigorous to follow welcomed such a leader.[49]

It was obvious that Western education, accompanied by imitation of Western culture, brought in its wake intellectual and cultural separation between the Muslim elite who were Westernized and loyal to the British Government, and the poorer classes of illiterate Muslims. Thus, according to Lady Minto's diary of 1910:

> The Aga Khan arrived to stay with us today. He seems to have had a triumphal progress through India amongst the Moslems. He says that the only real way to appeal to the feelings of Natives is by means of the superstitions of their religion, and consequently he has instructed the priests in every mosque to issue a decree that any Mahommedans who incite to rebellion, or go about preaching sedition, will be eternally damned.[50]

Western education created a chasm between Westernized Muslim leaders and those who were steeped in Islamic theology and thought. Muslim society thus came to be led by two rival groups of leaders—orthodox religious leaders, who were mostly ignorant of modern sciences and technology, and the modern educated classes who lacked Islamic fervour and had only a nodding acquaintance with their religion. Sir Sayyid was quite right when he suggested that religious reformation was essential. But who could undertake this task and build a bridge between Islamic traditions and Western sciences? Neither of the two groups of leaders was qualified to undertake such a task.

---

[48] W. S. Blunt, op. cit., p. 156.
[49] Nazir Ahmad, *Ibn ul Waqt*, Lahore: Sheikh Mubarak Ali, 1949, pp. 178–81.
[50] Mary Countess of Minto, op. cit., p. 383.

3 ATTEMPTS AT HINDU-MUSLIM UNITY, 1916–40

Sir Sayyid Ahmad Khan visualized enormous advantages accruing to the Muslim community if it followed faithfully his policy of unqualified loyalty to the British Government. In the early years he was interested in changing the British policy from that of hostility and suspicion towards Muslims to that of good-will and support for their interests. Later, when he saw that the Hindu community was not only ahead of Muslims in educational and economic fields, but also getting organized to obtain parliamentary institutions, he was shrewd enough to detect that this would ultimately result in the Hindu majority dominating the future Government of India. Again, the sovereign remedy he prescribed for all such evils was loyalty to the British Government who would either refuse to concede the Hindu demand for representative institutions or protect the Muslims from the Hindu majority. Nawab Viqar-ul-Mulk (1841–1917), one of Sir Sayyid's loyal followers, who also became Secretary of the Aligarh College, observed:

> We are numerically one fifth of the other community. If at any time, the British Government ceases to exist in India, we shall have to live as the subjects of the Hindus, and our lives, our property, our self-respect, and our religion will be all in danger. If there is any device by which we can escape this, it is by the continuance of the British Raj, and our interests can be safeguarded only if we ensure the continuance of the British Government![1]

Muslims did derive a number of advantages from Sir Sayyid's policy. But it suffered from three major weaknesses. It could not succeed indefinitely because the British Government had their own interests to pursue and protect. Having tried to educate and

---

[1] Cited in A. H. Albiruni, *Makers of Pakistan and Modern Muslim India*, Lahore: Ashraf, 1950, p. 109.

influence Indians on Western lines, the British Government could not indefinitely withhold from them parliamentary institutions. It soon became clear that they would not only have to concede representative government but also pay heed to the demands and grievances of the Hindus. Revocation of the partition of Bengal in 1911 was an example.

Secondly, as the Muslim community came increasingly under the impact of British education and culture, the educated Muslim elite felt that Hindus and Muslims should get together to evolve a common nationality and serve their country by awakening public opinion in support of political reforms. A man like Jinnah, who had studied closely the lives of British political leaders like Gladstone and Disraeli, probably was impatient to play a role in his country as great and useful as they had done in theirs. There were two obstacles in the way of such people—the British reluctance to concede political reforms and the lack of any genuine understanding between Hindus and Muslims. And men like Jinnah, in struggling to surmount such obstacles, were going against the grain of Sir Sayyid's policy.

Thirdly, there was an anti-British tradition in Muslim religious thought which continued unabated in orthodox religious circles. It was not necessarily reactionary. It did not reject Western ideas out of hand. It felt that Muslims could form a political alliance with Hindus without either going against the dictates of their faith or their interests. Its best exponent was perhaps Maulana Shibli Nomani (1857–1914). He was followed by Maulana Abul Kalam Azad (1888–1958). Maulana Muhammad Ali (1878–1931) stood between the two schools, that of Westernized parliamentarians like Jinnah, and orthodox leaders like Maulana Shibli and Azad. As Jawaharlal Nehru described him, he was 'an odd mixture of Islamic tradition and an Oxford education'. As it will be seen later, it was Islamic fervour which always had the upper hand over Western rationalism in Muhammad Ali's personality.

The annulment of the partition of Bengal in 1911 came as a severe shock to the followers of Sir Sayyid. Nawab Viqar-ul-Mulk pointed out, 'It is now manifest like the midday sun, that after seeing what has happened lately, it is futile to ask the Muslims to place their reliance on Government.' But despite such a rebuff, he would not recommend what he called 'the way to suicide', namely, joining the Congress as a result of such disappointments.[2]

Perhaps the most penetrating analysis of Muslim politics was given by Maulana Shibli in his series of articles entitled, *A Turning Point* in *Muslim Politics*.[3] Shibli's articles were stinging criticisms of the kind of political methods that the Muslim League pursued and its reactionary and short-sighted leadership. He said that Congress was engaged in pursuing a comprehensive and constructive economic and political programme. It demanded a wide measure of representative government, reduction in military expenditure, separation of the judiciary and the executive, increase in expenditure on social amenities, like university and technical education, holding of Civil Service examinations in India, etc. The Muslim League, on the other hand, was interested in demanding a larger share for Muslims in Government services, extension of the principle of separate electorates to Municipal and District Board elections, protection of Urdu and a thorough investigation of Muslim waqfs, etc. For Shibli, pursuit of such sectional and communal interests was not a political programme in the true sense of the term. For him, politics meant organized political parties under progressive leaders. He pointed out that the Hindu Congress had never elected its Presidents from the titled and landed gentry, whereas the leadership of the Muslim League was completely in the hands of such people, who could never be courageous enough to sacrifice their selfish and material interests by taking a firm stand against the Government. He laid great stress on organization. He suggested that all issues of public importance should be brought before the general body of Muslims through public speeches, publication of pamphlets and journals, and also by forming branches of political parties in every district. Above all, Shibli was a great believer in a concerted Hindu-Muslim effort to achieve some of these political objectives. He reminded Muslims of the bonds of unity which had prevailed between the two communities during the period of Muslim rule in India.

This was the old story. But even today go to the villages and see for yourself the brotherly feelings that exist between Hindus and

---

[2] Cited in ibid., pp. 110–2.
[3] Shibli Nomani, *Maqalat-i-Shibli*, Azamgarh: 1938, Vol. 8, pp. 148–81.

Muslims, and how the two communities participate in each other's functions as if they were related to each other by family ties.[4]

Shibli's denunciations were not only levelled at the Muslim League, but at the very roots from which the Muslim League had sprung, namely, Sir Sayyid's policy of loyalty to the British and his advice to Muslims to keep aloof from the Indian National Congress.

Shibli's writings were bound to fall on attentive ears. Muslims were bitter about the revocation of the partition of Bengal and apprehensive that their prestige and influence would weaken as a result of the steady decline of Muslim powers like Turkey and Iran. The Muslim League itself was being transformed by the emergence of Westernized middle-class leaders like Sir Muhammad Shafi (1869–1932) from Punjab and Mohammad Ali Jinnah (1876–1948). Sir Muhammad Shafi represented the right wing section of the Muslim League and the left was led by Jinnah. In March 1913, the Muslim League had come as far as 'the attainment under the aegis of the British Crown of a system of self-government *suitable to India*'. (Author's italics.) There was a motion to adopt the Congress formula of colonial self-government but it found no seconder.[5] And even Jinnah was unwilling to press for it, probably because there was hardly any chance of such a proposal being approved by a body which was dominated by extreme conservative and land-owning interests. Again, the League was trying to distinguish between the kind of unadulterated representative government that the Congress was agitating for, and the sort of representative government modified by reservations and separate electorates that the Muslim League believed in. As stated earlier, Westernized Muslim leaders like Jinnah were interested in working for a common Indian nationality. Both their education and admiration of British institutions made them believe that this was the objective that India should aspire to. Thus, writing about Jinnah's formal enrolment in the All-India Muslim League in the autumn of 1913, Mrs Sarojini Naidu wrote:

> His two sponsors were required to make a solemn preliminary covenant that loyalty to the Muslim League and the Muslim

---

[4] Ibid., p. 176.
[5] R. Coupland, *The Indian Problem*, New York: Oxford University Press, 1944, Part I, pp. 46–47.

interest would in no way and at no time imply even the shadow of disloyalty to the larger national cause to which his life was dedicated.[6]

I. THE CONGRESS-LEAGUE PACT OR LUCKNOW PACT OF 1916

If the annulment of the partition of Bengal awakened Muslim fears, the attitude of Italy and the Balkan countries towards Turkey confirmed Muslim suspicions about the perennial hostility of Western powers towards Muslims. Both the *Comrade*, started by Maulana Muhammad Ali in January 1911, and the *Al-Hilal* started by Maulana Abul Kalam Azad in June 1912, were in the forefront in reminding Muslims of the identity of interests of Muslims all over the world. They pointed out that only by a united action could they counteract the machinations of Western powers. A Muslim medical mission called the Red Crescent Mission was sent to Turkey under Dr Ansari to help that country in the Tripoli and Balkan wars. The comment of the London *Times* of this period was noteworthy:

> Young Mohummadans have already condemned the work of years, have brought great injury to the cause of Islam in India; turning a wise, well-directed movement into political agitation, calculated rather to strengthen sedition than to advance the legitimate claims of Mohummadans.[7]

The Aga Khan was also getting alarmed because the Muslim League had come considerably nearer the Congress goal of self-government for India when it passed the resolution for a system of self-government suitable to India in 1913. If this were to be pursued by gradual stages, he was not against it. 'But if it meant a mere hasty impulse to jump at the apple when only the blossoming stage was over, then the day that witnessed the formulation of the ideal will be a very unfortunate one in the annals of their country.'[8] He soon resigned the Presidentship of the Muslim League.

---

[6] See Mrs Naidu's pen portrait of Jinnah in *Mohomed Ali Jinnah: An Ambassador of Unity: His Speeches & Writings 1912–1917*, Madras: Ganesh, n.d., p. 11.

[7] Cited in Mohammad Noman, *Muslim India*, Allahabad: Allahabad Law Journal Press, 1942, p. 134.

[8] Cited in ibid., p. 135. For the growing opposition to the Aga Khan's leadership of the Muslim League see Badr-ul-Hasan, ed., *Mazameen Abul Kalam Azad*, Delhi: Hindustani Publishing House, 1944, Vol. II, pp. 130–131.

It seemed that the liberal wing of the Muslim League, led by Jinnah, was becoming increasingly powerful. It succeeded in persuading both the Congress and the Muslim League Parties to hold their annual sessions in Bombay in 1915. A large number of Muslims also felt that the British Government was turning against the Muslims once again. The British were not only fighting against Turkey in the war but also making Muslim soldiers in the Indian army fight against their fellow Muslim Turks. Muhammad Ali, Shaukat Ali, and Maulana Abul Kalam Azad had all been interned under the Defence of India Act and their papers suppressed under the Press Act. Thus this current bitter feeling against the British enabled Jinnah and Mazhar-ul-Huq to persuade the Muslim League to think in terms of coming to a longterm settlement with the Congress. The war was on and both the League and the Congress expected that the Government would soon be compelled to concede constitutional reforms to placate the political interests in the country. An unexpected incident made the League session perhaps look even more progressive than it actually was. Mazhar-ul-Huq, who presided over the Muslim League session, and Lord Sinha, who presided over the Congress session, had travelled to Bombay by the same train. Mazhar-ul-Huq, who was inclined to be very pro-Congress in his views, had probably no hesitation in showing his Presidential address to Lord Sinha, who also reciprocated such cordiality. According to one version, 'By some unfortunate mistake, Lord Sinha read out the halting and hesitating address of the ever loyal Muslim, while the ever loyal Muslim read out the piquant and pungent address of the ever disloyal Bengali.' The result was that in the Muslim League meeting 'the President of the session was described as a man who cannot be called a Mohammadan'.[9]

A resolution was moved by Jinnah calling upon the All-India Muslim League to appoint a committee entrusted with the task of formulating a scheme of reforms and authorized to confer with other political organizations. It was obvious that the League was moving away from its traditional and safe paths. Liberals and those forces who stood for India's constitutional progress and a settlement of the Hindu-Muslim problem were becoming increasingly influential. This meant that such a Muslim League could no longer be treated as a loyal supporter of the Government.

---

[9] Mohammad Noman, op. cit., p. 147.

On the contrary, it was likely to arouse the Government's suspicions. Jinnah was to complain later that the session of the All-India Muslim League in Bombay was allowed to be broken up under the very nose of the police.[10]

The atmosphere in Lucknow in 1916, where once again the All-India Muslim League and the Indian National Congress met to hold their annual sessions, was even more cordial. It was at Lucknow that the famous Congress-League Pact, otherwise known as the Lucknow Pact, was signed. As regards the brotherly feeling that existed between Hindus and Muslims at this time in Lucknow, no one can better Swami Shradhanand's description:

> On sitting on the dais [Lucknow Congress platform] the first thing that I noticed was that the number of Moslem delegates was proportionately fourfold of what it was at Lahore in 1893. The majority of Moslem delegates had donned gold, silver and silk embroidered chogas [flowing robes over their ordinary course [sic] suits of wearing apparel. It was rumoured that these 'chogas' had been put by Hindu moneyed men for Congress Tamasha. Of some 433 Moslem delegates only some thirty had come from outside, the rest belonging to Lucknow City. And of these majority was admitted free to delegate seats, board and lodging.... A show was being made of the Moslem delegates. Moslem delegate gets up to second a resolution in Urdu. He begins: Hozarat, I am a Mahomedan delegate. Some Hindu delegate gets up and calls for three cheers for Mahomedan delegates and the response is so enthusiastic as to be beyond description.[11]

Jinnah was the principal architect of the Lucknow Pact and was hailed as an ambassador of Hindu-Muslim unity. He presided over the League session at Lucknow in December 1916. It seemed that the liberal wing in the League was in complete ascendancy. Jinnah observed:

> Towards the Hindus our attitude should be of good-will and brotherly feelings. Cooperation in the cause of our motherland should be our guiding principle. India's real progress can only be achieved by a true understanding and harmonious relations between

---

[10] Jamil-ud-Din Ahmad, ed., *Some Recent Speeches and Writings of Mr. Jinnah*, Lahore: Ashraf, 1952, Vol. I, p. 525.

[11] Cited in B. R. Ambedkar, *Pakistan or The Partition of India*, Bombay: Thackers, 1946, p. 141.

the two great sister communities. With regard to our own affairs, we can depend upon nobody but ourselves.[12]

The agreement arrived at between the Congress and the League was the famous Lucknow Pact and was largely a product of concessions offered from both sides. It was obvious that Jinnah was at his best in composing constitutional differences and offering compromise solutions likely to be accepted by both sides. Congress conceded separate Muslim electorates and was even agreeable to their introduction in Provinces like Punjab and the Central Provinces where they had not existed before. Muslims were to get nine-tenths of the seats in Punjab to which they were entitled on a purely numerical basis. The result was that their representation rose from twenty-five per cent (under the reforms of 1909) to fifty per cent (as a result of the Pact). In Bengal, Muslim acquisition on the basis of separate representation was not so impressive. They were given only three-quarters of the seats to which they were entitled on their population basis. The result was that they obtained only forty per cent of the seats. Mr Fazl-ul-Huq was also a signatory of the Pact. Muslims were to complain later that particularly in Bengal (though also in Punjab) they were deprived of their majority position. The answer was that separate electorates had been conceded by the British to the Muslims as a minority. Therefore, they were not entitled to have separate electorates in provinces where they were in majority. The Muslim complaint was that their majority in such provinces was not very large and also that they were backward and grossly under-represented even in these majority provinces. However, in Muslim minority provinces, Muslims obtained a representation almost double that which they would have got on a purely numerical basis. Similarly, at the Centre they obtained one-third representation in the Council by separate Muslim constituencies. They, of course, had to give up their right to vote in general constituencies which had been accorded to them by the Reforms of 1909. The Congress also went so far as to concede that no bill or resolution concerning a community could be passed if three-fourths of the representatives of that community were opposed to it.

Most of these principles, as well as other constitutional features of the Lucknow Pact, were later incorporated in the Government

---

[12] *Mohammed Ali Jinnah: An Ambassador of Unity,* op. cit., p. 59.

of India Act, 1919. The Hindu-Muslim concordat of Lucknow was the high-water mark of Hindu-Muslim unity. It was obvious that it was all the work and creation of constitutionalists, both in the Congress and in the League. All this was to be swept away by tides which followed in the wake of the Amritsar tragedy and particularly the Khilafat agitation. During that time, constitutionalists like Jinnah were relegated to the background and men like Gandhi and Muhammad Ali, who were experts in extra-constitutional methods, were called upon to guide the political destinies of Hindus and Muslims.

II. THE KHILAFAT MOVEMENT—INTERMINGLING OF RELIGION AND POLITICS

The Lucknow Pact showed that it was possible for middleclass, English-educated Muslims and Hindus to arrive at an amicable settlement of Hindu-Muslim constitutional and political problems. The Khilafat movement was to show that all this work could be swept aside within a few years as a result of the injection of religious problems into politics and mass participation in political movements. Just as towards the end of the nineteenth century and during the time of the partition of Bengal Hindus had become acutely conscious of their separate religious and cultural identity, the Muslims also wanted to revive religious consciousness to counteract both against Western cultural penetration and Hindu revivalism.

The fact that anti-British agitation became more prominent submerging anti-Hindu consciousness, was largely attributable to external factors. Western powers, including Britain, were moving into the vacuum created by the incompetence and weakness of the Turkish government in Eastern Europe and the Middle East. This is not denying the fact that men like Maulana Shibli and Abul Kalam Azad from the very beginning took an anti-British stand in politics and stood for Hindu-Muslim unity. But neither should the fact that their ideas fell on willing ears largely because of the anti-Muslim policy followed by Western powers in international politics be underrated. It was not only Turkey but other Muslim countries like Afghanistan and Persia which had been reduced to mere playthings in the hands of British and Russian diplomats. Persian independence, for example, was recognized by both Britain and Russia, but this did not prevent the two powers from dividing Persia into their respective spheres of influence, the north being under Russian influence and the south under British. The situation was well illustrated by a cartoonist who represented Persia as a Persian cat and the two powers as the British lion and the Russian bear. The bear said to the lion, 'You stroke the tail while I stroke the head and we can both stroke the back'.[13]

It was in such an atmosphere that Muhammad Ali's *Comrade*, started on 1 January 1911, and Maulana Abul Kalam Azad's *Al-Hilal*, started in June 1912, came forward to awaken Muslims from the lull of loyalty to a furious indignation at the way Western powers were trampling the rights and interests of Muslims all over the world. Azad referred to 'those heretics and hypocrites who, during the last forty years, had cooperated with the Satans of Europe to weaken the influence of Islamic Caliphate and Pan-Islam'.[14] The obvious reference was to the Aligarh movement, which in his own words, had 'paralysed the Muslims'. As regards the Hindus, Azad's exhortation was as clear. He urged the Muslims to get rid of the fear of the Hindu majority. According to Azad, this had been deliberately planted in the minds of the Muslims by the British because they wanted to enlist Muslim support to consolidate their rule in India. And Muslims offered to play this role. The result was that Hindus were in the forefront of the struggle for Indian independence. Azad also warned that when historians wrote the history of India's struggle for independence, they would have to say that Muslims, like lifeless puppets, danced to the tune of the British Government and obstructed the efforts of those who were fighting for their country's independence.

Remember that patriotism demands from Hindus that they should struggle for their country's independence. But for Muslims, this is a religious duty, a *jihad*. You are fighters for God's battle and *jihad* includes every endeavour which is made in the name of truth and freedom. Today those people (Hindus) who are engaged in a struggle for their country's progress and independence are also waging a *jihad*. You should have been in the forefront of this *jihad*. Therefore, arise! God also wishes that you should wake up and discharge your duty to wage *jihad* relentlessly. You have not done anything in India,

---

[13] Percival Spear, ed., *The Oxford History of India*, London: Oxford University Press, 1958, p. 773.

[14] Cited in A. H. Albiruni, op. cit., p. 136.

but now your God desires that you should do here, too, what you are enjoined upon to do everywhere else.[15]

It was not only the ideas that Azad was propagating that were popular, but also the style in which they were conveyed that contributed considerably to their currency and the intensity with which they came to be held. Within two years of its publication, the circulation of *Al-Hilal* was 26,000 copies per week.[16] This does not indicate the number of people who came to be influenced by the newspaper for in Pakistan and in India, as the practice still exists, a newspaper would be read aloud to a number of illiterate townspeople and villagers. Similarly, Muhammad Ali's *Comrade* and *Hamdard* were also widely read. Zafar Ali Khan brought out the *Zamindar* of Lahore. According to one estimate, as many as 20,000 copies of this paper (twice a day) were in circulation.[17]

The antipathy to the British policy towards Turkey had also permeated the ranks of the Indian army in which Muslims formed a very high proportion. It has been reported: 'The Turks set in their front line mullahs whose voice rang out across the narrow No-Man's land at Sannaiyat, and elsewhere, reproaching the Mohammedans opposite.... Desertions were frequent, so were executions.'[18] Desertions among the Pathans from the Tribal Area were more frequent than among the Punjabi Musalmans. The result was that recruitment from the Tribal Belt (independent zone between the administered area and the Durand Line) was almost abandoned during the inter-war period owing to Pathan desertions in World War I.[18a] In contrast to this was the attitude of some of the members of the landed gentry like Nawab Sir Mohammad Akbar Khan, Khan of Hoti. *A History of the Hoti Family* proudly records that the Nawab of Hoti 'rendered very valuable services at Gallipoli and was the only Muslim of a

[15] Badr-ul-Hasan, ed., *Mazameen Abul Kalam Azad*, Delhi: Hindustani Publishing House, 1944, Vol. II, pp. 132–3.

[16] Maulana Abul Kalam Azad, *India Wins Freedom*, Calcutta: Orient Longmans, 1959, p. 8.

[17] W. C. Smith, *Modern Islam in India: A Social Analysis*, Lahore: Ripon Printing Press, 1947, p. 236.

[18] Edward Thompson, *The Reconstruction of India*, London: Faber & Faber, 1930, p. 121.

[18a] *The Times Book of India*, London: The Times Publishing Co., 1930, p. 61.

respectable family who fought in that theatre of war against the Turks....'[19] Hindu Jats from Punjab also came forward to fight the Turks, presumably because the Turks were Muslims.[19a] Muhammad Ali and Shaukat Ali were imprisoned during most of the war period. Azad was arrested towards the end of 1916 and was in prison until 31 December 1919. But Muslim concern for the future of Turkey and bitterness towards the British were infecting the more cautious and Westernized Muslim Leaguers. Fazl-ul-Huq, in his Presidential address to the Muslim League session at Bombay in 1918, declared: 'To me the future of Islam in India seems to be wrapped in gloom and anxiety. Every instance of a collapse of the Muslim powers of the world is bound to have an adverse influence on the political importance of our community in India.' He also urged the Muslims to abandon their traditional hostility towards Hindus and seek their cooperation, which was there for the mere asking, against the British bureaucracy.[20]

It was becoming increasingly obvious that one great result of Britain's anti-Turkish policy in the Middle East and repressive measures in India was to drive Hindus and Muslims into each others' arms. Thus they could forge a united front against the British Government. The British Prime Minister, Lloyd George, had given assurances that the Allies had no intention of breaking up the Turkish Empire and that after the cessation of hostilities, Turkey would be given back all its possessions. After his release at the end of 1919, Muhammad Ali led a deputation to Britain and tried to impress upon the British Government the fact that the Muslims could not disregard the commands of their Holy Prophet, who with his dying breath had bidden them never to surrender the *Jazirat-ul-Arab* (Arabia, Iraq, Syria and Palestine) to any non-Muslim government. Muhammad Ali argued that for Muslims to accept mandates over Iraq, Syria and Palestine would amount to a total disregard of the wishes of the Prophet. Muhammad Ali failed in his mission and returned empty-handed and bitter to India in October 1920.

The British had already done everything possible to antagonize both the Hindus and Muslims by following a repressive policy in India. During the war all classes of Indians had cooperated with the British. Even Gandhi had taken part in a recruiting campaign urging the Gujarati peasants to win *Swaraj* by joining the army. They felt that the Report of the Rowlatt Committee, published in the summer of 1918, was a poor reward for the sacrifices that India had made, both in men and money, to support the British cause. The Committee suggested that in the event of the Government being faced with anarchical and revolutionary movements, the Government could deprive a man of his liberty and intern him for a long period. The Government argued that the Rowlatt Act was not such a drastic piece of legislation as it was made out to be by Indians. The Government could take action against any individual only after a report had been received from a judicial officer concerning the case. And even after action had been taken, the Government had to submit within a month of such action the whole matter to an investigating authority consisting of three officers. The Rowlatt Report was published soon after the Montagu-Chelmsford Report which promised responsible government by measured stages. The two Reports were read together, and to the growing suspicion on the part of Indians that they had been tricked by the British, was added the anguish and tragedy of Amritsar.

Rioting started in Amritsar on 10 April 1919 following the deportation of two Nationalist leaders. It was true that two banks were attacked, and a few Europeans murdered. But the racial ferocity and complete callousness to human life that General Dyer displayed in opening fire on the densely packed crowd that had assembled in the Jallianwalla Bagh on 13 April have had few parallels in the history of British association with India. The number of people killed was 379 and the wounded numbered at least 1,200. This action was not only approved by the Provincial Government, but on the following day aerial bombing was resorted to at Gujranwalla where a crowd was burning and rioting. This was followed by the proclamation of Martial Law on 15 April which continued until 9 June. A series of orders deliberately designed to humiliate Indians were passed. As the Hunter Committee recorded later, men were made to crawl while passing through the street where Miss Sherwood, a missionary, was attacked. At Gujranwalla they had to offer their salaams to any commissioned officer. Public flogging was resorted to for any minor offence like 'the contravention of the curfew order, for failure to salaam a commissioned officer, for disrespect to a European, for taking a commandeered car without leave, or refusal to sell milk, and for similar contraventions'.[21]

However much the British might be accused by Indian politicians for having always attempted to foment differences and conflicts between Hindus and Muslims, the British certainly did everything possible to force Hindus and Muslims to unite against them in the period immediately following the end of the First World War. The first Khilafat Conference was held at Delhi on 23 November 1919. Gandhi was present and took upon himself the task of urging the Muslims to launch a non-cooperation movement for forcing the British to yield to their demands regarding the maintenance of the Khilafat in Turkey. Hindus had been invited by the Muslims to attend the Delhi Khilafat Conference. Similarly, at the conference held in June 1920 at Allahabad, non-Muslim leaders like Sir Tej Bahadur Sapru, Motilal Nehru, and Annie Besant were present. Gandhi, however, was the only Hindu leader who was prepared to take a clear and courageous stand as regards the Khilafat demands of the Muslims. He was the only Hindu leader included in the Executive Committee formed on 9 June 1920 to formulate a detailed programme of non-cooperation. On 22 June 1920, the Muslims sent a message to the Viceroy warning him that if the injustices imposed on Turkey were not removed by 1 August 1920, they would launch a non-cooperation movement. Again it was Gandhi who gave a notice to the Viceroy on 1 July 1920 that non-cooperation would start on the first of August. After this, Gandhi took upon himself the task of persuading the Congress to launch a non-cooperation movement in concert with the Khilafat Committees. Between 1 August and 1 September 1920 Gandhi went on an extensive tour of the country to rally the people behind the Khilafat cause.[22]

On 8 September 1920, Gandhi moved the historic resolution in the extraordinary session of the Indian National Congress at Calcutta. The resolution referred to the broken pledges of the British

---

[21] *Report of Hunter Committee 1920*, Cmd. 681, p. 85. Cited in Edward Thompson and G.T. Garratt, *Rise and Fulfilment of British Rule in India*. Allahabad: Central Book Depot, 1958, p. 548.

[22] B. R. Ambedkar, op. cit., pp. 138–40.

Government given to Muslims regarding the Khilafat, and also to the tragic events of April 1919. The only way to prevent a repetition of such wrongs was 'the establishment of *Swarajya*'. The policy of 'progressive, non-violent, non-cooperation' was to be given effect to in the following manner:

1. surrender of titles and honorary offices and resignation from nominated seats in local bodies;
2. refusal to attend Government Levees, Durbars, and other official and semi-official functions held by Government officials or in their honour;
3. gradual withdrawal of children from schools and colleges owned, aided or controlled by Government and in place of such schools and colleges establishment of National Schools and Colleges in the various Provinces;
4. gradual boycott of British courts by lawyers and litigants and establishment of private arbitration courts for the settlement of private disputes;
5. refusal on the part of the military, clerical and labouring classes to offer themselves as recruits for service in Mesopotamia;
6. withdrawal by candidates of their candidature for election to the Reformed Councils and refusal on the part of the voters to vote for any candidate who may, despite the Congress advice, offer himself for election;
7. boycott of foreign goods.[23]

B.C. Pall from Bengal, supported by other Bengalis, particularly C. R. Das, and leaders from other parts like Pandit Malaviya and Jinnah tried to oppose the resolution by suggesting that the masses should first be trained in the principles of non-cooperation before the actual launching of the movement. Pall also suggested that a mission selected by the All-India Congress Committee should be sent to the Prime Minister to lay before him India's grievances and its demand for immediate autonomy. Jinnah pointed out that he was not convinced of the practicability of Gandhi's scheme. He urged the delegates to take stock of the materials and forces of the country and follow the advice of C. R. Das, namely, to pause and consider the question carefully in all its aspects. Gandhi in his reply said that he had extended

---

[23] *The Indian Annual Register 1921*, Calcutta, 1921, Part III, pp. 106–8.

the hand of cooperation before but found no redress of the Khilafat and Punjab wrongs from the Government. It had become painfully clear to him that 'the British Ministers or the Government of India had never meant well by the people of India.' He reminded the audience that the Muslims were determined to boycott the Councils. 'Can the Hindus gain anything by a policy of obstruction if every believer in Islam boycotts the Council as he should boycott sin? This is a religious position. In Islam they consider it is sinful for them to go to the Councils and take the oath of allegiance. Let not practical India and practical politicians, who gather here from year to year, forget this settled fact.'[24] Gandhi's resolution of non-cooperation was adopted by 1,886 votes in favour with 884 votes cast against it. Dr B. R. Ambedkar has written: 'The late Mr Tairsee once told me that a large majority of the delegates were no others than the taxi drivers of Calcutta who were paid to vote for the non-cooperation resolution.'[25]

Gandhi, accompanied by the Ali brothers and Azad, undertook another extensive tour of the country. In December 1920, the Congress held its annual session at Nagpur. The Khilafat programme had become so popular that leaders like C. R. Das and Lala Lajpat Rai had to come round to the non-cooperation programme. But nothing could swerve Jinnah from the constitutional path that he was determined to follow. When asked by Gandhi to contribute his share to the new political life, he wrote bluntly that Gandhi's programme would lead to disaster and bring about conflict between Hindus and Muslims. According to him, Gandhi's 'extreme programme has for the moment struck the imagination mostly of the inexperienced youth and the ignorant and the illiterate. All this means complete disorganization and chaos.'[26] He conceded that the Government was entirely responsible for the current deterioration in the political situation. But on the other hand, he could not see how the movement could succeed. His approach was much too practical to be popular at a time when his community was surcharged with

[24] Ibid., p. 112(i).
[25] B. R. Ambedkar, op. cit., p. 141. See also Azim Husain, *Fazl-i-Husain*, Bombay: Longmans, Green, 1946, p. 124. According to this source, figures were 1,826 in favour, 800 against and 3,188 neutral on the Resolution.
[26] Matlubul Hasan Saiyid, *Mohammad Ali Jinnah: A Political Study*, Lahore: Ashraf, p. 186.

a religious zeal for the Khilafat and the whole country eagerly expecting that freedom was at hand and they had to make one final attempt to grasp it. He questioned the wisdom of withdrawing children from schools and colleges when no other institutions had been built to replace them and of boycotting foreign goods when they could not be replaced by domestically produced goods. It was during the Nagpur session in December 1920 that Jinnah resigned from the Congress.

The Khilafat movement was very largely a mass movement. It attracted Hindus and Muslims alike. The words 'Khilafat' and 'Swaraj' were on everybody's lips. 'Khilafat' was interpreted by rural people as a word originating from *khilaf,* which in Urdu meant 'against', and so they thought they were supposed to oppose the Government.[21] Hindu-Muslim unity was at its height. In 1921, at the time of the Baqrid (Muslim religious festival), Muslims voluntarily gave up the sacrifice of cows. Swami Shradhanand, one of the Hindu religious leaders, was allowed to enter the Jama Masjid of Delhi to deliver an address.[28]

But for Muslims it was primarily a religious movement. The *Jamiyat al Ulama-i-Hind* issued a *fatwa* signed by 925 eminent Muslim divines sanctioning the programme of non-violent non-cooperation.[29] Many Westernized Muslims who were once 'fondly proud of a well-trimmed moustache as a European girl of her curls, are now to be seen in some cases with the most ungainly beards turning grey with the dust of an Indian summer.'[30] The movement was dominated, as it has been suggested earlier, by religious ideas and religious leaders. This was not only a breaking away from the tradition of loyalty to the British Government started by Sir Sayyid, but also a complete eclipse of the leadership of Westernized leaders like Jinnah, Sir Muhammad Shafi, and Sir Fazl-i-Husain (1877–1936).

The idea that owing to the flagrant disregard of the law of Islam by the British Government, India had become a *dar-ul-harb* spread widely, particularly in the North-West Frontier and

---

[27] Jawaharlal Nehru, *An Autobiography,* London: The Bodley Head, 1958, p. 69.

[28] Rajendra Prasad, *India Divided,* Bombay: Hind Kitabs, 1947, pp. 122–3.

[29] Ibid., p. 121.

[30] Afzal Iqbal, ed., *My Life: A Fragment. An Autobiographical Sketch of Maulana Mohamed Ali,* Lahore: Ashraf, 1946, p. 65.

Sind. The result was that thousands of Muslims, as many as 18,000 in the month of August 1920 itself and mostly from Sind and the North-West Frontier, migrated to Afghanistan. They had sold their land and property and with their wives and children made their long trek in carts in the direction of the Khyber Pass. They had been told that the Afghan Government would welcome them with open arms and fertile fields. Afghan authorities, alarmed by such an enormous influx, were compelled to turn the *muhajarin* (emigrants) back. It is difficult to establish who was responsible for misleading such a large number of Muslims. According to one version, the idea of *hijrat* (migration) was originated by Maulana Abul Kalam Azad.[31]

It was on the 8th, 9th and 10th of July 1921 that the All-India Khilafat Conference met in Karachi. Nearly 5,000 people were present. The famous Karachi resolutions, for which the Ali brothers had to face trial and imprisonment later, were passed. Some of the salient resolutions were:

1. This meeting of the All-India Khilafat Conference declares allegiance of the Muslim population to His Majesty the Sultan of Turkey, the Commander of the Faithful, and gives him an assurance that they would not rest content until they had secured complete fulfilment of the Khilafat demands.

2. It records its sorrow at the death of Jan Mahomed who had led the Hijrat movement and sends its condolence to his family.

3. It further congratulates those workers in Sind who have undergone imprisonment in the cause of their religion and country and hopes that their efforts will meet with success.

4. This meeting of the All-India Khilafat Conference declares that so long as the demands of Indian Muslims regarding the integrity of the Khilafat and the preservation of the sanctity of Jazirat-ul-Arab and other holy places which are based upon their religious canons are not fulfilled, neither shall they rest in peace nor shall they leave it to the enemies of Islam; that the entire provinces

---

[31] Mazhar Ansari, *Tarikh-i-Muslim League,* Jamia Book Depot, p. 275: Cited in A. H. Albiruni, op. cit., p. 159.

of Thrace and Smyrna shall form the indissoluble components of the territories of the Turkish Sultan as they used to be before the war, and in no part of them shall Muslims tolerate the influence and interference of Greek or any other Power. The Muslims shall never agree to the conditions the Allies wish to impose upon the Turkish Government, or on its military, naval and air forces, or in connection with the financial, economic or judicial administration, as that would tend to interfere with the complete independence of the Khilafat and the Sultanate. This Conference calls upon local committees to make fresh declarations to the above effect so that no doubt be left as to the religious obligation of the Muslims.

5. Whereas Mesopotamia contains holy places, such as the burial places of the descendants of the Prophet and holy saints, and is in addition an integral part of the Jazirat-ul-Arab, the influence, residence or entrance of non-Muslim nations without the authority of Islamic Powers is not permissible by religion, and in case a colonization of the above character comes about, it would conflict with their holy Shariat. The Mussalmans are convinced the Americans [sic] would take advantage of their nearness to the holy places and revive their old enmities towards Islam. This Conference therefore demands that the above country be immediately vacated.

6. This meeting of the All-India Khilafat Conference heartily congratulates Ghazi Mustafa Kemal Pasha and the Angora Government upon their magnificent victories and the success of their most desperate (or self-sacrificing) endeavours in upholding the laws of Islam and this meeting prays to Almighty God that they may soon succeed in expelling the whole of the armies of the foreign Government from every nook and corner of the Turkish Empire. In addition this meeting clearly proclaims that it is in every way religiously unlawful for a Mussalman at the present moment to continue in the British Army or to induce others to join the army and it is the duty of all the Mussalmans in general and the Ulemas [sic] in particular to see that these religious commandments are brought home to every Mussalman in the Army.

Furthermore this meeting also announces that if the British Government were to take any military measures against the Angora Government, directly or indirectly, openly or secretly, then the Mussalmans of India will be compelled to commence the breaking of laws, that is civil disobedience, with the concurrence of the Congress and to proclaim in the complete independence of India and the Indians and the establishment of a Republic for the Government of India.

7. This meeting of the All-India Khilafat Conference calls upon all local Khilafat Committees to devise measures to absolutely stop drinking within their districts, and congratulates the workers and volunteers of places where the liquor traffic has diminished and further commands to them to put forth their best efforts to achieve greater success.

8. That this meeting of the All-India Khilafat Conference calls upon all Provincial, District and Village Committees to put forth their last efforts to enlist a crore of Khilafat members and collect forty lakhs of rupees to relieve the distress in Smyrna and aid the Muhajirin Relief Fund.

9. This Conference strongly appeals to the Pirs and Zamindars of Sind to take more interest in the Khilafat movement than they had done hitherto and request the former to command their disciples to do the same.'[32]

It was transparent that the whole Khilafat movement had taken a religious turn, and it was extremely doubtful whether Muslims could conduct their agitation and demonstrations purely on non-violent lines. And as it will be seen later, neither could Hindus remain completely non-violent. Hindu leaders like Pandit Malaviya and Swami Shradhanand were apprehensive about Muslim intentions. It had been alleged that Muhammad Ali in one of his speeches had said that if the Afghans were to invade India, Muslims would offer their help to them against the British. Later, when Muhammad Ali apologized for having given such an impression, he said that his apology was intended specifically for Pandit Malaviya who entertained fears of an Afghan invasion.[33]

[32] *The Indian Annual Register 1922*, Calcutta: 1923, Vol. I, pp. 172–4.
[33] Ibid., p. 172.

Swami Shradhanand was equally concerned about the Khilafat movement taking an anti-Hindu turn, even though it had started as an anti-British movement.

> There was another prominent fact to which I drew the attention of Mahatma Gandhi. Both of us went together one night to the Khilafat Conference at Nagpur. The Ayats [verses] of the Qur'an recited by the Maulanas on that occasion, contained frequent references to Jihad and against, [*sic*] killing of the Kaffirs. But when I drew his attention to this phase of the Khilafat movement Mahatmaji smiled and said, 'They are alluding to the British Bureaucracy.' In reply I said that it was all subversive of the idea of non-violence and when the reversion of feeling came the Mahomedan Maulanas would not refrain from using these verses against the Hindus.[34]

The Moplah rising in Malabar in August 1921 was a clear indication of both the intensity and the confused nature of the Khilafat movement. The Moplahs claimed to be descendants of Arab settlers and were fanatically religious. The Moplahs rose against Hindu *zamindars* and moneyed interests and also against the British. It could be said that the exclusion of Khilafat and Congress leaders from the Moplah territory meant that the Moplahs were cut off from the influence of Gandhian ideas of non-violence and their movement, being deprived of supervision from experienced leaders, had to fall back on purely local resources and grievances. But it could not be denied that the rugged outlines of the movement were in tune with the kind of emotional and religious ideology that the Khilafat movement was propagating.

About the middle of August 1921 agrarian riots broke out in Nilambur. Hindu *zamindars* redistributed their lands and the Moplahs, who had been suffering, rose in revolt. District authorities supported the rich landlords and the Moplahs thought that they had no choice except to fight against this apparent Hindu-British alliance. Mullahs who were preaching the orthodox doctrines about *kaffirs* and *jihad* were arrested and a British regiment arrived at Tiruvangadi. All this contributed to the frenzy and a crowd of 3,000 Moplahs came by train and a pitched battle was fought between the British regiment and the Moplahs. The railway station was looted, rails were cut, and in a couple of days Ernad Taluk cut itself off from British territory and a Khilafat

---

[34] Cited in B. R. Ambedkar, op. cit., p. 149.

kingdom was declared. This was followed by the havoc at Tirur in which 10,000 Moplahs set fire to the police station and the courts and plundered all arms and ammunition. Several Europeans were killed and European planters had to flee their plantations before the advancing Moplahs. Hindu houses were sacked, temples desecrated and thousands of Hindus converted. It was also alleged that women were attacked. The Moplahs were not only rising against Hindu *zamindars* and money lenders but were also converting by force those Hindus who did not help them or were suspected of being in league with the Government. It has been estimated that throughout the campaign British troops suffered casualties of less than a hundred while 4,000 Moplahs were killed in action and tens of thousands injured and captured. There was also considerable cruelty in the martial law administration that was declared on 26 August 1921. There was the notorious Moplah train tragedy. A hundred prisoners confined in a close and almost air-tight goods-van were transported by rail. When the door was opened, sixty-six Moplahs were found suffocated to death and the remaining thirty-four on the verge of collapse.[35]

In the Central Legislature it was disclosed that, according to the Madras Government, the number of conversions by force ran into thousands. But the Congress Working Committee did not want to hurt Muslim feelings by denouncing in too strong terms the Moplah outrages against Hindu religion, life and property. The Working Committee's resolution recorded its sense of deep regret over the deeds of violence perpetrated by the Moplahs in certain areas of Malabar, and referred to three cases of conversions forced upon Hindus by a fanatical group which had always been opposed to the Khilafat and non-cooperation movement. It has also been reported that Hindus in the Subjects Committee were shocked when an 'out-and-out Nationalist' like Maulana Hasrat Mohani opposed the resolution on the ground that the Moplahs being in a state of war (their country *dar-ul-harb*), were justified in suspecting the Hindus of collusion with the British Government. 'Therefore, the Moplahs were right in presenting the Quoran or sword to the Hindus. And if the Hindus became

---

[35] My account of the Moplah rising is based on *The Indian Annual Register 1922*, op. cit., pp. 187–8, and Sir Charles W. Gwynn, *Imperial Policing*, London: Macmillan, 1936, pp. 83–117.

Mussalmans to save themselves from death, it was a voluntary change of faith and not forcible conversion'.[36]

The Ali brothers were arrested in September 1921. Azad was already in prison. Between December 1921 and January 1922 there were as many as 30,000 arrests.[37] According to Subhas Chandra Bose, 'About the middle of 1920, anti-British feeling was stronger amongst the Mussalmans than amongst the rest of the Indian population.'[38]

But from the very beginning it was detected by shrewd observers that the Hindu-Muslim unity as stressed by Khilafat leaders and Gandhi was not based on firm foundations. The impression that the author has gathered is that the Muslims were not so much fighting for freedom for India as they were fighting for the maintenance of the Khilafat in Turkey, whereas for Gandhi the Khilafat was a weapon which he could use to accelerate India's advance towards *Swaraj*. One of the main Karachi resolutions clearly stated that if the British Government were to take any arbitrary action against the newly established Angora Government, the Muslims of India would, in retaliation and in cooperation with the Congress, proclaim the complete independence of India and the establishment of a Republic of India. The obverse of such a threat would be that Indian Muslims would not participate in a struggle for India's independence, at least at that time, if the British Government refrained from undertaking any arbitrary measures against the new Government of Turkey.

Gandhi on the other hand felt that Hindus, by supporting the Khilafat movement, would place Muslims in considerable indebtedness and thus mitigate their traditional hostility towards the Hindu religion. Thus Gandhi himself said: 'I claim that with us both the Khilafat is the central fact, with Maulana Mahomed Ali because it is his religion, with me because, in laying down my life for the Khilafat, I ensure safety of the cow, that is my religion, from the Mussalman knife.'[39]

Thus, it was not surprising that such a partnership could be

[36] B. R. Ambedkar, op. cit., p. 150.

[37] W. C. Smith, op. cit., p. 245.

[38] Subhas Chandra Bose, *The Indian Struggle*, Calcutta: Thacker, Spink, 1948, p. 62.

[39] M. K. Gandhi, *Communal Unity*, Ahmedabad: Navajivan, 1949, p. 26.

buffeted from its nationalist course by any hostile wind that blew either from the Government side or the communalists. It was felt that Gandhi might have aroused Muslim suspicions by seeking an interview with the Viceroy, who was after all, in the words of Gandhi himself, the head of a 'Satanic' Government. There were altogether six of these interviews in Simla between 13 and 18 May 1921. They were considered a diplomatic triumph for Lord Reading, who, through the good offices of Gandhi, was successful in extracting an apology from the Ali brothers for the violent speeches they had made.[40]

But the deadly blow came from the Moplah rising. This was followed by a number of communal clashes at Multan and Bengal in September 1922, both on the occasion of the Muharram festival. Thus, Hindus felt justified in starting movements like the *Shuddhi* and *Sangathan*. The *Shuddhi* movement was started by Swami Shradhanand to reconvert to Hinduism the Malkhana Rajputs and other low castes, who, though they had embraced Islam, yet retained a number of Hindu customs and practices. Another factor which triggered this movement was the sudden realization by the Hindus after the publication of census returns in the United Provinces that their numbers were declining in comparison with the Muslims.[41] The *Sangathan* movement was sponsored by Pandit Malaviya with two objects in view: firstly, to remove untouchability and, secondly, to popularize physical exercises and sword play among Hindus to enable them to protect themselves. Later Malaviya was willing to make a public announcement that he favoured the creation of inter-communal *akharas* (wrestling centres).[42] The *Shuddhi* movement has been defended by Rajendra Prasad on the score that Hindus had as much right to proselytize as Muslims and Christians without realizing that, though retaliatory, the movement was extremely ill-timed and was bound to increase communal conflict and bitterness.[43] The murder of Swami Shradhanand, the founder of the *Shuddhi* movement in December 1926, heightened Hindu-Muslim animosity and Hindus started threatening Muslims with

---

[40] *The Indian Annual Register 1922*, op. cit., Vol. I, pp. 164–5.

[41] *The Indian Yearbook 1925*, Bombay: The Times of India, n.d., p. 61.

[42] Afzal Iqbal, ed., *Select Writings and Speeches of Mohamed Ali*, Lahore: Ashraf, 1944, p. 307.

[43] Rajendra Prasad, op. cit., p. 123.

reprisals. Muslims also started the *Tabligh* and *Tanzim* movements. It has been claimed that the *Jamiyat al Ulama-i-Hind* was successful in converting more than 2,000 non-Muslims and in winning back 11,000 apostates.[44]

In February 1922 occurred the famous Chauri-Chaura tragedy in which twenty-one policemen were murdered. Gandhi had been dismayed by communal clashes, but this tragedy, though not communal at all, horrified him because his national volunteers were responsible for it and he called off the whole movement. This was to create intense bitterness among Congress leaders like C. R. Das and Motilal Nehru who formed the Swaraj Party. A few weeks after the suspension of the movement, the Government came to Gandhi's rescue, arrested him and sentenced him to six years' imprisonment. He was released two years later. But after 1923, Gandhi lived more or less in political eclipse and the Swaraj Party was in the ascendent until 1928.

Even though the Hindu-Muslim base of the Khilafat movement had been immeasurably weakened, the Government perhaps feared that Muslims were still capable of carrying on the Khilafat movement under their own steam. For, otherwise, one cannot understand why Lord Reading sent a telegram to Edwin Montagu, Secretary of State for India, recommending not only a revision of the harsh terms of the Treaty of Sèvres, but also the evacuation of Constantinople by the Allies and giving back to the Sultan Thrace and Smyrna and his former suzerainty over the Holy Places. The telegram reached the Secretary of State on 1 March 1922 and on the same day he was asked in a second telegram from the Government of India to give permission to publish their recommendations immediately. The Secretary of State privately telegraphed his consent, an indiscretion for which he had to offer his resignation later.[45] Lord Curzon protested that his hands had been weakened by the publication of such recommendations 'claiming far more for the Turks than even in their wildest moments they have dared to ask for themselves....'[46]

---

[44] Muhammad Miyan, *Jamiyat al Ulama Kia Hai?*, U.P.: Jamiyat al Ulama, n.d., pp. 39–40.

[45] Frank Owen, *Tempestuous Journey: Lloyd George—His Life and Times*, London: Hutchinson, 1954, pp. 603–4.

[46] Lord Ronaldshay, *The Life of Lord Curzon*, London: Ernest Benn, 1928, Vol. III, p. 286.

However, during the later negotiations at Lausanne during 1922–3 the Turks were not so much interested in claiming their Sultan's suzerainty over the Holy Places as they were in obtaining possession of the Vilayet of Mosul for its strategic and oil value. And again, their case was based on the claim that the people in the Vilayet were of Turkish origin. The Turks also suggested that the Kurds were also of Turkish race. Lord Curzon's counter arguments were again designed to prove that the Turks who lived in Mosul were not Osmanli Turks and that the Kurds were a people of Iranian race who spoke an Iranian language.[47] All such arguments couched in racial terms must have appeared very strange to Indian Muslim leaders like Muhammad Ali and Azad, if they had bothered to follow the proceedings of the conference. Here were Muslims in India prepared to lay down their lives for the maintenance of the *Khalifa's* sovereignty over the Holy Places in Arabia, Iraq, Syria and Palestine. And Turkish representatives, on the other hand, who were in a fairly strong position because they had driven the Greeks from Turkey, were prepared to hand over Arab lands as good riddance as mandates of the League of Nations to Britain and France. On 3 March 1924 the final and deadly blow was struck at the Khilafat movement by Ghazi Mustafa Kemal Pasha who exiled the *Khalifa*, Abd-ul-Majid, and abolished the Khilafat.

Thus, the Khilafat movement, being deprived of its main motive power, was bound to collapse. Professor, W. C. Smith has observed: 'It had petered out because it was a wrong ideology, romantic and out of touch with actualities.'[48] Professor F. Rahman suggest, '…It was, perhaps more semi-consciously, a bid for finding Muslim security in a future independent India over against a non-Muslim majority.'[49] All this was true. But there was something more than this in the Khilafat movement. The Khilafat movement was the first and the only movement in which both Hindus and Muslims had played a joint role on a mass scale. But as suggested earlier, freedom of India was not the first and only objective of the Muslim struggle. Muslims seemed

---

[47] Ibid., pp. 322–35.
[48] W. C. Smith, op. cit., p. 249.
[49] F. Rahman, 'Muslim Modernism in the Indo-Pakistan Subcontinent', *Bulletin of the School of Oriental and African Studies*, London: 1958, xxi, 1, p. 89.

to suggest to the Hindus through the Khilafat movement that they could become passionately interested in the freedom of their country only if it ensured the safety and glory of Islam both in India and Muslim countries. No one was more acutely aware of this than Gandhi.

> We both have now an opportunity of a life-time. The Khilafat question will not recur for another hundred years. If the Hindus wish to cultivate eternal friendship with the Mussalmans, they must perish with them in the attempt to vindicate the honour of Islam.[50]

And as it will be seen later, even a highly Westernized leader like Jinnah could evoke such tremendous support for Pakistan because he said that the freedom of a united India might bring about Hindu domination and endanger the safety of Islam.

Some of the Muslim League historians have tried to paint Gandhi as the arch-villain who deliberately directed the Khilafat movement with the sole purpose of causing maximum harm to Muslim interests and Muslim solidarity. His first aim was to persuade them to leave the Muslim League, and having succeeded in destroying their political organization, he carefully planned their educational and economic ruination. Thus Muslim lawyers and litigants boycotted the courts, and students and teachers deserted their schools and colleges. The Muslim community, which was already economically and educationally backward, was weakened still further. Even the migration that thousands of Muslims undertook was a trap set by Gandhi. 'The land of the *rishis* was being rid of the *malechhas*! Here was the crux of Gandhi's programme. Well might he rejoice over it!'[51] Another verdict based on the same premises was: 'Everything destructive of Mussalmans had the Mahatmaic blessing of Gandhi.'[52]

It is not quite fair to lay the whole blame on Gandhi and accuse him of having planned methodically the political and economic ruination of the Muslim community. Surely, what

---

[50] M. K. Gandhi, op. cit., pp. 5–6.

[51] A. B. Rajput, *Muslim League Yesterday and Today*, Lahore: Ashraf, 1948, p. 37.

[52] Zia-ud-Din Ahmad Suleri, *My Leader*, Lahore: Lion Press, 1946, p. 52.

Muslims were being called upon to do was in conformity with what their leaders thought were Islamic injunctions. If a political power like the British were waging war against the Muslim *Khalifa*, it was the sacred duty of Muslims in India either to paralyse that Government or migrate from the country. This code of action was not something which Gandhi had prescribed, but had come down to Muslims not only from their religion but also from the practices and traditions of Muslim leaders like Sayyid Ahmad Barelawi and Shah Abd-ul-Aziz.

It has also been suggested that though Gandhi was quite willing to let Muslims make tremendous sacrifices for the sake of the Khilafat and of India's independence, he did not demand the same services from Hindus. Thus, he was quite keen on the Aligarh University declaring its independence of Government control and grants, but did not do anything to persuade the Benares Hindu University to follow the example of Aligarh.[53] This argument does not take into account the fact that Gandhi did not exercise a complete and dominant hold over Hindus in the early twenties. He had recently emerged as an outstanding Congress leader, but he was trying to unite moderates and extremists in the Congress and to make the Congress a national organization. Congress had been divided before Gandhi's time; sometimes it was under the control of moderate leadership like that of Gokhale and sometimes under the influence of extremists like Tilak. It was Gandhi's role to unite these factions and guide them along a united course of action. Similarly, as it has been suggested earlier, he also tried to reassure Hindus of Muslim loyalty to India whenever orthodox Hindus insinuated that Muslims had extra-territorial loyalties and that in following the Qur'anic injunctions, they could turn against all non-Muslims, the British and Hindus alike.

Muslim leaders like Abul Kalam Azad and Muhammad Ali were responsible for exhorting Muslims to sacrifice their material possessions and interests for the sake of Islam. Azad's rhetoric created the climate for mental vacuity in which Muslims did not calculate the consequences of their actions.

---

[53] Ibid. According to Nehru, a very large number of students from the Benares Hindu University did participate in the non-cooperation movement. See Syed Sharifuddin Pirzada, ed., *Leaders' Correspondence with Mr Jinnah*, Bombay: Sh. Nazir Ahmad, 1944, p. 81.

Muslims should neither think of politics nor education, should neither praise freedom nor get entangled in the shackles of slavery. They are not supposed to think or decide on these things. It was God who had to decide on these things and He has decided. Their duty is only to act strictly in accordance with the commands of God which are incorporated in the Qur'an. They should empty their minds of all man-made ideas and national sentiments and surrender themselves to the instruction and guidance of the Supreme Educator. If Islam invites them to participate in politics, they should immediately get involved in it. If it tells them to keep aloof, then they should immediately withdraw from it. If Islam says that slavery and sycophancy are the two real means to achieve welfare, then Muslims should become living embodiments of slavery. If Islam says that freedom and demanding one's rights are the only sources of a nation's life and honour, then Muslims should immerse themselves in the struggle for freedom...Muslims have no desires of their own, no plans, no policy. Their desire and policy is to act completely according to the dictates of Islam.[54]

In such an intellectual climate it was relatively easy for Khilafat leaders and the *ulema* to ask the Muslims to give up their jobs, boycott the law courts, withdraw from the army and police, and even migrate from the country all in the name and defence of Islam.

Azad's autobiography states that soon after he reached the age of sixteen, that is during 1904–5, his views regarding religion underwent a radical change. He started asking: 'Why should each religion claim to be the sole repository of truth and condemn all others as false?' He 'passed from one phase to another and a stage came when all the old bonds imposed on my mind by family and upbringing were completely shattered.'[55] But in 1911–12 in the *Al-Hilal,* he was exhorting Muslims to pin their complete faith to Islam because it was the repository of all that was good and true in worldly and spiritual life. There was no need for them to adopt a political or an economic programme when Islam gave eternally valid answers to all these problems. This shows that either he had reverted to Islam or he was deliberately using Islam to excite Muslims into taking a vigorous anti-British stand in partnership with Hindus in Indian politics. As for Maulana Muhammad Ali, he admitted in the Indian

---

[54] Badr-ul-Hasan, ed., op. cit., p. 78–79.
[55] Maulana Abul Kalam Azad, op. cit., pp. 3–4.

Round Table Conference, 'Where Islam and India are concerned, I am mad.'[56]

The author is not suggesting that Abul Kalam Azad and Muhammad Ali should bear the entire blame for not having foreseen the consequences of the Khilafat movement. Both Muslims and their leaders thought and functioned in such emotional terms and Islam, as they understood it from the Qur'an, also beckoned them to place complete trust in God and not to think of the consequences or the strength of their enemy if their action and conduct were righteous and guided by highest motives.

Perhaps it is unfair to judge the roles of men like Azad and Muhammad Ali in terms of the consequences of their actions and pronouncements for they were political agitators and revolutionaries and not shrewd politicians. Azad always chastised Muslims for being timid and following the lead of Sir Sayyid when God commanded them to be fearless and struggle for truth and justice. It is only after the emergence of Jinnah as the dominant leader that Muslim politics becomes a politics of both methods and objectives. Jinnah could put on both dresses with equal ease. He could appear as a fiery Muslim Nationalist before the masses. And he could also function as a hard and shrewd negotiator with the Viceroy and Congress leaders.

III. The Nehru Report and Jinnah's Fourteen Points

As it has already been stated, Jinnah was opposed to Gandhi's non-cooperation movement on the plea that the Congress leaders had not considered carefully the practical consequences of such a movement. In the Nagpur session of the Congress in December 1920, protesting against the non-cooperation programme, he declared, 'Mine is the right way—the constitutional way is the right way.' Jinnah must have been equally opposed to the exuberance of uncontrolled and often misguided energy generated by the Khilafat movement. Jawaharlal Nehru has written:

> He felt completely out of his element in the khaki-clad crowd demanding speeches in Hindustani. The enthusiasm of the people outside struck him as mob-hysteria.[57]

---

[56] *Indian Round Table Conference, 12 November, 1930–19 January 1931, Proceedings.* Cmd. 3778, London: His Majesty's Stationery Office, 1931, p. 98.

[57] Jawaharlal Nehru, op. cit., pp. 67–68.

In the annual session of the All-India Muslim League at Lucknow in March–April 1923, Jinnah's resolution recommending entry into Councils and striving for attainment of Dominion status was vigorously opposed in the Subjects Committee by Dr Ansari and other leading Khilafat and non-cooperation leaders. It was reported that Jinnah's motion was rejected because many members of the Committee were absent. In the open session, both the parties, those who supported Jinnah, and those who were in favour of continued non-cooperation, were evenly balanced.[58]

As it has been indicated earlier, Jinnah believed passionately in the constitutional progress of his country. This, he thought, could only be built on the bedrock of Hindu-Muslim unity. Thus, if he opposed the temerity of non-cooperators, he was equally against the timidity of conservative Muslim leaders like Sir Muhammad Shafi. A major source of friction with the conservative section was Jinnah's emphasis on Hindu-Muslim unity and his persistent efforts to bring about such a settlement. All this crystallized on the issue of opposition to the Simon Commission. The British Government announced the constitution of a Commission under Sir John Simon in November 1927. The Commission, which had no Indian members on it, was being sent to investigate India's constitutional problems and make recommendations to the Government on the future constitution of India. The Congress decided to boycott the Simon Commission and accept the challenge of Lord Birkenhead, Secretary of State for India, to produce a constitution acceptable to the various elements in India. There was a clear split in the Muslim League. Sir Muhammad Shafi, who enjoyed the support of the Government and who wanted to cooperate with the Commission, decided to hold the Muslim League session in Lahore in December 1927. The other faction, whose moving spirit was Jinnah, and which stood for the boycott of the Commission, held the Muslim League session at the same time in Calcutta. In the Calcutta session of the All-India Muslim League it was resolved that the Muslim League Council should appoint a Subcommittee to confer with the Working Committee of the Indian National Congress and other organizations with a view to drafting a constitution for India. The Muslim League session also made it clear that it stood in favour of the following proposals:

---

[58] *The Indian Annual Register 1923*, Calcutta, 1923, Vol. I, p. 935.

1. The formation of a separate Province of Sind.
2. Introduction of reforms in the N-W. F. P. and in Baluchistan on the same footing as in other provinces.
3. Unless and until the above two proposals were implemented, the Muslims would never surrender the right of their representation through separate electorates. Muslims would be willing to abandon separate electorates in favour of joint electorates with reservation of seats fixed in proportion to the population of different communities, if the above two proposals were implemented to the full satisfaction of Muslims and also if the following proposals were accepted:
4. Hindu minorities in Sind, Baluchistan and the N-W. F. P. would be accorded the same concessions in the form of reservation of seats over and above the proportion of their population as Muslims would get in Hindu majority provinces.
5. Muslim representation in the Central Legislature would not be less than one-third.
6. In addition to provisions like religious freedom, there was to be a further guarantee in the constitution that on communal matters no bill or resolution would be considered or passed if a three-fourths majority of the members of the community concerned were opposed to it.[59]

It was significant that no mention was made of Punjab or Bengal in the above proposals. It had always been the contention of Muhammad Shafi that Muslim majorities, particularly where they were narrow as in Punjab and Bengal, were being sacrificed in order to get more seats for Muslims than were due to them on the basis of their population in Hindu majority Provinces. It must also be emphasized that under the influence of leaders like Jinnah, Muhammad Ali, and Sir Ali Imam, Muslims were prepared under certain circumstances to abandon separate electorates.

The policy of the British Conservative Government in Britain was to keep the initiative firmly in their hands and not to let it be seized by the Congress or Muslim Nationalist leaders like Jinnah.

---

[59] Resolution No. 4. (*Text of Resolutions Passed at the 19th Annual Session of the All-India Muslim League on the 30th and 31st December 1927 and 1st January 1928.*) *Resolutions of the All India Muslim League from May 1924 to December 1936*, Delhi, n.d.

Clear evidence of this may be found in Lord Birkenhead's letter
to the Viceroy, Lord Irwin, in February 1928.

> I should advise Simon to see at all stages important people who are not
> boycotting the Commission, particularly Moslems and the depressed
> classes. I should widely advertise all his interviews with representative
> Moslems. The whole policy is now obvious. It is to terrify the immense
> Hindu population by the apprehension that the Commission having
> been got hold of by the Moslems, may present a report altogether
> destructive of the Hindu position, thereby securing a solid Moslem
> support and *leaving Jinnah high and dry.* (Author's italics.)[60]

Thus, here was an opportunity for the Congress to negotiate
with Jinnah and arrive at an amicable and firm settlement with
the Muslim League that Jinnah and Muhammad Ali represented.
If the Congress had followed such a course, they could have
isolated the conservative factions in the Muslim League like those
led by Muhammad Shafi and supported by the British. But the
Nehru Report produced precisely the opposite result. It drove the
two factions in the Muslim League to unite.

It would not be fair to suggest that the entire Congress leadership was avowedly anti-Muslim. There is considerable evidence to
show that men like C. R. Das and Motilal Nehru did try to pursue
a non-communal policy. But the anti-Muslim elements in the
Congress and among Hindus triumphed in the end and forced
the Congress to follow a strong policy towards the Muslims.

In the special session of the Congress at Delhi held in
September 1923, leaders like C. R. Das and Motilal Nehru
succeeded in persuading the Congress to allow those Congressmen
who were eager to enter the Legislatures to stand as candidates.
They felt that Gandhi's methods of non-cooperation had been
tried and found not very successful. They felt that the Nationalists
should capture the Councils and paralyse the Government by
withholding supplies and passing motions of no-confidence. This
created two factions in the Congress; the Swaraj Party or 'Pro-
Changers', which stood for contesting the elections and for
entering the Councils, and the 'No-Changers' who followed
Gandhi and were in favour of continuing the boycott policy.

In the first elections that were held towards the end of 1923,

---

[60] The Earl of Birkenhead. *Frederick Edwin, Earl of Birkenhead; The Last Phase,*
London: Thornton Butterworth, 1935, p. 255.

C. R. Das created a stir in Bengal. He was not only an undisputed leader of the Hindus but also succeeded in creating a profound impression on the Muslims. Bengali Muslims, who constituted slightly more than fifty per cent of the population, held barely thirty per cent of the posts under the Government because of their backwardness. C. R. Das made a dramatic announcement when he declared that this disparity would be rectified under Congress rule when sixty per cent of all new appointments would be offered to the Muslims until such time that they would achieve adequate representation according to population in the Services. He was even more generous in the matter of Muslim share of Services under the Calcutta Corporation where he said eighty per cent of new appointments would be offered to Muslims. But the Swarajists entered the Councils to wreck the Government and not to form one. C. R. Das died on 16 June 1925. After his death, Hindu communalists became dominant. And as Maulana Azad has written, 'The result was that the Muslims of Bengal moved away from the Congress and the first seeds of partition were sown.'[61]

It was also significant that in the United Provinces and in Punjab, Hindu communalism was emerging as a dominant force in the Congress. Commenting on the elections of 1926, Motilal Nehru wrote to his son:

It was simply beyond me to meet the kind of propaganda started against me under the auspices of the Malaviya-Lala gang. Publicly I was denounced as an anti-Hindu and pro-Mohammedan but privately almost every individual voter was told that I was a beefeater in league with the Mohammedans to legalize cow slaughter in public places at all times.

In the same letter he went on to assert: 'The Malaviya-Lala gang aided by Birla's money are making frantic efforts to capture the Congress. They will probably succeed as no counter effort is possible from our side'.[62]

It might seem strange that Motilal Nehru, who was so concerned and gloomy about the communal situation towards the end of 1926, did not seem to display much caution and tact in tackling the communal problem in the Nehru Report in 1928. He

---

[61] Maulana Abul Kalam Azad, op. cit., p. 21.
[62] Jawaharlal Nehru, *A Bunch of Old Letters,* Bombay: Asia Publishing House, 1958, pp. 49–50.

was confident that, 'barring a few diehards of the Shafi school', Punjab would agree with the recommendations of the Report. As for Bengal, he relied on Maulana Abul Kalam Azad, who had assured him of even better results in that Province. Thus, he thought that having disposed of the Hindu-Muslim question in Punjab and Bengal, 'all that will then remain to settle the Hindu-Muslim question in the rest of India will I expect be easily settled by throwing a few crumbs here and there to the small minorities'.[63]

The Nehru Report was an answer to the challenge thrown to Indians by Lord Birkenhead that the composition of the Simon Commission had to be purely British because Indians were incapable of arriving at an agreed solution as regards the constitutional problem of India. The Committee which was called upon to draft a constitution for India was chaired by Pandit Motilal Nehru. It included spokesmen of the various communal points of view like those of the Muslims, the Hindu Mahasabha, non-Brahmins, Sikhs, and also those representing the Liberal viewpoint and the interests of labour.[64]

The Report referred to what it considered the illogical fear of Muslims of being dominated by the Hindu majority. But what was significant was the way Muslims were thinking of tackling this problem. They had made a novel suggestion that 'they should at least dominate in some parts of India.' Hindus, on the other hand, in spite of enjoying all-India majority, were fearful of Muslim majorities in Bengal, Punjab, Sind, Baluchistan and the North-West Frontier Province. But the Report ended on an optimistic note saying that once alien authority and intervention were withdrawn from India, people would start thinking in terms of the larger economic and political problems. In such a climate, political parties based mainly on economic grounds were a natural outcome.[65]

The Report conceded Muslim demands for the formation of separate Provinces of the North-West Frontier and Sind. Probably as a sort of compensating concession to the Hindu community,

---

[63] Ibid., p. 64.

[64] *All Parties Conference 1928. Report of the Committee appointed by the Conference to determine the principles of the Constitution for India,* Allahabad: General Secretary, All-India Congress Committee, 1928, p. 23.

[65] Ibid., pp. 28–9.

the Report suggested the creation of a new Canarese-speaking Province in Southern India. But on the issue of electorates, the recommendations of the Report were bound to antagonize most of the Muslim vocal interests. The Report not only rejected separate electorates, but also weightage for minorities. Reservation of seats was accorded to Muslims at the Centre and in the Provinces in which they were in a minority and to no other group except the non-Muslims in the North-West Frontier Province. But all this was to be in strict proportion to the size of the community. 'A minority must remain a minority whether any seats are reserved for it or not.' Muslims had always complained that even in Punjab and Bengal, where they enjoyed a small majority, they were educationally and economically so backward that without separate electorates and reservation of seats they would be in an extremely weak position. The Report tried to show by detailed examination of the distribution of the Muslim population in the various districts of Punjab and Bengal that Muslims without reservation of seats could certainly expect to have elected majorities at least in proportion to their numbers in these Provinces.

The Centre was to be constructed on a unitary basis. The Lower House was to be elected by general constituencies and the Upper House, though elected by Provinces, did not have equal representation for each Province. Thus, the Muslims could feel that the autonomy accorded to them in Muslim majority Provinces was weakened by a unitary Centre. And because of the absence of separate electorates and reservation of seats, they were not even sure of their majority in Punjab and Bengal. It was obvious that Muslim leaders were not likely to accept these proposals. According to the supplementary Report of the Committee, the Aga Khan had gone so far as to advocate independence for each Indian Province by suggesting that the position of each Province must be similar to that of Bavaria in the former German Confederation rather than that of an American state or a Swiss canton.[66]

Soon after the All Parties Conference in Lucknow in August 1928 (which met to consider the Report), Shaukat Ali expressed what, perhaps, a number of Muslim leaders felt about the Report.

---

[66] Pattabhi Sitaramayya, *History of the Indian National Congress*, Bombay: Padma Publications, 1946, Vol. I, p. 334.

'As a young man, he said, he had been a keen owner of greyhounds, but he had never seen greyhounds deal with a hare as the Hindus proposed to deal with the Muslims.'[67]

A Convention of all parties known as the All Parties National Convention met in Calcutta in the last week of December 1928, to consider the Nehru Report. Jinnah, who was at that time President of the Muslim League, put forward his famous Fourteen Points, which were amendments to the Report, before the open session of the Convention on 28 December 1928. His basic amendments were:

1. In the Central Legislature Muslims should have 33⅓ per cent of the seats.
2. That the residuary powers should vest in the Provinces and not in the Centre.
3. That Muslims in Punjab and Bengal should be represented on the basis of population for ten years subject to subsequent revision of this principle.

Jinnah pleaded for statesmanship and cited constitutional precedents in countries like Canada and Egypt where, he said, political adjustments were made not on a population basis, but on principles of equity. Jinnah's proposals were rejected *in toto*. M. R. Jayakar, who represented the Hindu Mahasabha point of view, pointed out that Jinnah, after all, represented only a small minority of Muslims and there was no guarantee that if the Convention agreed to his proposals, the rest of the Muslim community would abide by such an agreement. He also warned that, having with great difficulty restrained his Hindu supporters from rebelling against the Nehru Report, it would be impossible for him to persuade them to accept any more concessions to Muslims.[68]

According to Muhammad Azizul Huque, one of the Muslim League delegates who participated in the All Parties National Convention, Hindu and Muslim leaders could not reach an agreement in the Convention because of the unwillingness of the Congress and Hindu leaders to accept the Muslim demand for 33⅓ per cent of the seats in the Central Legislature put forward by Jinnah

---

[67] J. Coatman, *Years of Destiny: India 1926–1932*, London: Jonathan Cape, 1932, p. 214.

[68] Matlubul Hasan Saiyid, op. cit., p. 272.

on behalf of the Muslim League. According to the same source, Jinnah with great difficulty had persuaded the Muslim leaders to accept the principle of joint electorates with reservation of seats recommended by the Nehru Report. Muslim delegates from all over India, and particularly those from Bengal, were strongly in favour of separate electorates. Gandhi pointed out that he was inclined to concede the Muslim demand for 33⅓ per cent representation but since the Sikh leaders also demanded one-third representation in the Punjab, it was difficult to accept the Muslim League demand. All this meant that since the Nehru Report had already conceded 30 per cent of the representation in the Central Legislature to Muslims and since the Muslim League had accepted the principle of joint electorates with reservation of seats as recommended by the Nehru Report, the only reason why the Congress and Muslim League leaders could not reach a settlement was because of the unwillingness of Hindu leaders to concede the additional 3⅓ per cent seats that the Muslim League demanded in the Central Legislature.[69]

The result was that the refusal to accept any amendments to the Nehru Report on the part of the Congress and Hindu leaders at the All Parties National Convention united the different factions of Muslims in the All-India Muslim Conference held in Delhi under the Presidentship of the Aga Khan on 1 January 1929. Some of the noteworthy features of the Resolution passed in this Conference were:

1. The only form of government suitable to Indian conditions was a federal system with complete autonomy and residuary powers vested in the constituent states.
2. Muslims should not be deprived of the right to elect their representatives through separate electorates without their consent.
3. Muslims should continue to have weightage in the Hindu majority Provinces and they were willing to accord the same privilege to non-Muslim minorities in Sind, the N-W. F. P. and Baluchistan.
4. Muslims should have their due share in the Central and Provincial cabinets.

[69] For this version of the negotiations in the All Parties National Convention, see M. A. Mehtar, *Whys of the Great Indian Conflict*, Lahore: Ashraf, 1947, pp. 67–73.

5. Muslim majority in all Muslim majority Provinces (presumably with particular reference to Bengal and Punjab) should in no way be disturbed.[70]

Muslim demands were given a more cogent presentation in the famous Fourteen Points of Jinnah, an earlier draft of which had been presented before the All Parties National Convention in December 1928. The final draft of these Points was in the form of a resolution which Jinnah intended to move at the meeting of the All-India Muslim League on 28 March 1929. According to this resolution, no scheme for the future constitution of the Government of India would be acceptable to Muslims unless and until the following basic principles were incorporated in it:

1. The form of the future Constitution should be federal with the residuary powers vested in the Provinces.
2. A uniform measure of autonomy shall be granted to all Provinces.
3. All Legislatures in the country and other elected bodies shall be constituted on the definite principle of adequate and effective representation of minorities in every Province without reducing the majority in any Province to a minority or even equality.
4. In the Central Legislature, Mussulman representation shall not be less than one third.
5. Representation of communal groups shall continue to be by means of separate electorates as at present: provided it shall be open to any community, at any time, to abandon its separate electorate in favour of a joint electorate.
6. Any territorial redistribution that might at any time be necessary shall not in any way affect the Muslim majority in the Punjab, Bengal and the North-West Frontier Province.
7. Full religious liberty, i.e. liberty of belief, worship and observance, propaganda, association and education, shall be guaranteed to all communities.
8. No Bill or resolution or any part thereof shall be passed in any Legislature or any other elected body if three-

---

[70] Maurice Gwyer and A. Appadorai, *Speeches and Documents on the Indian Constitution 1921–47*, London: Oxford University Press, 1957, Vol. I, pp. 244–5.

fourths of the members of any community in that particular body oppose such a Bill, resolution or part thereof on the ground that it would be injurious to the interests of that community or in the alternative, such other method is devised as may be found feasible and practicable to deal with such cases.

9. Sind should be separated from the Bombay Presidency.

10. Reforms should be introduced in the North-West Frontier Province and Baluchistan on the same footing as in other Provinces.

11. Provision should be made in the Constitution giving Muslims an adequate share, along with the other Indians, in all the Services of the State and in local self-governing bodies having due regard to the requirements of efficiency.

12. The Constitution should embody adequate safeguards for the protection of Muslim culture and for the protection and promotion of Muslim education, language, religion, personal laws and Muslim charitable institutions and for their due share in the grants-in-aid given by the State and by local self-governing bodies.

13. No Cabinet, either Central or Provincial, should be formed without there being a proportion of at least one-third Muslim Ministers.

14. No change shall be made in the Constitution by the Central Legislature except with the concurrence of the States constituting the Indian Federation.[71]

When one reads the Nehru Report, one wonders why an experienced politician like Motilal Nehru could flout the views and interests of Muslims. Several answers are possible. Muhammad Ali attributed the indifference of the Nehru Report to Muslim interests to the political surrender of Motilal Nehru and Gandhi 'for the sake of their popularity to the Hindu Mahasabha.'[72] It is no doubt true that the Congress Party in the late twenties was not a unified machine. It had been split in 1923 between 'Pro-Changers' and 'No-Changers'. Gandhi's influence was not easily available because he had voluntarily and shrewdly withdrawn himself from political activities. Jawaharlal Nehru

---

[71] Ibid., pp. 245–7.

[72] Afzal Iqbal, ed. *Select Writings and Speeches of Mohamed Ali*, op. cit., p. 477.

and Subjas Chandra Bose were busy building up their support in youth movements and pressuring the Congress into taking a clear stand on complete independence as against Dominion status. Faced with such divisive forces, it was not easy for Motilal Nehru to produce a Report which satisfied most of the Muslim grievances. If he had yielded to Jinnah's amendments, it would have meant that he was yielding to one of the factions of Muslims, thereby antagonizing considerable Hindu sections. Muslims were not only disunited, but there were Muslim leaders like Dr Ansari, Abul Kalam Azad and Abdul Kadir Kasuri (Punjab) who were in whole-hearted agreement with the proposals of the Nehru Report.

But it must be emphasized that Motilal Nehru stood solidly behind his Report not merely because it was politically wise to do so. His intellectual and ideological sympathies were in complete accord with the spirit of the Report. He was a lawyer who believed in a liberal, democratic and constitutional government. To him, separate electorates were not only antithetical to all essential principles of responsible government, but had also accentuated the animosities that prevailed between the two communities. Indeed, even Jinnah, had he not aligned himself with Muslims in politics, would have fully reciprocated such sentiments. It was while giving evidence before the Parliamentary Select Committee in 1919 that Jinnah had given expression to such views. When he was asked whether he wished to see complete elimination of political distinctions between Muslims and Hindus, his answer was, 'Yes; nothing will please me more when that day comes.'[73] In the author's opinion, herein lay the crux of the problem. Leaders like Motilal Nehru in their total adherence to Western modes of thinking and forms of government were not taking into account the peculiar and unique political conditions in India. India was a heterogeneous subcontinent and in order to solve its problems, they were drawing on the practices and traditions of a unitary and homogeneous country like the United Kingdom. Jinnah realized this mistake later. But the Congress persisted in following the same course. This was clearly demonstrated in 1937 (as it will be seen later), when Motilal Nehru's son, Jawaharlal Nehru, took a firm stand against the inclusion of Muslim League representatives

---

[73] *Joint Select Committee on the Government of India Bill. Vol. II. Minutes of Evidence,* London: H.M. Stationery Office, 1919, p. 225.

in the Provincial Cabinet of the United Provinces on the plea that it should be a homogeneous and united team and not a weak coalition Cabinet.

Jinnah also learned a bitter lesson from the All Parties National Convention of 1928. He had played the role of a compromiser and negotiator successfully in composing Hindu-Muslim differences at Lucknow in 1916. He thought in 1928 he could play the same role in negotiating a compromise. But he was bluntly reminded that he had no right to speak on behalf of the Muslims because he did not represent them. There he learnt the lesson that political leadership did not rest merely on one's forensic ability to plead a political case. It also depended on political strength, that is, the actual support that one had among the masses of people. It was only when Jinnah acquired a large political following among Muslims and with his political astuteness (like Gandhi) succeeded in uniting different factions and interests of Muslims that he became a leader who was respected and feared by his opponents because he could veto any proposal that was not acceptable to the Muslim League.

IV. WIDENING OF THE CHASM, 1930–40

I. *The Round Table Conference and the Government of India Act, 1935*

Since the Simon Commission was composed purely of British members, attempts were made to consult Indian opinion as fully as possible. Such attempts did not meet with much success because of the Congress and League boycott (though the Shafi wing of the League cooperated). At a later stage the British Government assured Indian leaders that they would hold a Round Table Conference to which representatives of both British India, Indian States and British political parties would be invited. It may also be pointed out that Lord Irwin. while announcing the decision of the Government in October 1929, to hold such a Conference, also made the historic declaration wherein he stated on behalf of the British Government that the natural issue of India's constitutional progress was the attainment of Dominion status.

The Congress Party wanted a clear commitment from the Government that the purpose of the Round Table Conference would be to draft a scheme for Dominion status which would be implemented by the British Government. The Viceroy made it clear that the British Government would give no such undertaking as the Conference was being called to elicit the greatest possible measure of agreement for the final proposals which, again, would have to be submitted to Parliament for its approval. Whereupon the Congress at its annual session at Lahore in November 1929, decided that the Congress would not take part in the proposed Round Table Conference. The resolution also declared that the word 'Swaraj' in Article 1 of the Congress Constitution would signify complete independence and that the entire scheme of the Nehru Committee Report had lapsed. The Congress also decided to withdraw from the Central and Provincial Legislatures and boycott future elections. On 26 January 1930, Independence Day was celebrated and the resolution which was circulated by the Working Committee to be adopted in public meetings said, 'We hold it to be a crime against man and God to submit any longer to a rule that has caused this four-fold disaster (economic, political, cultural and spiritual) to our country.' The people were called upon to prepare for civil disobedience, including non-payment of taxes. The campaign of civil disobedience began in March–April 1930.

It was significant that Muhammad Ali called upon Muslims to remain aloof from the Congress movement at a meeting of the All-India Muslim Conference at Bombay in April 1930. His denunciation of the Congress and Gandhi was as follows: 'Mr Gandhi is working under the influence of the communalist Hindu Mahasabha. He is fighting for the supremacy of Hinduism and the submergence of Muslims.'[74] This was strong language and this view of Congress and Gandhi, as we shall see later, became the official and accepted view of the Muslim League under Jinnah. This bitterness also cast its shadow over the Round Table Conference. Gandhi was absent in the first session, November 1930–January 1931. He was present in the second session of the Round Table Conference in the autumn of 1931, after having suspended the civil disobedience movement in accordance with the agreement reached between himself and Lord Irwin.

In the Round Table Conferences there took place a long and

---

[74] Cited in Jamil-ud-Din Ahmad, ed., op. cit., Vol. I, p. 529. According to Gandhi, several thousands of Muslims went to jail in the Congress civil disobedience movement of 1930. See Maurice Gwyer and A. Appadorai, op. cit., p. 257.

bitter conflict as regards the number of seats that minorities should be given in various legislatures. Sir Muhammad Shafi asked for 33⅓ per cent representation for Muslims in the Central Legislature of British India. He argued that even though Muslims constituted a little over 25 per cent of the population of British India, yet so far as defence of the country was concerned, they bore the major burden. The logic was that seats could not be distributed among the various communities on the basis of pure numbers. Other factors, like the historical importance of the community and its share in the defence of the country, should be taken into account. This was reminiscent of the way the Aga Khan had put forward the Muslim case before Lord Minto in October 1906. Similarly, Shafi argued strongly for Muslim majority representation in Punjab and Bengal now that the Provinces were to be given provincial autonomy.[75] But no agreement could be reached on the question of minority representation. Gandhi tried his best, but 'with deep sorrow and deeper humiliation' he announced 'utter failure to secure an agreed solution of the communal question.' Even after their return to India, a representative body of the delegates to the Round Table Conference continued their efforts at Simla to arrive at an agreement on the communal question, but failed.

On 16 August 1932 Prime Minister Ramsay MacDonald announced the Communal Award. As regards separate electorates, the Prime Minister's statement said that 'Government had to face facts as they are, and must maintain this exceptional form of representation.' Muslim representation in various Provinces under the Award was as shown in the table overleaf.[76]

The Sikhs, who were 13.2 per cent of the population of Punjab, secured thirty-two seats in an Assembly of 175 members. The Hindu Depressed Classes were given a number of special seats to be filled from special Depressed Class electorates in the areas where these voters were concentrated. Gandhi in protest undertook a fast unto death and in September 1932 an agreement known as the Poona Pact was arrived at between

---

[75] *Indian Round Table Conference 12 November 1930–19 January 1931. Proceedings of Subcommittees (Part II) (Subcommittees II–IX)*, London: H.M. Stationery Office, 1931, pp. 98–99.

[76] V. P. Menon, *The Transfer of Power in India*, Princeton: Princeton University Press, 1957, p. 49.

Dr B. R. Ambedkar and Gandhi. According to this Pact, seats
were reserved for Depressed Classes in various Provinces on a
more generous scale than those awarded by the Communal
Award. For each of these seats, a panel of four Depressed Class
candidates would be elected by the Depressed Classes. These four
members would be candidates for election to each such reserved
seat and the candidate from these four would be elected by the
general non-Muslim electorate. In this way, Gandhi was successful
in avoiding what he considered the defection of Depressed Classes
from the Hindu community.

Province	Muslim Percentage of Population	Total Number of Seats	Number of Seats Reserved for Muslims
Madras	7.9	215	29
Bombay excluding Sind	9.2	175	30
Bengal	54.7	250	119
The United Provinces	15.3	228	66
The Punjab	57.0	175	86
The Central Provinces	4.7	112	14
Assam	33.7	108	34
Sind	70.7	60	34
N-W. F. Province	91.8	50	36
Bihar and Orissa	10.8	175	42

Another conflict was concerning the powers of the Centre. The
Muslim position was that the residuary powers, that is, the domain
over subjects not explicitly allocated to the Centre or the Provinces
or to the concurrent jurisdiction of both, should rest with the
Province. The Hindus were in favour of such powers being vested
in the Centre. It may be noted that according to Section 104 of
the Government of India Act, 1935, the residuary powers were
vested in the Governor General to be exercised in his discretion.

The Government announced their decisions after considering
the various views put forward in the Round Table Conferences
in the form of a White Paper in March 1933. In April, a joint
Committee of both Houses under Lord Linlithgow as Chairman
was set up to consider the White Paper proposals and make

recommendations regarding the future government of India. The Committee sat for eighteen months and examined numerous witnesses and also consulted a fairly representative delegation from British India and Indian states. The latter included men like the Aga Khan, Sir Tej Bahadur Sapru and Dr Ambedkar. In December 1934, the Government introduced a bill based on the recommendations of the Joint Select Committee. On 4 August 1935, the bill, having been passed by the Parliament, received the Royal Assent. And thus, the Government of India Act, 1935, came into being.

Elections for the Indian Legislative Assembly, which was still functioning under the provisions of the Government of India Act, 1919, were held towards the end of 1934. The results indicated that the strength of the parties in the Assembly was as follows:

Congress—44; Congress Nationalists (that section of Congressmen who repudiated the Communal Award and thus formed a separate group in support of the Hindu Mahasabha)—11; Independents (all except three, Muslims)—22; Europeans (representatives of the British business community)—11; Officials—26; Nominated members—13. The Government, with the support of Europeans, officials and nominated members, could muster in all fifty members. The Congressmen could probably, with the aid of eleven Congress Nationalists, depend upon the support of fifty-five members. Thus, the Muslims under the leadership of Jinnah held the balance between these two blocs.

Jinnah was not only in his element in such a setting, but pursued a non-communal policy which was more in line with the beliefs he had cherished and worked for in the past than it was with the course of action that he adopted in subsequent years. Of course his own explanation of such a course of action would be that he was willing and eager to play his old role of the ambassador of Hindu-Muslim unity as long as the Congress displayed a breadth of view which was non-communal and accommodating. When the Joint Select Committee's Report came up for debate in February 1935, the Congress motion was that the recommendations of the Report should be rejected completely because they were no more than the usual imperialist device to deprive the Indian people of the power to assume charge of their affairs. Muslims, led by Jinnah, did not agree with this approach and the Congress motion was defeated by 72 to 61. Jinnah put forward three resolutions. The first accepted the Communal Award until the Indians, by mutual agreement, could produce a substitute. The second resolution was critical of the scheme of provincial autonomy only in its details, but conceded that it represented a real advance in the sense that dyarchy was replaced by provincial autonomy. Jinnah's third resolution dealt with the plan of All-India Federation. He condemned this scheme as highly reactionary and devoid of any semblance of responsible government. 'I believe that it means nothing but the absolute sacrifice of all that British India has stood for and developed in the last fifty years in the method of progress in the representative form of government.' It was significant that Jinnah was successful in having all the three resolutions passed by the Assembly because of the Congress support that he received.

Muslims worked in alliance with the Congress on several other questions. Thus, this combined strength was successful in rejecting in early 1935 the trade agreement concluded between the British and the Indian governments. Budgets had to be certified by the Government because of the Congress-Muslim opposition both in 1935 and in 1936. The Criminal Law Amendment Bill was also rejected and had to be certified as well.[77] All this goes to show that given a spirit of compromise, Westernized constitutional lawyers like Jinnah and Bhulabhai Desai could work in reasonable harmony. But Indian politics could not be confined only to the calm and dignified atmosphere of the Indian Legislative Assembly.

Owing to the unwillingness of the Princes to accede to the Federation contemplated in the Government of India Act, 1935, and the opposition of the Congress and the League to what they considered an undemocratic and an irresponsible Centre in the Act, the British Government decided to postpone the implementation of the federal part of the Act. It was decided to put into effect the section dealing with the British Indian Provinces in the Act. This was also in keeping with the British policy of introducing responsible government by stages. Dyarchy of the Government of India Act, 1919, as being replaced by provincial autonomy of

---

[77] This account of Jinnah's cooperation with the Congress in the Central Legislative Assembly is based on R. Coupland, op. cit., Part II, pp. 9–10. For the full text of Jinnah's speech, see Jamil-ud-Din Ahmad, ed., op. cit., Vol. I, pp. 21–22.

the 1935 Act. Provinces were being used as training centres for Indians in the art of responsible government.

Provincial elections were held in the early part of 1937. The All-India Muslim League was by no means a well-organized body in the beginning of 1937. It had held its twenty-third annual session in November 1933, but the following twenty-fourth annual session, was held after nearly two and a half years, in April 1936. Jinnah had returned from his self-imposed exile in Britain and was trying his best to infuse a new life and vigour in the Muslim League. Even after the general elections, one of his admirers wrote, 'Surprising as it may seem, it is nevertheless true that Mahatma Gandhi and Pandit Jawaharlal Nehru are better known to the Muslim masses than Mr Jinnah.'[78] The Congress had an efficient organization, an elaborate machinery for publicity, and enjoyed enormous financial backing from the industrial magnates of Bombay and Ahmedabad. The League was inferior in all these respects. It had only one Muslim English daily, *The Star of India*, and whatever strength it had was chiefly confined to the Hindu majority Province.

The election speeches of Jinnah in 1937 were mostly couched in moderate terms expressing friendliness towards the Congress and his usual Stress on compromise and mutual accommodation.

> Ours is not a hostile movement. Ours is a movement which carries the olive branch to every sister community. We are willing to cooperate, we are willing to coalesce with any group or groups, provided their ideals, their objects are approximately the same as ours.

One of his statements from Bombay declared:

> The Moslem League stands for full national self-government for the people of India. Unity and honourable settlement between Hindus, Moslems and other minorities is the only pivot upon which national self-government for India of three hundred and eighty millions can be constructed and maintained.

In another speech he went so far as to say:

> There is no difference between the ideals of the Moslem League and of the Congress, the idea being complete freedom for India. There could not be any self-respecting Indian who favoured foreign

---

[78] *The Pioneer,* Lucknow, 26 September 1937.

domination or did not desire complete freedom and self-government for his country.[79]

In the Bombay session of the All-India Muslim League in April 1936, Jinnah was empowered to constitute a Central Election Board under his Presidentship to contest the approaching provincial elections. The Board issued a manifesto for the elections. It was obvious that this was entirely the handiwork of Jinnah. The social and economic programme was very similar to that of the Congress. There was only one difference and that was the League's opposition to any attempt at expropriation of private property. It condemned the Federal scheme and was equally unsparing of the Provincial scheme, except that the League, unlike the Congress, was not determined to wreck it, but to work it 'for what it was worth'. Another striking difference was the League pledge 'to protect and promote the Urdu language and script', the insinuation being that the Congress was determined to make Hindi the national language of India. Similarly, the Lucknow Pact of 1916 was hailed as 'one of the greatest beacon lights in the constitutional history of India' and as a 'signal proof of the identity of purpose, earnestness and cooperation between the two great sections of the people of India.'[80] Again, this could be interpreted to mean that the League stood solemnly by separate electorates, which was one of the central pillars on which the Lucknow Pact was based.

How was it that all this sweetness and light was over-shadowed by the bitterness and conflict of the post-election period? Some of the commentators, impressed by the Congress-League accord during the election period, failed to notice the conflict that was developing between Jinnah, as the principal exponent of the Muslim League point of view, and Jawaharal Nehru, the leading spokesman on behalf of the Congress.[81] During the election campaign itself, Jinnah had started putting forward his main point, which he was to reiterate and emphasize later, namely, that the

---

[79] For these extracts from Jinnah's speeches, see Sir Bijoy Prasad Singh Roy, *Parliamentary Government in India*, Calcutta: Thacker, Spink, 1943, pp. 366–7.

[80] R. Coupland, op. cit., Part II, p. 14.

[81] See R. Coupland, op. cit., Part II, pp. 11–16; Maulana Abul Kalam Azad, op. cit., pp. 160–1; and Sir Bijoy Prasad Singh Roy, op. cit., pp. 366–367.

Congress should not challenge the position of the Muslim League as the only representative organization of the Muslims and should confine itself to representing Hindus. Inaugurating the Muslim League election campaign in Bengal, Jinnah declared:

> I warn my Hindu friends and the Congress to leave the Moslems alone. We have made it clear and we mean it that we are ready and willing to cooperate with any group or groups of progressive and independent character, provided that their programme and our programme are approximately the same. We are not going to be the camp followers of any party or organization. Pandit Jawaharlal Nehru is reported to have said in Calcutta that there are only two parties in the country, namely, the Government and the Congress, and the others must line up. I refuse to line up with the Congress. There is a third party in this country and that is the Moslems. We are not going to be dictated to by anybody.[82]

Nehru was deeply disturbed by Jinnah's approach to politics and pointed out in his statement that it implied 'in politics and social and economic matters the Moslems must function separately as a group and deal with other groups as one nation deals with another.' According to him, the economic interests of the various classes of Muslims were indistinguishable from similar Hindu classes. He asserted that the League represented only the upper middle classes. 'I come into greater touch with the Moslem masses than most of the members of the Muslim League. I know more about their hunger and poverty and misery than those who talk in terms of percentages and seats in the Councils and places in the State service.'[83]

The results of elections for Provincial Assemblies indicated that Congress victories were won mainly in Hindu constituencies. Out of 1,585 seats, the Congress captured 711. Of these, only 26 were Muslim seats. On the other hand, the Muslim League showing was not very impressive. Out of 489 Muslim seats, the Muslim League captured only 104 seats. It won a substantial number of seats in the Hindu majority Provinces, but in the Muslim majority Provinces it did not create much of an impression. In Bengal, out of 119 Muslim seats, it won only 37. In Punjab, it won only one seat out of 86 Muslim seats. And in the N-W. F. P.

[82] *The Statesman* (Weekly, Overseas Edition), Calcutta, 7 January 1937.
[83] Ibid., 14 January 1937.

(36 Muslim seats) and Sind (37 Muslim seats), it did not win a single seat.[84] Out of the eleven Provinces, the Congress formed governments in seven and a year later one more Province was brought under Congress control. Fifteen out of the 26 Muslim seats it had won throughout India were in the N-W. F. P. It could form a Government in a Muslim majority Province like the N-W.F.P. because the other 21 Muslim seats in a House of 50 were divided among a number of parties and groups.

According to the Government of India Act, 1935, 'the safeguarding of the legitimate interests of minorities was one of the "special responsibilities" of the Governor'. This meant that the Ministers could offer advice on the subject of minorities, but it was up to the Governor to do what he deemed right. In the Instrument of Instructions issued to the Governor, he was called upon to select his Ministers who collectively commanded the confidence of the Legislature. But in so doing, he was expected to include in the Ministry as far as practicable members of important minority communities.[85] This matter came to a head particularly in the United Provinces. The Congress and the League had fought the Provincial elections on a common platform. The Muslim League was also supported by the *Jamiyat al Ulama* (which was sympathetic towards the Congress) because the latter expected that after the elections the Muslim League would work in close cooperation with the Congress. It was understood that the League would be offered two places in the Ministry. Out of 64 Muslim seats, the Muslim League had won 24, the Independent Muslims 30, the National Agricultural Party 9 and the Congress only one. According to one version, the Muslim League was not prepared to let its representative join the Congress Ministry because the Congress demanded from the Muslim League, as the price for its inclusion in the Congress Ministry, the complete

---

[84] For these figures, see *Returns Showing The Results of Elections in India 1935*, Cmd. 5589. In arriving at precise figures regarding Muslim League gains in the Provincial elections, only those seats have been included which were won by Muslim League candidates. Those won by Independents with Muslim League leanings have been excluded. This has been done because if Independents with Muslim League leanings were included in the Muslim League total then Muslim League candidates with Congress leanings in a Province like the U.P. would have to be excluded from the Muslim League total.

[85] Maurice Gwyer and A. Appadorai, op. cit., Vol. I, p. 371.

merger of the Muslim League Party in the Congress Party. It was also demanded that the Muslim League Parliamentary Board should be dissolved and no candidates set up by that Board at any later by-election.[86] According to Maulana Abul Kalam Azad, who was a member of the Congress Parliamentary Subcommittee and presumably in charge of Muslim affairs, the Muslim League refused to join the Ministry because Jawaharlal Nehru had written to Choudhry Khaliquzzaman, the U. P. Muslim League leader, that the Muslim League could get only one place in the Ministry. According to Azad, this could not be accepted by the Muslim League because the local political situation was such that both Nawab Ismail Khan and Choudhry Khaliquzzaman had to be taken into the Government and since only one seat was available, it was not possible for either of them to enter the Government alone However, when no Muslim Leaguer was included in the Congress Cabinet, the claim of the Muslim League that the Congress was out to establish Hindu Raj gained credence and currency among the Muslim masses. Hindu masses also probably felt that Congress rule was more or less the establishment of Hindu Raj. Thus, Sir Harry Haig, Governor of the United Provinces at that time, has recorded: 'The enthusiasm of the masses for Congress Raj melted imperceptibly into ideas of Hindu Raj, which were certainly prevalent throughout the Province. These ideas were deeply resented by the Muslims, who were invincibly determined not to be ruled by the Hindus.'[87]

Azad seemed to think that the Congress refusal to allow the Muslim League representatives to join the U.P. Congress Cabinet was largely dictated by the fact that the Congress was not prepared to give two places to the Muslim League in the Cabinet. The Congress would have given one place to the Muslim League had it agreed. Azad blamed Nehru for not being generous towards the Muslim League, an attitude which was partly responsible for the creation of Pakistan.[88] Nehru, while replying to Azad's criticism, remarked that in 1937 he was eager that the Congress

---

[86] *Returns Showing The Results of Elections in India 1935*, op. cit., pp. 62–6.

[87] 'The United Provinces and the New Constitution', *The Asiatic Review*, Vol. XXXVI, No. 127, pp. 428–9.

[88] Maulana Abul Kalam Azad, op. cit., p. 160–2.

should introduce land reforms in the United Provinces and therefore was averse to the idea of the Muslim League, which represented some big landowners, joining the Cabinet. He conceded, however, that the Muslim League had agreed to abide by the majority decisions of the Cabinet.[89] This is a more accurate representation of the Congress point of view than Azad's version. Azad looked at the problem in terms of places in the Cabinet and personalities, whereas for Nehru the real problem was the implementation of the Congress programme through a homogeneous and united Cabinet. Congress, from the beginning (as it has been made clear in the case of the Nehru Report) took its stand on the theory of British parliamentary government. It regarded a homogeneous Cabinet drawn from a single party based on an economic and political programme as an ideal instrument of a democratic form of government. The situation in India was not the same as it was in a homogeneous and unitary state like the United Kingdom. In India, because of its infinite diversities, a coalition Cabinet drawn from more than one political party would have created more confidence among the minorities. This was probably the reason why the British Governors were charged both in the Constitution and in their Instrument of Instructions to include in their Ministries members of important minority communities. The Joint Committee on Indian Constitutional Reform thus pointed out: 'A Ministry thus formed must tend to be the representative, not, as in the United Kingdom, of a single majority party or even of a coalition of parties, but also of minorities as such.'[90]

2. *The Growing Strength of the Muslim League*

As is has been suggested earlier, there was probably no one in India who could excel Jinnah as a skilful negotiator and possibly also as a constitutional expert. Even as early as 1917, Mr Montagu, the Secretary of State for India, had written: 'Jinnah is a very clever man, and it is, of course, an outrage that such a man should have no chance of running the affairs of his own country.'[91] But it cannot be denied that Jinnah, despite his

[89] *The New York Times*, 8 February 1959.

[90] *Joint Committee on Indian Constitutional Reform Report*, London: H.M. Stationery Office, 1934, Vol. I, Part I, p. 63.

[91] Edwin S. Montagu, *An Indian Diary*, London: William Heinemann, 1930, p. 58.

personal courage, lacked the dynamism and pugnacity of a leader of the Muslim masses. Pandit Nehru had sarcastically remarked: 'There was as much difference between him and the Indian masses as between Savile Row and Bond Street and the Indian village with its mud huts.'[92] A Muslim Leaguer, probably in his bitterness for having been removed from the All-India Muslim League Council, criticized Jinnah's deliberate aloofness from some of the past political movements. 'No national or religious crisis, however stupendous, can move him. Jalianwala Bagh does not affect him. The great clash of Khilafat of the heart-rending disintegration of the Islamic brotherhood does not move him.'[93] All these verdicts were probably true of Jinnah during the years prior to 1937. But it looked as if after the election campaign of 1937 and during the subsequent years when Jinnah came in fairly close contact with the Muslim masses, he was deeply influenced by the enthusiasm and the sense of unity that the Muslim masses displayed when he appealed to them to follow the programme and policy of the Muslim League. It was true that here was a mass of people who, perhaps, responded more readily to the call of leadership than any other community. But it was also true that the cold-blooded logician, as Jinnah had once described himself, was moved by the emotional warmth and religious fervour of the Muslim masses.

The annual session of the Muslim League, held at Lucknow in October 1937, was probably the first indication of the growing sense of solidarity among the Muslims of India. The Muslim League had won less than a quarter of the Muslim seats in the Provincial elections. Particularly its showing in the Muslim majority Provinces was most unimpressive. But at Lucknow it looked as if Jinnah had snatched victory from the jaws of defeat. On the day he appealed to the Muslims to get organized for 'politics meant power and not relying only on cries of justice or fair-play or good-will,' Sir Sikander Hyat Khan, the Premier of Punjab, Fazl-ul-Huq, Premier of Bengal, and Sir Muhammad Saadullah, Premier of Assam, declared in the League session that they were advising the Muslim members of their respective political parties to join the Muslim League. No better tonic

[92] Jawaharlal Nehru, *An Autobiography*, op. cit., p. 68.
[93] *The Pioneer*, Lucknow, 26 September 1937.

could have invigorated the Muslim League than those declarations.

What was significant was that after the Congress rebuff to the Muslim League on the question of the inclusion of League representatives in the Congress Cabinets, Jinnah had not adopted a completely communal attitude. He was still thinking in terms of forging a united front of the minorities against the totalitarian Congress. Thus, the resolution condemning the formation of Congress Ministries, which were exclusive of genuine minority representatives, referred to the spirit of the Government of India Act, 1935, and Instrument of Instructions of Governors and spoke of 'the safeguards of the interests of the Mussalmans and other important minorities.' Another resolution said that the object of the Muslim League was the 'establishment in India of Full Independence in the form of a federation of free democratic states in which the rights and interests of the Mussalmans and other minorities are adequately and effectively safeguarded.'

But one could see clear signs of the growing Muslim hostility to what the League alleged as aggressive Hindu nationalism practised by Congress Governments. Thus, one of the resolutions of the Lucknow session condemned the foisting of *Bande Mataram* as a national anthem upon the country. It characterized the anthem as 'positively anti-Islamic and idolatrous in its inspiration and ideas.' One could also detect the signs of closing of the ranks and intolerance towards anti-League Muslims. Maulana Zafar Ali Khan, while speaking at the Lucknow session, said that the people who had deserted the League would be answerable for their action to the Creator.[94]

It was natural that after winning such an impressive support in eight out of the eleven Provinces in the Provincial elections that the Congress Party found the intoxication of power a bit too exhilarating. The Congress Party men wanted to reform and control the official machinery. They found the British members of the Indian Civil Service hostile to their movement. They also resented the favourable positions that Muslims enjoyed in the subordinate public services of the United Provinces. The Congress High Command felt that if the Congress could obtain support from a great majority of Hindus now that the Party was in power, they could use their prestige and the economic and political programme of the Congress to enlist support among the Muslims

---

[94] Ibid., 16 October 1937.

through an extensive Muslim mass contact campaign. The Congress leaders did not see the contradiction in the two-pronged offensive of their Party. Interference in administration by Congress Party officials and particularly any diminution in authority and influence of Muslim subordinate officials in the districts were bound to be resented by Muslims. And this resentment was likely to defeat the Congress Muslim mass contact. In addition to this was the propaganda against the Congress launched through an increasingly efficient Party machine of the Muslim League.

The local Congress committees were converted to the status of more or less a parallel administration in the districts. There cannot be more authoritative and convincing evidence to substantiate this than the letter written by the Chief Secretary of the U.P. Government to all District Magistrates. The letter referred to frequent reports which had reached the Secretariat about the 'embarrassing attitude' towards the district authorities adopted by Congress supporters and also to the complaints of Congress workers against the behaviour specially of the lower grades of Government officials. Nevertheless, the letter emphasized the importance of 'the establishment of relations of mutual confidence between the district authorities and the leaders of the Congress organization'.[95] Thus, a climate was set for the Congress Party officials to set up their parallel and probably dominant authority in the districts. There were reports that the Congress committees, overwhelmingly Hindu, took advantage of the advent of their Party government 'to work off their private grudges'.[96] There were also reports that Congress police stations were set up in some districts and Congress policemen were busy investigating crimes on their own.[97] There were also complaints by Muslim members in the Assembly that Congressmen in the U.P. were interfering in religious matters.[98]

Side by side with this the Congress Muslim mass contact movement was launched. Congress leaders tried to impress upon the poor Muslim villagers the fact that the more prosperous and

[95] *Proceedings of the Legislative Assembly of the United Provinces 1938*, Vol. III, No. 13, pp. 1443–4.

[96] Sir George Schuster and Guy Wint, *India and Democracy*, London: Macmillan, 1941, p. 179.

[97] R. Coupland, op. cit., Part II, p. 104.

[98] *Proceedings of the Legislative Assembly of the United Provinces 1938*, Vol. III, No. 14, p. 1476.

urban class self-seeking Muslim politicians might lose under the Congress dispensation, but certainly not the Muslim poorer classes whose interests were identical with those of Hindu poorer classes. It was also stressed that Congress was a non-communal organization which pursued a social and economic programme. Thus, the real champion of the Muslim poor classes were the Congress leaders and not the landlords and lawyers of the League. At the same time, it was made clear to Muslim lawyers and landlords that their political future and material prosperity lay in associating themselves with the Congress Party and not in condemning themselves 'to a lifetime in the wilderness' by joining the League. It was true that these tactics could not work in Muslim majority Provinces. But the aim of the Congress Party was to nip the Muslim League in the bud by weakening it in the Hindu majority Provinces from where it drew its principal support.

The Muslim League, on the other hand, grew from strength to strength. It lost the first by-election in the United Provinces towards the end of 1937, but the three subsequent by-elections were won by the League. Jinnah started building the League organization throughout India. As indicated above, he was helped considerably in this task by the short-sighted policy that the Congress Governments and the Congress High Command followed. In addition to this, he was probably helped by the village *mullahs* who saw in the Congress Muslim mass contact campaign a threat to their own authority, as well as a challenge to the traditional Muslim belief that Islam pervaded every sphere of human activity in that the Congress advocated a secular politics. In the urban areas, Jinnah could depend upon his own organizing ability as well as that of his lieutenants. Muslim students from Aligarh and other urban areas gravitated towards the Muslim League, partly attracted by Jinnah's dynamic personality and partly by the fears aroused by the Congress rule as regards their future material interests in the Services and commercial life. But there is no clear authoritative account of how Jinnah built up his party machine almost from nothing. According to one account, soon after the League session at Lucknow in October 1937, as many as 90 branches of the League were established in the United Provinces and 40 in the Punjab. Nearly 100,000 new members were enrolled in the United Provinces.[99]

---

[99] R. Coupland, op. cit., Part II, p. 183.

In 1938, beginning from 18 January, there followed a correspondence between Jinnah and Jawaharlal Nehru which dragged on until December 1939. Jinnah had correspondence with other leaders like Subhas Chandra Bose, Gandhi, and Sir Tej Bahadur Sapru, but the correspondence between Nehru and Jinnah was, perhaps, the most illuminating so far as the basic Hindu-Muslim differences were concerned. In addition to Jinnah's Fourteen Points, a number of other important problems were also discussed like the issue of *Bande Mataram*, the alleged imposition of Hindi by Congress Ministries, the issue of cow slaughter, and above all, Jinnah's persistent claim that the Muslim League should be recognized as the sole authoritative organization of the Muslims.

On the issue of *Bande Mataram*, Nehru argued that the two stanzas that had been recommended by the Working Committee to be used as a national anthem did not contain any phrases or references which were likely to cause any offence to anybody. The Congress could not compel large numbers of people to abandon what they had come to treasure for so long.[100] This was true, but it was difficult to see how Muslims would reconcile themselves to an anthem which was derived from such a blatantly anti-Muslim novel as *Anandamath*.

As regards the language question, Nehru put forward the official Congress point of view that he was in favour of Hindustani written both in *Nagri* and *Urdu* scripts. Azad also informed the Congress Premiers of the official policy of the Congress as regards the language question.

> The Congress has decided that, for the national and inter-provincial language the name 'Hindustani' should be adopted, which has been used for this language since the seventeenth century; and both scripts should be accepted for writing purposes, that is, Deonagri and Urdu.... You should henceforth use the word 'Hindustani' for 'Hindi' and 'Urdu', whenever you want to refer to the 'national' and 'inter-provincial' language of India, for which both Deonagri and Urdu scripts have been adopted.[101]

The Muslims were not prepared to give up Urdu, which they claimed had been developed by the joint efforts of both Hindus

---

[100] Syed Sharifuddin Pirzada, ed., *Leaders' Correspondence With Jinnah*, Bombay: Sh. Nazir Ahmad, 1944, pp. 119–20.

[101] *The Statesman* (Weekly, Overseas Edition), Calcutta, 12 May 1938.

and Muslims. They often quoted Sir Tej Bahadur Sapru, who said that Urdu 'had served the remarkable purpose making Hindus grasp Muslim culture and making Muslims grasp Hindu culture and thereby promote fellowship and common citizenship.'[102] Urdu was, after all, the language in which some of the best Muslim literary output in India had appeared and the Muslim élite were not likely to accept any compromise. The controversy degenerated into the usual intransigence on both sides, Muslim leaders clinging to a Persianized Urdu and the Congress Ministries, contrary to Azad's instructions, trying to propagate Hindi.

Throughout the correspondence, Jinnah constantly harped on the point that before any negotiations could start the Congress should recognize the Muslim League as the authoritative and representative organization of the Muslims of India. Nehru could not admit this contention because it would reduce Congress to a completely Hindu organization. Nehru claimed that there were about 100,000 Muslims on the Congress rolls.[103] It was clear that Jinnah at this stage was not keen on coming to a final settlement with the Congress because he wanted to wait and build up the strength and organization of the Muslim League to such a level that the Congress and everybody else would be compelled to treat the Muslim League on a footing of complete equality and until that happened, he said, 'We shall have to wait and depend upon our inherent strength which will "determine the measure of importance or distinction that it possesses"'.[104] The Congress circles were also probably marking time and certainly in 1938 and 1939 they were optimistic about the success of the Muslim mass contact campaign launched by the Congress.[105]

How did Jinnah plan to weld the different classes and sections in the Muslim community into a united and monolithic organization? As suggested earlier, Jinnah had learnt his lesson that one could not play a dominant role in politics by merely functioning as a negotiator or a compromiser. As he himself had said in his speech to the Lucknow session of the Muslim League, politics

---

[102] Ibid., 10 March 1938.
[103] Syed Sharifuddin Pirzada, ed., op. cit., p. 124.
[104] Ibid., p. 132.
[105] The Statesman (Weekly, Overseas Edition), Calcutta, 21 April 1938.

meant power and not relying only on cries of justice or fair-play. He knew that the Muslim community, divided though it was into different Provincial, economic and even religious groups, should get together on a broad and common programme for there was no other way of compelling his opponents to treat the Muslim League with respect. At the Patna session of the Muslim League in December 1938, dealing with the accusation that the Muslims were allied with British imperialism, Jinnah said:

> I say the Muslim League is not going to be an ally of anyone, but would be the ally of even the devil if need be in the interests of Muslims. It is not because we are in love with imperialism; but in politics one has to play one's game as on the chess-board.[106]

Sir Muhammad Iqbal complained to him that the Sikander-Jinnah Pact was causing damage to the prestige of the Muslim League in Punjab and that Sikander Hyat was trying to capture the Muslim League with the help of his landlord supporters. 'Knowing the opinion of the province as I do I cannot take the responsibility of handing over the League to Sir Sikander and his friends. The pact has already damaged the prestige of the League in this province and the tactics of the Unionists may damage it still further.'[107] Jinnah had to follow the dictates of politics and continue his alliance with Sikander Hyat for the sake of Muslim solidarity. Jinnah has been quoted as writing to the poet, 'I fully agree with you that the political objective of the Indian Muslims must be stated fully and unequivocally but there are practical difficulties in the way of doing so at this stage.... I want to pull them (Muslims) up step by step and before making them run I want to be sure that they are capable of standing on their own legs.'[108] To Barkat Ali of Punjab Jinnah wrote:

> I hope you will show this letter to Sir Mahomed Iqbal and Ghulam Rasool. I have appointed some members to the Central Parliamentary Board which was suggested by Sir Sikander Hyat, but that does not mean that I am not going to appoint some other members representing Punjab which may be suggested by Sir Mahomed Iqbal, Malik Zaman Mehdi Khan, Ghulam Rasool and yourself.[109]

---

[106] Jamil-ud-Din Ahmad, ed., op. cit., Vol. I, p. 87.

[107] Mohammed Noman, ed., *Our Struggle 1857–1947*, Karachi: Pakistan Publications, n.d., Appendix II, p. 32.

[108] *Dawn*, Karachi, 25 December 1955.

[109] Ibid.

Similarly, later on, referring to the charge that the League was against the *zamindars*, he said, 'The League is not against any interests among the Muslims.'[110] Before the Provincial elections of 1937, realizing the weakness of the Muslim League in Bengal, Jinnah brought about a compromise between the Bengal Proja Party, led by Fazl-ul-Huq, and the Muslim League Parliamentary Board. As a shrewd politician, interested in building up the strength and power of the Muslim League as the sole spokesman of the Muslims of the whole of India, he did not follow Iqbal's advice that he should concentrate on building up the unity of Muslims in North-West India and Bengal and ignore Muslim minority Provinces.[111]

But at the same time Jinnah methodically built up popular support among the Muslim masses and became their Quaid-i-Azam. And there came a stage, particularly after he was associated in the public mind as the supreme founder and architect of Pakistan, when it was not easy for a Sikander Hyat or a Fazl-ul-Huq to defy the orders of the Quaid-i-Azam. And whenever they did, he turned fiercely against them with the full support of the Muslim 'nation' and in the name of Muslim solidarity.

Like the Congress, the Muslim League began to draw increasing support from certain economic interests. Both in Bengal and Punjab Muslims were agriculturalists whereas the Hindus represented the more prosperous urban interests—merchants, shopkeepers, lawyers and doctors, and above all, the hated moneylenders. Even in the predominantly Muslim East Bengal, Hindu teachers, lawyers, and doctors were not only the dominant interests in the cities but the majority of the population in the cities were also Hindu. In Punjab, even though, unlike Bengal, there was a considerable number of prosperous Muslim landowners, nevertheless, as will be seen later, the interests of all agriculturalists, both small *zamindars* as well as big *zamindars*, were opposed to the urban Hindu classes. Thus, the Punjab Land Alienation Act of 1900, the Restitution of Mortgaged Lands Act, 1938, the Registration of Money-lenders Act, 1938, and the Relief of Indebtedness Act, 1940, were one and all regarded by the Hindu opposition as deliberately designed to penalize their interests.

---

[110] Jamil-ud-Din Ahmad, ed., *Speeches and Writings of Mr. Jinnah,*, Lahore: Ashraf, 1964, Vol. II, p. 46.

[111] Mohammed Noman, ed., op. cit., Appendix II, pp. 28–29.

This conflict of interests became so intense that when towards the end of 1940 the Punjab Government introduced measures like tax on urban immovable property, a bill restricting urban rents and a general sales tax, the local Congressmen were supported even by the Congress High Command in offering strenuous resistance to such measures.

It was also alleged that Muslim interests being chiefly agricultural would lose by the new commercial policy of high tariffs and the fostering of industries. The argument was that this policy, which was being supported by the Congress, was against the interests of Muslim agricultural producers of cotton and jute and in favour of the Hindu mill owners and capitalists. It has been reported that when the Cotton Bill was being discussed in the Central Assembly, Jinnah did not realize the conflict of interests between Hindu mill owners and Muslim producers of cotton and supported a high tariff policy which was in favour of the cotton manufacturing interests of Bombay and Ahmedabad. Sikander Hyat rushed to Delhi to impress upon the Quaid-i-Azam that as leader of the Muslims he should support the interests of Muslim cotton growers and not the mill owners. When Jinnah was informed of this, he was quite disturbed and asked Sikander Hyat to assure the *zamindars* of Punjab that such a mistake would not occur again.[112]

It would not be fair to say that there were no Muslim merchants and industrialists at all. Before Pakistan was established, Muslims had also produced the Adamjees and Ispahanis as opposed to the Hindu Dalmias and Birlas. But the competition between these two groups was also taking a communal turn. Particularly as the prospects of the establishment of Pakistan improved, Muslim capitalists, bankers, merchants, all looked forward to the time when competition would be less fierce and the prospects of making high profits infinitely brighter. Resolutions urging Muslims to consume goods manufactured or sold by Muslims were passed by the Provincial Muslim Leagues and also by the All-India Muslim League.[113] The conflict was perhaps

---

[112] Abdul Majeed Salik, *Yaran-i-Kohan*, Lahore: Chatan Publications, 1955, p. 98.

[113] *Indian Annual Register 1938*, Calcutta, n.d., Vol. II, p. 356, and *Resolutions of the All-India Muslim League from March, 1940 to April, 1941*, Delhi, n.d., p. 26.

at its sharpest on the matter of Government jobs. This was understandable because in the Indian subcontinent so many of a citizen's interests were determined by the decisions of Provincial and Central Servants. The conflict was also heightened by the fact that in the United Provinces where Muslims were in a minority, they occupied a favoured position in the subordinate public services whereas in Bengal where they were in a majority, the Hindus held most of the posts in the subordinate public services. In the United Provinces, the Muslim League could point out that under the Congress regime Hindus were determined to oust the Muslims from their favoured positions and in Bengal the Muslim League could point the accusing finger at the Hindus for having deprived the Muslims of their share in public services even though the latter were in the majority.

What was the way out of this tangle? Gandhi suggested that all these problems could be satisfactorily settled once the vicious role of the British was terminated. Hindus and Muslims should jointly struggle for India's *Swaraj* and once that was achieved, most of the difficulties would disappear. It was obvious from the very beginning that Gandhi could never hope to exercise any profound hold over the Muslims. During the Khilafat movement, he operated very largely through the popularity of the Khilafat cause itself and the organizing ability and leadership of Maulana Muhammad Ali. Later on, he was becoming increasingly aware of his limitations so far as the Muslims were concerned. It was not only the separate culture and interests of the Muslims that stood in his way, but also his own Hindu approach to politics. Being a devout Hindu himself, he was quite justified in giving a Hindu twist and turn to his political methods. He also felt that that was perhaps the most effective way of evoking an enthusiastic response from the Hindu masses. We have already seen Motilal Nehru expressing his helplessness at the emergence of the communal hatred in the Congress ranks and the Malaviya-Lala interests aided by Birla's money trying to capture the Congress. His son, Jawaharlal Nehru, also found Gandhi's frequent use of Hindu phrases in politics as strange and wrong.

> Even some of Gandhiji's phrases sometimes jarred upon me—thus his frequent reference to *Ram Raj* as a golden age which was to return. But I was powerless to intervene, and I consoled myself with the thought that Gandhiji used the words because they were well

known and understood by the masses. He had an amazing knack of reaching the heart of the people.[114]

This was equally true of the way Congress Governments functioned during 1937–9. Thus, the Congress educational scheme introduced in the Central Provinces was given a Hindu name and a Hindu form. The scheme of *Vidya Mandirs* (Temples of Learning) was bitterly opposed by the three per cent Muslim minority but their protests were disregarded. Their complaint was that Muslims could scarcely cooperate with a scheme which had a Hindu name like *Mandirs* (Hindu temples). For Muslims, a Hindu temple was a place where idols were worshipped and this, they thought, was a deliberate affront to Islam's prohibition and condemnation of idolatry. Further, according to the scheme, the schools were to be managed by committees chosen by joint electorates. Muslims complained that no provision was made for separate Muslim schools or for the training of Urdu speaking teachers. Their feelings ran so high that, ignoring the directions of the Muslim League Working Committee, they resorted to direct action over the *Vidya Mandirs* scheme.[115] Muslim children were forced to sing *Bande Mataram* with folded hands and offer reverence before the Mahatma's portrait. In the eyes of the Muslim League these were all clear manifestations of the tyranny of Hindu brute majority over the helpless Muslim minority. This was how the famous Pirpur Report catalogued the alleged injustices and oppressions of the Congress Governments.[116] It could be argued that the Muslim League was exaggerating Congress injustices, but the fact remained that the Congress Governments during 1937–9 tended to look at social and educational problems from a Hindu point of view.

What were the other avenues available for resolving these differences? An alternative method of arriving at a Hindu-Muslim settlement was that suggested by Jinnah. Jinnah believed that the

---

[114] Jawaharlal Nehru, *An Autobiography,* op. cit., p. 72. See also A.R. Desai, *Social Background of Indian Nationalism,* Bombay: Geoffrey Cumberlege, 1948, pp. 366–7.

[115] Maurice Gwyer and A. Appadorai, op. cit., Vol. I, p. 417.

[116] The Pirpur Report was entitled *The Report of the Inquiry Committee Appointed by the Council of the All-India Muslim League to Inquire into Muslim Grievances in Congress Provinces,* Delhi: All India Muslim League, 1938. For details, see Part III of the Report.

method followed in the Lucknow Pact of 1916 was the best possible method. The Congress, representing the Hindus, and the Muslim League, representing the Muslims, should negotiate at the summit through their leaders armed with full powers to arrive at any settlement they considered best in the interests of their respective communities. Year after year the annual session of the Muslim League armed Jinnah with full powers to adopt whatever steps he deemed appropriate or necessary for the furtherance of Muslim interests. The Congress rejected such a method because it would have reduced the Congress to a Hindu organization and also because leaders like Nehru felt that Jinnah and the Muslim League represented probably only the upper urban crust of the Muslim community. And by the time they became aware of the fact that this was no longer so, Jinnah had moved on to the demand for Pakistan.

But as indicated earlier, Congress insistence on forming one-party Cabinets in the Provinces was a serious error. If they had realized that the model of British parliamentary democracy borrowed from a homogeneous and unitary state was not likely to work as effectively in an essentially plural society like that of India, much of the communal rancour could have been avoided. The Swiss pattern, where racial and linguistic groups were represented in a composite Cabinet, was not unknown to them. There was also a suggestion that matters which were of particular significance to certain communities, such as their social customs, religious establishments, language and literary traditions, should not be subject to legislation by the common Central or Provincial Legislature, but should fall within the domain of special bodies or guilds, each of which represented one cultural or religious group.[117]

On 3 September 1939, Britain's declaration of war on Germany was followed by Lord Linlithgow's announcement that India was also at war with Germany. The Congress Working Committee in its resolution of 15 September demanded that the issue of peace and war must be decided by the Indian people and that India could not fight for the cause of freedom unless she herself was free. Lord Linlithgow, in his statement of 18 October 1939, tried to defend the British position by saying that the

---

[117] See P. Spear, *Communal Harmony*, Bombay: Oxford University Press, 1940.

British Government stood firmly by their pledge of conferring Dominion status on India. The Viceroy also spoke of the establishment of a consultative group consisting of representatives of all major political parties and of the Indian Princes. The object of setting up such a body was to associate public opinion in India with the conduct of the war. The Working Committee of the Congress saw in all this nothing but the pursuit of the same old imperialist policy and declared in its resolution of 22 October that it was determined to combat such a policy. It called upon all the Congress Ministries to tender their resignations. By the end of October, all the Congress Ministries had resigned. Sir Samuel Hoare, Secretary of State, came forward with the conciliatory gesture that the Viceroy's Executive Council should be expanded to include in it representatives of major political parties. The Viceroy accordingly held negotiations with the Congress and Muslim League leaders and suggested to them that if they reached an agreement in the Provincial field, they could then suggest to him ways and means by which the representatives of the two organizations could participate in the Central Government as members of the Executive Council.

While these discussions were going on between the Viceroy and the Congress and Muslim League leaders in November 1939, Jinnah offered five terms for an interim settlement with the Congress for the duration of the war. These terms were: firstly, establishment of coalition Ministries in the Provinces; secondly, Congress acceptance of the formula that no legislation affecting Muslims would be passed by a Provincial Lower House if two-thirds of the Muslim representatives in that House were opposed to it; thirdly, an undertaking from the Congress not to fly their flag on public institutions; fourthly, an understanding as regards the singing of *Bande Mataram*; fifthly, a Congress undertaking to cease its hostile campaign against the Muslim League. According to Jinnah, he tried to persuade the Congress leaders to agree to the Viceroy's proposal to expand the Executive Council subject to a settlement with the League in the Provincial field. But the Congress was adamant in their stand.[118]

22 December 1939 was celebrated as what Jinnah called 'The Deliverance Day' by the Muslim League throughout India. The

---

[118] V. P. Menon, op. cit., p. 72.

resolution that was passed by Muslim League meetings on this day said:

> That the Congress Ministry both in the discharge of their duties of the administration and in the Legislatures have done their best to flout the Muslim opinion, to destroy Muslim culture, and have interfered with their religious and social life, and trampled upon their economic and political rights; that in matters of differences and disputes the Congress Ministry invariably have sided with, supported and advanced the cause of the Hindus in total disregard and to the prejudice of the Muslim interests.[119]

Thus the day was celebrated as the Day of Deliverance from, tyranny, oppression, and injustice during the last two and a half years.' This action of Jinnah was bitterly resented by the Congress. Jawaharlal Nehru, writing to Jinnah in December 1939, rightly remarked, 'It thus seems that politically we have no common ground and that our objectives are different. That in itself makes discussion difficult and fruitless.'[120]

It could be said that Jinnah's mind was groping for a new solution to India's constitutional and political problems. His basic approach as regards the parties to a settlement was the same, namely, that the representatives of the Muslim League and the Congress, representing the two communities in India, should negotiate at the summit. But as regards the terms of the settlement, it was becoming clear by the end of 1939 that Jinnah was drifting away from the traditional methods and pattern of thinking. In a statement to the *Manchester Guardian* in October 1939, he decried the folly of foisting British parliamentary democracy on India. He referred to Muslim apprehensions regarding the introduction of democratic institutions in India. Muslim insistence on separate electorates, weightage and statutory safeguards from 1909 onwards was a clear indication of the fear that they would be reduced to a perpetual minority under a democratic rule. As regards the obstacles to the working of democracy in India, he pointed out:

> Having regard to the 35 millions of voters, the bulk of whom are totally ignorant, illiterate and untutored, living in centuries old superstitions of the worst type, thoroughly antagonistic to each other, culturally and socially, the working of this Constitution has clearly

---

[119] Jamil-ud-Din Ahmad, ed., op. cit., Vol. I, pp. 118–9.
[120] Syed Sharifuddin Pirzada, ed., op. cit., p. 147.

brought out that it is impossible to work a democratic parliamentary government in India.[121]

Democracy in Canada and Australia could work because the people there were mainly British in stock. But there were doubts as to how it could work in South Africa where the differences between the rival communities like the Boers and the British had to be composed. According to Jinnah, even these differences were not so fundamental as those between Hindus and Muslims.

But what was novel and noteworthy was his thesis that Muslims should not be described as a minority when they were 'in a majority in the North-West and in Bengal, all along the corridor stretching from Karachi to Calcutta.' When asked about the new proposals and schemes that were being put forward, he said that the League had appointed a subcommittee to examine the entire constitutional and political problem of India.[122]

In the only article he ever wrote, Jinnah carried his thesis forward and claimed that Hindus and Muslims were two different nations. He advocated the setting up, both at the Centre and in the Provinces, Governments that represented all the segments of Indian society and decried party government as unsuitable to Indian conditions. The Muslim League was irrevocably opposed to any federal objective because it would bring about Hindu majority rule. He suggested that the British Government should revise the entire problem of India's future constitution *de novo*. But according to him, no new constitutional scheme for India should be evolved and implemented without the consent and approval of the All-India Muslim League. One could see in what direction his mind was working. 'To conclude, a constitution must be evolved that recognizes that there are in India two nations who both must share the governance of their common motherland.'[123] This was on 19 January 1940, and on 23 March 1940 the historic Pakistan Resolution was passed. The ambassador of Hindu-Muslim unity had ceased to think in terms of composing differences. He had taken the view that these differences should be recognized as hard facts and that Hindus and Muslims should settle down in their respective homelands to construct their politics on lines best suited to their own genius and traditions.

---

[121] Jamil-ud-Din Ahmad, ed., op. cit., Vol. I, p. 99.
[122] Ibid., p. 102.
[123] Ibid., p. 138.

4 THE EMERGENCE OF PAKISTAN—I

---

1. First Faint Glimmerings of Pakistan

The origin of the idea of Pakistan as well as the composition of the word Pakistan have often provided lively subjects for controversy among scholars and publicists. Jinnah, in his interview with Beverley Nichols, pointed out that the idea of dividing India was not new for it had occurred to John Bright in 1877.[1] Talking about the distant future when the British Government might have to withdraw from India, Bright urged that the peoples of different Provinces in India should be encouraged to regard themselves as citizens of different states so that at the time of transfer of power there might be five or six great successor States.[2] It would be interesting to speculate whether John Bright was prescient or history was playing tricks for in May 1947, before the plan of 3 June 1947 was announced, the British Government put forward a plan whereby power could be transferred to several successor States. This plan had to be abandoned because of the bitter opposition it evoked from the Congress.[2] Similarly, Communist writers have credited Stalin with foreseeing as early as 1912 the break up of India into diverse nationalities. 'In the case of India, too, it will probably be found that innumerable nationalities, till then lying dormant, would come into life with the further course of bourgeois development.'[4]

The idea of Muslims forming a separate state in India was mooted as early as December 1883. It was Wilfrid Scawen Blunt who suggested in Calcutta that in his view practically all the

---

[1] Beverley Nichols, *The Verdict on India*, Bombay: Thacker, 1944, p. 192.

[2] Quoted in R. Coupland, *The Indian Problem*, Part I, Oxford University Press, New York, 1944, pp. 50–51.

[3] V. P. Menon, *The Transfer of Power in India*, Calcutta: Orient Longmans, 1957, pp. 361–5.

[4] Quoted in R. Palme Dutt, *India Today and Tomorrow*, London: Lawrence and Wishart, 1955, p. 239.

Provinces of Northern India should be placed under Muslim Government and those of Southern India under Hindu Government. In this scheme, the British would continue as the controlling power drawing their support from British troops stationed in each of the Provinces, but 'the whole civil administration, legislation, and finance should be let to native hands.'[5]

After the inauguration of the Government of India Act, 1919, it became clear that the British seriously contemplated the transfer of political power by stages to Indian hands. This created a feeling of uneasiness among Muslims as regards their share of power. It was significant that even at that stage Muslims regarded themselves and their problems as somewhat separate from the rest of India. Thus, Maulana Muhammad Ali, speaking on the resolution that reforms should be introduced in the North-West Frontier Province of India in the annual session of the All-India Muslim League held in Bombay in December 1924, said:

> If a line be drawn from Constantinople to Delhi on the map of the world it would be found that at least right up to Saharanpur, there was a corridor of purely Muslim people or Muslims were in clear majority. This gave them the clue for understanding the backward condition in which the Frontier and the Punjab were purposely kept by those in power.[6]

One gets another glimpse of Muslim apprehensions and their separatist tendencies in the Nehru Report of 1928. The Report recorded: 'The Muslims being in a minority in India as a whole fear that the majority may harass them, and to meet this difficulty they have made a novel suggestion—that they should at least dominate in some parts of India.'

All this, at best, was a hazy and uncertain groping towards a separate state. A clear conception was given by Sir Muhammad Iqbal in his Presidential Address at the Allahabad session of the All-India Muslim League in December 1930. Iqbal's conception was not only clear but comprehensive in the sense that it was based on both geographical and ideological factors. 'I would like to see the Punjab, North-West Frontier Province, Sind and Baluchistan amalgamated into a single state. Self-government within the

---

[5] W. S. Blunt, *India Under Ripon: A Private Diary*, London: T. Fisher Unwin, 1909, pp. 107–8.

[6] *The Indian Annual Register 1924*, Vol. II, Calcutta, p. 478.

British Empire or without the British Empire, the formation of a consolidated North-West Indian Muslim state appears to me to be the final destiny of the Muslims at least of North-West India.'[7]

It may be noted that Iqbal was thinking only of North-West India and not of Bengal. Secondly, he suggested the exclusion of Ambala Division and those districts where non-Muslims were in a majority from this North-Western Muslim state. In a way he was clearer than the formulators of the Lahore Resolution of 1940. West Pakistan of the future was to cover roughly the territory outlined by Iqbal. Thirdly, Iqbal was agreeable to the idea of the North-Western Muslim state forming a part of the Indian Federation, if 'residuary powers' were left entirely to self-governing states.

However, what was most noteworthy in Iqbal's conception was the ideological basis of his state. His idea was not inspired by fear or hostility towards the Hindus.

> A community which is inspired by feelings of ill-will towards other communities is low and ignoble. I entertain the highest respect for the customs, laws, religious and social institutions of other communities.... Yet I love the communal group which is the source of my life and my behaviour; and which has formed me what I am by giving me its religion, its literature, its thought, its culture, and thereby re-creating its whole past, as a living operative factor, in my present consciousness.[8]

At this stage it should also be made clear that Iqbal's conception of Islamic State was extremely liberal and flexible. He declared in the same Presidential Address: 'Nor should the Hindus fear that the creation of autonomous Muslim states will mean the introduction of a kind of religious rule in such states.' He went on to assert that in certain cases a Muslim state could adopt such a flexible approach as to impose no restrictions on the realization of interest on money loaned.

> I therefore demand the formation of a consolidated Muslim state in the best interests of India and Islam. For India it means security and peace resulting from an internal balance of power, for Islam an opportunity to rid itself of the stamp that *Arabian Imperialism* [author's italics] was forced to give it, to mobilize its law, its education,

---

[7] Dr Sir Muhammad Iqbal, *Presidential Address*, Allahabad Session, *December, 1930*, Delhi: All-India Muslim League, 1945, p. 12.

[8] Ibid., pp. 10–11.

its culture, and to bring them into closer contact with its own original spirit and with the spirit of modern times.[9]

This is a highly revealing statement which has escaped the notice of many writers. It not merely indicates how liberal Iqbal was in his conception of Islam (a fact which is well known to those who have read the Sixth Lecture entitled 'The Principle of Movement in the Structure of Islam' in his *Reconstruction of Religious Thought*), but also that he was in favour of Muslims in India continuing in the liberal and tolerant traditions that Indian Islam had nurtured so assiduously in contrast to its Arabian counterpart. It should not be too difficult to demonstrate on the basis of this statement that the conception of Islam that men like Iqbal had was different from that of Muslim religious leaders like Maudoodi, who in their zeal to purify it of Moghul or Indian impurities, wanted to cast it in a rigid Arab mould.

Choudhry Rahmat Ali is considered the originator of the word Pakistan. The word was first used in a four-page leaflet entitled *Now or Never*, published in January 1933, and signed, besides by Rahmat Ali, by three other students in Cambridge. Explaining the composition of the word Pakistan, Choudhry Rahmat Ali wrote later:

'Pakistan' is both a Persian and an Urdu word. It is composed of letters taken from the names of all our homelands—'Indian' and 'Asian'. That is, **P**unjab, **Af**ghania (North-West Frontier Province), **K**ashmir, **I**ran, **S**indh (including Kachch and Kathiawar), **T**ukharistan, **Af**ghanistan and Balochista**N**. It means the lands of the Paks—the spiritually pure and clean. It symbolizes the religious beliefs and the ethnical stocks of our people; and it stands for all the territorial constituents of our original Fatherland. It has no other origin and no other meaning; and it does not admit of any other interpretation.[10]

Tracing the origin of his scheme, Choudhry Rahmat Ali attributed to Divine guidance its due role. 'I observed *chillahs* and prayed for Allah's guidance…. I carried on till, at last, in His dispensation Allah showed me the light, and led me to the name "Pakistan" and to the Pak Plan….'[11]

---

[9] Ibid., p. 15.

[10] Chaudhry Rahmat Ali, *Pakistan the Fatherland of the Pak Nation*, London: The Pak National Liberation Movement, 1947, p. 225.

[11] Ibid., p. 225.

There were two basic differences between Iqbal's scheme and that of Rahmat Ali. Unlike Iqbal's scheme, the Provinces which constituted Rahmat Ali's Pakistan were to have a separate Federation of their own. Secondly, Rahmat Ali published a map of India which showed three independent Muslim nations forming a triple alliance. They were: Pakistan in the North-West, Bang-i-Islam consisting of Bengal and Assam in the North-East, and Usmanistan in the South formed by the state of Hyderabad.

II. LEADING UP TO THE LAHORE RESOLUTION OF 23 MARCH 1940

The schemes discussed in the previous section were of a speculative nature and no large body of Muslims considered them as practical propositions. It was only after it became clear that the federal part of the Government of India Act, 1935, was not likely to work in view of the opposition of the Congress, the Princes, and the Muslim League that Partition became a serious and practical alternative. It seems that some of the Congress leaders condemned the Government of India Act, 1935, without reading its full text. This was presumably because they were antagonized by the presence of discretionary powers given to the Governor General and the Governors in the Act. Their worst fears were confirmed by the way safeguards were pushed out of scale by men like Churchill in the British Parliamentary debates on the Act.[12] It has been reported that Gandhi confessed to the Viceroy, Lord Linlithgow, in 1942 that he had just read for the first time the Government of India Act, 1935, and that had he read it when it was first passed, the course of recent Indian history might have been very different for the Act could have given India an she desired.[13] There is much room for speculation on the part of future historians as regards what would have happened if the Congress had accepted the Government of India Act, 1935, and the British Government, in its turn, persuaded the Princes to adopt a similar approach. One thing was clear, Jinnah and the Muslim League were in no position to offer much resistance. It may be recalled that in 1936 Jinnah had tried his best to gain a foothold for himself and the League in the Punjab, but Sir Fazl-i-Husain had such a complete hold over the Punjab that it

---

[12] The Earl of Halifax, *Fulness of Days*, London: Collins, 1957, p. 125.

[13] Cyril Philips, 'Tradition and Experiment in Asia', *The Listener*, 25 February 1954, p. 326.

was reported that Jinnah left in disappointment saying, 'I shall never come to the Punjab again. It is such a hopeless place.[14] The resolution passed by the Sind Muslim League Conference held at Karachi in October 1938, gave a clear picture of the way the minds of Muslim League leaders were working at that time. The resolution catalogued all the alleged wrongs and injustices that the Congress Governments had inflicted on Muslims. It went on to argue that nothing better could be expected from 'the caste-ridden mentality and anti-Muslim policy of the majority community'. But the resolution also suggested that such differences and conflicts had arisen not merely because of the narrow outlook of the Hindu community. They had arisen 'also on account of acute differences of religion, language, script, culture, social laws and outlook on life of the two major communities and even of race in certain parts.' For the first time Hindus and Muslims were described officially by the Muslim League as two distinct nations.

> This Conference considers it absolutely essential in the interests of an abiding peace of the vast Indian continent and in the interests of unhampered cultural development, the economic and social betterment, and political self-determination of the *two nations known as Hindus and Muslims* [Author's italics], to recommend to All-India Muslim League to review and revise the entire question of what should be the suitable constitution for India which will secure honourable and legitimate status due to them, and that this conference therefore recommends to the All-India Muslim League to devise a scheme of Constitution under which Muslims may attain full independence.

The resolution also expressed 'emphatic disapproval of the scheme of the All-India Federation as embodied in the Government of India Act, 1935' and urged the British Government to refrain from enforcing it as it was detrimental particularly to the interests of the Muslims of India.[15]

This was followed by a resolution passed at the annual session of the All-India Muslim League held in Patna in December 1938, whereby the President was authorized to adopt such course as

---

[14] Azim Husain, *Fazl-i-Husain*, Bombay: Longmans, 1946, p. 310.
[15] *Resolutions of the All-India Muslim League from October 1937 to December 1938*, Delhi: All-India Muslim League, 1944, pp. 78–82.

might be necessary with a view to exploring a suitable alternative to the Government of India Act, 1935, which would safeguard the interests of Muslims and other minorities.

The next stage was when the Working Committee of the All-India Muslim League, in its meeting at Meerut on 26 March 1939, resolved that a Committee examine and report on the various draft schemes 'already propounded by those who are fully versed in the constitutional developments of India and other countries and those that may be submitted hereafter to the President and report to the Working Committee their conclusions at an early date.[16] The Committee appointed by the Working Committee consisted of the following: M. A. Jinnah (President), the Hon. Sir Sikander Hyat Khan, Nawab Mohammad Ismail Khan, Syed Abdul Aziz, Sir Abdoola Haroon, the Hon. Sir Khwaja Nazimuddin, Abdul Matin Choudhri, Sardar Aurangzeb Khan, Nawabzada Liaquat Ali Khan (Convener). The above resolution of the Working Committee was placed before the Council of the All-India Muslim League for its ratification in April 1939. Jinnah, while speaking before the Council in New Delhi, said:

> In regard to Federation, there were several schemes in the field including that of dividing the country into Muslim and Hindu India. These schemes were before the Committee which had been set up by the Working Committee of the League. The Committee was not pledged to any particular scheme. It would examine the whole question and produce a scheme which according to the Committee, would be in the best interests of the Muslims of India.[17]

The Muslim League Committee presumably examined a number of schemes. The schemes put forward by Sir Muhammad Iqbal and Choudhry Rahmat Ali have already been outlined in the previous section. There was also the scheme of Dr Syed Abdul Latif of Hyderabad, Deccan, which he published in 1939.[18] According to this scheme, the Indian Federation was to consist of

---

[16] *Resolutions of the All India Muslim League From March 1939 to March 1940*, Delhi: All India Muslim League, n.d., pp. 1–2.

[17] *The Indian Annual Register 1939*, Vol. I, Calcutta, p. 374.

[18] Sir Maurice Gwyer and A. Appadorai, eds., *Speeches and Documents on the Indian Constitution 1921–47*, Vol. II, Oxford University Press, London, 1957, pp. 444–5.

four Muslim cultural zones and eleven Hindu cultural zones. The Muslim cultural zones were:

1. The North-West bloc embracing Sind, Baluchistan, the Punjab, North-West Frontier Province and the Indian states of Khairpur and Bahawalpur and consisting of 25 million Muslims.
2. The North-East bloc of Eastern Bengal and Assam of over 30 million Muslims.
3. The Delhi-Lucknow bloc extending from the Eastern border of Patiala to Lucknow. This zone was designed to attract Muslims from adjacent areas, particularly from the areas of the United Provinces and Bihar.
4. The Deccan bloc embracing the state of Hyderabad and including a strip of territory in the South with an opening to the sea was to include more than 12 million Muslims in number.

The rest of India was to be divided into eleven Hindu cultural zones. A novel feature of this scheme was that being a Hyderabadi, Dr Latif wanted the creation of a Muslim zone in the state of Hyderabad, even though Muslims were not in majority there. Being an Urdu-speaking Muslim and with cultural affinities with the Urdu-speaking Muslims of the United Provinces and Bihar, he wanted the creation of a Muslim zone called the Delhi-Lucknow bloc. Creation of such cultural zones was to be effected through exchanges of populations. Dr Latif underestimated the difficulties of such exchanges because he thought that there would be considerable voluntary movement and above all that the modern multiple means of easy transit would reduce the difficulties involved in migration.

The scheme provided for a weak Centre, restricted to Defence, Foreign Affairs, Commerce and Communications with residuary powers in the Provinces. Another noteworthy feature was the idea of a composite and stable Executive that it put forward. Since the Executive could not be removed by an adverse vote of the Parliament, it was stable. Dr Latif ruled out a Parliamentary Executive for India based on the support of a majority party in the Parliament because in practice it would often amount to a permanent communal Executive responsible to a permanent communal majority. The recent experience of Congress Hindu

Governments was also fresh in the minds of Muslims. Therefore, Dr Latif provided for a composite Executive drawn from all parties or groups in the Parliament.

Another scheme which must have engaged the attention of the League Committee was that of Professor Syed Zafarul Hasan and Dr Mohammad Afzal Husain Qadri of the Aligarh Muslim University.[19] In this scheme, British India was to be divided into three independent, sovereign states. There were the predominantly Muslim states of North-West India and Bengal and the Hindu state called Hindustan comprehending the rest of British India. The Muslim state of North-West India was to be a separate Federation known as the Pakistan Federation, whereas Bengal was to constitute a separate Muslim Federation. There were a number of striking features in this scheme all of which were designed to protect Muslim interests. Hyderabad with its old dominions of Berar and Carnatic was to be created a sovereign state. There were to be newly constituted Provinces of Delhi and Malabar in Hindustan deliberately designed to protect Muslim interests in those areas. Muslims would not be in a majority for they would constitute 28 per cent in Delhi and 27 per cent in Malabar. Delhi would be close to the Muslim Federation of Pakistan and it was hoped that the Malabar Muslims, being a virile race and an important minority, would be able to look after their interests. Another way of protecting Muslims in Hindustan was to give the status of free cities or boroughs to large towns as Muslims lived in considerable numbers in cities in Hindustan. Similarly, Muslims in the rural areas of Hindustan were to be induced to migrate to villages with large Muslim populations. There were to be no restrictions on the migration of Hindus and Muslims to their respective national states. Muslims in Hindustan were to be recognized as minority nations which formed part of a larger Muslim nation inhabiting Pakistan and Bengal.

Nawab Sir Muhammad Shah Nawaz Khan of Mumdot, President of the Punjab Provincial Muslim League, published his scheme, *The Confederacy of India*, in the summer of 1939.[20] In his scheme India was divided into what he called five 'countries':

1. The Indus Regions.
2. Hindu India lying in the central region and including all the territory not covered by the other 'countries'.

---

[19] Ibid., pp. 462–5.
[20] R. Coupland, op. cit., Part II, pp. 203–4.

3. Rajistan comprising the states of Rajputana and Central India.
4. The Deccan states built around the states of Hyderabad and Mysore.
5. Bengal, excluding the Hindu districts in it, but including parts of Assam and other states.

Transfer of population was ruled out as highly expensive and inconvenient. Even though each of the 'countries' would constitute a Federation by itself, yet there would be a Confederacy embracing all the five 'countries'. The author took a stand against the idea of Muslims forming a separate Federation by themselves. Muslim ambitions should not be extra-territorial. 'The foreign element amongst us is quite negligible and we are as much sons of the soil as the Hindus are. Ultimately our destiny lies within India and not out of it.' The subjects assigned to the Confederacy were not clearly defined. Fiscal policy was not to be controlled by it because it would amount to further strengthening of the existing Hindu domination in economic matters. As regards the cost of defence, it was proposed that this should be shared equally among the five members of the Confederacy. The scheme provided no details as regards the domestic federal constitutions of the members.

Two of the members of the League Committee appointed to consider various constitutional proposals, Sir Abdoola Haroon and Sir Sikander Hyat Khan, put forward their own schemes. Sir Abdoola Haroon's scheme envisaged the division of India into two separate Federations, each drawing its major support from one of the major communities. In his letters to the Aga Khan in November and December 1938, Sir Abdoola pointed out that the Muslim League circles had begun drifting in the direction of 'a separate federation of Muslim States and Provinces so that we are free, once and for all, from the Hindu molestation.'[21] The Muslim Federation was to comprise the North-Western part of India and Kashmir. Strangely enough, the future of Bengal and Hyderabad was left out of this scheme.

Sir Sikander Hyat's scheme, published in July 1939, turned out to be most influential.[22] It envisaged a two-tier Federation—a

[21] Alhaj Mian Ahmad Shafi, *Haji Sir Abdoola Haroon; A Biography*, Karachi: Begum Daulat Anwar Hidayatullah, n.d., pp. 138, 140.

[22] Sir Maurice Gwyer and A. Appadorai, eds., op. cit., pp. 455-62.

regional and an All-India Federation. India was divided into the following seven zones:

Zone 1. Assam, Bengal (excluding one or two Western districts in order to approximate the size of this zone to other zones), Bengal States and Sikkim.

Zone 2. Bihar and Orissa (plus the area transferred from Bengal to Orissa).

Zone 3. United Provinces and U.P. States.

Zone 4. Madras, Travancore, Madras States, and Coorg.

Zone 5. Bombay, Hyderabad, Western India States, Bombay States, Mysore and C.P. States.

Zone 6. Rajputana States (minus Bikaner and Jaisalmer), Gwalior, Central India States, Bihar, Orissa States, C.P., and Berar.

Zone 7. Punjab, Sind, N-W. F. Province, Kashmir, Punjab States, Baluchistan, Bikaner, and Jaisalmer.

Each zone was to have a regional Legislature consisting of representatives of both British Indian and Indian States' units comprising that zone. The representatives in the various regional Legislatures were to collectively constitute the Central Federal Assembly consisting of 375 members (250 from British India and 125 from the Indian States). It was also laid down that the Muslims would constitute a third of the total number of representatives in the Federal Assembly.

The Federal Executive, to be headed by the Viceroy, was to include at least one representative from each zone and at least a third of the Ministers so appointed were to be Muslims. The Federal Government was allocated subjects like Defence, External Affairs, Communications, Customs, Coinage, and Currency, etc. Subjects other than these, which were at present included in the Federal list, were to be transferred to the units or zones. Similarly, residuary powers were to vest in the units. One can see that most of these proposals came to be reproduced later in the famous Cabinet Mission Plan of May 1946.

It was significant that all the schemes which envisaged an All-India Federation recommended a weak Centre and fully autonomous Provinces. It could be said that these features were primarily designed to help those Provinces where Muslims were in majority to protect themselves against the encroachment of a

Centre dominated by Hindus. As regards those schemes which recommended separate Muslim Federation or Federations, none of them visualized a Federation embracing both North-Western India and Bengal as Pakistan turned out to be.

It was true that the League Committee examined the details of all these schemes, but there is no evidence to suggest that the Committee had recommended a particular scheme of its own to the Muslim League Working Committee. A day before the Lahore Resolution was passed on 23 March 1940, Jinnah indicated in his Presidential Address that no final scheme had as yet emerged from the Committee (of which he himself was the President). The only authoritative version of what transpired in the Working Committee before the Lahore Resolution emerged is that of Sir Sikander Hyat Khan.

> I have no hesitation in admitting that I was responsible for drafting the original resolution. But let me make it clear that the resolution which I drafted was radically amended by the Working Committee, and there is a wide divergence in the resolution I drafted and the one that was finally passed. The main difference between the two resolutions is that the latter part of my resolution which related to the centre and co-ordination of the activities of the various units, was eliminated.[23]

This explains why the Lahore Resolution said that the 'North-Western and Eastern zones of India should be grouped to constitute "Independent States" in which the constituent units shall be autonomous and sovereign.' This could be interpreted to mean that there were to be two 'Independent States', each of which would have a Federal constitution in which the constituent units would be autonomous and sovereign. This interpretation was also confirmed by the final paragraph of the resolution which read: 'This Session further authorizes the Working Committee to frame a scheme of Constitution in accordance with these basic principles, providing for the assumption finally by the respective regions of all powers such as defence, external affairs, communications, customs and such other matters as may be necessary.'

Was the Muslim League deliberately making provision for the establishment of two states and expecting at the same time that these two states would come together later under some sort of a

---

[23] *The Punjab Legislative Assembly Debates,* 11 March 1941.

Federal arrangement? Or was the vagueness due to poor draftsmanship? If Sir Sikander's version is correct, it seems that the Working Committee removed the federal elements from his resolution and made the Muslim zones in the North-West and in the North-East 'Independent States', which had no federal relationship with an Indian Federation. This probably explains the origin of the term 'Independent States'. The Committee might have also felt that since the two zones were separated from one another by Indian territory, it would not be easy to make them units of a single federation and therefore each of them was likely to emerge as an independent state. However, the resolution later created considerable confusion and misunderstanding. Those Bengali leaders who felt after Partition that the Centre, dominated by West Pakistanis, was not looking after the interests of Bengal, claimed that the original Lahore Resolution visualized two independent Muslim states, one of West Pakistan and the other of East Bengal.

Choudhry Khaliquzzaman, a member of the Working Committee of the All-India Muslim League, in his book, *Pathway to Pakistan,* claims that in 1939 in his interview with Lord Zetland, Secretary of State for India, he proposed the establishment of three or four Federations of Provinces and States. From the records he has produced in this book, Choudhry Khaliquzzaman suggested the formation of a 'federation of Muslim Provinces and States in North-West India' and 'a further federation of Bengal and Assam, and possibly more than one further federation of the other Provinces and States in the remaining part of India'. It may be noted that Khaliquzzaman envisaged the coordination of the three or four Federations by a small central body and pointed out that the object of this scheme was 'to give the Muslims as great a measure of control at the Centre as the Hindus'.[24] This shows that Khaliquzzaman was thinking of not one Muslim state, but two Federations of Muslim Provinces, and secondly, the Muslim Federations would not be separate and independent entities but linked to a confederal Centre consisting of three or four Federations. In his interview with Lord Zetland, Khaliquzzaman also pointed out that the Muslim League in its next session would pass a resolution to this effect. This means that he must have been

---

[24] Choudhry Khaliquzzaman, *Pathway to Pakistan,* Lahore: Longmans. 1961, p. 207.

authorized by Jinnah to seek such an interview and put forward these ideas.

All this confirms the point that we have made in an earlier paragraph, namely, that Muslim League leaders at the time of the passing of the Lahore Resolution did entertain the idea of the formation of two Muslim states—one in the North-West and the other in the Eastern part of India. Khaliquzzaman refers to a discussion of the Partition proposals in the Muslim League Working Committee meeting held on 4 February 1940. According to Khaliquzzaman, in this meeting Sir Sikander Hyat favoured the idea of a confederation whereas it seems Khaliquzzaman had changed his point of view for he had advocated a confederal scheme in his interview with Lord Zetland. Khaliquzzaman states that in the Muslim League Working Committee meeting of 4 February 1940, Jinnah opposed the idea of confederation put forward by Sir Sikander Hyat and 'entered in his notebook my suggestion with approval'.[25] It would not be possible to accept this claim without Jinnah's papers being available. However, it may be said to the credit of Khaliquzzaman that he wrote to Jinnah in October 1942, expressing his apprehension as regards the future interpretations of the phrase 'such territorial readjustments as may be necessary' in the Lahore Resolution. He pointed out that the term 'territorial readjustment' could be interpreted to mean that those divisions or subdivisions in which Muslims were not in majority could be detached from the Muslim Provinces of Punjab and Bengal. If this were to happen, Muslims would lose a valuable port like Calcutta. According to Khaliquzzaman, if Muslims had tenaciously held to the idea of claiming the whole of that Province as a part of Pakistan in which they were in majority, they would have been able to claim the whole of Punjab. If this position had been accepted, the whole of Punjab would have become a part of Pakistan and in this way a state like Kashmir would have been deprived of any direct communication with Indian territory.[26]

The sort of confusion that prevailed among League ranks before Partition was indicated by the resolution that the Sind Legislature passed in support of Pakistan in March 1943. The resolution pointed out that the Muslims, differing from Hindus in vital matters like religion, philosophy, social customs, literature,

[25] Ibid., p. 234.
[26] Ibid., Appendix VIII, pp. 424–7.

traditions, political and economic theories were 'entitled to the right as a single, separate nation, to have *independent National States* [author's italics] of their own, carved in the zones where they are in majority in the subcontinent.' Again, after declaring that the Muslims would not accept a constitution which established one Central Government in India, the resolution continued. 'It is necessary for them to have *independent National States* (author's italics) of their own....'[27] This resolution, moved by G. M. Sayed, was open to confusing and dangerous interpretation. Similarly, Abul Hashim, a famous Muslim League leader from Bengal, made a passionate plea in favour of creating a separate Muslim state of East Bengal in the Subjects Committee of the Muslim League Legislators Convention in April 1946. He pointed out that the Lahore Resolution was clearly capable of such an interpretation.

As opposed to this, it can also be argued that the Lahore Resolution envisaged a union of the two 'Independent States' of the North-Western and Eastern zones. The key phrase which suggests such interpretation is to be found in the Resolution itself. The Resolution says that the North-Western and Eastern zones of India 'should be *grouped* [author's italics] to constitute "Independent States"'. At the annual session of the League in Madras in 1941, a major portion of the Lahore Resolution, drafted in slightly different terms, was adopted as one of the aims and objects of the All-India Muslim League thereby amending the League constitution.[28] In this draft, it is interesting to note that the word 'together' was added after the word 'grouped'. The draft said that the 'North-Western and Eastern zones of India shall be *grouped together* [author's italics] to constitute Independent States as Muslim Free National Homelands in which the constituent units shall be autonomous and sovereign.' However, it could still be claimed that both the Lahore Resolution and the draft which was incorporated in the League Constitution spoke of 'Independent States'. Thus, according to the Muslim League Constitution, the Muslim League was committed to the establishment of two Muslim 'Independent States' in the North-Western and Eastern zones of India.

---

[27] G. M. Sayed, *Struggle for New Sind*, Karachi: 1949, pp. 93–94.
[28] *Resolutions of the All India Muslim League From March 1940 to 1941*, Delhi: All India Muslim League, n.d., p. 35.

In the subsequent statements and speeches of the League leaders, this confusion was glossed over and the impression that one gathered was that what the League really meant by the Lahore Resolution was the establishment of a single Muslim state including both the North-Western and the Eastern zones.[29] However, the first official statement by the Muslim League Organization that by the term 'Pakistan' in the Lahore Resolution they meant the establishment of a single sovereign state and not two independent states was made in the form of a resolution passed in the Muslim League Legislators Convention in April 1946. The resolution demanded that the 'zones comprising Bengal and Assam in the North-East and the Punjab, the North-West Frontier Province, Sind and Baluchistan in the North-West of India…where the Muslims are a dominant majority, be constituted into a sovereign state…'; that 'two separate Constitution-making bodies be set-up by the peoples of Pakistan and Hindustan for the purpose of framing their respective constitutions.'[30]

It may also be pointed out that the Lahore Resolution did not specify the areas in the North-Western and Eastern zones where Muslims were in majority. Sir Muhammad Iqbal did try to delimit the area of the North-West Muslim state by suggesting that Ambala Division and some of those districts where non-Muslims predominated could be excluded. Similarly, the scheme put forward by Professor S. Z. Hasan and Dr M. A. H. Qadri delimited the area of the Bengal Muslim Federation as that which included the adjacent District of Purnia (Bihar) and the Sylhet Division (Assam), but excluded the South-Western Districts of Howrah and Midnapore and the North-Western district of Darjeeling. It may be suggested that the vagueness of the Lahore Resolution was perhaps deliberately designed. Some writers have argued that this gave room to League leaders for bargaining and manoeuvring. It has been reported that Lord Mountbatten pointed out to the League leaders that the area of Pakistan as envisaged in the Lahore Resolution did not include the entire Provinces of Punjab, Bengal and Assam because the Lahore Resolution carefully used the phrase 'areas in which the Muslims are numerically in

---

[29] *Jinnah-Gandhi Talks* (September 1944), Delhi: All India Muslim League, 1944, pp. 40, 44, 75.

[30] *Resolutions of the All-India Muslim League from January 1944 to December 1946*, Delhi: All-India Muslim League, n.d., pp. 46–47.

a majority as in the North-Western and Eastern zones of India.' If the framers of the Lahore Resolution had been clear and confident about Muslim majority in the entire Provinces of Punjab, Bengal and Assam, they would have been more specific. Accordingly, Lord Mountbatten argued, the Muslim League could not oppose the partition of Provinces like Punjab and Bengal, as this was clearly hinted at by the Lahore Resolution itself, which used the term 'areas' without clearly defining what Provinces the term 'areas' constituted.

The origin of the word Pakistan has already been dealt with. In the Lahore Resolution there was no mention of the word Pakistan. Mr Jinnah made it clear in his Presidential Address in the Delhi session of the League in 1943 that it was not the Muslim League or Quaid-i-Azam who had coined it. It was originally coined by 'some young fellows in London' in 1929–30 and they applied it only to the North-Western part of India. The opponents of the Muslim League 'started damning this resolution on the ground that it was Pakistan', their propaganda being that Jinnah was working for the North-West and Eastern zones which were *Pak* (clean) and the others *Na-Pak* (unclean), and also that Pakistan meant alliance with other Muslim countries against Hindu India.

> You know perfectly well that Pakistan is a word which is really foisted upon us and fathered on us by some section of the Hindu press and also by the British press. Now our resolution was known for a long time as the Lahore resolution, popularly known as Pakistan. But how long are we to have this long phrase? Now I say to my Hindu and British friends: We thank you for giving us one word.[31]

III. Towards Partition

1. *The Cripps Mission, 1942*

Soon after the Lahore Resolution was passed in March 1940, there came a reassuring statement from the Viceroy, Lord Linlithgow, on 8 August 1940, which clearly stated that the British Government 'could not contemplate the transfer of their present responsibilities for the peace and welfare of India to any system of government whose authority is directly denied by large and powerful elements in India's national life. Nor could they be

---

[31] Jamil-ud-Din Ahmad, ed., *Speeches and Writings of Mr. Jinnah,*, Vol. I, Lahore: Ashraf, 1960, p. 509.

parties to the coercion of such elements into submission to such a Government.'

The next stage was reached with the announcement of the Cripps proposals in March 1942. The Muslim League could claim that in the Cripps offer, 'the possibility of Pakistan is recognized by implication by providing for the establishment of two or more independent Unions in India.'[32] It was also laid down in the Draft Declaration which Sir Stafford Cripps brought with him that the British Government was particularly concerned about the problem of protecting the rights of racial and religious minorities in a free India. It was clearly stated that the British Government would not impose any restriction on the power of the Indian Union to decide their relationship with other member States of the British Commonwealth in a treaty that would be negotiated between the British Government and the constitution-making body after the war. But the treaty would make provision, 'in accordance with the undertakings given by His Majesty's Government for the protection of racial and religious minorities.'[33]

The Congress Working Committee in its resolution of April 1942, expressed its unhappiness at these proposals. 'The acceptance beforehand of the novel principle of non-accession for a Province is also a severe blow to the conception of Indian unity and an apple of discord likely to generate growing trouble in the Provinces, and which may lead to further difficulties in the way of the Indian States merging themselves into an Indian Union.' But still it did not want to veto any Province's or people's right of self-determination if they were determined to exercise it. The resolution of the Working Committee conceded this right in a grudging fashion.

> Nevertheless, the Committee cannot think in terms of compelling the people of any territorial unit to remain in an Indian Union against their declared and established will. While recognizing this principle, the Committee feel that every effort should be made to create conditions which would help the different units in developing a common and cooperative national life.[34]

---

[32] *Resolutions of the All India Muslim League From April 1942 to May 1943*. Delhi: All India Muslim League, n.d., p. 2.

[33] Sir Maurice Gwyer and A. Appadorai eds., Vol. II, op. cit., p. 520.

[34] Ibid., p. 525.

There was a strong section in the Working Committee of the Congress led by Gandhi which adopted a negative attitude towards the Cripps proposals. Gandhi's reported reaction to the Cripps Mission was that it was 'a post-dated cheque on a bank that was obviously failing.' The British were being conciliatory because they were in a precarious position. According to Azad, Gandhi argued against acceptance of the Cripps proposals in the Working Committee because of his opposition to war. But there were others, like Nehru and Azad, who adopted a more constructive approach.[35] The latter section was willing to come to a settlement with the British Government if they would concede to the Provisional Government that would be formed during the war the status of a National Cabinet with full powers rather than a glorified Viceroy's Executive Council. The British Government, on the other hand, was against the idea of introducing a Cabinet system in the Viceroy's Executive Council even by convention for a Cabinet nominated by the major political organizations would be 'responsible to no one but itself, could not be removed and would in fact constitute an absolute dictatorship of the majority.' Again, the British Government took its stand on the pledges given to minorities. 'This suggestion would be rejected by all Minorities in India, since it would subject all of them to a permanent and autocratic majority in the Cabinet.'[36]

It would not be quite accurate to suggest, as Azad and other Congress leaders have suggested, that the problem of the transfer of Defence portfolio to Indian hands constituted an intractable difference of approach between the British and the Congress. The Congress regarded the problem of defence vital because due to the war situation the whole country had to be mobilized in order to support the war effort. The British Government were prepared to concede substantial control over the Defence portfolio and also were willing to transfer subjects like war finance, supplies for all forces and munitions, propaganda and publicity, civil defence, internal security, etc.—subjects which were all related to the general problem of defence—to Indian Executive Councillors.[37] This would have given to the Congress most of what it wanted.

---

[35] Maulana Abul Kalam Azad, *India Wins Freedom*, Calcutta: Orient Longmans, 1959, p. 50.

[36] Sir Maurice Gwyer and A. Appadorai, eds., Vol. II, op. cit., p. 537.

[37] Ibid., p. 536.

The Congress agreed with the British Government that the Commander-in-Chief would be allowed to have full control over the technical and operational sides of the war and also 'that the higher strategy of the war should be controlled by the War Cabinet in London, which would have an Indian Member.' Thus, the negotiations between the Congress and the Government failed not so much because the Congress wanted substantial control over Defence but because the Congress was keen on acquiring *de facto* power in the Executive Council by transforming it into a Cabinet Government. This, as it has been pointed out earlier, the British Government was not prepared to concede.

As for the Muslim League, it was obvious that it was not in a very strong position, and it was widely believed that the League took a clear stand against the acceptance of the proposals after it became known that the Congress had rejected the proposals. Jinnah also complained that 'the talks had been carried on with the Congress leaders over the heads of the Muslims, and other parties had been utterly ignored.'[38] The League expressed its gratification that the possibility of Pakistan was recognized by implication. But it complained about how handicapped the Muslim majority Provinces were in the channels that were available to them to express their non-accession to India. In the Legislative Assemblies of Bengal and the Punjab, Muslims were in a minority. The Sind and Frontier Assemblies were so small and the weightage given to the non-Muslims so heavy, that a majority could not be easily manipulated. In the Provinces in which the Muslims could not obtain a majority in the Legislative Assemblies in favour of non-accession, the prescribed procedure was that a plebiscite would be held of the entire adult population and not of the Muslims alone. The League Working Committee regarded this as a denial of the right of self-determination to Muslims.[39] This was presumably a bargaining attitude, for how could the non-Muslims in the non-acceding Provinces be coerced into throwing their lot in with the Muslims when the Muslims of those Provinces had voted in favour of non-accession to India? What the League could have suggested was that the Muslim majority Provinces be demarcated in such a way that the districts or

[38] V. P. Menon, op. cit., p. 133.
[39] *Resolutions of the All India Muslim League From April 1942 to May 1943*, op. cit., p. 5.

divisions in which Muslims were not in majority could be separated from them. Muslims of the demarcated areas could then be asked to vote on the question of non-accession. But probably Jinnah did not want to weaken his bargaining position by disclosing all his cards.

2. Gandhi-Jinnah Talks, 1944

The Gandhi-Jinnah talks took place during the month of September 1944. They were brought about largely by the efforts of C. Rajagopalachari, the former Congress Premier of Madras, to resolve the Congress-League deadlock on the issue of Pakistan. Ever since April-May 1942, Rajagopalachari had been trying to persuade the Congress to acknowledge the Muslim League's claim for separation. Such a long-term arrangement, he thought, might enable the Congress and the League to come to an immediate understanding as regards the formation of a national administration to tackle the present war situation. He moved a resolution to this effect before the All-India Congress Committee when it met during April-May 1942. But the resolution was rejected.[40] The Congress Committee passed another resolution which stated:

> ...That any proposal to disintegrate India by giving liberty to any component state or territorial unit to secede from the Indian Union or Federation will be highly detrimental to the best interests of the people of the different States and Provinces and the country as a whole and the Congress, therefore, cannot agree to any such proposal.[41]

Rajagopalachari continued with his efforts and it was being increasingly felt on the part of other leaders as well that the League and Congress should make an earnest effort to arrive at an understanding. Jinnah's complaint was that the Congress by passing the 'Quit India' Resolution in August 1942, had deliberately tried to coerce the British Government at a time when they were engaged in fighting the war into handing over the reins of the Government of India to the Congress. However, responding to the appeals that were being made to him that he should take the initiative in opening negotiations with the Congress, he

---

[40] Sir Maurice Gwyer and A. Appadorai, op. cit., p. 547.
[41] Ibid., pp. 547-8.

declared in his Presidential Address to the League in Delhi in April 1943:

> Nobody would welcome it more than myself if Mr Gandhi is even now really willing to come to a settlement with the Muslim League on the basis of Pakistan.... If he has made up his mind, what is there to prevent Mr Gandhi from writing direct to me?...I cannot believe for a single moment—strong as this Government may be in this country—you may say anything you like against this Government—I cannot believe that they will have the daring to stop such a letter if it is sent to me.[42]

Gandhi did write a letter to Jinnah from prison but the Government refused to forward the letter and merely conveyed the gist of the letter saying that Gandhi wished to meet Jinnah. When a section of the Hindu press commented sarcastically on Jinnah's reluctance to take a firm stand against the Government when they had, despite his challenge, refused to forward the letter, Jinnah's explanation was: 'This letter of Mr Gandhi can only be construed as a move on his part to embroil the Muslim League to come into clash with the British Government solely for the purpose of helping his release, so that he will be free to do what he pleases thereafter.'[43] Jinnah further continued:

> I, therefore, suggested that if Mr Gandhi were to write to me a letter indicating that he was prepared to retrace his steps and abandon his policy and programme culminating in the resolution of the A.-I.C.C. of 8 August, and was even now willing to come to a settlement with the Muslim League on the basis of Pakistan, we were willing to bury the past and forget it. I still believe that the Government will not dare to stop such a letter if it came from Mr Gandhi.[44]

Jinnah was at his best in this sort of tactical warfare. He was not satisfied with a mere desire on the part of Gandhi to meet him and explore the possibilities of a settlement. He wanted at first a total surrender from Gandhi on fundamentals, and once this was made, he was prepared to negotiate on details. This again goes to show that he was in no hurry to arrive at a compromise agreement with the Congress on some of the basic issues but probably

---

[42] Jamil-ud-Din Ahmad, Vol. I, op. cit., pp. 499–500.
[43] Ibid., pp. 514–5.
[44] Ibid., p. 516.

wanted to wait until he was politically much stronger to obtain the best terms that the League and the Muslims could get.

The correspondence that took place on the points at issue between the two leaders during the talks at Bombay also confirmed the impression that Jinnah was biding his time. First of all, Jinnah pointed out that it was difficult to negotiate with Gandhi when he had openly stated during the talks that he had come to discuss the Hindu-Muslim settlement in his individual capacity and not as a representative of the Hindus or the Congress. It would be difficult to deny that this did present a formidable difficulty to the League leader. On the other hand, Gandhi himself could not have adopted any other position for the members of the Congress Working Committee were in jail and therefore he could only speak as an individual who would try to persuade the Congress to accept any understanding arrived at between himself and the League leader.

Jinnah contended that the Rajagopalachari formula, on the basis of which Gandhi wanted to continue his discussions, did not fully concede the basic demands of the Lahore Resolution. The formula suggested that the North-Western and Eastern areas of India should be demarcated so that the wishes of the inhabitants of the area might be ascertained. Jinnah insisted that Gandhi should first concede that the two zones of Pakistan would comprise the six Provinces of Sind, Baluchistan, the North-West Frontier Province, the Punjab, Bengal and Assam.

In fairness to Gandhi, it may be pointed out that Gandhi did concede that the North-Western and Eastern zones would comprise the six Provinces that Jinnah referred to. All that Gandhi insisted was that Muslims could get only that part of the Punjab 'where they are in absolute majority over all the other elements and in parts of Bengal and Assam where they are in absolute majority, desire to live in separation from the rest of India.'[45] Thus, there was really no serious difference in the views held by Jinnah and Gandhi in so far as the area of Pakistan was concerned. And indeed, the area of Pakistan that came to be established after August 1947 was about the same area that Gandhi was willing to concede in September 1944. Where Gandhi did strike a note of disagreement was with regard to the claim of the Lahore Resolution that Muslims were a separate nation. He was

---

[45] *Jinnah-Gandhi Talks,* op. cit., p. 37.

willing to accord to the Muslims the right of separation, not because they formed a separate nation but only because they wanted to separate themselves from 'one family consisting of many members.'[46]

If one started from the position that Muslims were a separate nation, then it followed that they would form a separate national state of their own. This was Jinnah's position and presumably that of the Lahore Resolution. On the other hand, if one started from Gandhi's point of view that India was a sort of joint family, some of whose members were breaking away from the family, then one would think in terms of a confederal or federal arrangement under which the separated members would still come together by a treaty or some other arrangement to 'provide for the efficient and satisfactory administration of foreign affairs, defence, internal communications, customs, commerce and the like, which must necessarily continue to be the matters of common interest between the contracting parties.'[47] This probably created the suspicion in Jinnah's mind that Gandhi was still thinking in terms of some sort of a federal or confederal arrangement and not in terms of two sovereign, separate and independent States.[48]

However, even this difference in approach was not an insurmountable obstacle to a compromise or an understanding. If the Muslims unitedly and clearly were to insist on total separation (as they actually did and thus won Pakistan), no amount of Hindu or Congress opposition could have stopped them. What must have made Jinnah reluctant to come to any definite and clear understanding with Gandhi at that time was his own position as a leader of the Muslims. In September 1944 Jinnah was not sure whether he could produce overwhelming support for his demand among the Muslims if a plebiscite were to be held. Secondly, there was no guarantee that if Gandhi had come to a definite understanding with the League on these issues, that the Congress leaders, after coming out of jail, would abide by the terms of agreement. Finally, as a lawyer and as a hard-headed negotiator, Jinnah could not visualize Pakistan being achieved only because the Congress and the League had agreed to divide the country. The party who had the power, namely, the British Government, was not in the picture. Gandhi suggested that this difficulty could

---

[46] Ibid.
[47] Ibid., p. 38.
[48] Ibid., p. 44.

be overcome by the Congress and the League, immediately on the acceptance of an agreement, deciding on a common course of action for the attainment of independence for India.[49] This approach, Jinnah probably thought, was fraught with risks and dangers. There was the sad experience of the joint struggle waged for the Khilafat and Indian independence. It was likely that another struggle might also degenerate into communal warfare.

Why did Jinnah agree to hold these talks when he probably knew that nothing concrete or useful would emerge from these discussions? The answer lay in the great tactical and political victory that Jinnah snatched from these talks. For the first time, it was clearly and publicly recognized that here were two leaders, Gandhi representing the Hindus, and Jinnah representing the Muslims, meeting, as it were, at the summit, to resolve the political deadlock in India. The image of himself and the Muslim League as the sole representative of Muslim India that Jinnah was so assiduously trying to establish in India and abroad assumed a concrete shape after these talks and a precedent once established was duly followed in subsequent talks.

3. *The Wavell Plan and the Simla Conference, 1945*

It has already been seen that the Cripps proposals envisaged the formation of a provisional popular government in India so that during the war India might be able to bring about a more efficient mobilization of its moral and material resources. Rajagopalachari had the same objective when he tried to persuade the Congress to concede in substance the Muslim League demand of Pakistan. Similarly, an attempt was made in the beginning of 1945 to bring about an understanding between the Congress and the League so that the two parties might participate in the formation of an Interim Government at the Centre. It was hoped that such an interim arrangement might create the climate for a better and long-term understanding between the two parties. This was the Desai-Liaquat Pact which started taking shape towards the end of 1944. It was a Pact between Bhulabhai Desai, the Leader of the Congress Party in the Central Legislature, and Liaquat Ali Khan, the Deputy Leader of the Muslim League Party in the Central Legislature.

---

[49] Ibid., pp. 38–39.

There is no accepted authoritative text of the Pact.[50] The broad outlines of the Pact were that the Congress and the League would join on the basis of parity in forming an Interim Government at the Centre. Representatives of minorities like the Scheduled Castes and the Sikhs would also be included in the Government. The Government would function within the framework of the Government of India Act, 1935. According to the text of the draft published by Liaquat Ali Khan, it was agreed that if the Cabinet could not get a particular measure passed in the Legislative Assembly, it would not seek recourse to the reserve powers of the Governor General. Again, the same version of the Pact also laid down that the Interim Government should secure the release of the Congress Working Committee members. All the versions of the Pact agreed as regards the provision that the Interim Government would take steps to secure the withdrawal of Section 93 administrations in the Provinces and have them replaced by coalition Ministries consisting of both Congress and League elements.

Bhulabhai Desai obtained Gandhi's blessings for his attempts to bring about this Pact. The Viceroy, Lord Wavell, also was in favour of such a plan and got in touch with the Secretary of State to obtain his reactions. The British Cabinet sought clarification on a number of points before giving their full approval. They wanted to know whether there had been a change in the attitude of the Congress Party, whether they would support Desai, and how far the members of the proposed Interim Government would be subject to control by their Party caucuses. Lord Wavell, having obtained Desai's assurance that Gandhi would support the Pact, asked Sir John Colville, the Governor of Bombay, to contact Jinnah on his behalf to find out what his reactions were. Jinnah had already made a public statement to the effect that he had no knowledge of the Desai-Liaquat Pact. 'Sir John Colville saw Jinnah, who stated that he knew nothing about the talks between Desai and Liaquat Ali Khan and that the proposals had been made without any authority from the League.'[51]

---

[50] A text entitled 'Text of the Draft Desai-Liaquat Ali Pact, 1944 as published by Nawabzada Liaquat Ali Khan' is in Sir Maurice Gwyer and A. Appadorai, eds., Vol. II, op. cit., pp. 566–7. A different text is given in V. P. Menon, op. cit., pp. 176–7.

[51] V. P. Menon, op. cit., p. 178.

This meant that Liaquat Ali Khan had come to some sort of a clandestine understanding with Desai without informing Jinnah. If this were true, he had committed breach of trust and also flouted the clear directives of the Muslim League Party. Each year it was the President who was given the authority till the next session by the annual session of the Muslim League to conduct negotiations with other parties or take any steps that he deemed necessary for the furtherance of the objectives of the League. In this scheme, Liaquat Ali Khan had not only overstepped his powers, but also, as Secretary of the Muslim League, had not kept the President informed of such a serious proposal as the Desai-Liaquat Pact. According to the verbal evidence that was made available to the author by several members of the then Muslim League Working Committee as well as by persons who were very close to Jinnah, Quaid-i-Azam expressed his strong disapproval to Liaquat for his conduct in this episode. The author understands that Liaquat's own explanation was that it was high time that an understanding should be brought about between the two major communities because the British were likely to leave any moment. Jinnah and Gandhi, being older men, had so far adopted a rigid attitude and thus, not been able to bring about a Hindu-Muslim agreement. Liaquat felt that younger men should make an attempt.

Lord Wavell was basically a soldier. As a soldier, he thought that India's defence could best be organized and maintained if it continued as a united political and administrative country. In an address to the Central Legislature in February 1944, he declared, 'You cannot alter geography. From the point of view of defence, of relations with the outside world, of many internal and external economic problems, India is a natural unit.... That two communities and even two nations can make arrangements to live together in spite of differing cultures or religions, history provides many examples.'[52] Lord Wavell's hope was that if he could get the various party leaders to work together in an Interim Government, he might be able to persuade them by patience and tact to come to some sort of a long-term agreement which would preserve the unity of the country. He hoped that problems like the successful conclusion of the war against Japan, and, above all, preparations of plans for the post-war agricultural and industrial

---

[52] Sir Maurice Gwyer and A. Appadorai, op. cit., p. 557.

development of India, would once and for all inject into the thinking of political leaders a sense of realism and an awareness of the enormity of the problems that faced India. Thus, instead of being absorbed in day-to-day partisan bickerings, the new administrative problems and the result of working together to solve them would infuse into them a constructive and tolerant point of view. But as a soldier and as an administrator, he underrated the enormous political chasm that divided the Congress and the League.

Lord Wavell visited England towards the end of March 1945. In June 1945, L. S. Amery, Secretary of State for India, announced that as a result of the discussions that were held between the Government and the Viceroy, it was proposed that the Executive Council should be reconstituted to include leaders of Indian political parties in such a way that a balanced representation was given to the main communities, including an equal proportion of Muslims and Caste Hindus. This would not entail any change in the existing constitution except for one amendment to the Ninth Schedule to the Government of India Act, 1935. According to a provision in that Schedule, not less than three members of the Executive Council must have put in at least ten years' service under the Crown in India. Presumably, if the Congress and the League agreed to join the Council, this clause would have to be amended. All the members of the Executive Council would be Indians, except the Viceroy and the Commander-in-Chief, who would retain his position as War Member. This meant that the defence of India would continue to be a British responsibility. Similarly, no change in the relations of the Crown with the Indian States through the Viceroy as Crown representative was contemplated.

The Viceroy, in order to place these proposals before the Indian leaders and explore the possibilities of the formation of a reconstituted Executive Council, called a Conference at Simla which began its deliberations on 25 June 1945. From the very beginning it was clear that there was a fundamental disagreement between the Congress and the League as regards the right of the Congress and other non-League groups to nominate Muslim members to the Executive Council. Jinnah took the stand that the Congress could include only Hindu members in its quota to the Executive Council. This was challenged by Azad in the Conference. Lord

Wavell also agreed that the position of the Muslim League was not reasonable. According to Azad, the provisional list which Lord Wavell had himself prepared had four names, in addition to the quotas of five each allotted to the Congress and the Muslim League respectively. The four additional members in the provisional list consisted of a representative of the Sikhs, two from the Scheduled Castes and the fourth was Malik Khizr Hyat Khan Tiwana, the Unionist Premier of the Punjab.[53] Azad's version regarding the inclusion of Malik Khizr Hyat Khan Tiwana in Lord Wavell's provisional list is not correct. Lord Wavell was prepared to accept four Muslim Leaguers in the proposed Executive Council nominated by Jinnah, and the fifth Muslim member would not be Malik Khizr Hyat Khan Tiwana himself but his nominee representing Punjab Muslims. This meant that the Muslim League would be allowed to nominate only four members and the fifth Muslim member would be a non-League Muslim.[54] Jinnah rightly thought that such an outcome would have been a deadly blow to the Muslim League *vis-à-vis* Pakistan because it would have meant that a non-League Muslim would have been included in the Executive Council as a representative of the Punjab, which was the heart of Pakistan. Jinnah also complained that the Muslim League would be reduced to a minority of one-third in the Executive Council as the representatives of the Scheduled Castes, Sikhs, and Christians were likely to vote with the Congress. 'Ethnically and culturally, they are very closely knitted to Hindu society.'[55]

When Lord Wavell announced the failure of the Simla Conference on 14 July 1945, it was clear that, despite Lord Wavell's statement that the responsibility for the failure of the Conference was his, it was Jinnah's uncompromising attitude which had wrecked the Conference. Lord Wavell said, '...He was so

---

[53] Maulana Abul Kalam Azad, op. cit., p. 114.

[54] This information, that Lord Wavell suggested that the fifth Muslim member should be a non-League nominee of Malik Khizr Hyat Khan Tiwana, has been furnished to the author by Sir Francis Mudie in a personal communication. According to Sir Francis, the non-League member would have been Sir Muhammad Nawaz Khan, Sardar of Kot. The fact that Lord Wavell suggested that he would be a non-League nominee of the Punjab Premier is also borne out by Jinnah's statement after the breakdown of the Simla Conference. Jamil-ud-Din Ahmad, ed., Vol. II, 1964, p. 188.

[55] Ibid., p. 187.

decided that I felt that it would be useless to continue the discussions.'

It would be interesting to speculate as to whether the Muslim League was completely united behind Jinnah's implacable opposition to the Viceroy's proposals. V. P. Menon has written that Husain Imam, a member of the League Working Committee who attended the Conference as Leader of the Muslim League Party in the Council of State, urged him to see Liaquat Ali Khan in order to find a way out of the impasse. 'He gave me the impression that the members of the Working Committee of the Muslim League were far from unanimous in rejecting the Viceroy's offer.'[56] Husain Imam presumably referred to that minority in the Working Committee who were keen to come to an understanding with the Congress. They were quite opposed to Khizr Hyat Khan or his nominee being included in the Interim Government, but were probably not averse to the idea of the Congress nominating a Muslim in their quota. There was also a feeling in the League Working Committee that Jinnah had pitched his demands far too high in asking for parity for Muslims with Caste Hindus when Muslims were only about 25 per cent and the Caste Hindus about 60 per cent of the population. All this goes to show that had it not been for the so-called 'intransigence' of Jinnah, Pakistan might not have been achieved within slightly more than seven years of the Lahore Resolution.

Why did Jinnah 'wreck' the Simla Conference? Was he trying to wreck it deliberately from the very beginning? First of all, it was clear that whatever the differences in the League Working Committee, they were unanimously behind Jinnah's unshakable opposition not to let Khizr Hyat or his nominee be included as a representative of the Punjab Muslims in the Interim Government. Once Jinnah came to know that the Viceroy wanted to include a non-League Muslim from the Punjab, he was determined to wreck the Conference. He knew that once it became clear to all the Muslim leaders and particularly the Muslim leaders of Punjab that they were not likely to get any prize offices by remaining outside the Muslim League, they would all have to flock to the Muslim League.

It has also been suggested that Jinnah was confident that his opposition would seal the failure of the Conference because he

---

[56] V. P. Menon, op. cit., p. 214.

had been advised by a member of the existing Viceroy's Executive Council to stand firm.[57] One can only guess as to who this member was. It was probably Sir Firoz Khan Noon, the Defence Member of the Executive Council, who had always been deferential towards the Quaid-i-Azam, who suggested to Jinnah that the Viceroy was not likely to go ahead with his plans without Jinnah's support.

One may also advance the view that probably Jinnah was not very keen that the Simla Conference should succeed because his claim that the Muslim League was the sole representative organization of the Muslims had not yet been established through general elections. The Muslim League had grown popular, but it was still not strongly entrenched in so far as the Provincial governments in Muslim majority Provinces were concerned. The Frontier Province was under a Congress Ministry, Bengal was under Section 93, whereas Punjab had a Unionist Ministry. The Sind Ministry, under Sir Ghulam Hussain Hidayatullah, depended on Congress support. Therefore, it may be argued that Jinnah wanted fresh elections to be held so that the Muslim League might be given a chance to capture some of these Ministries. He was probably confident that as the prospects of Pakistan became brighter, the Muslims in Punjab and particularly the Muslim officials, would do everything to unseat the Unionist Ministry. Thus, it was in the interests of the Muslim League that the Simla Conference should fail.

Dawn, the official organ of the Muslim League, in its editorial of 15 June 1945 said that 'with regard to the Muslim moiety, the Musalmans will tolerate no infiltration of non-League stooges to humour any party.' This challenge was answered by the Congress Working Committee when it declared in its instructions issued to its representatives attending the Conference that the idea of the Muslim League exercising the exclusive right to nominate all the Muslim members of the National Government should be firmly resisted.[58]

In fairness to Jinnah, it must be said that when he argued that the Muslim League was the sole, authoritative representative of the Muslim nation, he did not mean that it represented each and every Muslim. Even though Pakistan was not yet a reality, he was thinking along the lines that the Muslim League represented

[57] Ibid.
[58] Sir Maurice Gwyer and A. Appadorai, op. cit., p. 561.

the Muslim nation in the same sense that a British party government represented the British nation.

Azad was right when he said that, 'The Simla Conference marks a breakwater in Indian political history.' The Congress was beginning to realize that the achievement of Indian independence was not simply a matter of forcing the British Government to agree to their demands, but that there was an equally important third party, the Muslim League, without whose consent no long-term settlement of the Indian problem could be brought about.

5 THE EMERGENCE OF PAKISTAN—II

I. THE CABINET MISSION PLAN, 1946

The Viceroy and the British Government had so far tried to create a better atmosphere for a long-term settlement by bringing about a short-term agreement. The best instrument of achieving the latter, they thought, was the formation of an Interim Government in which the party leaders would be expected to look at the various administrative problems from a broad point of view. This approach had borne no fruit, and Sir Stafford Cripps, commenting on the failure of the Simla Conference, hinted at the direction in which the mind of the Government was working. '...It is obviously desirable not to waste further time trying to arrive at a temporary arrangement, which is mixed up inexplicably with problems of permanent settlement, especially with that of the unity of British India.' The previous Conservative Government had mostly talked in terms of not allowing the majority to ride roughshod over the interests of the minorities in India. The present Labour Government, though suspected by the Muslim League of pro-Congress sympathies, was very keen to evolve some sort of a long-term arrangement without being partial to one side or the other. Thus, Sir Stafford in the same statement pointed out: 'It would not be right to allow any Minority, however large and important, to hold up the attainment of self-government in India, any more than it would be right to force the Muslim Majority Provinces into a new constitutional arrangement to which they took fundamental objection.' In spite of this tightrope walking, it was becoming clear that the issue of Pakistan could not be avoided. Sir Stafford Cripps quite frankly admitted that in arriving at a permanent settlement, Pakistan must form a major issue. He urged the necessity of holding new elections in India, 'to form from the representatives so elected a Constituent Assembly to work out a new free self-government Constitution for British India or such part of it as was ready to consent to such a Constitution.'[1]

This was followed by elections to the Central and Provincial Legislatures which started towards the end of 1945. The election results of the Central Legislative Assembly were available towards the end of December 1945. The Muslim League won every Muslim seat and the Nationalist Muslims, who opposed it, forfeited their deposits in many cases. The success of the Congress was also very impressive in general constituencies and many opposing candidates withdrew in these constituencies. In the Central Legislative Assembly, the party position was as follows: Congress—57; Muslim League—30; Independents—5; Akali Sikhs—2; and Europeans—8. The total number of elected seats was 102. In the Provinces, Congress successes enabled it to form Ministries in Assam, Bihar, the United Provinces, Bombay, Madras, the Central Provinces, Orissa and the North-West Frontier Province. The Muslim League achieved an equally impressive success, but could form governments only in Bengal and Sind. In the Punjab, the Muslim League obtained 79 out of a total of 86 Muslim seats, but since the 79 Muslim seats it had won did not have a clear majority in a House of 175 and also owing to the opposition of other non-Muslim parties, the Muslim League could not form a Ministry. A Ministry was formed by Khizr Hyat Khan with the help of Congress and Sikh support. It should also be noted that the Congress success in forming a Ministry in the North-West Frontier Province was a serious blow to the Muslim League. The Congress had won 19 Muslim seats as opposed to 17 Muslim seats won by the Muslim League. The Muslim League could claim that this was largely because of the personal influence of the Khan brothers. The Muslim League did succeed in making the Ministry unpopular by launching Province-wide agitation later on the issue of Pakistan.[2]

After his discussions with the British Government in London, the Viceroy announced in December 1945 that it was the

---

[1] Sir Maurice Gwyer and A. Appadorai, eds., *Speeches and Documents on the Indian Constitution, 1921–1947*, London: Oxford University Press, 1957, Vol. II, p. 566.

[2] Maulana Azad has written, 'The actual position in 1946 was that the Khan brothers did not enjoy as much support in the Frontier as we in Delhi thought.' Maulana Abul Kalam Azad, *India Wins Freedom*, Calcutta: Orient Longmans, 1957, p. 171.

intention of the British Government to convene a Constitution-making body soon after the elections. In this connection, the Viceroy proposed to hold discussions with the elected representatives in the Legislative Assemblies as well as with the representatives of Indian States to ascertain whether the Cripps proposals of 1942 were acceptable or whether they preferred an alternative or modified scheme. It was also proposed that a new Executive Council should be formed which had the support of the main Indian parties. On 19 February 1946, Lord Pethick-Lawrence, Secretary of State for India, announced in the House of Lords that the Government had decided to send a Cabinet Mission to assist the Viceroy in these deliberations. The Cabinet Mission was to consist of Lord Pethick-Lawrence, the Secretary of State for India, Sir Stafford Cripps, President of the Board of Trade, and Mr A.V. Alexander, First Lord of the Admiralty.

The Cabinet Mission, soon after its arrival in New Delhi on 24 March 1946, plunged itself into a series of discussions with the representatives of the Congress, the Muslim League, the Sikhs, and the Hindu Mahasabha. Liberal leaders like Sir Tej Bahadur Sapru and M.R. Jayakar were also interviewed. While the Cabinet Mission was holding these discussions, both the Congress and the League were busy digging their trenches in order to drive as hard a bargain as possible. The Congress made it clear that it would never agree to the partition of India. The Muslim League, through a Convention held in 7–9 April 1946 of over 400 Muslim Legislators who had been elected on the Muslim League ticket to the various Assemblies, declared that 'the Muslim nation will never submit to any constitution for a united India and will never participate in any single constitution-making machinery set up for the purpose.' It demanded that the zones comprising Bengal and Assam in the North-East and the Punjab, the North-West Frontier Province, Sind and Baluchistan in the North-West of India should be constituted into the sovereign State of Pakistan.

It was obvious that the two parties approached the constitutional problem from opposite points of view. Jinnah's solution was to dismantle the existing Central structure of the Government of India and reconstruct it on the basis of Pakistan. After the establishment of Pakistan, he was prepared to arrive at an amicable arrangement with the rest of India on a treaty basis. Once

Pakistan was conceded, he was not averse to the idea of a super Centre on an agency basis entrusted by both states to look after certain common subjects.[3] The Congress position was diametrically opposite. They would start with the existing Centre and were willing to subtract from the Central list certain subjects in which the Provinces wanted to be autonomous. The Cabinet Mission pointed out to Jinnah that he could not have the six Provinces in their entirety, claiming full sovereignty for the proposed State of Pakistan. There were a number of districts in the area that he claimed which had non-Muslim majorities. If he wanted full sovereignty, he should be satisfied with a Pakistan which was much smaller. If he wanted the whole area, then he should be willing to relinquish some part of the sovereignty to a Union Centre. In other words, in the latter case, there would be a sort of three-tier Federation with Provinces at the lowest level, followed by Federations or groups, which in their turn would be linked for certain common subjects to a Union Centre. Jinnah was not agreeable to the three-tier Union scheme, but it was obvious that he was bargaining for the best deal. He suggested that if the Congress viewed his demand of six Provinces in their entirety as excessive, they should tell him what he ought to have.

The Cabinet Mission found that they were getting nowhere, either with the League or with the Congress. Jinnah was demanding more or less his full, sovereign Pakistan. The Congress, on the other hand, was even opposed to the creation of an All-India Union on a three-tier basis. The Mission thought that perhaps the best way to resolve this tangle was to proceed on a new line of approach. Their scheme was that a new Interim Government should be formed which would be entrusted with the task of setting up an All-India Commission from the elected members of the Provincial and Central Assemblies. This Commission would be called upon to determine principally whether there should be one or two sovereign States in British India. If the Commission failed to arrive at an agreement on this matter within thirty days, the question would be decided by taking votes. If the dissenting minority amounted to more than a certain prescribed percentage, the question whether they should be allowed to form a separate State would be decided as follows: the Muslim

[3] V. P. Menon, *The Transfer of Power in India*, Calcutta: Orient Longmans, 1957, p. 247.

representatives in each of the Legislative Assemblies of Sind, the
North-West Frontier Province, the Punjab, and Bengal (with the
addition of the district of Sylhet from Assam) would meet
separately to decide whether they would like to separate from the
rest of India. Baluchistan would also be separated if the contiguous
Provinces voted for separation. Similarly, if the Muslim
representatives of the North-West Frontier Province voted against
separation, the Province would still have to be separated if the
surrounding Provinces voted for it. It would be possible for the
non-Muslim representatives of districts in which the non-Muslims
were in majority and which were contiguous to the main part of
India to vote whether these districts should be separated from
their parent Provinces and attached to the territory of India. If
75 per cent of the Muslim representatives voted for separation
they would have a Constituent Assembly to frame a constitution
for their own area. Even this ingenious scheme was turned down
both by the Congress and the Muslim League.[4]

The Cabinet Mission once again turned towards the three-tier
scheme as a possible way out. It may be recalled that the Congress
had already expressed their opposition to the latter scheme, but
probably Azad, who wanted to avoid partition at any cost,
persuaded the Congress to agree to accord maximum autonomy to
Provinces as a better alternative than the partition of the country.
He issued a lengthy statement on 15 April 1946 in which he tried
to show that Pakistan would be detrimental to the interests of
Muslims themselves. He pointed out that all the Muslim fears of
Hindu domination at the Centre would cease to exist if the
Congress were to agree to grant full autonomy to the Provincial
units. He suggested that there could be two lists of Central subjects,
one, compulsory, and the other, optional. The Provincial units could
administer all the optional subjects except a minimum of
compulsory subjects delegated to the Centre.[5] The Cabinet Mission
felt encouraged by this reaction. When Jinnah was informed of this
development, he was not enthusiastic about the scheme, but was
willing to discuss the proposal with the Congress after seeking the
approval of his Working Committee. The concrete proposal that
the Mission put forward in writing to the Congress and the League
was that the three-tier Federation would be constructed as follows:

[4] Ibid., p. 253.
[5] Maulana Abul Kalam Azad, op. cit., p. 144.

1. The All-India Union Government and Legislature would deal with Foreign Affairs, Defence, Communications, Fundamental Rights and would have the necessary powers of taxation to raise the finances required for these subjects.
2. In the Government and the Legislature of the Union equal representation would be given to the Muslim majority Provinces or their group and to the Hindu majority Provinces or their group. In addition to these, there would be representatives from the States.
3. The residuary powers would vest in the Provinces. Provinces could form groups and such groups would determine what Provincial subjects they should deal with in common.
4. There would be a provision both in the constitutions of the Union and the groups whereby any Province, if a majority in its Legislative Assembly so desired, could call for a reconsideration of the terms of the constitution after an initial period of ten years and at ten yearly intervals thereafter.

The Cabinet Mission also put forward its proposals as regards the composition of the Constituent Assembly. The most important of these dealt with the meetings of three sections of Provinces— one section each for Hindu and Muslim majority Provinces and the third for the States. It was laid down that after the preliminary meeting of the Constituent Assembly at which the general order of business would be settled, the Assembly would divide itself into the three sections of Provinces. The two sections representing Hindu and Muslim majority Provinces would meet separately to decide the Provincial constitutions for their group and, if they so desired, a group constitution. This was a major concession to the Muslim League in the sense that the Muslim Provinces would be allowed to meet in their sections and decide their respective constitutions as well as their group constitutions. But once these were settled, any Province which did not wish to remain in the original group to which it was assigned could opt out of that group, join another group or remain outside all groups. This was presumably a concession to the Congress for a Province like Assam which had a Hindu majority but which was likely to be placed in a Muslim group. Finally, the three sections were to meet as the Constituent Assembly to settle the constitution for the Union on the lines suggested by the Cabinet Mission in the previous paragraph. Another major concession to the Muslim League was that the Constituent Assembly could not by a simple majority write into the Union Constitution any provision which involved a communal issue. Such provisions could only be considered to have been passed by the Assembly if a majority of both the two major communities voted in its favour.[6]

Discussions dragged on and despite a special conference that took place between the 5th and 12th of May, the gulf between the two parties had still to be bridged. This was well reflected in the proposals that the two parties had put forward to the Cabinet Mission. Some of the salient points in the demands put forward by the Muslim League were significant because for the first time Jinnah was submitting something in writing which compromised his demand for Pakistan. The six Muslim Provinces known as the 'Pakistan Group' would have a separate constitution-making body which would frame constitutions for the group and the Provinces in the groups. This constitution-making body would determine the list of subjects that would be vested in the constituent Provinces and the list of subjects that the Pakistan Federation would be entrusted with. The two Federations, the Pakistan Group and that formed by the Hindu Provinces, would come together under a Union which would deal with subjects like Foreign Affairs, Defence and Communications necessary for defence. It was also stipulated in the League memorandum that there should be parity of representation between the two Federations in the Union Executive and the Legislature, if they were formed.[7]

The proposals submitted by the Congress differed fundamentally from those of the League. The Congress suggested that the first step should be for the Constituent Assembly for the whole of India to meet and later on it could be decided if the Provinces desired to form groups. It was made clear that it was up to the Provinces to function as a group and let the group frame their constitutions. It was pointed out that Assam could not belong

---

[6] *Papers Relating to the Cabinet Mission to India 1946*, Delhi: The Manager of Publications, 1946, pp. 14–15.

[7] Ibid., pp. 20–21.

to the Muslim group. Nor was the North-West Frontier Province in favour of joining the Muslim group, as the elections had indicated. The Congress was similarly opposed to the principle of parity of representation between groups of Provinces, either in the Union Executive or in the Legislature. They were of the opinion that the provision that on no major communal issue could a decision be taken by the Constituent Assembly unless a majority of the members of the community concerned present and voting in the Constituent Assembly were in its favour was an adequate safeguard for all minorities.[8]

The Cabinet Mission announced their plan on 16 May 1946. They had to put forward their own proposals because they said that even though the Congress and the League 'had made considerable concessions', there still remained a gap to be filled between the positions of the two parties. They turned down the demand for a sovereign State of Pakistan as impracticable and unworkable. First of all, the six Provinces claimed by the League would have a non-Muslim minority of 37.93 per cent in the North-Western area and 48.31 per cent in the North-Eastern area. In this respect, they were not being quite fair to the League because the Muslim League did agree, as the statement itself admitted, to consider adjustment of boundaries. Another argument against Pakistan in the view of the Mission was that even if it were established, twenty million Muslims would still remain as minorities dispersed in the remainder of British India. The Cabinet Mission pointed out that they had also considered a smaller sovereign Pakistan confined to the Muslim majority areas alone. They were not prepared to recommend this either because it would involve a radical partition of the Punjab and Bengal contrary to the wishes and interests of a considerable proportion of the inhabitants of these Provinces. They also referred to administrative, economic and military disadvantages of dividing the country.

The Cabinet Mission also turned down the Congress scheme under which those Provinces who desired could cede to the Centre certain optional subjects in addition to the compulsory ones like Foreign Affairs, Defence and Communications. Presumably the Congress was hoping that some Hindu majority Provinces might make such concessions to the Centre in order to take part in economic and administrative planning on a large

---

[8] Ibid., pp. 22–23.

scale. The Cabinet Mission pointed out that this would involve a cumbrous and confusing arrangement in which some Ministers in charge of compulsory subjects would be responsible to the whole of India whereas some who dealt with optional subjects would be responsible only to those Provinces who had ceded control over these subjects to the Centre. As regards the Princely States, it was hoped that they would offer their cooperation to an independent India because 'the relationship which has hitherto existed between the Rulers of the States and the British Crown will no longer be possible. Paramountcy can neither be retained by the British Crown nor transferred to the new Government.'

Some of the salient recommendations made by the Mission were as follows:

1. A Union of India comprising both British India and the States with its domain over Foreign Affairs, Defence and Communications and with powers necessary to raise the finances required for these subjects.

2. Union Executive and Legislature to be constituted from the British India and States' representatives. The Provision regarding parity of representation in the Union Legislature and Executive between Hindu and Muslim majority Provinces or groups was deleted. The Muslim fear of a Hindu majority was met by the provision that on a major communal issue a decision by the Legislature would require a majority of the representatives present and voting of each of the two major communities as well as a majority of all the members present and voting.

3. All the residuary subjects would vest in the Provinces.

4. Provinces would have a right to join groups and each group would be allowed to determine the Provincial subjects to be administered in common.

5. In the Cabinet Mission Plan itself three sections were provided, each having its own Provinces. Section A had Madras, Bombay, the United Provinces, Bihar, the Central Provinces and Orissa. Out of 187 representatives in Section A, 167 were general or non-Muslim and 20 Muslim. Section B had the Punjab, the N-W. F. P. and Sind in which, out of 35 representatives, Muslims had 22, Sikhs 4 and general 9. Section C had Bengal and Assam

in which out of 70 representatives, Muslims had 36, and general 34. Thus, the total number of representatives for British India was 292 on the basis of one representative for every million of the adult population. The maximum for Indian States, provided on the same basis, was 93.

6. The representatives chosen above would meet to draft the new constitution. After the preliminary business like the election of the chairman, other officers, and an Advisory Committee on the Rights of Citizens, Minorities and Tribal and Excluded Areas, the Provincial representatives would divide up into three sections as indicated above—A, B, and C.

Thereafter, these sections would formulate Provincial constitutions for the Provinces included in each section. The question whether there should be any group constitution for those Provinces and what Provincial subjects would be entrusted to the group would also be taken up by these sections. It was also laid down that Provinces could opt out of groups in which they were placed if the Legislatures of those Provinces decided to do so after the first general election under the new constitution.

Was this another tactical triumph for Jinnah? Later on, when the League rejected the Cabinet Mission proposals, Jinnah said,

> The League, throughout the negotiations, was moved by a sense of fairplay and sacrificed the full sovereign state of Pakistan at the altar of the Congress for securing the independence of the whole of India. They voluntarily delegated three subjects to the Union and by doing so, did not commit a mistake.[9]

It was not like Jinnah to make such a fundamental concession. Why was he making it? Presumably because, short of complete sovereignty, he had achieved his Pakistan. The Cabinet Mission Plan offered a weak Centre and an opportunity to large Muslim majority Provinces like the Punjab and Bengal to dominate in their respective sections. These sections were allowed to formulate both group and Provincial constitutions. Provinces were given the right to opt out, but only after the first general elections and probably under the terms of the constitution settled by the

---

[9] Jamil-ud-Din Ahmad, ed., *Speeches and Writings of Mr. Jinnah,*, Lahore: Ashraf, 1964, Vol. II, p. 315.

respective section. In addition to all this, under Sections B and C, Jinnah was getting the entire territory of Provinces like the Punjab, Bengal and Assam in parts of which non-Muslims were in majority. The only problem was, perhaps, the slender majority that Muslims had in Section C. But given separate electorates, Muslims would probably present a united front and angle for support among the Scheduled Castes and other minority groups. Thus, the resolution of the Council of the All-India Muslim League, justifying its acceptance of the Cabinet Mission Plan, said:

> ...In as much as the basis and the foundation of Pakistan are inherent in the Mission's plan by virtue of the compulsory grouping of the six Muslim Provinces in Section B and C, is willing to cooperate with the constitution-making machinery proposed in the scheme outlined by the Mission, in the hope that it would ultimately result in the establishment of complete sovereign Pakistan, and the consummation of the goal of independence for the major nations, Muslims and Hindus, and all the other people inhabiting the vast subcontinent.
>
> It is for these reasons that the Muslim League is accepting the scheme and will join the constitution-making body, and it will keep in view the opportunity and right of secession of Provinces or groups from the Union, which have been provided in the Mission's plan by implication.[10]

Thus, the League wanted to have the best of both worlds—compulsory grouping of the Provinces, and, if the groups or Provinces were not satisfied, the right of secession from the Union itself.

The text of the Cabinet Mission Plan lent itself to equivocal interpretation. Paragraph 15(5) said that Provinces should be free to form groups'. But Paragraph 19(v) empowered sections to settle Provincial constitutions and also the group constitution. Clause viii of the same paragraph said that Provinces could opt out of the group only after the first general election had taken place under the new constitution. Later on, when the Congress Working Committee asserted the right of the Provinces to make the choice in the beginning itself whether or not to belong to the section to which they were assigned the Cabinet Mission pointed

---

[10] *Resolutions of the All-India Muslim League from January 1944 to December 1946*, Delhi: All-India Muslim League, n.d., pp. 50–51.

out that such an interpretation 'does not accord with the Delegation's intention.' The statement also pointed out: 'The reasons for the grouping of the Provinces are well known and this is an essential feature of the scheme and can only be modified by agreement between the parties.'[11]

What were the reasons for the grouping of the Provinces which the Cabinet Mission claimed were well known to the Congress and the League representatives? It must have been clear to Jinnah that the Congress was not altogether happy with the Cabinet Mission Plan. The Congress had opposed grouping of Provinces as such and the Cabinet Mission Plan had gone as far as providing for compulsory groupings of Provinces. This meant that a Province like the North-West Frontier Province, in which a Congress Government was functioning, would be compelled to join Section B, and a Province like Assam, which had a Hindu majority, would be compelled to join Section C. Jinnah himself had said that the Plan was a sugar-coated pill for the Congress and that without the sugar, it was still a pill. He wanted to know from the Viceroy what the Government would do if one party accepted the scheme and the other rejected it. He extracted the following personal and confidential assurance from the Viceroy on 4 June 1946:

> I can give you on behalf of the Cabinet Delegation my personal assurance that we do not propose to make any discrimination in the treatment of either party; and that we shall go ahead with the plan laid down in the statement so far as circumstances permit if either party accepts; but we hope that both will accept.[12]

This was followed by the acceptance of the Cabinet Mission Plan by the Council of the All-India Muslim League through their resolution of 6 June 1946.

The Congress, from the very beginning, was aware of the dangers and pitfalls in the Cabinet Mission proposals. A few days after the announcement of the Cabinet Mission Plan, Azad wrote a letter to Lord Pethick-Lawrence expressing his fear on behalf of the Congress that Provinces like the Punjab in Section B and Bengal in Section C would dominate the smaller Provinces. 'It may even conceivably lay down rules, for elections and otherwise, thereby nullifying the provision for a Province to opt out of

---

[11] *Papers Relating to the Cabinet Mission to India 1946*, op. cit., p. 24.
[12] Ibid., p. 36.

a group.'[13] Similarly, the Working Committee resolution also complained that as regards grouping, 'a measure of compulsion is introduced which clearly infringes the basic principle of provincial autonomy.' To the Congress plea that it read Paragraph 15 of the Plan to mean that in the first instance, the respective Provinces would make their choice whether or not to join the section in which they were placed, the Cabinet Mission pointed out clearly again and again that this was not the interpretation that the Cabinet Mission itself placed on its Plan. However, the Congress clung to its own interpretation. The All-India Congress Committee, meeting in early July 1946, in Bombay ratified the resolution of the Working Committee which had accepted the long-term proposals of the Cabinet Mission, particularly with regard to the compulsory grouping of Provinces, with its own interpretations, and rejected the proposals for the formation of an Interim Government. Soon after the meeting of the All-India Congress Committee, Jawaharlal Nehru, who had then become the President of the Congress, held a press conference in which he was blunt in his opposition to the group scheme put forward in the Cabinet Mission Plan.

> The big probability is, from any approach to the question, there will be no grouping. Obviously section A will decide against grouping. Speaking in betting language, there is a four to one chance of the North-West Frontier Province deciding against grouping. Then group B collapses. It is highly likely that Bengal and Assam will decide against grouping, although I would not like to say what the initial decision may be since it is evenly balanced. But I can say with every assurance and conviction that there is going to be finally no grouping there, because Assam will not tolerate it under any circumstances whatever. Thus you see this grouping business, approached from any point of view, does not get on at all.[14]

Nehru further asserted that the Congress would enter the Constituent Assembly 'completely unfettered by agreement and free to meet all situations as they arise.'...Azad has commented that this statement was most unfortunate.

> I must place on record that Jawaharlal's statement was wrong. It was not correct to say that Congress was free to modify the Plan as it pleased.... We had further agreed that there would be the three

---

[13] Ibid., p. 33.
[14] Sir Maurice Gwyer and A. Appadorai, eds., op. cit., p. 613.

Sections, viz. A, B and C in which the provinces would be grouped. These matters could not be changed unilaterally by Congress without the consent of other parties to the agreement.[15]

It is interesting to note that the Congress, despite its objection to the grouping plan, would not commit itself either to total rejection or acceptance of the Cabinet Mission Plan. In the first resolution of the Working Committee dated 24 May 1946, the Committee said that they were unable to give a final opinion at that stage. In its resolution of 25 June 1946 the Committee said: 'These proposals fall short of these objectives. Yet the Committee has considered them earnestly in all their aspects because of their desire to find some way for the peaceful settlement of India's problem and the ending of the conflict between India and England.' Jawaharlal Nehru was even a shade better. 'We have committed ourselves on no single matter to anybody. Naturally, even though one might not agree to commit oneself, there is a certain compulsion of facts which makes one accept this thing or that thing. I do not know what that might be in a particular context.' In a letter to Lord Wavell dated 25 June Azad wrote, 'While adhering to our views we accept your proposals and are prepared to work them with a view to achieve our objective.'[16] This evasiveness aroused Muslim League suspicions. The League feared that the Congress was planning to change the Cabinet Mission Plan to suit their interests in the Constituent Assembly where they had a great majority.

Azad has charged that Nehru's opposition to the proposals regarding grouping was wrong and turned out to be disastrous so far as the future of India's unity was concerned. But there was a method in this opposition. It was becoming increasingly clear to the Congress that Jinnah, in surrendering his demand for sovereign Pakistan, had extracted valuable concessions from the Cabinet Mission, like the compulsory grouping of the Provinces, and a weak Centre. And there was no guarantee that he would merely stop at that. In its resolution of 6 June 1946 the League Council, even though accepting the Cabinet Mission Plan, had openly asserted that the basis and the foundation of Pakistan were inherent in the Mission Plan by virtue of the compulsory grouping

---

[15] Maulana Abul Kalam Azad, op. cit., p. 155.

[16] Sir Maurice Gwyer and A. Appadorai, eds., op. cit.; see pages 610, 612, and 609, respectively, for these statements.

of the six Muslim Provinces. It also said that the Plan was being accepted 'in the hope that it would ultimately result in the establishment of a complete, sovereign Pakistan.' The Muslim League had also achieved spectacular success in the recent elections on the issue of Pakistan. It may be argued that Congress leaders were probably justified in fearing that with separate electorates continuing and with the help of disgruntled minorities and the Princes, the Muslim League might succeed in paralysing any majority government in India. But probably Nehru and the Congress did not foresee that Jinnah would resort to 'Direct Action' after withdrawing the League acceptance of the Cabinet Mission Plan. Jinnah had always given the impression of being a constitutionalist and his declaration to 'bid good-bye to constitutional methods' came as a complete surprise. The Muslim League Council in a resolution passed on 29 July 1946 declared that 'now the time has come for the Muslim Nation to resort to Direct Action to achieve Pakistan, to assert their just rights, to vindicate their honour and to get rid of the present British slavery and the contemplated future caste-Hindu domination.' Thus, once again both parties were digging their trenches and getting ready for another round of battle.

II. Formation of the Interim Government

It may be argued in defence of the Muslim League that though in its Council resolution of 6 June it had suggested that the struggle for Pakistan would continue, yet so far as the actual proposals of the Cabinet Mission were concerned, it had accepted them.[17] The Congress, on the other hand, as has been seen earlier, had not accepted the Cabinet Mission proposals with regard to compulsory grouping of the Provinces. This probably

---

[17] *Resolutions of the All India Muslim League,* op. cit., pp. 49–51. Thus, as far as the League was concerned, there was no evidence to warrant the statement: 'Neither the Congress nor the League ever really accepted the plan, though both placed their formal approval on record for bargaining purposes.' Michael Brecher, *Nehru: A Political Biography,* London: Oxford University Press, 1959, p. 317. The Congress itself never accused the League of not having accepted the Cabinet Mission Plan. It was only after the League Council had passed its resolution withdrawing acceptance of the Mission Plan in July 1946, that the Congress insisted on the League withdrawing this resolution if it wanted to remain in the Interim Government.

explains why Lord Wavell was keen to bring the Muslim League, along with the Congress, into the Interim Government. He perhaps thought that once the League entered the Interim Government and started administering India's problems in concert with the Congress and other parties, there was an even chance that the Pakistan demand might recede into the background. Moreover, since the League had established its representative capacity as the spokesman of an overwhelming majority of Muslims, the Viceroy felt that perhaps the League insistence that the Congress should not be allowed to nominate Muslims to the Interim Government was not unjustifiable.

The result was that the Cabinet Mission and the Viceroy issued a statement on 16 June outlining their proposals regarding the formation of an Interim Government. In the list of persons who were invited by the Viceroy to serve in the Interim Government, there were six Congress members, including the Scheduled Caste representative, Jagjivan Ram. There were five Muslim Leaguers including Jinnah. Sikhs, Parsis and Indian Christians had a representative each. Thus, there was no Muslim from the Congress side. Paragraph 8 of this statement pointed out that if the Congress or the League, or both of them, were found to be unwilling to enter the Interim Government, the Viceroy intended to go ahead with the formation of an Interim Government which would be as representative as possible of those that accepted the Cabinet Mission Plan of 16 May.

Jinnah complained that the parity formula between the League and the Congress had been changed in the sense that the Congress had six representatives as opposed to the five of the Muslim League. But he extracted a valuable assurance from the Viceroy that if any vacancy occurred in the future among the seats allotted to minorities, he would consult both the main parties before filling them. Similarly, no decision involving a major communal issue would be taken by the Interim Government if a majority of either of the main parties were opposed to it.[18] Armed with such reassurances, the League Working Committee in its resolution of 25 June agreed to enter the Interim Government.

The Congress Working Committee, on the other hand, in its

---

[18] *Papers Relating to the Cabinet Mission to India 1946*, op. cit., pp. 46–47.

resolution of 25 June rejected the proposals for the formation of an Interim Government as contained in the statement of 16 June. The resolution made it clear that the Congress could never be denied the right to nominate a Muslim to the Interim Government or made to accept an artificial and unjust parity or agree to the right of a communal party like the Muslim League to be consulted in filling minority seats in the Government.

The result was that the Viceroy was placed in a predicament. According to Paragraph 8 of the statement of 16 June, he was supposed to invite the Muslim League Party to join the Interim Government since they had accepted his proposals. Presumably, he felt that if he had followed this course he would have offered an affront to the position of the Congress. It was likely that such a course would have hardened the Congress opposition to the Cabinet Mission Plan, ultimately resulting in its total rejection. The Muslim Leaguers, placed in power in the Interim Government, would have very likely provoked the Congress into bitter opposition to both the Interim Government and the British Government. In short, such a course would have embittered the future relations between the British Government and Indian leaders to such an extent that British strategic and commercial interests would have been adversely affected for a long time to come. Thus, the Viceroy decided to adjourn the negotiations for a short interval and set up in the meantime a temporary caretaker government of officials. When questioned by Jinnah as to how he could justify his action in view of the clear assurance that he had given in Paragraph 8 of the statement of 16 June, the Viceroy tried to wriggle out of the difficult position by suggesting that the later part of the paragraph said that in the event of one of the parties not joining the Interim Government, the Viceroy would form the Government as far as possible from those parties who had accepted the statement of 16 May. Thus, the Viceroy was stretching the text of the statement to mean that since the Congress and the League had accepted the plan of 16 May, negotiations should continue so that both might join the Government. If the League joined the Government and the Congress remained outside, the Interim Government, in that case, would not be 'as representative as possible of those willing to accept the statement of 16 May.' It was obvious that the Viceroy, in his eagerness to form the Interim Government, had given assurances to the Muslim League which he could not honour without antagonizing the Congress and thus hurting British interests. *The Scotsman* of 21 July 1946 wrote: 'It grieves us that the venerable and idealistic Secretary of State, a fine Viceroy, and their two eminent colleagues of Britain's new and good Cabinet should at this last stage have descended—as we see matters—to similar swithery courses.'

Lord Wavell resumed his negotiations for the formation of an Interim Government towards the end of July, 1946. In a letter addressed to the Presidents of the Congress and the Muslim League dated 22 July 1946 the Viceroy suggested that the Interim Government, consisting of fourteen members, would be constituted as follows: six members (including one Scheduled Caste representative) to be nominated by the Congress, five by the Muslim League, and three representing minorities to be nominated by the Viceroy; one of these representatives to be a Sikh. The Viceroy made it clear that neither the Congress nor the Muslim League would be allowed to object to the names submitted by the other party. This was a clear hint to Jinnah that the Muslim League would have no right to object to the Congress nominating a Muslim in their quota of six.

It may be noted that when the Muslim League Council passed its resolution declaring that the time had come for the Muslims to resort to 'Direct Action', the Muslim League leaders suspected that the Viceroy was thinking of going ahead with the formation of an Interim Government even if the Muslim League refused to cooperate. The Viceroy's letter, announcing the terms of the Interim Government, was written on 22 July and the 'Direct Action' resolution was passed on 29 July.

How could the Labour Government have agreed with the Congress that it had accepted the Cabinet Mission Plan in its entirety, when the Cabinet delegation itself had pointed out to the Congress that its interpretation as regards compulsory grouping of Provinces was not correct? Similarly, how could the Viceroy go back on his clear statement of 16 June that he would invite whichever party accepted his proposals regarding the Interim Government to form a Government? Jinnah's reading of the situation was that the British Government wanted to appease the Congress because they were afraid of the Congress launching a civil disobedience movement against them. Particularly as the

Labour Party, which was in power then, had all along supported the Congress and would not like to be placed in a position in which its representative, the Viceroy, would have to suppress the Congress movement. The result was that Jinnah took a leaf from the Congress book and thought that the only way of compelling the British Government to treat the Muslim League as an equally important party was the threat of 'Direct Action'. Jinnah's view had always been that the Congress had launched the 'Quit India' movement to coerce the British Government during the war to surrender power to them. He thought that this was the most effective way of dealing both with the British Government and the Congress.

> Our motto should be discipline, unity and trust in the power of our own nation. If there is not sufficient power, create that power. If we do that, the Mission and the British Government may be rescued, released and freed from being cowed down by the threats of the Congress that they would launch a struggle and start non-cooperation. Let us also say that.[19]

Jinnah felt that the Viceroy did not fear the League as much as he feared the Congress. He had not only gone back on his assurances to the League, but had also been coerced by the Congress into abandoning positions which he had taken earlier. In a letter to the Congress President dated 22 June 1946, the Viceroy had clearly stated that it would not be possible for the Cabinet Mission or himself to accept the Congress request to include a Congress Muslim among their representatives in the Interim Governrnent.[20] But in his letter to the League President of 22 July, he made it clear that it was not open to the League to object to the Congress nominating a Muslim in their quota. Jinnah's position was that if he were to concede on this issue, it would mean that the Muslim League was not the sole representative organization of the Muslims. It would also allow discontented Muslim leaders from the League to seek shelter in the Congress. Thus, in his letter dated 31 July Jinnah on his own initiative turned down the Viceroy's offer to join the Interim Government

---

[19] Mohammad Ashraf, ed., *Cabinet Mission and After*, Lahore: Ashraf, 1946, p. 291.

[20] *Papers Relating to the Cabinet Mission to India 1946*, op. cit., pp. 48–49.

saying that there was no chance of his Working Committee accepting that proposal.

Though the formation of the Congress Interim Government was announced on 24 August 1946, negotiations had started between the Congress and the Government much earlier and it was well known that the Congress had been invited to form the Government. On 16 August 1946, when the League had called upon Muslims to celebrate that day as the 'Direct Action' day, Nehru made it clear that 'Direct Action' would have to be suppressed for otherwise the Government would be swept away.[21] He was quite correct in his reading of the situation for it was obvious that if 'Direct Action' were launched by the League, it would be aimed at and against the Congress Government. Many of the commentators on the extremely unfortunate results of the 'Direct Action' day seem to forget that this was precisely the nature of Indian politics at that time, namely, that it had degenerated into an open Hindu-Muslim warfare and struggle for power. Nehru's statement was interpreted as a threat. Maulana Shabbir Ahmad Osmani, President of the All-India *Jamiyat al Ulama-i-Islam*, probably represented Muslim reaction to both Nehru's statement and the installation of the Congress Interim Government when he said that a Muslim could not be crushed. 'Living he is a *ghazi* (victor in battle) and killed in action, he is a martyr.'[22] It was obvious that the whole atmosphere was surcharged with communal frenzy.

The Government knew that the Viceroy's decision to install the Congress Interim Government was fraught with serious dangers. They were aware that the programme and the popularity of Jinnah and the Muslim League had captured the imagination

---

[21] At first Nehru was reported to have said: 'If the Government is strong, "Direct Action" goes under, but if the Government is weak, the Government will go under.' This was interpreted by League circles to mean that if the Muslim League started 'Direct Action', it would be crushed. Later on, Nehru suggested that this was not an accurate interpretation. He explained: 'I was asked what would happen if there was "Direct Action" against the Government. I replied that wherever there is such "Direct Action", there can be only two results: Either the success or partial success of that action which means the Government being swept away or coming to terms with it, or that "Direct Action" fails.' Mohammad Ashraf, ed., op. cit., pp. 359–360, 371.

[22] Quoted in Mohammad Ashraf, ed., op. cit., p. 369.

of all sections of Muslims, including Muslim officers. The proportion of Muslims in the police in Sind and the Punjab was at least 70 per cent; they were 50 per cent in the United Provinces; and they also held a dominant share in East Bengal. Jinnah's call for 'Direct Action' would be instantly obeyed, particularly in Muslim Provinces. V. P. Menon, who was constitutional adviser to the Viceroy, wrote: 'What stood out clearly was that, especially in the Muslim Provinces, any attempt to go ahead with constitution-making without Muslim participation would have very serious results.'[23] Thus, the installation of the Congress Party in power at the Centre was extremely ill-timed in view of such clear dangers of the outbreak of communal warfare. The Viceroy should have carried on his negotiations further in order to bring the League into the Interim Government. But unfortunately, he realized his mistake too late for it was only after the Calcutta riots had taken place and the situation in Bihar and Noakhali had become alarming that the Viceroy succeeded in bringing the Muslim League into the Interim Government.

The view that the Muslim League decision to celebrate 16 August as 'Direct Action' day, followed by the announcements by the Muslim League Governments of Sind and Bengal that 16 August would be a holiday, triggered the horrible Calcutta killing is held among many sections.[24] The Muslim League answer to this charge was that the Muslim League leaders had given clear instructions to the various Provincial Leagues that 16 August should be utilized only for the purpose of explaining to the Muslims the political situation that they were faced with and the Muslim League stand on it *vis-à-vis* the Council resolutions passed on 29 July 1946. Jinnah, in his statement issued two days before the 'Direct Action' day made it clear: 'But the 16th of August is not for the purpose of resorting to direct action in any form or shape; therefore, I enjoin upon the Muslims to carry out the instructions and abide by them strictly and conduct themselves peacefully and in a disciplined manner and not to play into the hands of the enemies.'[25]

H. S. Suhrawardy, the Premier of Bengal, was also charged by

---

[23] V. P. Menon, op. cit., p. 290.

[24] See, for example, Michael Brecher, *Nehru: A Political Biography*, London: Oxford University Press, 1959, p. 319.

[25] Mohammad Ashraf, ed., op. cit., p. 372.

some with actual complicity in the riots and by others with flagrant negligence of his responsibilities. Suhrawardy's answer to these charges was that it was actually the Congress who had started the trouble in Calcutta with the sole aim of creating a situation which might ultimately bring about the dismissal of the League Ministry and the imposition of Section 93.[26] *Dawn's* correspondent also made similar charges and tried to prove that it was the Hindus who took Muslims unawares and Muslim retaliation followed later.[27] *The Statesman* of Calcutta of 20 August, on the other hand, accused the Muslim League of having brought about 'the worst communal riot in India's history.' Sir Francis Tuker, who was in charge of the military operations during the riots, has held all the three, the Congress, the Muslim League and the Sikhs, responsible for the Great Calcutta Killing. 'They could hardly have done better if they had had a combined committee to arrange the grisly tournament.'[28] A very alarming factor in the situation was the growing hostility between Hindu and Muslim officers in the police and in the army. Commenting on the infiltration of communal politics into the army, Sir Francis wrote: 'Directly the British officer left, the mixed mess of Hindu and Muslim officers would part into two cliques and the parting would soon be reflected among the men.'[29]

Maulana Azad laid the entire responsibility at that time for all that had happened on the League Ministry. Later, in his book, he was of the opinion 'that it had followed inexorably from the opportunity given to the Muslim League to reopen the whole question of political and communal settlement.'[30] This controversy will rage in this partisan fashion for a long time to come until all the documents and the facts have been disclosed. But one cannot escape the impression that it was not so much the Congress shortsightedness in its blunt opposition to the Cabinet Mission Plan (as Azad suggests), but the haste of Lord Wavell in inviting the Congress to form the Interim Government and leaving the Muslim League out that precipitated the whole series of communal riots.

It would be needless to dwell at any length on the gruesome

---

[26] Ibid., p. 375.

[27] Ibid., pp. 377–80.

[28] Lieut. General Sir Francis Tuker, *While Memory Serves*, London: Cassell, 1950, p. 156.

[29] Ibid., p. 162.

[30] Maulana Abul Kalam Azad, op. cit., pp. 159–60.

details of riots that took place in Noakhali in East Bengal during the second week of October 1946, which took a heavy toll of Hindu lives, followed by the Bihar riots towards the end of October and early November 1946, in which an even greater number of Muslims died. Amidst all this communal carnage, Gandhi, actuated by highest humanitarian motives, brought solace and succour to the suffering people among both communities. Probably he was the most disappointed man in India for these riots were the complete negation of all that he had stood and struggled for.

Battle between the Muslim and the Congress in the Interim Government

It was obvious that Lord Wavell was not happy about the Muslim League remaining outside the Interim Government and the country steadily slipping into a state of civil war. At Calcutta, where he had gone to assess the havoc caused by communal riots, he was informed by Khwaja Nazimuddin, a former Premier of Bengal and a senior member of the Muslim League Working Committee, that the League would be willing to reconsider its rejection of the Cabinet Mission Plan if the Government were to meet some of its minimum demands. The Viceroy was told that the League would be satisfied only if either the Congress were to give a clear assurance that it would not be open to Provinces to opt out of groups except after a certain period when the first elections had taken place, or failing that, if the Viceroy were to give a guarantee that the Congress would not be allowed to interpret the Cabinet Mission Plan in a way contrary to that of the Mission itself. Nazimuddin also suggested that the inclusion of a Nationalist Muslim from the Congress side would not pose an insurmountable difficulty if the League were allowed to fill the Muslim quota of five seats.[31] It is difficult to assess the accuracy of this version of the Wavell-Nazimuddin talks for surely there was no doubt about the Muslim League being allowed to nominate five Muslims in its quota, because the Viceroy in his letter to the League President, dated 22 July, had clearly stated that five members would be nominated by the Muslim League. However, it was significant that according to Nazimuddin, the Muslim League was not adamant about the exclusion of a 'Nationalist

---

[31] V. P. Menon, op. cit., p. 301.

Muslim' from the Interim Government. Did this indicate that Jinnah's mind had already started thinking in terms of outwitting the Congress?

Another version of the League entry into the Interim Government was offered later by Nehru to Mountbatten. According to Nehru, Jinnah had capitulated on the issue of entering the Constituent Assembly in a 'private Moslem League meeting.'[32] It was Wavell who made the serious blunder of inviting the Muslim League to come into the Interim Government. If he had waited a little longer, the Muslim League would have itself begged to be invited in. According to the evidence that the author has gathered from various members of the then Muslim League Working Committee, it was not correct to say that the League President had made any capitulations as regards the long-term plan of the Cabinet Mission.

On the other hand, there was considerable and visible evidence to show that Jinnah was in a strong position. The country was on the brink of a civil war and more trouble was feared if the Muslim League were left outside the Interim Government to fulminate both against the Congress and the British. It was impressed by such dangers that the Viceroy wanted to go to any length, as far as the Cabinet Mission Plan was concerned, to dispel the apprehensions of the Muslim League. He wanted the Congress to come out with a clear declaration that it accepted the compulsory grouping of Provinces whereby a Province could not exercise any option concerning their membership of the sections or of the groups, if formed, until a decision regarding this was taken by the new Legislature of the Province after the first general election under the new constitution. The Viceroy tried to pressure the Congress into accepting this position by warning them that he would not undertake to summon the Constituent Assembly until the Congress gave a clear assurance that they would abide by the grouping plan. Both Gandhi and Nehru expressed surprise and bitterness at this change in the Viceroy's attitude. The Viceroy tried to reason with the Congress leaders by pointing out that the Plan would be wrecked if the Congress persisted in its own interpretation that Provinces were free to opt out of groups, if formed, in the beginning itself. The

---

[32] Alan Campbell-Johnson, *Mission With Mountbatten*, London: Robert Hale, 1951, p. 44.

Congress, however, were not willing to abandon the position that they had taken. The British Government in London were in general accord with the Viceroy and supported his efforts to bring about a *rapprochement* between the Congress and the League. 'At the same time, His Majesty's Government felt that the Viceroy should not take any steps which were likely to result in a breach with the Congress.'[33]

This also explains why Jinnah wanted his party to enter the Interim Government. He probably felt that the British Labour Government, in order to save the Cabinet Mission Plan, were not likely to go to the length of antagonizing the Congress. Therefore, the best course for him would be to continue his battle by occupying positions of vantage in the Interim Government. And in the negotiations, true to form, he went about extracting maximum concessions from his opponents.

The first one represented a great tactical victory for the Muslim League. During a meeting with Gandhi which was brought about by the efforts of the Nawab of Bhopal, he very cleverly made Gandhi sign the following formula:

> The Congress does not challenge but accepts that the Muslim League now is the authoritative representative of an overwhelming majority of the Muslims of India. As such and in accordance with democratic principles they alone have today an unquestionable right to represent the Muslims of India. But the Congress cannot agree that any restriction or limitation should be put upon the Congress to choose such representatives as they think proper from amongst the members of the Congress as their representatives.[34]

Jinnah had once again scored a great point and the Congress were very unhappy about it. Nehru, in his letter to Jinnah, pointed out that 'my colleagues and I did not accept the formula agreed to by Gandhiji and you.' Gandhi himself at his prayer meeting said that he was thoroughly ashamed of having been over-hasty in signing the formula. 'No public servant has a right to act in this way.'[35]

In his letters to Nehru and the Viceroy, Jinnah put forward his proposals in the form of Nine Points. They included his demands that the Congress should not include a Muslim in their

---

[33] V. P. Menon, op. cit., p. 305.

[34] Sir Maurice Gwyer and A. Appadorai, eds., op. cit., p. 648.

[35] Mohammad Ashraf, ed., op. cit., p. 415.

quota and that a clear convention should be established that no decision would be taken on major communal issues if the majority of Hindu or Muslim members of the Executive Council were opposed to it. Jinnah also wanted the office of the Vice-President to rotate between the two major communities, and that there should be an equal distribution of the most important portfolios between the two major parties.

The Viceroy, in his letter dated 4 October 1946, pointed out that he could not agree to Jinnah's demand that no Muslim should be included in the Interim Government from the Congress side. 'Each party must be equally free to nominate its own representatives.' On 12 October both the Viceroy and the Congress were taken aback when Jinnah suggested that just as the Congress were keen on including a Muslim in their quota, he could also nominate a representative of Scheduled Castes in the League quota. In the subsequent correspondence that followed between Jinnah and the Viceroy, Jinnah not only nominated the members of the Executive Council on behalf of the League, but also indicated how the portfolios allotted to the League should be distributed amongst them. The League nominees, with their portfolios, were: Liaquat Ali Khan (Finance), I. I. Chundrigar (Commerce), A. R. Nishtar (Post and Air), Ghazanfar Ali Khan (Health), and Jogendranath Mandal (Legislative).

It was noteworthy that Jinnah had carefully selected only those League leaders who in his opinion were likely to put up a fight in the Council for League interests. Men like Nawab Ismail Khan, Chairman of the Committee of Action, and Choudhry Khaliquzzaman were not included, probably because they represented that section in the League which was anxious to come to terms with the Congress. Husain Imam, who was the Leader of the Muslim League Party in the Council of State, was not selected. The loyal Chundrigar from Bombay, with his years of legal practice on the commercial side, was sent in as Commerce member. The ever obedient Nazimuddin was left out to give place to Jogendranath Mandal, a Scheduled Caste Minister in the Muslim League Ministry of Bengal. In order to counter the Congress claim that they had the support of the Frontier, Abdur Rab Nishtar was sent, He was probably the only capable Muslim Leaguer available from that Province even though he had not been returned in the recent Provincial elections. The Punjab Muslims were represented by Ghazanfar Ali Khan, by no means brilliant but certainly loyal and pugnacious.

As regards the distribution of important portfolios, it seems that Jinnah again played his hand very skilfully. He gave the impression from the very beginning that he was not much interested in the matter of portfolios but was more concerned about the position of the Vice-President. He thought that he would get the best of the bargain if he let the Viceroy do the bargaining for him. Thus, it was the Viceroy who suggested to the Congress that they might perhaps give up the Home Department held by Sardar Patel. The Congress strategy was that the League should, under no circumstances, be given portfolios like Home and Defence because of the strong position already enjoyed by Muslims in these spheres. Muslims were not inadequately represented in the army, and as suggested earlier, they were well entrenched in the police departments, not only in Muslim Majority Provinces, but also in a Province like the United Provinces. On the other hand, they thought that if a portfolio like Finance were offered to the League, they might refuse it because of the proverbial Muslim inability to handle matters like Finance. If they accepted it, the Congress thought they would make fools of themselves.[36] Similarly, when the League asked that the office of the Vice-President should be made rotational, they were told that this would be a difficult arrangement and a League member was offered the position of Vice-Chairman of the Coordination Committee of the Cabinet. Again, perhaps it was thought that since the Coordination Committee dealt with economic and industrial questions, no League member was likely to be competent enough to handle such a post.

It was obvious that the Congress had made a great tactical mistake. Liaquat, with Chaudhri Mohamad Ali as his extremely able assistant, not only managed his portfolio efficiently, but caused maximum annoyance to Congress Ministers.[37] Particularly Patel was chagrined. 'Whatever proposal he made was either rejected or modified beyond recognition by Liaquat Ali.'[38] Liaquat dealt another severe blow at the Congress when he

---

[36] Maulana Abul Kalam Azad, op. cit., p. 166.

[37] Chaudhri Mohamad Ali at that time was Financial Adviser to the Military Finance Department.

[38] Maulana Abul Kalam Azad, op. cit., p. 167.

presented the Budget. Drawing on the technical ability of Chaudhri Mohamad Ali he imposed heavy taxes on the high incomes of the rich Hindu industrialists who financed the Congress. In addition, he proposed the setting up of a Commission to investigate charges of tax evasion made against businessmen and industrialists.

Liaquat knew that if he disclosed any details of his Budget in the Cabinet meeting there would be fierce opposition from the Congress side. Therefore, he proceeded to obtain the assent of the Cabinet to the general principles of his Budget. He tried to disarm the opposition from the Congress side by pointing out that had it not been for the clear stand of Nehru and Azad against businessmen evading taxes on their huge war profits, the whole idea of taxing these incomes and setting in motion an investigation machinery might never have occurred to him. It seems that the Congress group fell for such a trap and they only realized the mistake they had made when Liaquat announced all the details of his Budget in the Assembly. It was obvious to the Congress group that Liaquat's primary purpose was to deal a severe blow at the financiers of the Congress. Congress leaders later argued that Liaquat's aim was also to cripple commerce and industry, which were again largely concentrated in Hindu hands.[39]

Even though the Muslim League had joined the Interim Government and League members were engaged in administering their portfolios, for Jinnah the larger issue had not changed and the battle for Pakistan was to continue unabated. It has been said that no political leader in the subcontinent could excel Jinnah in the ferocity and biting sarcasm with which he attacked his political opponents. Nehru wanted the Interim Government to function as a Cabinet in the full parliamentary sense. He was also desirous that his position as the Vice-President of the Interim Government should emerge as that of a Prime Minister. Jinnah interpreted this desire of Nehru as a part of the Congress tactics to establish Congress hegemony in the country. He reminded the Congress that the Interim Government was after all a Viceroy's Executive Council functioning on the basis of the Government of India Act, 1919. He also pointed out that the position of the Vice-President was not the same as that of a Prime Minister and that there had been Vice-Presidents ever since 1919 whose sole function was to preside over the Council

---

[39] Ibid., p. 176.

meeting only when the Viceroy was absent. Whenever Nehru tried to hold informal meetings of the Council at his residence, League members would absent themselves and attend informal meetings of League members of the Interim Government held at Liaquat's residence.

A few samples of Jinnah's brutal bluntness would not be out of order. When Jinnah was told that the Viceroy himself had called the Interim Government a 'Cabinet', Jinnah pointed out that the Viceroy had done so in order to please Nehru. 'Little things please little minds and you cannot turn a donkey into an elephant by calling it an elephant.'[40] When asked to comment on Patel's challenging speech that 'sword would be met with sword', Jinnah said, 'Sardar Patel is a strong man as they said and therefore he uses strong language but words do not break bones.... Where has Sardar Patel got his sword?'[41] This was rather an unkind reference to the common belief that a Hindu lacked fighting qualities. Nehru was equally unsparing in his criticism of the League attitude. He said that the League, through its efforts not to let the Government function as a Cabinet, had played the role of a 'King's Party' and thereby increased the influence and power of the Viceroy.

In justification of its attitude the Muslim League could argue that the Congress had never accepted the Cabinet Mission Plan in its entirety. Therefore, how could the League extend its hand of cooperation when the Congress itself was determined to bring about defections in Sections B and C by encouraging and supporting Provinces like Assam to withdraw from their respective sections during the initial stages? The Congress, on the other hand, constantly reminded the Viceroy that since the Muslim League had withdrawn its acceptance of the Cabinet Mission proposals and had also asked the Muslim League members of the Constituent Assembly not to attend the Assembly meetings, the Muslim League should be asked to resign from the Interim Government. The Viceroy realized that these recriminations would only result in further bitterness inside the Government and fresh outbreaks of communal violence outside. The British Government thought that perhaps a new effort should be made to resolve the dead-lock by summoning the Congress and the League leaders to meet in London. The meeting in London was attended by

---

[40] Jamil-ud-Din Ahmad, op. cit., Vol. II, p. 375.
[41] Ibid., p. 376.

Nehru on behalf of the Congress, Baldev Singh, the Defence Minister, on behalf of the Sikhs, and Jinnah and Liaquat on behalf of the League.

The Congress contention was that a Province like Assam could stay out of its Section C from the very beginning and frame its constitution independently. In other words, the fundamental point was that the Provinces should start as units and it was entirely up to them whether to join a group or not. The League argued that the Provinces must first join the group and later on, after the first elections, if they wished, they could withdraw from the group. Had it not been for the grouping plan and restricted powers allotted to the Centre, the League Council would not have accepted the Mission Plan. The League scored another victory when the British Government issued a statement on 6 December 1946, saying that the League interpretation was correct.

> The Cabinet Mission have throughout maintained the view that decisions of the Sections should, in the absence of an agreement to the contrary, be taken by a simple majority vote of the representatives in the Sections. This view has been accepted by the Muslim League, but the Congress have put forward a different view. They have asserted that the true meaning of the statement, read as a whole, is that the Provinces have the right to decide both as to grouping and as to their own Constitutions.
>
> His Majesty's Government have had legal advice which confirms that the statement of 16 May means what the Cabinet Mission have always stated was their intention. This part of the statement, as so interpreted, must, therefore, be considered an essential part of the scheme of 16 May for enabling the Indian people to formulate a Constitution which His Majesty's Government would be prepared to submit to Parliament. It should, therefore, be accepted by all parties in the Constituent Assembly.[42]

This statement also failed to put an end to recriminations between the Congress and the League. The All-India Congress Committee, in its resolution of 5 January 1947, though saying that it would 'advise action in accordance with the interpretation of the British Government in regard to the procedure to be followed in the sections', did not deviate even an iota from its former position. 'It must be clearly understood, however, that this must

---

[42] Sir Maurice Gwyer and A. Appadorai, eds., op. cit., p. 660.

not involve any compulsion of a province, and the rights of the Sikhs in the Punjab should not be jeopardized.' The Muslim League Working Committee in its resolution of 31 January 1947, took grave exception to the qualifying clauses in the Congress resolution and pointed out that the Congress was not only encouraging 'a province' to exercise the right of veto within the section but also 'a part of a province' to exercise a similar right. It pointed out that the Congress had not accepted the Cabinet Mission Plan and therefore the Working Committee would not call the Council of the League to reconsider its decision of July 1946.

The Constituent Assembly started meeting on 9 December 1946, and the Muslim League members were absent. The Congress demanded the resignation of the League representatives from the Interim Government on the grounds that the League had rejected the Cabinet Mission scheme, absented itself from the Constituent Assembly and was also committed to a programme of 'Direct Action'. Liaquat retaliated that it was presumptuous on the part of the Congress and minority members of the Executive Council to demand the resignation of their Muslim League colleagues when the Congress had not accepted the Cabinet Mission Plan. This was followed by the threat of Patel that the Congress would withdraw from the Interim Government if the Muslim League were allowed to remain in it. 'The Viceroy was in sympathy with the Muslim League contention and was himself of the view that the Congress had not in fact accepted the Cabinet Mission Plan.'[43] However, events had reached such a crucial stage that the British Government had to make up their mind as to whether they should ask for the resignation of the League or let the Congress withdraw from the Interim Government. It was obvious that either course was fraught with dangerous consequences. Attlee felt that in such circumstances a bold policy as well as a new Viceroy were needed to save the situation. On 20 February 1947, he announced the appointment of Admiral the Viscount Mountbatten. He also declared that it was the definite intention of the Government to transfer power to responsible Indian hands by a date not later than June 1948. If by that date it became clear that a Constitution based on the Cabinet Mission Plan could not be worked out, the Government would then

---

[43] V. P. Menon, op. cit., p. 336.

think in terms of transferring power 'to some form of Central Government for British India, or in some areas to the existing Provincial Governments.'

III. ARRIVAL OF PAKISTAN

When Lord Wavell was in London in connection with the conference of Indian leaders regarding the correct interpretation of the Cabinet Mission Plan, he suggested to the British Government that there were two ways of solving the Indian problem. The first was what he called a 'phased withdrawal of British authority and British military forces from India,' with power being transferred on 31 March 1948. The withdrawal was to take place in phases. At first the British would withdraw from the Indian peninsula and the Congress-controlled areas and later the final withdrawal would be preceded by a 'concentration of British administrative and military forces in northern India.' This presumably meant that the British would withdraw from Pakistan last. The alternative plan that he suggested was that the British should make up their minds to re-establish British power and rule the country for a further period of at least fifteen years.[44]

The reaction of the British Government was completely opposed to either of the two courses. The British Prime Minister felt that the Viceroy was probably inclined to favour the Muslim League and was too much of a soldier to understand the political implications of his first course of action. King George recorded in his diary on 17 December 1946:

> Attlee told me that Lord Wavell's plan for our leaving India savours too much of a military retreat and does not realize it is a political problem and not a military one. Wavell has done very good work up to now but Attlee doubts whether he has the finesse to negotiate the next step when we must keep the two Indian parties friendly to us all the time.[45]

Attlee was convinced that the only way of resolving the Indian tangle was a speedy British withdrawal from India. He thought that such a decision would force the Indian leaders to realize that if they did not arrive at an agreement, the alternative would be

---

[44] John Connell, *Auchinleck: A Critical Biography*, London: Cassell, 1959, p. 852.

[45] Cited in ibid., p. 852.

complete chaos from which neither side would gain. 'Unless these men were faced with the urgency of a time limit, there would always be procrastination.'[46] In his statement of 20 February 1947, Attlee set the time limit of the British withdrawal following transfer of power as June 1948.

An indication of how time was the essence of the problem was given by the detailed instructions that Mountbatten was given before he left London. He was told in clear terms that the British Government still desired the setting up of a unitary Government for British India and the Indian States, 'if possible within the British Commonwealth.' Nevertheless, it was not their policy to bring this about by force. 'If by the 1st October Mountbatten considers there is no prospect of reaching a settlement on the basis of unitary Government, he is to report to the British Government on the steps he considers should be taken for the hand-over of power on the due date.'[47]

It seemed Mountbatten from the very beginning was highly sceptical about the prospects of a Central Government being established for the whole of India on the lines suggested by the Cabinet Mission Plan. One often wonders whether Mountbatten came somewhat convinced to India that the Partition of the country could not be avoided. As has been seen already, the bitter differences between the two parties in the Interim Government had become practically irreconcilable. V. P. Menon has recorded that either late in December 1946, or early in January 1947, that is, before Lord Mountbatten's arrival as Viceroy, he had succeeded in persuading Patel to agree to Partition. Menon had also sent the outline of his plan to the Secretary of State and also written to say that the Congress was likely to accept his proposals. Before coming to India, Mountbatten had seen Menon's proposals.[48] There is considerable evidence which goes to suggest that soon after Mountbatten's arrival in Delhi on 22 March 1947, most of the opponents of Partition had veered round to the idea that Pakistan was inevitable. Azad, who met Patel soon after Mountbatten's arrival, 'was surprised and pained when Patel in reply said that whether we liked it or not, there were two nations in India.' Similarly, 'Jawaharlal Nehru asked me in despair what

---

[46] Cited in ibid., p. 853.
[47] Alan Campbell-Johnson, op. cit., p. 31.
[48] V. P. Menon, op. cit., pp. 358–9.

other alternative there was to accepting partition.' As for Gandhi, at first he said that Partition 'will be over my dead body.' But within a few days, 'he too had changed.'[49] This change in Gandhi took place on 2 April 1947. Before Gandhi's conversion, Mountbatten had already succeeded in converting Patel and Nehru to the idea of Partition by playing on Patel's eagerness to get rid of the Muslim League. Both Patel and Nehru were impressed by the argument that it would be better to hand over a few provinces in the North-Western and Eastern parts of India to Muslims than to endanger Indian unity and strength by trying to work with the Muslim League.[50] Thus, barely two weeks had elapsed after Mountbatten's arrival when it became clear that India would be divided.

Mountbatten from the very beginning did not conceal his predilections towards Partition. Within the third week after his arrival in India on 8 April, Mountbatten was discussing Liaquat's paper on the division of the Armed Forces.[51] On 19 April, during a discussion at the Viceroy's Staff meeting, Lord Ismay, Chief of the Viceroy's Staff, stressed the difficulty of two physically separated Pakistans in the West and in the East. Mountbatten's reply was 'that whatever its implications he was beginning to think that Pakistan was inevitable.' On 27 April, when concern was expressed over leakage of the Government's intentions to the press, Mountbatten pointed out: '…The more the papers speculate about partition, the more they are preparing public opinion for its arrival.'[52]

From the evidence that has so far appeared, one wonders whether Mountbatten ever seriously tried to bring about an understanding between the Congress and the League on the basis of the Cabinet Mission Plan.[53] He never put forward the Cabinet Mission Plan as a serious proposition. He did talk now and again of resurrecting it, but it was never brought out of cold storage to

[49] For these statements, see Maulana Abul Kalam Azad, op. cit., pp. 185–7.
[50] Ibid., pp. 187–8.
[51] John Connell, op. cit., p. 872.
[52] For these statements, see Alan Campbell-Johnson, op. cit., pp. 67, 73.
[53] See V. P. Menon, op. cit., p. 353. But Azad was more emphatic: 'It is also possible that Lord Mountbatten did not feel so strongly about the Cabinet Mission Plan, as this was not the child of his brain.' Maulana Abul Kalam Azad, op. cit., p. 188.

be aired thoroughly. At best it was an alternative solution but entirely dependent upon complete Congress approval of it, which Mountbatten and his advisers knew could not be easily elicited. At one time Mountbatten did talk about a modified version of the Cabinet Mission Plan at a Staff meeting. He thought that a serious flaw in the Cabinet Mission Plan was that Hindus would have a permanent majority in the Centre to keep the Muslim minority in subjugation. He thought that if Pakistan and Hindustan were to come together on the basis of parity, Provinces like the Punjab, Bengal and Assam would not have to be partitioned. 'My object is to create the effect of two sovereign States or separate blocs negotiating at the centre rather than having a system of majority voting.'[54] But all these proposals never went beyond the discussion stage. Mountbatten knew that the Cabinet Mission Plan had collapsed before his arrival. As suggested earlier, the Congress had never liked the Cabinet Mission Plan. Their strategy had succeeded in forcing Jinnah to withdraw his acceptance of the Plan. At first, they argued in terms of championing the cause of tiny Assam being dragged into Section C against its will. Later, they played on the traditional Sikh hostility towards Muslims and said that Sikhs would never like to be subjugated under Muslim rule in Section B of the North-West Provinces.

The haste with which Mountbatten was acting was largely dictated by the alarming situation that was developing. Lord Mountbatten himself had never had any experience with the administration in India. The Chief of his Staff, Lord Ismay, had been out of touch with Indian administration since 1936 when he left India after being Military Secretary to the Viceroy, to work in the British Civil Service. To both Mountbatten and Ismay, Hindu-Muslim conflict looked extremely dangerous and ugly. They probably did not think, as a Deputy Commissioner or a Home Secretary would have done, that law and order could be brought about by using extremely ruthless and drastic methods. Instead of taking the view that power should be transferred only after law and order had been brought about, they thought that the situation might deteriorate into anarchy for which the British would be blamed. As Lord Ismay told the author, 'The British had all the responsibility but no power. Once you say you are going, you must go at once. Muslim or Hindu policemen may act

---

[54] Alan Campbell-Johnson, op. cit., p. 71.

against their co-religionists (to maintain peace) but when their boss is going they have to ensure their future.' Sir George Cunningham, who had been Governor of the North-West Frontier Province as well as Private Secretary to the Viceroy, commenting on the Punjab disturbances, wrote to the author:

> This, again, was the result of Mountbatten's unwisdom in accelerating the date of Partition so suddenly. I am sure that if the Punjab had been given time (say 8 or 9 months) to sort out their services properly—Muhammadan and Hindu—the terrible massacres of Aug-Sept-Oct would never have happened *in anything approaching* the scale that they did assume.

In defence of Mountbatten's haste, it could be pointed out that the political complexion of Provinces like the Punjab and the Frontier had so completely changed in favour of the Muslim League that any attempt to postpone the granting of power to the Muslim League would have resulted in more lawlessness and communal conflict. Even though the League had not done well in the Provincial elections in the Frontier and the Congress had assumed office, by the beginning of 1947 the Muslim League had become so popular that they had launched a Province-wide agitation against the Congress Ministry. According to Azad, 'The actual position in 1946 was that the Khan brothers did not enjoy as much support in the Frontier as we in Delhi thought. When Jawaharlal reached Peshawar, this discovery came to him with an unpleasant shock.'[55] In the Punjab, the Muslim League had won overwhelming support in the elections, but because of the slender majority of Muslim seats over the rest in the Assembly, they had not been able to form the Government. But their agitation against Khizr Hyat Khan's Ministry had succeeded in toppling it.

Mountbatten's first plan was to hand over power to the Provinces or to such confederations of Provinces as the latter might decide to form. The plan also envisaged the partition of Bengal and the Punjab for which the procedure proposed was that representatives of predominantly Muslim and non-Muslim areas would meet separately in two parts in each of the Provinces. If it were found that both sections of these Provincial Assemblies were in favour of Partition, that Province would be partitioned. If the decision in Bengal were in favour of Partition, the predominantly

---

[55] Maulana Abul Kalam Azad, op, cit., p. 171.

Muslim district of Sylhet would be given the option of joining the Muslim Province of Bengal. As regards the N-W. F. P., fresh elections were proposed to ascertain the wishes of the people.

Mountbatten encountered oppositio.n to these proposals from a number of sources. Two of these were Governors of Bengal and Punjab and the Muslim League leader, Jinnah. Sir Evan Jenkins, the Governor of the Punjab, opposed Partition on the plea that the divided Provinces would still be saddled with minorities. The Governor of Bengal argued that division of Bengal would make East Bengal a rural slum. Jinnah also pointed out that division of the Punjab and Bengal would destroy the administrative and economic fabric of the Provinces which for nearly a century had been reared on the basis of single and autonomous Provinces. He suggested exchange of populations which would eventually take place as a way out, thereby hinting that Bengal and Punjab should be emptied of their large Hindu minorities and subsequently filled with the migrating Muslims. He argued that if the Punjab and Bengal were partitioned, other Provinces as well where Muslims lived in large numbers in certain areas should be partitioned. Jinnah's statement was followed by a resolution passed by the Hindu and Sikh Legislators of the Punjab and the non-Muslim members of the Central Assembly and Constituent Assembly from that Province demanding a just and equitable division of the Punjab as the only solution.

Mountbatten sent his plan to London with Ismay and his Secretary, George Abell, urging the Government to let him have their approval by 10 May. He was thinking of presenting the approved plan before a meeting of party leaders on 17 May. Mountbatten's plan came back from London with several important amendments which he felt had dimmed the prospects of the plan being accepted by Indian leaders. By that time he had become very friendly with Nehru who was staying at Simla as his guest. He showed the amended version of the plan to Nehru who turned it down saying that the Congress would categorically reject it. His basic opposition was that the draft plan did not recognize the fact that the Indian Union was the successor authority to the British Government in India from which certain States wanted to secede. The draft plan proposed the transfer of power to a large number of successor States who could unite, if they desired, into two or more States. Similarly, the idea that each of these successor States could conclude separate treaties with the British Government would bring about the Balkanization of India. Particularly some of the major Princely States would try to emerge as independent kingdoms. When Mountbatten found that Nehru was bitterly opposed to the draft that he had received from London, he decided that another approach should be made to resolve the deadlock. He turned to the plan of V. P. Menon who, as suggested earlier, had drafted a scheme according to which transfer of power would take place on the basis of Dominion status to India and such other areas as wanted to separate from India and form another State. He had already obtained Patel's approval of this scheme. Mountbatten suggested that Nehru should examine it. Nehru was not averse to the plan according to which power would be transferred to two Central Governments on the basis of Dominion status. Menon also kept Patel fully informed who 'was delighted by the turn of events.'[56] It was significant that while these crucial discussions were taking place, Jinnah and the League were in the dark as to how the final plan was being evolved. What emerges from the evidence so far made available is that Jinnah and the League were not close friends of the Viceroy, but represented forces which had to be persuaded or overcome.[57] Unlike Nehru, they did not seem to enjoy the confidence of the Viceroy.

V. P. Menon was justified in thinking that he was the first to obtain Patel's approval to the idea of Partition and transfer of power on the basis of Dominion status. But so far as Dominion status was concerned, there was another claimant. 'Krishna Menon takes credit as the first to have suggested an early transfer of power to India on this basis [Dominion status].'[58] Even V. P. Menon's claim that he was the original author of the Partition plan, as finally announced and accepted in the form of the 3 June 1947 plan of transfer of power, could be admitted only with certain qualifications. First of all, the idea of Pakistan without the Hindu majority districts of Bengal and the Punjab and without the Hindu areas of Assam had been put forward as early as September 1944, by C. Rajagopalachari during the course of the

---

[56] V. P. Menon, op. cit., p. 365.

[57] This is clear in Alan Campbell-Johnson, op. cit., and V. P. Menon, op. cit.

[58] Alan Campbell-Johnson, op. cit., p. 88.

Gandhi-Jinnah talks. Similarly, the detailed mechanics of ascertaining the wishes of the Muslim areas of the Punjab, Bengal and Provinces like Sind, the N-W. F. P., Baluchistan and a district like Sylhet had been spelled out by the Cabinet Mission in April 1946, before they put forward their final plan of 16 May. The idea of partitioning the Punjab and Bengal, the holding of fresh elections in the N-W. F. P., and the inclusion of Sylhet in Muslim Bengal were there in the plan that Mountbatten sent with Ismay and George Abell to London on 2 May 1947. Thus, it could be said that V. P. Menon's main contribution was in incorporating all these ideas into a new plan which might be acceptable to both parties. The fact that this was not altogether a difficult task is hinted at by V. P. Menon himself. 'I had only two or three hours in which to prepare an alternative draft plan and I set to work on it at once.'[59] As regards his claim that he was the first to persuade Patel to agree to Partition, it should also be qualified by the fact that Patel was in a receptive mood because of the bitter conflict that was taking place in the Interim Government and the continuous eruption of communal warfare outside. However, there was no doubt that V. P. Menon played an important role in the sense that he was an excellent draftsman who could incorporate a number of ideas into his scheme and thus increase the chances of it being accepted by the party leaders. His draft of 'Heads of Agreement' of 16 May 1947, was an outstanding example.

The 'Heads of Agreement' were eight in all and suggested that in the event of a decision that there should be two sovereign States in India, the Central Government of each State would assume power and be responsible to its respective Constituent Assembly on a Dominion status basis. The Government of India Act, 1935, would be modified to conform to Dominion status position and would form the Constitution of each Dominion in the initial stages. The present Governor General would be reappointed as a common Governor General for both Dominions. A Commission would be appointed for the demarcation of boundaries. There would also be a division of the Armed Forces. It was stipulated that the units recruited from the territory of the Dominion concerned would be allocated to that Dominion. But in the case of mixed units the separation and redistribution was to be

---

[59] V. P. Menon, op. cit., p. 365.

entrusted to a committee chaired by Field-Marshal Sir Claude Auchinleck and the Chiefs of the General Staff of the two Dominions. The committee was to function under the supervision of a Council constituted by the Governor General and the two Defence Ministers.

The Congress agreement to these 'Heads of Agreement' was obtained in writing, but Jinnah and Liaquat were not willing to commit themselves beyond accepting the general principles. Mountbatten tried to pressure Jinnah by suggesting that if his complete agreement was not forthcoming he might have to resort to the alternative of demitting power to the Interim Government on a Dominion status basis. But the Viceroy found that Jinnah had a very steady nerve. Jinnah probably knew that these were bluff and threat tactics. The Viceroy left for London on 18 May and the British Government, after a full appraisal of the situation from the Viceroy, issued their 'Statement regarding the method of transfer of power, 3 June 1947.'

Some of the noteworthy proposals in the statement were with regard to the partitioning of the Provinces of the Punjab and Bengal, the setting up of a Commission to demarcate the boundaries, and the hint that the British Government were willing to transfer power before June 1948. It was clear that power was to be transferred to two Central authorities responsible to their respective Constituent Assemblies. The work of the existing Constituent Assembly was not to be interrupted. A new Constituent Assembly consisting of the North-West Frontier Province, Sind, British Baluchistan, West Punjab and such other Muslim districts, East Bengal and the district of Sylhet, could be established if a decision in favour of Partition and the creation of such a Constituent Assembly were obtained in the manner prescribed in the statement of 3 June 1947.

The Provincial Legislative Assemblies of the Punjab and Bengal were to meet in two parts, one consisting of the representatives of the Muslim majority districts and the other representing the rest of the Province, to decide by a simple majority whether the Province concerned should be partitioned. If either part decided in favour of Partition, the Province would be partitioned. A Commission for each of the two Provinces was to be set up by the Governor General to demarcate the boundaries of the two parts of the Punjab and Bengal after ascertaining the contiguous majority areas of Muslims and non-Muslims. The Commission was also to be instructed to take into account other factors. A referendum was to be held in the North-West Frontier Province in the event of the whole or any part of the Punjab deciding not to join the existing Constituent Assembly to ascertain the wishes of the people of the Province regarding the Constituent Assembly they would like to join. British Baluchistan was also to be given an opportunity to decide whether it would like to join the existing Constituent Assembly or a new Constituent Assembly consisting of Muslim majority areas. A referendum was also to be held in the district of Sylhet to determine whether in the event of the partition of Bengal, the people of Sylhet would like to be amalgamated with the Muslim part of Bengal.

Both the Muslim League and the Congress had carried on bitter and lengthy negotiations and if some decision were not taken at this stage, they knew that the alternative would be carnage and chaos. The League was not altogether jubilant about obtaining a Pakistan stripped of East Punjab and West Bengal. The Muslim League Council, which met in New Delhi on 10 June, passed a resolution saying that though it could not agree to the partition of Bengal and the Punjab, it had to consider the plan of 3 June for the transfer of power as a whole. The resolution authorized Jinnah to accept the Partition scheme as laid down in the 3 June statement 'as a compromise'. Jinnah was also armed with all the powers necessary to take all steps and decisions with regard to the implementation of the Partition plan. The All-India Congress Committee meeting on 14 June 1947 was more dramatic. As Azad noted later, there was a touch of irony in the situation, for arrayed against the resolution accepting the plan of 3 June were both Nationalist Muslims and those 'men who have posed as nationalists but who are in fact utterly communal in outlook.'[60] Azad was referring, perhaps, to men like Purshottamdas Tandon, who in an impassioned speech said that acceptance of the resolution would mean abject surrender to the British and to the Muslim League. 'The Working Committee had failed India, but India with the strength of millions behind her must reject this resolution.' It looked as if neither Pandit Pant's (who moved the resolution) persuasiveness nor Patel's unemotional clarity could overcome the feeling of bitterness that

---

[60] Maulana Abul Kalam Azad, op. cit., p. 197.

pervaded the Committee. Gandhi had to intervene, posing before the Committee the unpleasant consequences of rejecting the plan. 'The consequences of such a rejection would be the finding of a new set of leaders who could constitute not only the Congress Working Committee but also take charge of the Government.' The Committee endorsed the official resolution by 157 votes to 29 in a House of 218. The resolution pointed out: 'The A.I.C.C. earnestly trusts that when present passions have subsided India's problems will be viewed in their proper prospective [*sic*] and the false doctrine of two-nation [*sic*] will be discredited and discarded by all.'[61] Thus, Partition had arrived not with a bang but with a whimper.

---

[61] I. S. Jehu, ed., *The Indian and Pakistan Year Book 1948*, Vol. XXXIV, Bombay: Bennett, Coleman, n.d., p. 945.

6 THE MUSLIM LEAGUE.
ITS ROLE AND ORGANIZATION

There are many people in Pakistan, particularly among the Services, who tend to dismiss the contribution of the Muslim League towards the achievement of Pakistan as one of little consequence. They often quote, out of context, the statement of Jinnah that his 'entire equipment was confined to an attache-case, a typewriter, and a personal assistant.'[1] It is obvious that such glib statements lack both reflection and historical perspective. Jinnah, with all his adroitness, needed an organization like the Muslim League to impress upon the British and the Congress that he enjoyed universal Muslim support. He also needed the Muslim League for winning elections. In fact the Muslim League bridged the gulf that yawned between the illiterate Muslim masses and the highly Westernized Muslim elite at the top.

What was the state of the Muslim League before Jinnah undertook its reorganization? In 1927, the total membership of the Muslim League was 1,330.[2] During the years 1931–3, its annual expenditure did not exceed Rs 3,000.[3] In the 1930 Allahabad session, when Sir Muhammad Iqbal presented his historic address demanding the establishment of a North-Western Muslim state in India, the League meeting did not even have its quorum of 75 members. Hafiz Jalandhari was asked to read his famous

---

[1] Jamil-ud-Din Ahmad, ed., *Speeches and Writings of Mr. Jinnah,*, Vol. I, Lahore: Ashraf, 1960, p. 132. This statement is from a speech made in 1940 in which Jinnah urged Muslims to strengthen the Muslim League organization and pointed out that it was only after Muslims were well organized that he would give them marching orders. This meant that he attached great importance to the organization of the Muslim League.

[2] R. Palme Dutt, *India Today and Tomorrow,* London: Lawrence and Wishart, 1955, p. 234.

[3] *Annual Report of the All India Muslim League for the Years 1932 and 1933*, Delhi: n.d., p. 10.

poem, *Shahnama-i-Islam,* to keep those who were present entertained while the organizers were busy enrolling new members in the town. During this time, the annual sessions of the Muslim League were often held in private houses. The annual session of 1931, held at Delhi, was described as 'a languid and attenuated House of scarcely 120 people in all.'[4] During this session the annual subscription was reduced from Rs 6 to Re 1 and the admission fee of Rs 5 was abolished to attract new members.[5] The League's declining strength was also reflected in the resolution which reduced the quorum at the annual sessions from 75 to 50.

When Jinnah started reorganizing the Muslim League in early 1935, Sir Fazl-i-Husain had retired from the Executive Council and returned to the Punjab to resuscitate the Unionist Party. Jinnah, who had been elected President for three years, very shrewdly invited Fazl-i-Husain to preside over the annual session of the Muslim League. Fazl-i-Husain declined the request and made it clear to Jinnah that he should desist from setting up a Central Parliamentary Board of the Muslim League because Muslims in Provinces like the Punjab might like to work with non-communal organizations in which case a Central Muslim Parliamentary Board would hamper their efforts in creating communal harmony. Fazl-i-Husain, writing to Sikander Hyat, said, 'I have also asked Ahmad Yar (Daultana's father) to strongly press on him (Jinnah) the advisability of keeping his finger out of the Punjab pie.'[6] Jinnah did not make any headway in the Punjab, even though he was reported to have made promises of procuring large election funds from Bombay millionaires and the Raja of Mahmoodabad. At that time the prospects of Jinnah's success were obviously so dim that even a former founder of the Muslim League like the Aga Khan lent his financial support to the Unionist Party.[7] The weakness of the League was reflected in the elections of 1937 when it won only 4.6 per cent of the total Muslim votes.

---

[4] *The Hindustan Times,* Delhi, 30 December 1931.

[5] Ibid. Also *Annual Report of the All India Muslim League,* op. cit.

[6] Azim Husain, *Fazl-i-Husain,* Bombay: Longmans, 1946, p. 309.

[7] Ibid., p. 312. The Aga Khan wrote to Fazl-i-Husain, 'My agents have sent you the first part of my grant (i.e. Rs 10,000) due to my horse *Mahmud* winning the Derby, otherwise I should not have been able financially to help you.' Ibid., p. 312.

But in April 1938, Jinnah was claiming that during the last six months the Muslim League had enrolled members by hundreds of thousands.[8] Even though the Congress had launched its Muslim mass contact movement, by January 1938 it could claim the support of only a hundred thousand (or 3.3 per cent) Muslims out of its 3.1 million members.[9] Thus, the great majority of politically conscious Muslims were joining the Muslim League. In 1944, the Muslim League officially claimed a membership of some two millions.[10] Its organization had penetrated the countryside and those Muslims who openly remained hostile to the Muslim League were not considered Muslims by their co-religionists. By the end of 1944, the Bengal Muslim League claimed a membership of about half a million and the Sind and Punjab Leagues had 200,000 members each. But the most convincing testimony of the Muslim League's strength came from the 1945–6 election results. The Muslim League polled about 4.5 million or 75 per cent of the Muslim votes in the elections.[11] It won 460 out of the 533 Muslim seats in the Central and Provincial elections.

The question arises that if the organization and power of the Muslim League were entirely due to the drive and organizing ability of Jinnah, why was it that the Muslim League prior to the thirties, when Jinnah was one of its leading figures, was a dormant body? Jinnah had been President of the Muslim League during the years 1919–30. The Secretary of the League, lamenting Jinnah's decision to leave the country in 1931, said in his annual report: 'Mr M. A. Jinnah had been the life and the moving spirit of the League for many years and the success of the institution during the last 9 years was due to his earnestness, devotion and statesmanship.'[12] Did the Muslim League receive new impetus first as a result of the shortsightedness of the Congress in excluding Muslim League representatives from the Provincial Congress Cabinets in 1937, and later owing to the alleged persecutions that the Muslims suffered during the Congress

---

[8] *The Indian Annual Register 1938*, Vol. I, Calcutta, p. 382.

[9] R. Palme Dutt, op. cit., p. 235.

[10] Ibid., p. 234.

[11] The 4.5 million votes cast for the Muslim League do not indicate the total number of votes that might have been cast in favour of the League if the 40 uncontested seats had been contested. See the table of these election results in *The Indian Annual Register 1946*, Vol. I, Calcutta.

[12] *Annual Report of the All India Muslim League for the Year 1931*, Delhi: n.d., p. 1.

regimes of 1937–9? and Choudhry Khaliquzzaman seem to think that the former was the main cause which helped the League to rally the Muslims under its banner.[13] There is no doubt that this did help the League. But how was it that the Muslim League did not achieve its maximum strength during these years of alleged Congress persecutions? It was only after the Lahore Resolution was passed and the demand for a separate Muslim State came to the forefront that Muslims in their thousands flocked to the Muslim League. Thus, neither Jinnah's organizing ability nor the alleged Congress misrule by themselves could have transformed the League into a mighty force. The demand for Pakistan reminded Muslims of their past glory and opened before them vast and fascinating vistas of future greatness. It was this stimulant which put life and vigour into the Muslim League.

Those who think that Pakistan was entirely a product of Hindu hostility to Muslims not only exaggerate Hindu responsibility for it but also forget that Muslims were just as hostile. In addition to all this, they have not appreciated the demand for Pakistan in its historical perspective. Muslims had ruled India and they could not understand why under a democratic system they should be deprived of power and influence. Thus, it was this desire for power and unwillingness to live under those whom they had governed which largely explains the demand for Pakistan. Jinnah was groping towards this even before the demand for Pakistan was launched.

> Muslims have made it clear more than once that besides the question of religion, culture, language and personal laws, there is another question of life and death for them and that their future destiny and fate are dependent upon their securing definitely their political rights, their due share in the national life, the Government and the administration of the country.[14]

Muslim educated classes were not so much concerned about their religious and cultural rights as they were about their share in the government of the country. The tremendous following that Jinnah had among these classes lay in the fact that he offered to them political power under a new Muslim State.

---

[13] Choudhry Khaliquzzaman to the author in an interview in Karachi on 3 June 1960. See also Maulana Abul Kalam Azad, *India Wins Freedom*, Calcutta: Orient Longmans, 1959, pp. 160–2.

[14] *The Indian Annual Register 1938*, Vol. I, op. cit., p. 384.

Which government claiming to be a civilized government can demolish our mosque, or which government is going to interfere with religion which is strictly a matter between God and man? The question is that Musalmans are a nation, distinct from the Hindus.... It is a historical fact that the Musalmans are a separate nation and hence we must have our own States.[15]

But a great majority of the two-anna members of the Muslim League were not Westernized educated Muslims.[16] They were simple rural folk or the poorer sections of the urban Muslims who were told time and again by their *Mullahs* that power would be given to them by God if they became good Muslims. Thus, the idea of establishing a Muslim State was not new. Less sophisticated and anti-League Muslim organizations like the *Ahrar* and the *Khaksar* had talked about it. The *Ahrars* put forward the idea of *Hakumat-i-Ilahia* (Government of God) and the *Khaksars* claimed that their aim was *Istikhlaf fi al-Ard* (Establishment of Khilafat [Islamic Government] on earth).[17] Thus, when the League demanded Pakistan, it was responding to this inner urge for political power among the Muslims. The Muslim League was, on one hand, satisfying a craving for power and influence free from Hindu competition among the Muslim intelligentsia and, on the other, the more vague and religious urge for power among the Muslim masses. The League, in this sense, had become a more comprehensive and representative organization than the Khilafat movement which did not attract the full support of Westernized and educated Muslims.

The Muslim League, like the Congress, was not a political party in the ordinary sense of the term. It was a national movement whose aim was the establishment of the separate, sovereign State of Pakistan. Any man who stood against the Muslim League was called a traitor or quisling by the Quaid-i-Azam. Some of the Muslim Leaguers went so far as to say that any Muslim who opposed the Muslim League had betrayed the cause of Islam itself.[18] As long as Pakistan remained unachieved, all

---

[15] Jamil-ud-Din Ahmad, ed., Vol. I, op. cit., p. 469.

[16] The annual subscription for primary members was 2 annas

[17] Zakir Husain Faruqi, *Muslim League Kiyyun?*, Bombay: Maktaba-i-Sultani, 1947, pp. 230-1.

[18] Fazl-ul-Huq in a speech to the Sind Muslim League Conference in Karachi, 1938. *The Indian Annual Register 1938*, Vol. II, Calcutta, p. 355.

Muslims were supposed to subordinate their personal and ideological difference to the national goal.

We shall have time to quarrel ourselves and we shall have time when these differences will have to be settled, when wrongs and injuries will have to be remedied. We shall have time for domestic programme and policies, but first get the Government. This is a nation without any territory or any government.[19]

Thus, within the Muslim League could be found feudal landowners, industrialists, the *ulama*, the lower middle classes, industrial workers and peasants. In it were Socialists like Mian Iftikharuddin and extreme leftist elements like Danyal Latifi, who had joined the League after it had become clear that the goal of Pakistan was within sight. The leadership of Jinnah and the organization and discipline of the Muslim League were such that all these heterogeneous elements could be kept within the League without impairing its unity. Similarly, the passionate zeal for Pakistan was such that Bengalis and Punjabis, though conscious of their differences, were willing to work together for the common goal.

Jinnah very cleverly kept himself and the League scrupulously out of all controversial issues. He himself was a Shi'ah and a Khoja by origin, but always said that he was only a Muslim and also offered his public prayers with the Sunni Muslims. The simple doctrine that he preached was that Islam transcended all petty sectarian differences. Since there was no state, no debates about what form of Islam should be established or practised could arise. And the sort of Islam that the Muslim League put forward was simple and straightforward, free of all theological and doctrinal subtleties, which the ordinary Muslim masses could understand. This intellectual naiveté was such that it pervaded not only the Muslim masses but infected the leaders as well.

The growth of the Muslim League was also helped considerably by the total absence of any competition from other political parties, particularly after 1942 when the Congress leaders were in jail. Jinnah himself frankly admitted that he shuddered when he considered what was going to happen in 1939. 'There was going to be a deal between Mr Gandhi and Lord Linlithgow. Providence helped us. The war which nobody welcomes proved to be a

---

[19] Jamil-ud-Din Ahmad, ed., *Speeches and Writings of Mr. Jinnah,*, Lahore: Ashraf, 1964, Vol. II, p. 199.

blessing in disguise.'[20] On the other hand, it could also be argued that the Congress Muslim mass contact movement had not proved successful earlier and was not likely to produce any different results if tried later. Moreover, if the Congress had remained in power, there might have arisen differences between the Congress High Command and the Provincial Ministries or between leaders in the High Command itself like Nehru and Patel. Congressmen, by going to jail and taking a stand against the British Government, created for themselves such support and sympathy that even the Communists, who tried to infiltrate into every segment of Indian political life, could not make much headway.

The Congress Party has been criticized for its unitarian structure and the way it nullified Provincial autonomy by controlling the Provincial Governments.[21] Sometimes Gandhi's interference in Congress affairs and his comparisons of the Congress structure with that of an army also created the impression that the Congress was imitating Fascist methods.[22] Jinnah was also quick to detect such Fascist features in the Congress organization. But he has also been subjected to the same sort of criticism in the sense that when the League organization became powerful, he saw to it that the Muslim League Provincial Parliamentary Parties and Governments carried out the instructions issued to them from the Centre. He was also sometimes fond of comparing the Muslim League with an army with himself as the general. Thus, he talked of giving marching orders when the Muslims were disciplined and ready.[23] When his mission of achieving Pakistan was accomplished in June 1947, he was reported to have said: 'I have done my job. When the Field Marshal leads his army into victory, it is for the civil authority to take over.'[24]

When Jinnah started reorganizing the Muslim League during 1935–7, he proceeded very cautiously and wanted to enlist as much support as possible of the influential Muslim leaders. Thus, as noted earlier, he invited Sir Fazl-i-Husain to preside over the annual session of the Muslim League in 1935. In the Lucknow

[20] Ibid., p. 245.

[21] R. Coupland, *The Indian Problem*, Part II, New York: Oxford University Press, 1944, pp. 120–5.

[22] Ibid., pp. 91–93.

[23] Jamil-ud-Din Ahmad, ed., Vol. I, op. cit., pp. 132–3.

[24] *Dawn*, Delhi 18 August 1947.

session in 1937, the Muslim League acquired tremendous strength when Fazl-ul-Huq, the Premier of Bengal, and Sir Sikander Hyat Khan, the Premier of Punjab, declared their support for the Muslim League and brought over their parties to the Muslim League ranks. At that time, Jinnah's main concern was to build the Muslim League as a powerful and well-organized party and the power he enjoyed depended very much upon the support that he obtained from powerful Muslim groups in the various Provinces.

It was in 1941 that one got the impression for the first time that the power of the President was not only dependent upon the League as a party but had also acquired a personal character. The Quaid-i-Azam had emerged. One cannot help admiring the strategy that Jinnah followed in building up his power and prestige as the League President. In July 1941, the Viceroy announced that the Premiers of the Punjab, Bengal, Assam and Sind had been invited to join the National Defence Council. The Muslim League had been following a very shrewd and cautious policy whereby it neither cooperated whole-heartedly with the British war effort nor did it take any steps to obstruct it. But it certainly did not want to create the impression that, unlike the Congress, it lacked national fervour for the freedom of the country. When the invitations to the Provincial Premiers to join the National Defence Council were issued, Jinnah knew that the Viceroy had made a tactical mistake by inviting them as representatives of the Muslim community. The Premiers of the Punjab, Bengal and Assam were under the impression that they had been invited to represent their Provinces and indicated their willingness to join the National Defence Council. (At that time Sind did not have a Muslim League Ministry.) When Jinnah issued peremptory orders to them to resign from the National Defence Council, they were resentful. But when he confronted Sir Sikander Hyat, the Premier of Punjab, with the text of the message that the Viceroy had sent to him through the Governor of Bombay, Sir Sikander Hyat had no choice except to tender his resignation from the National Defence Council because the message indicated that he had been invited as a representative of the Muslim community.[25] This was followed by the resignation of Sir Saadullah,

[25] *Resolutions of the All India Muslim League from March* 1941 *to April* 1942, Delhi: All India Muslim League, n.d., pp. 1–2.

the Premier of Assam. Fazl-ul-Huq at first was extremely resentful and reluctant, but later he had to resign as well. He complained that Jinnah had known of their selection at least a day before the names were published but did not care to indicate his disapproval immediately. 'He kept waiting and watching till our names were published and then he came out with his thunder that he had decided to take disciplinary action against us.' He 'took us unawares as if he was anxious to make a public exhibition of his authority.'[26] Similarly, Begum Shah Nawaz, who had joined the National Defence Council, was called upon to resign but when she refused, she was expelled from the Muslim League for five years. This was followed by the expulsion of Sir Sultan Ahmad for having joined the Viceroy's Executive Council contrary to the decision of the Muslim League and its general policy. This 'exhibition of authority' made the Muslims realize how powerful their Quaid-i-Azam was in the sense that powerful Muslim leaders could not easily flout his instructions without incurring the wrath of Muslim public opinion.

I. ORGANS OF THE MUSLIM LEAGUE. POWERS AND FUNCTIONS

I. *President, Working Committee and Council*

The Muslim League was not the only party in the subcontinent which developed the cult of leadership. As has been suggested earlier, the Congress had also built up the charismatic authority of Gandhi. But there was a difference between the two concepts of leadership. Gandhi was the Mahatma, who was associated in the Hindu mind with a sort of semi-divine authority. Jinnah was only the Quaid-i-Azam and particularly because of his Western habits and temperament, could never claim to be a religious leader or a holy man. In Muslim history, particularly in political matters, Muslims had been content to follow leaders who were not very religious but politically or militarily capable or successful. Thus, Jinnah was presented as a man of great wisdom, courage and such shrewdness that Hindus were afraid of him. The common belief was that his predecessors, like Maulana Muhammad Ali, had not been very shrewd and had often been out-witted by Hindu leaders. For the intelligentsia, Jinnah had

---

[26] *The Statesman* (Weekly Overseas Edition), Calcutta, 18 September 1941.

certain outstanding qualities. He was a brilliant and a wealthy lawyer and a constitutionalist who could lecture to them perhaps better than anyone else on the art of parliamentary government. For those who were wealthy like the Memon, the Khoja and the Bohri merchants, he was not only a man of unimpeachable integrity but being a Gujarati, was one of them.[27] But Jinnah was not content to derive his authority merely from popular acclaim. His mind worked along constitutional channels. For him, the basic source of his authority was the Constitution of the All-India Muslim League.

As one reads through the Constitutions of 1940, 1941, 1942 and 1944, one notices a steady centralization of power in the hands of the President and his Working Committee. Article 33 of the 1944 Constitution stated: 'The President shall be the principal head of the whole organization, shall exercise all the powers inherent in his office and be responsible to see that all the authorities work in consonance with the Constitution and Rules of the All-India Muslim League.'[28] What were the instruments available to the President to see that all the organs of the League worked in accordance with the Constitution and the Rules? The process of amassing power in the hands of the President and the Working Committee had started in 1940. According to the Constitution, the President was to be elected every year by the Council from amongst those who had been nominated by different Muslim Leagues. Could it be said that the Provincial Muslim Leagues could determine the choice of the President in the sense that they nominated the various candidates? The power of the Provincial League *vis-à-vis* the Centre was only nominal because in the annual session in 1940 the Constitution of the League was amended and the Working Committee was empowered 'to control, direct and regulate all the activities of the various Provincial Leagues.' Similarly, the Working Committee could suspend, dissolve or disaffiliate any Provincial League which failed in its duties or acted contrary to the decisions or directions of the

---

[27] Memons, Khojas and Bohras are Muslim traders whose communities are concentrated in Gujarat, Bombay, Cutch and Kathiawar. Jinnah's father was a Khoja merchant from Karachi.

[28] This article was first inserted in the Constitution of 1944. *The Constitution and Rules of the All India Muslim League,* Delhi: p. 17. The Constitution of 1944 was exactly similar to the Constitution of 1946.

Working Committee or the Council of the All-India Muslim League. Thus, it was the Working Committee which exercised ultimate and effective power over the Provincial Leagues.

The Working Committee was a creature of the President in the sense that its members were nominated by the President each year at the time of the annual session from amongst the members of the Council. It could be said that the Working Committee was responsible to the Council of the All-India Muslim League in which were represented the various Provinces. Article 24 of the 1942 Constitution said that all resolutions passed by the Working Committee would be subject to the approval of the Council of the League. But the process of concentration of power had altered this balance because Article 23 of the 1944 Constitution clearly laid down that: 'All resolutions passed by the Working Committee will be placed before the Council of the League for its information.'

There is no clear and authentic account of the way decisions were arrived at in the Working Committee. R. G. Casey, Governor of Bengal, 1944–6, probably drew his information from Khwaja Nazimuddin, for some time his Chief Minister, when he wrote:

> Mr. Jinnah is credited with ruling the working committee of the Muslim League with a rod of iron. He is said to tell them what's what, and that they invariably fall into line. At any signs of intransigence on what he considers a major point he is said to threaten resignation, after which the argument ceases....[29]

Most of the members of the then Working Committee that the author interviewed strongly denied the 'rod of iron' theory. But when they tried to explain to the author that the Quaid-i-Azam allowed free and full discussion in the Working Committee and that he always respected those who held their beliefs honestly and sincerely, they more or less always came back to the view that the power, experience and personality of the Quaid-i-Azam were such that invariably his decision was accepted. It was reported that the Quaid seldom spoke first. He often encouraged the members of the Working Committee to put forward their views clearly and completely. He often used to say, 'Why don't you argue?

---

[29] R. G. Casey, *An Australian in India*, London: Hollis & Carter, 1947, pp. 64–65.

I may be wrong.' But after the discussion was over, he would indicate how the Working Committee should deal with the particular matter on hand.

There were certain members like the Secretary, Liaquat Ali Khan, and I. I. Chundrigar (from Bombay) whom Jinnah called to his residence to discuss certain matters on the agenda before the Working Committee meeting. His method was to discuss every problem threadbare before a decision was reached. He would often tell Chundrigar, 'You take the British or Congress point of view and argue with me.' Jinnah often treated Nawab Ismail Khan with respect. He was the only member of the Working Committee who was addressed with his honorific 'Nawab' while others were addressed by their first names. There was a group in the Working Committee which strongly believed in coming to terms with the Congress. This group consisted of Chaudhry Khaliquzzaman, Ismail Khan, Husain Imam, and for some time, G. M. Sayed (from Sind). Jinnah's point of view was that since ultimate power was held by the British and it was they who could confer or transfer power, why should he go out of the way to come to terms with the Congress? Both the Congress and the League were engaged in extracting maximum power from the British. The best course that was open to the League was to consolidate its own position and deal with the Congress and the British from a position of strength.

There was some suspicion in the Working Committee that several important matters discussed in the Committee sometimes leaked out to the opponents of the League. Thus, when the Working Committee was in session during the Simla Conference in 1945 and when the Cabinet Mission was holding discussions with the Indian parties in 1946, the Working Committee would sometimes keep its position fairly flexible so that there might be enough room to manoeuvre from one position to another. It was suspected that the League's opponents had come to know of these decisions. This must have hampered free discussion and it was likely that at certain moments Jinnah did not feel safe to take the whole Working Committee into his confidence and probably consulted only some of his close and trusted lieutenants.

Liaquat Ali Khan, as Secretary of the Muslim League, built up his position slowly and steadily. He was a prosperous land owner whose family was originally from the Karnal District of

East Punjab, but who had moved over to the United Provinces. He was affable by nature and seldom antagonized anybody. He carefully kept himself aloof from all intrigues and soon outpaced Choudhry Khaliquzzaman, his most formidable rival, and also Nawab Ismail Khan, Chairman of the Committee of Action, in rising to a position next to Jinnah. Jinnah himself had described him as his 'right hand'. After getting elected to the Central Legislative Assembly he moved to New Delhi where the All-India Muslim League had its Central Office. He also became the deputy Leader of the Muslim League Party in the Central Legislative Assembly. When *Dawn*, the Muslim League newspaper, started in 1942, he was appointed its Director. *Dawn* gave him considerable publicity as an active and efficient Secretary of the All-India Muslim League. As Chairman of the Central Parliamentary Board, he occupied another influential position. But his main source of strength was the trust that his leader placed in him. Had it not been for this fact, the clever Khaliquzzaman or the dynamic Suhrawardy might have supplanted him.

The members of the Working Committee during 1945–7 were:

N-W. F. P.	1. Sardar Abdur Rab Nishtar.
	2. Sardar Aurangzeb Khan.
Baluchistan	3. Qazi Muhammad Isa.
Punjab	4. Mian Bashir Ahmad.
	5. Nawab Iftikhar Husain Khan of Mamdot.
	6. Malik Barkat Ali (died in 1946).
Sind	7. Muhammad Ayub Khuhro.
Bombay	8. I. I. Chundrigar.
Madras	9. Abdul Sattar Sait.
Central Provinces	10. Syed Abdur Rauf Shah.
United Provinces	11. Nawab Muhammad Ismail Khan.
	12. Choudhry Khaliquzzaman.
	13. Raja Muhammad Amir Ahmad Khan of Mahmoodabad.
	14. Begum Muhammad Ali (died in 1946).
Bihar	15. Husain Imam.
	16. Latifur Rahman.

Bengal   17. Maulana Akram Khan.
                  18. Khwaja Nazimuddin.
                  19. M. A. H. Ispahani.
Assam   20. Sir Muhammad Saadullah.
                  21. Abdul Matin Choudhri.

G. M. Sayed was removed from the Working Committee after his expulsion from the Muslim League towards the end of 1945. There were two office bearers who were ex-officio members, M. A. Jinnah, President, and Liaquat Ali Khan, Secretary.

From the Constitution itself it was obvious that the Council was neither an active nor an effective body. First of all, it had 475 representatives from various Provinces and if the ex-officio Members of the Indian Legislative Assembly, the Council of State, the President and Secretaries of the various Provincial Muslim Leagues and the President's 20 nominees were to be taken into account, it would be a much larger body. In the official list of the members of the League Council of 1941, there were as many as 513 members. The quorum in the Council meetings was 50, but usually as many as 200 members were present. Jinnah's admirers have assured the author that the Quaid-i-Azam accorded the fullest latitude to the Councillors for expressing their opinions. But they added that the personality of their leader was so towering and awe-inspiring that nobody could sway the opinion of the Council once it was clear what the Quaid desired. There were, of course, members like Z. H. Lari and Syed M. Rizwanullah, both from the U. P., who were daring enough to speak their minds. There was also Hasrat Mohani, often provocative and fearless. Barkat Ali from Punjab was perhaps the most logical and convincing speaker. But there were other veterans who vied with one another in agreeing with the Quaid-i-Azam.

The Council was empowered to disaffiliate Provincial Leagues if they acted in contravention of the League policy and programme and also to take disciplinary action against any members of the League who violated its decisions. These powers were also invested in the Working Committee and normally that was the body which took the initiative in these matters and the Council was expected to ratify its decisions.

2. Committee of Action

The Committee of Action was set up for the first time during the annual session of the Muslim League in Karachi in December, 1943. Jinnah, addressing the session, said that the organization of the Muslim League had grown so unwieldy that it was not possible for any one man to attend to its multifarious activities.

> If you were to know what I have to attend to all alone, you will be astonished. All over India, today this thing happening in Patna; tomorrow that thing happening in Bengal; the day after tomorrow this thing happening in N-W. F. P.; the day after that this thing happening in Madras.... Now it is not possible for one single man to do justice to all this.[30]

This revealed that decision-making on a number of small as well as complex matters was concentrated in the hands of the President. Secondly, he could not assemble his Working Committee off and on at different places to resolve problems as they arose from place to place. Another matter which must have taxed Jinnah's mind was the future constitutional problem of India. He probably expected that the war would soon be over or even before that the British might make some major policy decisions as regards the constitutional problem in India. This was indicated by the resolution that was passed regarding the appointment of a Committee of Action by the President of not less than five and not more than seven members. The aim was 'to prepare and organize the Muslims all over India to meet all contingencies, resist the imposition of an all-India Federation or any other constitution for the United India, and prepare them for the coming struggle for the achievement of Pakistan.'[31] All this was to be done by tightening the organization of the Muslim League. Formerly, the Working Committee was in exclusive charge of controlling and directing the various Provincial Muslim Leagues or taking disciplinary action against such members and Provincial Leagues who acted against the directives of the Central organization. All these functions were delegated to the new Committee of Action.

---

[30] Jamil-ud-Din Ahmad, ed., Vol. I, op. cit., p. 555.
[31] *Resolutions of the All India Muslim League from May 1943 to December 1943*, Delhi: All-India Muslim League, n.d.

The Committee of Action was another instrument devised by the Central Muslim League to tighten its control over the Provincial Muslim Leagues with a view to setting up a well-disciplined and monolithic organization. Thus, if and when the League were faced with a particular situation, all that the President had to do was to give his orders and they would be duly carried out by every Provincial Muslim League. The Committee of Action, therefore, suggested a model constitution for all Provincial Muslim Leagues. According to this constitution, the Presidents of the various Provincial Muslim Leagues would nominate members of their Working Committees from amongst the members of the Council of that Provincial Muslim League. Thus it was suggested that each Provincial Muslim League should be modelled on the pattern of the Central Muslim League. In Bombay, for example, according to the Constitution of the Provincial Muslim League, the office bearers and the members of the Working Committee of the Provincial Muslim League were to be elected at the annual general meeting from among the members of the Provincial Muslim League.[32] This meant that it was possible that many members of the elected Provincial Working Committee might not see eye to eye on a number of problems with the President. This often led to friction and presumably the Committee of Action had been called upon from time to time to resolve disputes arising from such a situation. As a result of the suggested change, it was hoped that if the Provincial Working Committees were made creatures of their President, the latter would be in a position to have the orders of the Central League efficiently and promptly carried out.

In the same manner the Committee of Action recommended to the Working Committee that all the Muslim Members of the Legislative Assembly and Council of a Province as well as all Muslim Members of the Central Legislative Assembly and Council of State elected from that Province should be ex-officio members of the Council of that Provincial Muslim League. The former provision was probably designed to ensure good relationships between the Parliamentary Party and the Provincial Muslim League, and the latter with a view to making the Provincial Council amenable to Central influence. By suggesting

[32] *The Constitution and Rules of the Bombay Provincial Muslim League*, Bombay: Aziz Gafur Kazi, 1944, Article 58, p. 18.

such a model constitution, it was also intended that each Provincial Muslim League would be organized on roughly the same lines instead of the different Provincial Muslim Leagues following a host of different constitutions of their own. The Working Committee accepted these suggestions and passed a resolution to this effect in May 1946.[33]

The Committee of Action was also entrusted, after the 'Direct Action' Resolution had been passed in July 1946, with drawing up a programme of 'Direct Action'. Probably nothing much came out of this because of the Working Committee's decision to enter the Interim Government in October 1946.

Usually, the various Committees of the Muslim League were dominated by Muslim Leaguers either from the minority Provinces or sometimes from those of the United Provinces alone. In the Committee of Action, however, one could see that there were three members out of six from the North-Western Muslim Provinces. They were: G. M. Sayed from Sind, Iftikhar Husain Khan of Mamdot from the Punjab, and Qazi Muhammad Isa from Baluchistan. The other three were from Muslim minority Provinces—Ismail Khan (Chairman) and Liaquat Ali Khan from the United Provinces, and Abdul Sattar Sait from Madras.

3. *Central Parliamentary Board*

The Central Parliamentary Board, according to the Constitution, was to be set up by the Working Committee. It was not clear from the resolutions of 1945 whether the President was given the power to appoint all the members of the Central Parliamentary Board for the elections of 1945–6. But the earlier Parliamentary Boards had been set up by the President who by a resolution of the Working Committee passed on 12 April 1941 was empowered to name the personnel of the Parliamentary Committee(the name given to the Central Parliamentary Board at that time). In July 1945, the rules and regulations of the Central Parliamentary Board were framed by the Working Committee. The Central Parliamentary Board was given a very wide range of powers which reduced the status of the Provincial Parliamentary Boards to that of subservient and subordinate bodies. It was the Central Parliamentary Board which was given the power

---

[33] *Resolution of the All India Muslim League from January 1944 to December 1946*, Delhi: All India Muslim League, n.d., p. 43.

to supervise and control the various Muslim League Provincial Parliamentary Parties. It was the tribunal which decided all disputes arising between a Provincial Parliamentary Board and a Provincial Muslim League or a Muslim League Parliamentary Party. Similarly, it was laid down that the Provincial Parliamentary Board would be under the general supervision, control and direction of the Central Parliamentary Board. A candidate could appeal against the decision of the Provincial Parliamentary Board to the Central Parliamentary Board whose decision was final and binding on the Provincial Parliamentary Board.[34]

Even before these rules were framed, the Council of the Sind Provincial League, in its meeting of 3–4 June 1945, protested against 'the convention established by the All-India League, which aims at divesting the Provincial Leagues of all their inherent powers of control and supervision over Provincial Assembly Parties and Ministries.' The resolution took a stand against such excessive centralization which 'definitely militates against the principle of provincial sovereignty.'[35] Sind had always been a hot-bed of intrigue and instability. The Central Muslim League was of the view that the Muslim League Members in the Provincial Legislature often crossed the floor for purely selfish considerations and there was no discipline in the party. The Central Parliamentary Board was anxious that there should be a fully-fledged Muslim League Ministry in a Muslim majority Province like Sind. In March 1945, the Central Parliamentary Board sent detailed instructions to Sir Ghulam Hussain Hidayatullah as to how he should constitute his Ministry. Moula Bukhsh, one of the Ministers, had refused to join the League. Sir Ghulam Hussain was called upon by the Central Parliamentary Board to submit the resignation of his Ministry to the Governor and reconstitute it when invited to form a Ministry by the Governor in such a way that no Muslim was taken in unless he were a Muslim Leaguer.[36]

Over and above all these organs like the Working Committee, the Committee of Action, and the Central Parliamentary Board stood the personal power of the Quaid-i-Azam as President of the

---

[34] *Rules and Regulations of the Muslim League Central and Provincial Parliamentary Boards*, Delhi: All India Muslim League, n.d., pp. 1–5, 16–17.

[35] G. M. Sayed, *Struggle for New Sind*, Karachi: 1949, pp. 131–6.

[36] *The Indian Annual Register 1945*, Vol. I, Calcutta, p. 204.

Muslim League. Thus, according to a resolution of the Working Committee passed on 22 October 1939, the President was empowered 'to advise, guide and issue instructions to Muslim League Parties in the various Provincial Legislatures in the event of some sudden emergency arising.' In October 1942, the Sind Muslim League Parliamentary Party had negotiated an agreement with Sir Ghulam Hussain Hidayatullah, who had been commissioned by the Governor to form a Ministry, that the party would support the Ministry if the latter would work under the supervision and control of the League Assembly Party and the Provincial Working Committee. According to the terms of the agreement, it was also agreed that the Ministry would sponsor the passage of Bills like the Tenancy Bill, the Moneylenders Bill and the Land Alienation Bill in the Assembly. When Jinnah was informed of these developments, he was doubtful whether such an arrangement would work and was also angry that he had not been consulted. The text of his telegram dated 19 October 1942 and addressed to the Provincial League read:

> Muslim League Party Provincial League its executive no power take decision without my approval see resolution number two twenty-second October 1939 it is binding on you Party bound carry out give effect my instructions come Delhi yourself immediately before accepting office joining Ministry cant follow nor understand terms from your telegram vague surprised you say my telephone not working am receiving calls perfect order.[37]

In the meantime, matters had gone so far that certain Muslim League members had already been sworn in as Ministers in the new Cabinet. Sind Muslim League leaders like G. M. Sayed, Khuhro and M. H. Gazder were summoned to Delhi to present their case before the Working Committee which met on 8 November 1942. The Muslim League Working Committee had to accept the *fait accompli* and its resolution only regretted that the Executive of the Sind Provincial Muslim League had failed to carry out the instructions of the President regarding the formation of a Ministry. The Subcommittee that was appointed by the Working Committee to look into the matter visited the Province in December and they also felt that the arrangement arrived at between Sir Ghulam Hussain and the Provincial League could continue undisturbed. This showed that in spite of the enormous

---

[37] G. M. Sayed, op. cit., p. 92.

powers and prestige that the President enjoyed, he could not dictate the course of events in the face of certain realities and a determined opposition from the Provincial League.

In the Madras session of 1941 the President was 'authorized till the next Annual Sessions to take every necessary action or steps in furtherance of and relating to the objects of the Muslim League, as he may deem proper, provided that they are consistent with the goal and policy of the League or any resolution expressly passed by the sessions of the All-India Muslim League.' This practice was continued in subsequent years. In the Allahabad session of April 1942, Maulana Hasrat Mohani protested that Jinnah should not be invested with such dictatorial powers because there was a possibility that he might take a wrong decision, accept the Cripps proposals, and thus act contrary to the established creed of the Muslim League, namely, the establishment of independent zonal States. But the resolution arming Jinnah with all the powers was passed with the single dissenting vote of Hasrat Mohani.[38]

One could see that Hasrat Mohani's fears were not purely imaginary. In June 1947, when the Congress had approved Mountbatten's plan of Partition, Jinnah was pressed by the Viceroy to give a categorical undertaking that the League would accept the plan. Jinnah made it clear that he could give no such undertaking without obtaining the approval of the Council. Mountbatten did not succeed in getting a clear undertaking from Jinnah even when he threatened that he might lose his Pakistan. The Viceroy wanted such an assurance from the League leader because of the Congress suspicion that Jinnah might use such delaying tactics to extract further concessions. Jinnah would not budge and said, 'What must be, must be.' However, he agreed later that he would try his best to persuade the Muslim League Council to accept the plan.[39] This meant that if the League Council had decided to reject the plan, it would have placed the Muslim League leader in an extremely embarrassing position in the sense that they would have let him down after he had indicated to the Viceroy that in all probability he would be able to persuade the Council.

---

[38] *The Indian Annual Register 1942*, Vol. I, Calcutta, pp. 320–1.

[39] Alan Campbell-Johnson, *Mission With Mountbatten*, London: Robert Hale, 1952, pp. 102–3.

Thus, it could be said that the Muslim League Constitution conferred enormous powers on the Central organs to supervise, control and regulate the Provincial Muslim Leagues. But over and above the Central organs stood the august and awe-inspiring personality of the Great Leader, who controlled the Central organs. The Working Committee was his creature. He more or less nominated the Central Parliamentary Board. The Committee of Action carried out his wishes and the Council, with some minor protests here and there, put a stamp of its formal approval on his behests. The great mystery was not that he had so much power but that he had not been corrupted by such excessive power.

II. METHOD AND MACHINERY OF PROPAGANDA

It has been shown already how the All-India Muslim League built up an elaborate mechanism to control the activities of the various Provincial Leagues. It has also been seen how the various Provincial Leagues were asked to model themselves on the pattern of the Central organization. This meant that there was a chain of command extending right from the President and his Working Committee or the Committee of Action to a Primary League in a Province. How this system operated at the Provincial level may be illustrated from a constitution like that of the Bombay Provincial Muslim League. It was stated that one of the main duties of the Provincial Muslim League was to 'supervise and control the work of the District and Primary Muslim Leagues and ensure that the instructions, policy and programme of the All-India Muslim League are carried out.' Similarly, a District Muslim League had to carry out the instructions received from time to time from the Provincial Muslim League and supervise and control the work of the Primary Muslim Leagues within its District. Finally, this was rounded off by the provision that a Primary Muslim League should carry out the instructions issued by the District Muslim League and was subject to its general supervision and control.[40]

It was obvious that the Muslim League had been doing considerable propaganda work to expand its membership and increase its popularity. But before 1940, its programme could have

---

[40] *The Constitution and Rules of the Bombay Provincial Muslim League*, op. cit. See Articles 63, 43, and 31.

been presented only in negative terms, the main plank in the programme being an outright denunciation of alleged persecutions of Muslims under the Provincial Congress Governments. After the Lahore Resolution of March 1940, it was imperative that the Muslim League should try to rally support for the idea of Pakistan by explaining what benefits would accrue to Muslims if it were achieved. But there was no clear indication, at least through the official resolutions passed during 1940–2, whether the League was strenuously engaged in popularizing the idea of Pakistan. It was during March-April 1943, that one saw for the first time that the League was thinking of embarking on an organized mass campaign through methods like sending out missions of speakers and propagandists and producing literature for the propagation of its objectives. However, according to the official records, the resolution embodying these proposals was referred to the Subjects Committee of the thirtieth annual session of the League held at Delhi in April 1943.[41] But it was never put forward and passed in the annual sessions. Therefore, one has to rely on the sort of propaganda that emerged in the form of speeches made by League leaders as well as the campaigns conducted by students and the *ulama* and also on the publicity of the League programme through the pro-League newspapers and the official literature.

What exactly was the problem involved in carrying out the League propaganda to popularize the idea of Pakistan? The League's propaganda had to be organized on two fronts. Muslims in Hindu majority Provinces had to be reassured that Pakistan would not necessarily result in their isolation and helplessness under Hindu domination. The League did not want a cleavage between the Muslims in Hindu majority Provinces and the Muslims of Pakistan Provinces, for the Quaid-i-Azam needed all his 'hundred million Musalmans' to fight against both the Congress and the British. But the sort of response that the Muslim League had achieved in the Muslim majority Provinces, particularly in the Punjab and the Frontier, was not very reassuring. The Muslim League did not obtain a majority in the Frontier even during the 1945 elections. It was after a good deal of hard work and per-severance that public opinion turned in the League's favour in

---

[41] See *Resolutions of the All India Muslim League from April 1942 to May 1943*, Delhi: All India Muslim League, n.d., pp. 23–24 and 27–28.

the Frontier. Similarly, the Punjab, which was described by Jinnah as the 'corner-stone of Pakistan', was by no means a solid Muslim League stronghold. In the Delhi session, addressing the Punjab delegates, Jinnah appealed, '...Please substitute love for Islam and your nation, in place of sectional interests, jealousy, tribal notions and selfishness.'

It was no doubt true that the Quaid-i-Azam was an indispensable asset of the League. He had unmistakably become, as his admirers said, a symbol of Muslim regeneration. He often appeared in public meetings in his *sherwani*, and, if the legends that have grown around him are to be believed, the Quaid-i-Azam frowned on any Muslim Leaguer attending the Council or public meetings in Western clothes. He was remote and aloof and often gave the impression of being arrogant and autocratic, but it seemed that with all his Western training and temperament, he understood his people extremely well. He knew that the ultimate focus of loyalty of an overwhelming majority of Muslims was Islam. Many of the Muslim League lawyers and landowners were by no means devout Muslims. Similarly, a great majority of the rural masses did not practise the tenets of Islam strictly. They had been influenced by their Hindu environment with its customs and traditions. Nevertheless, all these classes had in their minds a vague feeling that they would all become better Muslims once a Muslim State was established. The Quaid-i-Azam also knew that Pakistan could not be achieved unless his followers, particularly in the countryside, were assured that an Islamic form of government based on the laws of the *Qur'an* and the *Shariat* would be established in Pakistan. Without the help and intervention of the Pir of Manki Sharif, the Muslim League could not have built up its position in the Frontier and ultimately won the referendum in that Province. It seemed that the Pir Sahib demanded an assurance from Jinnah before he would offer his cooperation. In a letter to the Pir of Manki Sharif, the League leader clearly stated in November 1945: 'It is needless to emphasize that the Constituent Assembly which would be predominantly Muslim in its composition would be able to enact laws for Muslims, not inconsistent with the *Shariat* laws and the Muslims will no longer be obliged to abide by the Un-Islamic laws.'[42]

---

[42] *Constituent Assembly of Pakistan Debates,* 9 March 1949, Vol. V, No. 3, p. 46.

In the League meetings that the Quaid-i-Azam addressed, particularly in the Muslim majority areas, Islam with its symbols and slogans figured very prominently in all his speeches. Addressing the Pathans, he said:

> Do you want Pakistan or not? (shouts of Allah-o-Akbar) (God is great). Well, if you want Pakistan, vote for the League candidates.
>
> If we fail to realize our duty today you will be reduced to the status of Sudras (low castes) and Islam will be vanquished from India.
>
> I shall never allow Muslims to be slaves of Hindus. (Allah-o-Akbar.)[43]

With all his surging popularity, there were several limitations that the Quaid-i-Azam suffered from. He did not have a strong constitution and could not stand the dust and din of Muslim League campaigns in the countryside. The League also did not want to tax his energy too much because he was irreplaceable at the summit in the League's negotiations with the Congress and the British. He did not speak Urdu fluently and as a result of increasing mass participation in League meetings, particularly in the annual sessions, his speeches had to be translated, often by that gifted orator, Nawab Bahadur Yar Jung from Hyderabad (Deccan), President of the All-India States Muslim League. Further, the opponents of the League were also busy accusing the League leaders and particularly the Quaid-i-Azam of hypocrisy in their professions of loyalty to Islam and the *Shariat*. Thus, even, the *Jama'at-i-Islami* leader, Maulana Maudoodi, who could not be accused of pro-Congress sympathies, wrote: 'From the League's Quaid-i-Azam down to the humblest leader, there was no one who could be credited with an Islamic outlook and who looked at the various problems from an Islamic point of view.'[44] In subsequent years, the denunciations became even more bitter. Thus, Maulana Husain Ahmad, President of the *Jamiyat al Ulama-i-Hind*, gave a *fatwa* in October 1945, forbidding Muslims from joining the Muslim League on the grounds that such an action was contrary to the dictates of Islam. He also labelled the Quaid-i-Azam as 'Kafir-i-Azam' (the great heathen).[45]

---

[43] Jamil-ud-Din Ahmad, ed., op. cit., Vol. II, pp. 240, 241 and 243.

[44] Cited in Munshi Abdur Rahman Khan, *Tamir-i-Pakistan aur Ulama-i-Rabbani*, Multan: Idarah Nashar Al-Maarif, 1956, p. 122.

[45] Cited in Maulana Shabbir Ahmad Osmani, *Khutbat-i-Osmani*, Lahore: n.d., p. 48. Jinnah was also attacked on the charge that he had amended

The Muslim League relied quite heavily in its campaign among the masses both in the rural and urban areas upon the voluntary efforts of students, particularly from the Aligarh Muslim University. These students would often go to the remotest villages armed with the League's dialectics to do propaganda work. Later, the All-India Muslim Students Federation was formed which was very active in the Punjab. Particularly during the summer vacations, the Muslim students carried on extensive rural propaganda in the Punjab and were successful in enlisting support for the Muslim League. In 1942, they campaigned against some of the prominent Unionist Party members for having cooperated with the British war effort by joining the National Defence Council in defiance of the League policy. Their contributions to the general elections in 1945–6 were even more valuable. According to one source, over a thousand young Muslim students from Aligarh were sent particularly to Provinces like the Punjab and Sind, after having been trained at a centre for electioneering work. Jinnah was in touch with the leaders of these students and they constantly kept him informed of the developments in the election campaign.[46]

The Muslim League also relied very heavily on the services of its highly gifted orators like Nawab Bahadur Yar Jung and Maulana Zafar Ali Khan. Particularly Bahadur Yar Jung during the years 1940–4 rendered yeoman services in carrying the League message to the remotest corners of the Punjab and the Frontier. It is said that he learned Pushtu so well that he could speak it fluently. He was responsible for making the first dent in the Frontier which was considered as a Congress stronghold

---

radically the *Shariat* Bill brought before the Legislative Assembly. Maulana Sayyid Husain Ahmad Madani, *Khutba-i-Sadarat Fourteenth Annual Session of the Jamiyat al Ulama-i-Hind*, Delhi, 1945, pp. 46–47. It may be pointed out that the charge that Jinnah took a stand against the *Shariat* Bill or altered its spirit by his amendment was not true. Jinnah pointed out that the Bill could not abolish the existing law and therefore should be designed specifically to remove those usages and customs which were being enforced by the courts. Even though it might seem that his amendment restricted the scope of the Bill, yet it covered a wide field. *The Legislative Assembly Debates, Vol. V,* 1937, Delhi, pp. 1831–3 and 1842.

[46] Jamil-ud-Din Ahmad, *Glimpses of Quaid-i-Azam,* Karachi: 1960, pp. 20–22.

because of Abdul Ghaffar Khan's influence.[47] But his chief forte was his oratorical power in Urdu which could hold even the most critical audiences in Lucknow and Delhi spell-bound. It is difficult to recapture in translation the magnificent orations of this truly remarkable man.[48]

In addition to all this, the Muslim League had built up a very strong press, particularly in Urdu. Delhi had *Anjam*, *Jung*, and *Manshoor* in Urdu and *Dawn* in English. Lahore produced *Inqilab*, *Nawa-i-Waqt*, *Paisa Akhbar* and *Zamindar* in Urdu. Lucknow had its *Hamdam*. Calcutta produced *Asre-Jadid* in Urdu, *Azad* in Bengali, and *Star of India* in English. There were many others besides these prominent newspapers. There were also Gujarati pro-Muslim League newspapers. There were Nationalist or pro-Congress newspapers like the *Al-Jamiat* from Delhi and *Madina* from Bijnor. But in most of the Provinces, particularly during the later years, the Muslim League newspapers far exceeded those that were pro-Congress and also had a much greater circulation.

The author has been unsparing in Chapter II in showing how Hindu newspapers, novels, and other publications heralded Hindu revivalism and fanned the flames of Hindu-Muslim conflict towards the end of the nineteenth and the beginning of the twentieth century. Now the Muslims were in an aggressively bitter mood. The *Pirpur Report*, which catalogued the alleged Congress injustices and persecutions towards Muslims has already been referred to in an earlier chapter. The story that the *Pirpur Report* had begun was carried forward and presented with even more lurid and gruesome details of Congress oppression. Thirty-two articles were published in *Dawn* and *Manshoor* under the series entitled *It Shall Never Happen Again*. They described how Muslims were forbidden to eat beef, their prayer meetings and mosques disturbed and sometimes attacked and desecrated, and how Muslims suffered a much heavier toll of life and property in the riots that took place during the two and a half years of Congress administration.

Was it strange, then, that tragedy followed, tragedy and blood flowed instead of the milk of human kindness? Was it strange that Terror

---

[47] Ghulam Muhammad, *Quaid-i-Millat*, Hyderabad, Deccan: Nafis Academy, 1947, p. 122.

[48] For extracts from his original Urdu speeches, see ibid., pp. 220–7.

stalked the countryside and rendered the helpless outnumbered few despairing and desperate?

Here and there the worm did turn and not all the conflicts were one-sided. But so indeed could the German historian accuse the Poles for turning upon the aggressive and death-dealing Nazi hordes![49]

This could perhaps be characterized as an exaggerated sense of outrage at some of the wrongs that Muslims had suffered. In Muslim majority Provinces like Bengal there was a note of aggressive confidence in the attitude of Muslims. A poem recited at a Muslim League Conference in the district of Mymensingh in March 1941, and published later in the Bengali daily, *Azad*, indicated this attitude.

> The oppressed remain silent by seeing the hypocrisy
> Of the idolatrous Hindus—oh death-like eddy!
> O victorious soldiers; march forward on our
> Religious pilgrimage to the Kaaba under the banner of
>   The League....

> We want Pakistan, a proper division
> If it cannot be achieved by words, Muslims
> Are not afraid to use swords and spears.

> Where are the Muslim youths? We shall attain
> The desire of their hearts by tying down the wild tiger.
> Come quickly—break down Somnath....[50]

Role of the Pirs and Ulama

Sir Malcolm Darling, who had spent nearly all his working life in intimate contact with the peasants of the Punjab, once wrote:

> The peasantry, almost to a man, confess themselves the servants of the one true God and of Muhammad his Prophet, but in actual fact they are the servants of landlord, money-lender, and pir. All the way down the Indus from far Hazara in the north to Sind in the south these three dominate men's fortunes; and though they are found in greater or less degree all over the province, nowhere are they so powerful.[51]

---

[49] *It Shall Never Happen Again*, Delhi: All India Muslim League, 1946, p. 3.
[50] *The Indian Annual Register 1941*, Vol. I, Calcutta, pp. 127–8.
[51] M. L. Darling, *Rusticus Loquitur*, London: Oxford University Press, p. 214.

The Muslim League could justifiably say that since they were engaged in the struggle for the establishment of Pakistan, they were entitled to enlist all important and useful support they could muster for the achievement of their goal. Thus, in 1946, a *Masha'ikh Committee*, consisting of eminent *pirs* and *masha'ikh* was appointed. It included religious leaders like Pir Sahib of Manki Sharif, Pir Jama't Ali Shah, Khwaja Nazimuddin of Taunsa Sharif, Makhdum Raza Shah of Multan, etc.[52] But included in this Committee were political leaders with dubious pretentions to piety. '...Khan Iftikhar Husain Khan of Mamdot was described as Pir Mamdot Sharif, Sirdar Shaukat Hayat Khan as Sajjada Nashin of Wah Sharif, Malik Feroz Khan Noon of Darbar Sargodha Sharif and Nawab Muhammad Hayat Qureshi as Sajjada Nashin of Sargodha Sharif....'[53] Some of the League leaders, when interviewed by the author, denied completely the above allegation that political leaders like Mamdot, Noon and Shaukat Hyat were presented as *pirs* before the masses to win their votes during the elections. However, the League in defence could argue that the stakes were high and the campaign of abuse and slander that its opponents had resorted to justified such methods.

How hard-pressed the League was to obtain all available support during the elections was indicated by the fact that several prominent *ulama* had been persuaded to campaign on behalf of the League. A highly respected leader like Maulana Shabbir Ahmad Osmani lent his whole-hearted support to the Muslim League election campaign. He defended the Quaid-i-Azam against the attacks of other *ulama* and religious leaders and pointed out that whatever might be alleged about the landlords, the Nawabs and other titled gentry in the League, there was not a shadow of doubt that Jinnah's integrity was irreproachable. He exhorted the Muslims to vote for the Muslim League because it was fighting for the establishment of a Muslim State in which there would be a possibility of establishing a government based on Islamic law and traditions. The opponents of the League were enemies of Islam and the true interests of Muslims. '...Any man who gives his vote to the opponents of the Muslim League,

---

[52] *Report of the Court of Inquiry Constituted Under Punjab Act II of 1954 to Enquire into the Punjab Disturbances of 1953*, Lahore, 1954, p. 255.
[53] Ibid.

must think of the ultimate consequences of his action in terms of the interests of his nation and the answers that he would be called upon to produce on the Day of Judgement.'[54] As regards the charges that the Muslim League leaders, not being devout Muslims, were not likely to work for the establishment of an Islamic Government in Pakistan, Maulana Osmani said that if these charges were true, it was all the more important that all sincere and God-fearing Muslims should join the League in order to transform its character. Not being a politician, he did not realize that the powerful Westernized groups inside the League would not allow the *ulama* or other religious groups to change its ideology, for such a change would result in their group losing power in the League. Maulana Osmani's technique was to compare present Muslim politics with the political conditions of Muslims during the Prophet's time. This was a usual method with the *ulama*. Dealing with the argument that after the formation of Pakistan, Muslims in India would live under the domination of a hostile Hindu Government, he pointed out that the Prophet had migrated from Mecca to establish an Islamic State in Medina and had left behind infirm and old Muslims in Mecca. In the same manner, he pleaded that the thirty million Indian Muslims should not stand in the way of the welfare and happiness of seventy million Muslims in Pakistan. If Pakistan were not established, the result would be that all the hundred million Muslims would have to live under a Hindu Government.[55] Liaquat himself in a letter addressed to Maulana Zafar Ahmad Osmani acknowledged the great contribution that the *ulama* had made in the Central Legislative Assembly elections and particularly for their support to him in his constituency.[56]

Similarly, the *ulama* rendered great services to the League in the Provincial elections of Sind, the Punjab and the Frontier. Again, how heavily was the League drawing on their support was indicated by their participation in the Sylhet referendum as well as that of the Frontier during June-July 1947. According to

[54] Shabbir Ahmad Osmani, op. cit. See his Presidential Address at the Muslim League Conference at Meerut, p. 11.

[55] Ibid. See Part I, pp. 46–47. Muslim League leaders often assumed that the total population of Muslims in India was 100 million when according to the 1941 census it was only 94.4 million. In 1944–5, with the net population increase, it might have reached the figure of 97.5 million.

[56] Munshi Abdur Rahman Khan, op. cit., pp. 134–5.

Maulana Zafar Ahmad Osmani, it was Jinnah himself who requested the *ulama* to help the League in these campaigns. Maulana Zafar Ahmad Osmani went to Sylhet and Maulana Shabbir Ahmad Osmani was assigned the Frontier referendum. Both in Sylhet and in the Frontier religion played the most important role. Muslim voters in Sylhet were told that anyone who voted for Sylhet to stay in Assam was an 'unbeliever'.[57] As regards the Frontier, as pointed out earlier, the Muslim League could not have won the referendum without the intervention of the Pir of Manki Sharif and the help accorded to it by the *ulama* like Maulana Shabbir Ahmad Osmani and Maulana Abdul Sattar Khan Niazi. The sort of logic that these leaders used was best summarized in one of the speeches of Maulana Abdul Sattar Khan Niazi.

> We have got two alternatives before us, whether to join or rather accept the slavery of Bania Brahman Raj in Hindustan or join the Muslim fraternity, the federation of Muslim provinces. Every Pathan takes it as an insult for him to prostrate before Hindu Raj and will gladly sit with his brethren in Islam in Pakistan Constituent Assembly. A Pathan is a Muslim first and a Muslim last.[58]

Had the Muslim League undergone a metamorphosis as compared to the period when Jinnah presented his Fourteen Points as amendments to the Nehru Report in December 1928? During those days he used to argue in terms of percentages of Muslim seats in the Legislatures, cultural and religious safeguards for the minorities and the retention of separate electorates if Sind and the Frontier were not constituted as separate Provinces. Even as late as 1938, he was taking credit for having 'removed the unwholesome influence and fear of a certain section who used to pass off as Maulanas and Moulavis.'[59] But the realities of Muslim politics during the years 1945–7 were such that the assistance of *Maulanas* had been deliberately sought. In this way it could be said that the Muslim League had become much more representative of the Muslim people than it had been during the previous decades. But the price it paid for this metamorphosis was that it had become much more of a heterogeneous organization.

---

[57] Sir Francis Tuker, *While Memory Serves*, London: Cassell, 1950, p. 345.
[58] *Dawn*, Delhi, 2 July 1947, p. 8.
[59] *The Indian Annual Register 1938*, Vol. I, op. cit., p. 382.

As long as the crusading spirit was there and the objective still unattained, the landlord and the peasant or the *pir* and the professor or the landlord and the lawyer were willing to work together. The bond of Islam had united them against the fears of Hindu domination. But even during the thick of the battle some people had started asking the fundamental question: What role would Islam play in purifying Muslim society of corruption, social inequality, superstition and ignorance? Islam had been used to fight against the Hindus. Would it be used to fight against the landlords, the *pirs*, and the *mullahs?* Those who asked such questions were either told that the time was not appropriate or that they had raised them to pursue partisan interests.

III. GROUPS AND FACTIONS IN THE LEAGUE

It has already been suggested that the Muslim League had become a heterogeneous organization drawing its support from different classes and groups but united under one leader with Pakistan as its goal. The sense of unity arising largely from the goal it pursued and the leadership it had was strong enough to keep together classes and groups whose interests in normal circumstances would have been opposed to one another. First of all, particularly after the Muslim League pledged itself to the goal of Pakistan, there was a feeling of uneasiness, sometimes bordering on resentment, among the leaders of the Muslim majority Provinces that the Muslim League was dominated by leaders from the Muslim minority Provinces. In the Council of the All-India Muslim League for the year 1942, out of a total membership of 503, there were 245 members from the Muslim minority Provinces. Even though Muslims in the Muslim majority Provinces outnumbered those in the Muslim minority Provinces, there were only 258 members from the Muslim majority Provinces in the Council.[60] The balance was even more tilted in favour of the minority Provinces in the far more powerful organ of the League, the Working Committee. During 1945–7 there were only 10 members from the Muslim majority Provinces in a Working Committee of 23 members (including the President and the Secretary).

It has often been remarked that the Muslim League was dominated by landowners and the titled gentry. Congress leaders

---

[60] *List of the Members of the Council of the All India Muslim League 1942,* Delhi: n.d. The figures have been worked out from this list.

like Nehru often labelled the League as a reactionary organization, largely under the influence of Nawabs and Nawabzadas from the Punjab and the United Provinces. The Secretary of the Muslim League was Nawabzada Liaquat Ali Khan, a big landowner from the United Provinces. Nawab Ismail Khan, another big landowner from the United Provinces, was President of the U.P. Provincial Muslim League and also Chairman of the Committee of Action of the All-India Muslim League. Nawab of Mamdot was President of the Punjab Provincial Muslim League. There was also a thin sprinkling of knights in the Muslim League. Sir Muhammad Saadullah was President of the Assam Provincial Muslim League and had also been Premier of Assam several times. Similarly, Sir Abdoola Haroon had been President of the Sind Provincial Muslim League until his death in 1943. In addition, there were several knights who were Muslim League members in the Central Legislative Assembly.

Landlords represented the largest single group in the Muslim League Council. Out of a total membership of 503 members, there were as many as 163 landlords. Punjab contributed the largest share of 51, followed by the United Provinces and Bengal. Proportionately, Sind's share was the highest in the sense that out of 25 members in the Council, 15 were landlords.[61] Bengal did not have many big landlords like Tiwana, Daultana, Mamdot and Leghari from Punjab or like the Talpurs from Sind.

The next largest group in the Council was that of lawyers who were about 145 in number.[62] Commercial classes like merchants, bankers and industrialists were increasing, but they were far from influential in terms of numbers in the Council. The Provinces of Bombay and Bengal, because of the two commercial centres, Bombay and Calcutta, contributed a substantial share. But a good number of army and government contractors and general merchants were to be found in the Punjab, Delhi and the U. P. groups. It may be pointed out that Jinnah, besides being a

[61] Ibid. One can only be approximately correct in these figures because the particulars regarding the profession of each Councillor are not given in every case. Therefore, the author had to draw on the information given to him by former office-bearers and members of the Working Committee of the All-India Muslim League.

[62] Ibid. A few of the Councillors who had legal qualifications and are therefore listed as lawyers, were not practising lawyers. Again these figures are approximately correct.

Gujarati by origin, had a reputation for complete honesty and was therefore trusted by the prosperous trading Gujarati and Bombay communities like the Memons, the Khojas, and the Bohras. He often addressed meetings of Memon merchants and Chambers of Commerce and they were his principal supporters. A large number of Memon merchants were retailers and they often requested the Muslim League leaders not to publicize their contributions because they were afraid that the Hindu wholesalers would penalize them for their support to the League. The financial contributions of Muslim majority Provinces were not substantial. Even during the elections of 1945–6 substantial sums of money were contributed by the merchants and industrialists of Bombay and Calcutta to the League election campaign in the Muslim majority Provinces.[63]

As the Muslim League leaders, particularly the young intelligentsia, came increasingly in contact with the masses, they were shocked by the poverty and social inequalities that stared them in the face wherever they went in the countryside. They had also been influenced in their universities by socialistic ideas. Out of all this was born that impatient idealism which one noticed in the annual sessions of the Muslim League, in some of the manifestos that were published during the Provincial elections of 1945–6, and also in the conflicts between progressives and conservatives that smouldered in Provinces like Sind, the Punjab and Bengal. Nawab Bahadur Yar Jung, speaking at the Karachi session in December 1943, declared that he was a Communist 'if Communism means to efface poverty and class distinctions and to provide bread and clothing to the poor.' He qualified this remark by saying that he did not draw his inspiration from Karl Marx, who denied the existence of God. He hoped that the Muslim League Planning Committee would produce an economic plan based on Qur'anic justice. Addressing the Quaid-i-Azam, he said, 'We have understood Pakistan in this light. If your Pakistan is not such we do not want it.'[64] The manifesto of the Punjab

---

[63] According to information made available to the author, the total funds collected by the League were about Rs 6.7 million of which 3.6 million were for the Bihar Relief Fund, 2.4 for the Election Fund and Rs 700,000 for the Muslim League Fund.

[64] Abdul Hamid, ed., *Thirty-first Session of the All India Muslim League (Karachi) December 1943*, Lahore: The Eastern Times Book Depot, 1944, p. 111.

Provincial Muslim League declared that there should be nationalization of key industries and banks beginning with immediate nationalization of all public utility services, public control of private industry, a ceiling placed on land holdings, and an equalization of the burden of taxation involving the imposition of additional taxes on large landowners. The manifesto was adopted unanimously by the Working Committee of the Provincial Muslim League and published by an extreme left-wing leader, Danyal Latifi.[65] Similarly, it was reported that Abul Hashim, the young socialist General Secretary of the Bengal Provincial Muslim League, was waging a battle royal inside the Bengal Provincial League against the group led by the Nawab of Dacca and Khwaja Nazimuddin and probably supported by Muslim merchants and industrialists. G. M. Sayed, President of the Sind Provincial Muslim League during 1943–5, was also indignant that the Muslim League High Command constantly supported those whom he considered reactionaries like Sir Ghulam Hussain Hidayatullah. He had also seen and been moved by the destitution and squalor in which the *haris* of Sind lived, and his bitter outburst was:

> Do not forget that Islamic society actually in existence is that in which religious head is an ignorant Mulla, spiritual leader an immoral Pir, political guide a power intoxicated feudal lord and whose helpless members are subjected to all the wordly forces of money and influence. If the really important question about the abolition of Jagirdari and Zamindari system crops up or the prohibition of intoxicants becomes the issue of the day, what would not a rich Jagirdar or an aristocratic member of a sophisticated club do to use his influence, as also that of the Mulla and the Pir, to resist this threat to what is essentially an immoral and un-Islamic cause?[66]

Jinnah himself had thundered against the exploitation of the common people by landlords and capitalists. 'There are millions and millions of our people who hardly get one meal a day. Is this civilization? Is this the aim of Pakistan? ...If that is the idea of Pakistan I would not have it.'[67] He had encouraged men like

---

[65] *Manifesto of the Punjab Provincial Muslim League 1944*, Delhi: Danyal Latifi, pp. 13–14, 19 and 24.

[66] G. M. Sayed, op. cit., p. 216.

[67] Jamil-ud-Din Ahmad, ed., Vol. I, op. cit., p. 507.

Abul Hashim and G. M. Sayed to use their crusading spirit for organizing the Muslim masses under the League flag. He had counselled them to be patient and fight their battles inside the League with a view to transforming it. But the realities of Muslim politics forced even a domineering personality like Jinnah to work with the existing powerful social forces like the landowners and the new industrial magnates. Jinnah knew that the Muslim masses were too ignorant to be fully aware of their interests and too content to follow their *pirs* and landlords. The simmering of ideas that the activities and speeches of the fiery young idealists had produced was a phenomenon confined only to the top. It never went below the Provincial Working Committee or the Provincial Council. Thus Jinnah could not afford to antagonize the influential groups only to satisfy the wishes of the angry young men of the League. Referring to the charge that the League was against the *zamindars*, he said in Punjab, 'The League is not against any interests among the Muslims.'[68]

The Muslim League was sometimes faced with Provincial conflicts. Jinnah's technique was to avoid all controversial issues which might divide Muslims into conflicting Provincial groups. Thus in the Lucknow session of the Muslim League in 1937 a resolution was brought forward recommending that Urdu should be made the *lingua franca* of Muslim India. In addition to that, the resolution called upon the All-India Muslim League to make Urdu its official language. Bengali delegates were vehemently opposed to the idea of the Muslim League adopting Urdu as its official language. They pointed out that Muslims of Bengal constituted more than a third of the total Muslim population of India and if Urdu were adopted as an official language, it would hamper the propaganda work of the Muslim League among Bengali Muslims. Jinnah, with characteristic political correctness, suggested that he was not in favour of the resolution in its present form. The resolution as adopted read that the annual session only recommended to the All-India Muslim League, 'to make all efforts possible' to make Urdu the *lingua franca* of the Muslim League.[69] There were other signs which suggested that there might be a likelihood in the future of the Bengali Muslims not getting along with the Urdu-speaking Muslims of other areas.

[68] Jamil-ud-Din Ahmad, Vol. II, op. cit., p. 46.
[69] *The Pioneer*, Lucknow, 17 October 1937.

It has already been seen how the phrase 'Independent States' of the Lahore Resolution created confusion and encouraged some of the Bengali Muslim leaders to demand a separate and independent Muslim State of Bengal. There were other examples which indicated that this conflict was smouldering. Speaking on the Calcutta Municipal (Amendment) Bill, 1939, which sought to introduce separate electorates in the Calcutta municipal elections, Abu Husain Sarkar, a Congressman at that time and who later became Chief Minister of East Pakistan during 1955–6, expressed his bitterness as follows:

> Under the false cry of representing Muslim interest in the Calcutta Corporation, the non-Bengali elements are trying to perpetuate their hold in Calcutta, and that is also in the premier self-governing institution in Bengal. Unfortunately, Sir, the Urdu-speaking non Bengalis, the Iranis, the Suhrawardys, the Siddiquis, the Adamjis and the Currimbhoys—are in majority in Muslim Calcutta. Most of them are wholesale agents for selling cheap German, Japanese and Italian goods.[70]

However, all this went unnoticed. The League leaders knew that these differences and debates touched only the upper fringe of the Muslim community. The masses in their devotion to Islam were content to follow the call of the Quaid-i-Azam. As for the Quaid, the need of the hour was unity. He warned that the enemy was at the gate and Muslims should not dissipate their energies in doctrinal differences or Provincial wranglings.

IV. MUSLIM LEAGUE AND PARLIAMENTARY GOVERNMENT

The Muslim League campaign before 1940 was that Islam was in danger and therefore all Muslims should join the Muslim League which was fighting for the preservation of Muslim religion and culture. After 1940, its campaign was that in Pakistan lay the future glory of Islam and therefore all Muslims should support the demand for Pakistan. In either case, opposition was ruled out as anti-national. Any Muslim who opposed the Muslim League was an enemy of Islam. Thus, the Muslim League Party was not a party in the normal sense of the term. It was a movement which represented the whole nation. And its leader himself declared many times that anyone who acted

---

[70] *Bengal Legislative Assembly Proceedings*, Vol. LIV, Fifth session, 1939, pp. 29–30.

against the interests of the Muslim League was a quisling or a traitor.

When Jinnah reorganized the Muslim League during 1935–7, he knew that in the struggle for power that was taking place in India, Muslims would not amount to anything unless they organized themselves through a powerful political organization. 'If Wardha makes any decision and issues orders tomorrow, millions of Hindus will follow and obey. I ask you, suppose the Muslim League were to issue any order, what will happen to it?'[71] Thus, Jinnah's conception of a political organization was that it was like an army in which once orders were given by the High Command, they should be carried out.

For the Muslim League, parliamentary democracy was not an ideal but only an instrument through which it was trying to achieve its major objective. The Muslim League had come into being prior to most of the Legislatures and therefore the primary focus of loyalty was not to the Parliament or a parliamentary form of government but to the Muslim League. No matter who stood on the ticket of the Muslim League, 'we should support League candidate even though he may be lamp-post'.[72]

During the years the League was busy enlisting mass support, it did not have much of a programme but relied heavily on simple slogans. These slogans served their purpose in attracting thousands of Muslims to the League fold. But this intellectual vacuity, combined with the cult of leadership, infected the leaders at the top as well. The result was that particularly whenever, they were called upon to assume office, not being united by any concrete programme or ideology, the League leaders soon fell a prey to squabbling and petty intrigues. In addition to this, the majority that the Muslims had in the Provincial Assemblies of Bengal and the Punjab was very slender. In Bengal, even though Muslims were 54.6 per cent of the Provincial population, they had only 47.6 per cent of the total seats in the Legislative Assembly. In the Punjab, their population was slightly over 55 per cent but they had only 49 per cent of the seats in the Legislative Assembly. The result was that the Muslim League by itself could not possibly produce a majority in either of the Assemblies. It had to co-operate with the other parties. Since the Muslim League

---

[71] Jamil-ud-Din Ahmad, ed., Vol. I, op. cit., p. 44.
[72] Jamil-ud-Din Ahmad, ed., Vol. II, op. cit., p. 247.

was committed to pursuing primarily Muslim interests, non-Muslim parties or representatives were reluctant to cooperate with it. This explains why the Unionist Party in the Punjab was not willing to merge itself completely in the Muslim League organization. In Bengal, the Muslim League managed to form Governments largely because of the support it received from the Europeans.

In Bengal, though Muslims were in a slight majority, they were extremely backward as compared with the Hindus. In Government offices, professions and trade, they were outnumbered by Hindus. East Bengal, where they were in a considerable majority, was the backward hinterland of Calcutta where the Muslim peasants lived under the domination of Hindu landlords, lawyers and merchants. In many cities of East Bengal, Hindus were in the majority. This was the state of affairs when Fazl-ul-Huq assumed office as Premier in 1937, and the conditions had not altered very much when Partition came in 1947.

After the Provincial elections of 1937, Fazl-ul-Huq, the leader of the Proja Party (Peasants), formed a coalition Ministry with the support of the Muslim League, the Scheduled Caste Party, and a small group of Independent or non-Congress Caste Hindus. He also received support from the European group. In the Lucknow session of the Muslim League in 1937, he announced, along with the Premiers of the Punjab and Assam, that he would advise all the Muslim members in his coalition Party to join the Muslim League. He asserted that his Ministry was determined to support the Muslim cause and that he and his Govermnent would not remain silent spectators if Muslims in Hindu majority Provinces were persecuted. It may also be recalled that it was Fazl-ul-Huq who moved the Lahore Resolution in March 1940, in the League session at Lahore. In 1941, he had differences with Jinnah and the League Working Committee over the issue of his joining the National Defence Council. He agreed to resign from the National Defence Council but protested against Muslim League interference in Bengal politics. This brought about differences between himself and his Muslim League colleagues and demonstrations against him in Calcutta. Later, towards the end of 1941, Fazl-ul-Huq joined a new 'Progressive Coalition Party' and refused to join the Muslim League Party in the Legislative Assembly. He was expelled from the

Muslim League, but he retaliated by forming a new Ministry with the support of Hindu groups in the Assembly. The Premier, who not too long ago was a champion of Muslim separatism, had now agreed to work with Dr Shyama Prasad Mookerjee, a Hindu Mahasabha leader of Bengal. This was a great political mistake that Fazl-ul-Huq had made. Even though he was a fiery Bengali orator and an extremely popular figure among the Muslim masses in Bengal, Jinnah turned the full force of Muslim public opinion against him for having cooperated with the Hindus. The Muslim League won all the seven by-elections that were held after 1938. By 1942, it was clear that Fazl-ul-Huq could not work with his Hindu colleagues and particularly Dr Shyama Prasad Mookerjee, who was determined to follow a very pro-Hindu course in politics. Fazl-ul-Huq's Ministry continued until the end of March 1943. In April 1943, Khwaja Nazimuddin, leader of the Muslim League Parliamentary Party in the Bengal Legislative Assembly, was invited by the Governor to form a Ministry.

Khwaja Nazimuddin was an extremely affable man and completely loyal to the Quaid-i-Azam. It was well known that he was weak, indecisive and depended entirely on the counsels of his shrewd brother, Khwaja Shahabuddin. In 1943 his Ministry was faced with the disastrous Bengal famine. Distribution of food was a trade which was entirely in the hands of Hindus. When war and famine conditions of 1943 disrupted the normal channels of trade, the Provincial Government intervened to control the distribution of food through Government-appointed agents. The Muslim League Ministry thought that this was a great opportunity to establish their supporters and other Muslim traders in the lucrative business of distributing food involving a capital of millions of rupees. The Government not only supplied the capital but also met the losses incurred by the traders in the initial stages. Hindu Members in the Assembly accused H. S. Suhrawardy, the Minister for Civil Supplies, of corruption and favouritism towards members of his community. The Ministry was also charged for having extended its patronage to the Ispahani Company. Suhrawardy's defence was that he was perfectly justified in redressing the balance in distributive trade in favour of the Muslim community because even though Muslims were in a majority in the Province, Muslim traders had been completely kept out of the distributive trade. The Woodhead Commission, however, pointed out that in an emergency like the Bengal famine, 'administrative action should not be delayed by attempts to observe rules fixing communal ratios'.[73] However, the result was that the Hindu traders and professional classes in Bengal had become bitterly opposed to the Nazimuddin Ministry.

In March 1945, there suddenly occurred an acute cloth shortage in the city. As the prices rose, cloth began to disappear from the shops to reappear again at phenomenal prices from under the counter. The Ministry got alarmed because of the processions and demonstrations organized by the Communist Party in Calcutta. They clamped severe controls on the cloth trade and the result was that the powerful cloth merchants of Calcutta turned against the Ministry. Members started changing sides. At that time the Budget Demands were being considered by the Assembly. On 29 March, Demand for Agriculture was rejected by the House by 106 votes to 97. On the day this happened, there was a considerable uproar and disorder in the House. When the Speaker put the Demand under Agriculture to vote, Suhrawardy and other Government supporters rushed to the Speaker's table and snatching the Speaker's microphone, tried to address the House. This was followed by the Opposition Members rushing to the Speaker's table to grab the microphone from the hands of the Government Party Members to place it before the Speaker's seat.[74] It may be pointed out that such scenes were re-enacted in the East Pakistan Assembly in September 1958 with more disastrous results. However, it was clear that it was difficult for the Muslim League Party to keep its majority intact. First of all, the Muslims had only 119 seats in a House of 250. Secondly, Hindus were much better organized and also wealthier than the Muslims. R. G. Casey, who was Governor of Bengal at that time, recording his impressions on the day the Ministry was defeated, wrote: 'The result was that there was an uproar in the Assembly; members again started changing sides; those who took a poor view of human nature said that a good deal of money changed hands in the process, and one day in March 1945 the Ministry was defeated, and I found myself without a Ministry and with no prospect of getting another.'[75]

---

[73] Cited in *The Indian Annual Register 1944*, Vol. II, Calcutta, p. 42.

[74] *The Indian Annual Register 1945*, Vol. I, Calcutta, pp. 196–9.

[75] R. G. Casey, op. cit., p. 22.

Section 93 continued in Bengal until 1946 when Suhrawardy formed a Muslim League Ministry after the elections. The Muslim League Ministry could hardly do any constructive work. Communal riots broke out in August 1946, in Calcutta, followed later by riots in Noakhali. In such an atmosphere, the traditions and conventions of parliamentary government could hardly thrive. The Muslim League was engaged in a desperate struggle and it had to cling to power. The Congress and other Hindu groups could hardly think of functioning as a normal opposition in a climate of communal frenzy.

It has been said that the British had climbed to power on the backs of Hindu Bengalis, but had preserved it by organizing the Punjabis to defend the North-West frontiers of India.[76] No book gives a better insight into the workings of politics in the Punjab during pre-Partition times and West Pakistan after Partition than Lepel H. Griffin's *The Panjab Chiefs*. There one can see how the ancestors of the Nawab of Mamdot, Khizr Hyat Khan Tiwana, and Nawab Muzaffar Ali Khan Qizilbash (Minister in Punjab, 1943–7) had all served the British during the Mutiny of 1857 and other wars.[77] The policy of benevolence initiated by Sir Henry Lawrence in the Punjab before the Mutiny and that of firmness initiated by General Nicholson, who died during the Mutiny, paid handsome dividends. Muslim and Sikh landlords and peasantry became solid bulwarks of British power in India. Defence strategy demanded that the Punjab and the Frontier should be insulated from the tides of political agitation. The policy worked admirably in the Punjab, but with only partial success in the Frontier.

How rural was the composition of Muslim membership in the Punjab Legislative Assembly could be seen from the fact that out of 86 Muslim seats, 77 were rural and 9 urban.[78] The Unionist Party was built up entirely as a result of the rural support it acquired, predominantly from Muslims and Sikhs. It has been seen that Sir Fazl-i-Husain succeeded in insulating Punjab politics from the external, communal influence of the Muslim League

---

[76] Sir Walter R. Lawrence, *The India We Served*, London, 1928, pp. 264–5.

[77] Lepel H. Griffin, *The Panjab Chiefs*, Lahore: T.C. McCarthy, 1865. See pp. 57, 116, 534, 567.

[78] *The Punjab Legislative Assembly Debate*, Vol. I, 1937. pp. 1–6.

on the plea that Muslims could never muster a clear majority in the Provincial Assembly without seeking the support of non-Muslim groups. Sir Sikander Hyat tried to follow this policy, but the gusts of communal politics from outside had become so strong that he could not isolate Punjab and keep the Unionist Party free from communal tension. Thus, even during his Ministry (1937–1942), legislation like the three Acts amending the Punjab Alienation of Land Act, 1900, the Registration of Money-Lenders Act and the Relief of Indebtedness Act created the impression that the Ministry was penalizing Hindu money-lenders. Other legislative measures like a tax on urban immovable property, restriction of urban rents and a general sales tax were also interpreted by the Congress and other Hindu groups as having been specifically designed to hurt Hindu urban interests.

After Sir Sikander Hyat's death in December 1942, Khizr Hyat became the Chief Minister. In 1944, Jinnah demanded from Khizr Hyat Khan that the Muslim League members of the Unionist Party should owe allegiance to the Muslim League and to no other party. Jinnah also wanted that the name of the Unionist Party should be changed to the Muslim League Coalition Party. Khizr Hyat refused to accept these proposals and reminded Jinnah of the Jinnah-Sikander Pact, according to which the Muslim League was not to interfere in the internal politics of the Punjab on the understanding that Sikander Hyat and his Muslim Ministers would follow the policy of the Muslim League in all-India matters. Jinnah denied the existence of such a Pact. It was obvious that the Muslim League was trying to mobilize Muslim support in the Punjab because they knew that without such support the demand for Pakistan would have no firm basis. There was a final breakdown in Jinnah-Khizr negotiations in April 1944. In the Provincial elections of 1945–6, the Muslim League captured 79 out of 86 Muslim seats. The Unionist Party had lost the confidence of an overwhelming majority of Muslims. Even though the Muslim League was the largest party in the Assembly, it could not form a Ministry because the Sikhs and Hindus would not cooperate with it. Khizr Hyat formed a Ministry with the cooperation of the Congress and the Sikhs. In March 1947, he had to resign because of the Muslim League civil disobedience campaign against his Ministry which had paralysed the administration. The Muslim League campaign was organized primarily to show that no Ministry could function in the Punjab without their cooperation. The Muslim League would rather have Section 93 in the Province than to accept Khizr Hyat as the Chief Minister.

Thus, when Pakistan came into being in August 1947, there was only one Minister in the newly constituted West Punjab Ministry who could claim to have had some experience in Provincial administration. This was Shaukat Hyat Khan who had been a Minister under Khizr Hyat but who had been dismissed in 1945 on charges of corruption and mal-administration. The Chief Minister, Iftikhar Husain Khan of Mamdot, had been President of the Punjab Provincial Muslim League but had had no administrative experience. Even in matters like the organization of the Party, his experience was extremely limited. As President of the Punjab Provincial Muslim League, he had organized the campaign against Khizr Hyat's Ministry, but he could not draw on this sort of experience to tackle matters of administration and parliamentary government. Later, it was disclosed that he and other members of the Working Committee of the Punjab Provincial Muslim League had been busy in October 1946, in purchasing and collecting arms and ammunition for the forthcoming communal riots.[79] It was true that this had happened on both sides. But the fact remained that traditions and conventions of parliamentary government could not be reared on these foundations.

Sind provided the spectacle of a steady see-saw for political power between the big landlords of Sind. Between 1937 and 1942, there were as many as five Ministerial changes. It was like a game of musical chairs in which some landlords won and some lost. There were no differences between the contestants. Ghulam Hussain Hidayatullah, a wealthy lawyer and a landowner, was in practically every Ministry until October 1942, after which date he was the Chief Minister of Sind until Partition. Allah Bukhsh and Bandeh Ali Khan Talpur, who were the other two contestants, were both large landowners. Only in 1946 could the League claim that it had secured a firm stronghold in Sind. But the subsequent story of intrigues and instability, accompanied by mounting corruption, was a repetition of what had happened before.

---

[79] *Dawn*, Karachi, 22 October 1949.

In the North-West Frontier, the Muslim League had never been able to form a stable Ministry. A Congress Ministry under Khan Sahib was in power even when Pakistan came into being. For the first time a League Ministry was formed by Sardar Aurangzeb Khan in May 1943. This was entirely because a number of Congress members were in jail. In 1945, when they were released, Khan Sahib was back in power. During the elections of 1945–6, the Muslim League again failed to produce a majority in the Legislative Assembly. It was only from 1946 that the tide of public opinion turned in favour of the League.

Speaking in the Karachi session of the Muslim League in December 1943, when the Muslim League could claim to be in power in the North-West Frontier Province, in Sind, in the Punjab and in Bengal, Jinnah said: 'This is only a part, which will make a contribution to the whole of our organisational field.... Well, we are trying the experiment. Let us see what emerges from this laboratory.'[80] It was clear that not very sound political or administrative material had emerged from this laboratory. Pakistan started in August 1947, with great hopes but with very poor raw material in terms of political leaders and administrators.[81]

---

[80] Jamil-ud-Din Ahmad, ed., Vol. I, op. cit., pp. 573–4.

[81] For the number of Civil and Army Officers that Pakistan inherited from the Government of India, see Appendix I.

PART TWO

CONTINUATION OF THE VICEREGAL SYSTEM IN PAKISTAN, 1947–8

'Our freedom is the reward of the services and efforts of a single man, and that you know is our most beloved Quaid-i-Azam.'

Liaquat Ali Khan

At a public meeting in Rawalpindi on 17 January 1948

'No succeeding Governor General can quite fill his place, for as the "father of the nation" his prerogatives were enlarged by popular acclaim far beyond the limits laid down in the Constitution.'

The Times, 13 September 1948

7 JINNAH'S APPOINTMENT AS GOVERNOR GENERAL OF PAKISTAN

I. CIRCUMSTANCES LEADING TO JINNAH'S APPOINTMENT AS GOVERNOR GENERAL

There is no clear written evidence as to when it was decided among Muslim League circles that Jinnah's name should be suggested to His Majesty's Government for appointment as Governor General of Pakistan. The Congress had proposed Lord Mountbatten's name as joint Governor General of both Dominions. Many people thought that the Muslim League also had in mind a common Governor General. It looks as if Mountbatten was under the same impression. Campbell-Johnson, who was at the time Mountbatten's Press Attache, has written in his book, *Mission With Mountbatten*, that only when Mountbatten was in London 'did it become apparent that Jinnah wanted three Governors General, one of India, one of Pakistan, and one, Mountbatten himself, in an overall position as Supreme Arbitrator for the division of assets, most of which, of course, are in India'.[1] The British Government did not accept this proposal. Perhaps they found the constitutional difficulties much too formidable.

It looks as if in the beginning Jinnah had not made up his mind as to whether Mountbatten should be the joint Governor General of India and Pakistan, or if he should put forward his own name for the office of Governor General of Pakistan. Addressing the Council of the All-India Muslim League on 9 June 1947 at New Delhi, Jinnah was reported to have said: 'I have done my job. When the Field Marshal leads his army into victory, it is for the civil authority to take over.'[2] Two conclusions may be drawn from this: firstly, Jinnah was thinking of retiring altogether.

---

[1] Alan Campbell-Johnson, *Mission With Mountbatten*, London: Robert Hale, 1952, p. 115.

[2] Editorial, 'Freedom and After', *Dawn*, Delhi, 18 August 1947, p. 4.

There were even rumours that he would stay in India to fight for the rights of Muslims in India. His health had broken down quite a few times. For one month during February 1947, he had suffered a nervous breakdown at Malir where he was not allowed even to listen to the news on the radio.[3] Secondly, because of his declining health he was thinking of handing over all powers to his Prime Minister, Liaquat Ali Khan, and he himself remaining in the background as Governor General to exercise overall control. *Dawn* had reconciled itself to the fact that there would be a common Governor General 'to tide over the initial period when there will have to be continuing adjustments between the affairs of the two countries'. But it made it clear, 'We trust that the leaders of Pakistan will not agree to the continuance of this temporary makeshift beyond the period of absolute practical necessity.'[4]

It is obvious that Jinnah must have carefully weighed all the aspects of the problem before he finally decided to accept the position of Governor General of Pakistan.[5] If Mountbatten were to become common Governor General of both Dominions and remain in Delhi in contact with Nehru's government, he would be unduly exposed to exclusive Congress influence. If he moved to and fro between Delhi and Karachi, his official duties would suffer from the waste of time and energy. Then there was the overriding consideration that if there were a joint Governor General, an impression would be created abroad that the Indian subcontinent still somehow retained its oneness. 'Such an impression would have been fatal to the dignity and prestige of Pakistan.'[6] On 29 June in an article in *The Sunday Times* the New Delhi correspondent reported that an authoritative Muslim League spokesman said in an interview with him that once the division of India were complete, Pakistan would on no account accept a common Governor General with India, 'in order to avoid the remotest suggestion that the two countries have anything in common.'

---

[3] Hector Bolitho, *Jinnah: Creator of Pakistan*, London: John Murray, 1954, p. 174.

[4] Editorial, 'Divide and Quit Bill', *Dawn*, Delhi, 7 July 1947, p. 4.

[5] According to Campbell-Johnson, op. cit., on 2 July 1947, Mr. Jinnah 'came clean' and Jinnah's verdict went in favour of Jinnah, p. 127.

[6] Editorial, 'From Founder to Builder', *Dawn*, Delhi, 13 July 1947, p. 4.

Neither did Jinnah relish the idea of advising Mountbatten as his Prime Minister of Pakistan. First of all, there is fairly convincing evidence to show that the two did not altogether like each other. Jinnah met Mountbatten for the first time on 5 April 1947. Mountbatten's reaction to this first meeting was: 'My God, he was cold. It took most of the interview to unfreeze him.'[7] Jinnah must have also brooded over the problems of Kashmir and the North-West Frontier Province. Perhaps he knew Mountbatten's mind enough not to expect any help from him so far as Kashmir was concerned. Jinnah must have thought that a joint Governor General might not be able to tackle these problems in the best interests of Pakistan. Ian Stephens, writing about his meeting with the Mountbatten when the Kashmir conflict between the two Dominions was at its worst, said that he was 'startled by their one-sided verdicts on affairs.' They seemed to have 'become wholly pro-Hindu.'[8] This is also confirmed by Sir George Cunningham, who wrote in his diary:

> MESSERVY came up from 'PINDI for a talk; just back from England. He was in DELHI two days ago and was surprised to find MOUNTBATTEN directing the military operations in KASHMIR. M.B. is daily becoming more and more anathema to our Muslims, and it certainly seems as if he could see nothing except through Hindu eyes. (7 November 1947.)[9]

One gathers the impression in Campbell-Johnson's *Mission With Mountbatten* that the Muslim League circles from the very beginning suspected Lord Mountbatten of pro-India leanings. Again, to quote Cunningham's diary regarding communal massacres:

> JINNAH says this was known in June 1947; that MOUNTBATTEN was aware of it and decided in July to round up all the leaders, but put it off and off, and finally said he would do it simultaneously with the publication of the Border Commission Report; so he was able to play out time until after the 15th Aug, and thus did nothing. JINNAH says he has documentary proof that the Report was in MOUNT-BATTEN's hands by 7th Aug, and could have been published then if M. B. had not held it up. JINNAH very bitter about the whole thing. (9 February 1948.)[10]

---

[7] Campbell-Johnson, op. cit., p. 56.

[8] Ian Stephens, *Horned Moon*, London: Chatto & Windus, 1950, p. 109.

[9] Sir George Cunningham's Diary 1947–8, p. 23.

[10] Ibid., p. 34.

Secondly, Jinnah might have been suspicious that if he were to allow a common Governor Generalship, there might be some difficulties in future for Pakistan to establish its separate and complete sovereignty. In passing, it may be noted that the Labour Government had considered the idea of retaining certain common links between India and Pakistan and the structure of the Austro-Hungarian dual monarchy united by the link of the Hapsburg Crown had been discussed as a possibility for the subcontinent. The author has also learned that it was suggested to a British political scientist by a leading member of the Labour Government that he should study the structure of the Austro-Hungarian Empire and constitutions of some of the international bodies which had functioned under the League of Nations when he was appointed as an adviser to Lord Mountbatten. However, soon after his arrival, the British political scientist found that the idea had disappeared and he was not consulted very much as an adviser. Thus, a number of such considerations might have influenced Jinnah's mind when he calculated the risks of a common Governor Generalship.

John Connell, the biographer of Field-Marshal Auchinleck, has also recorded that 'long before Partition he [Mountbatten] had lost the trust of Jinnah and the Muslim League'.[11] In spite of all this, there are many Pakistanis who still doubt the wisdom of Jinnah in refusing to accept Mountbatten as the common Governor General of both Dominions. They rest their case on the plea that had this happened, Mountbatten would have been in a much stronger position to persuade and pressure India to adopt a more just and reasonable attitude towards Pakistan, particularly on the matter of division of assets of the former Government of India. They also suggest that had Mountbatten been a common Governor General, he would have been in a better position to maintain law and order in the two Punjabs and thus could have saved thousands of Muslims lives. But the evidence so far offered in this book seems to suggest that there was no firm basis for such optimism. Indians and Pakistanis were in such a state of communal frenzy that no arbitrator, however impartial he might be, could have maintained the even balance of justice between the two States. This was borne out by the accusations that the Indian Government levelled at Auchinleck as the Supreme Commander

---

[11] John Connell, *Auchinleck*, London: Cassell, 1959, p. 913.

in charge of partition of the Armed Forces and military stores. Mountbatten himself, writing to Auchinleck in September 1947, admitted: 'One of the most balanced and level-headed Ministers complained recently that you seemed to regard yourself as the champion of Pakistan's interests; such is the reward of strict impartiality!'[12]

Auchinleck also wrote in a note that he sent to the British Prime Minister that the Indian Government was determined to 'prevent Pakistan receiving her just share, or indeed anything of the large stocks of reserve arms, equipment, stores, etc. held in the arsenals and depots in India.'[13] Mountbatten in a letter to Auchinleck regretfully admitted that he was powerless to prevent the Indian Government demanding in the Joint Defence Council (of which Mountbatten was the Chairman) the removal of Auchinleck and the winding up of the Supreme Headquarters.[14] All this once again goes to show that in such an atmosphere Mountbatten, even if he had been trusted by the League, probably would not have been allowed to function as an impartial arbitrator. He enjoyed enormous prestige and popularity in India and yet he could not enable Auchinleck to discharge the task entrusted to him in an impartial manner. It is difficult to see how Mountbatten could have functioned in a more effective manner had he been made a common Governor General of both India and Pakistan.

Perhaps equally important was Jinnah's own position and prestige. He was not merely a party leader in the Western sense of the term. He was the Quaid-i-Azam—the Great Leader of a national movement. And now that he had won Pakistan within the incredible period of seven years, he had achieved something which no other Muslim leader had even dreamt of. Muslims, specially in Northern India, regarded him as a successor of great Moghul Emperors, Emperors like Babur and Aurangzeb. Indeed, soon after the announcement of the Partition scheme on 3 June 1947, he was hailed in New Delhi by Muslims as the Emperor of Pakistan. *Dawn* wrote a few years after his death: 'The populace had already begun to greet the Quaid-i-Azam as "Shahinshah-e-Pakistan". Had he so desired, 80 million willing hands would have rejoiced to put a Crown upon his head.'[15]

[12] Ibid., p. 916.
[13] Quoted in ibid., pp. 920–1.
[14] Ibid., p. 913.
[15] Editorial, 'Homage', *Dawn*, Karachi, 11 September 1950, p. 5.

Jinnah admonished his admirers not to call him Emperor. He could not conceive of becoming a Prime Minister either. In accordance with his own temperament and the tenor of the times, he agreed to his name being put forward for the position of Governor General of Pakistan.

It is also conceivable that a large number of Jinnah's own followers urged him to be at the helm of affairs because the position of the Muslim League was far from strong in the North-West Frontier Province and even in Provinces like Sind and West Punjab there were serious rifts and rivalries between League leaders themselves. In fine, his tremendous prestige and leadership were needed to consolidate Pakistan in its initial stages. *The Round Table* wrote:

> Mr. Jinnah said at the meeting of the Council of the League on June 9, when the plan was accepted, that he had 'done his job'. It is not surprising that they refused to part readily with one who, though aging and lately ill, surpasses them and, possibly everybody else in India, in practical political intelligence. From their point of view his recommendation as Governor General of Pakistan may be readily understood—though Mr Gandhi thinks that a different decision was taken earlier, perhaps before the N-W. F. P. problem was presented in a new form and Lord Mountbatten visited Kashmir.[16]

Jinnah did anticipate difficulties in the matter of division of assets. That was why he had come forward with the highly ingenious proposal that Mountbatten should be appointed as Supreme Governor General, in addition to and over the two Governors General of India and Pakistan. This would have created as many problems as it was designed to solve. If a neutral and Supreme Governor General disagreed with one of the two, the latter could always appeal to the British Government for arbitration. And this would place the British Government in an embarrassing position. Secondly, a neutral Governor General would certainly have to live within his own self-made enclave of neutral territory. Perhaps because of these formidable difficulties, Jinnah's proposal was not regarded as practicable in Whitehall.

---

[16] *The Round Table, 1946–7,* Vol. XXXVI, p. 372.

II. Constitutional Implications of Jinnah's Appointment as Governor General

The fact that an active politician had been appointed as Governor General of Pakistan caused considerable concern among many circles in England. Campbell-Johnson, giving a résumé of his editorial interviews in London to Mountbatten, wrote:

> Lord Layton said that in his view Jinnah's decision would be widely regarded as a selfish and ambitious act, and that it would involve a marking down here with the British Press of his reputation, which was at its peak during his visit to England in December last.[17]

It was also pointed out that Jinnah was not eminently suitable for this post because of his known autocratic ways. Thus, *The Economist* commented:

> The constitutional theory of a Governor General in a Dominion is that he represents the King and bears the same relation to the Ministers forming the Government as the King does to his Ministers in the United Kingdom. It is recognized that the rights of a Dominion include the right of recommending a person for appointment as Governor General. But that the Governor Generalship should be held by an active party politician who frankly states his intention of continuing his political leadership after assuming the office, is an innovation which radically alters the nature of the Dominion bond. The development is the more serious because Mr Jinnah's rule gives promise of being a very thinly veiled dictatorship. His motive in demanding the office of the Governor General is no doubt to obtain the position which belongs to it in the eyes of the Indian masses. The Viceroy as Governor General has been hitherto, even though to a restricted degree in recent years, the supreme executive ruler and his Ministers have been simply the members of his Executive Council. By force of mental habit the man in the street will continue to think of the Governor General as being more important than his Prime Minister.[18]

As shown before, it is difficult to see how Jinnah could have put forward any name other than his own for Governor Generalship. *The Times* appreciated his difficulties when it said: 'Yet those who will be called to rule Pakistan may hold that the relatively undeveloped qualities that make up much of its territory

---

[17] Campbell-Johnson, op. cit., p. 133.
[18] Article, 'Is It Well With India?', *The Economist*, 19 July 1947, pp. 93–94.

must be guided by a Governor General capable of exercising the functions of higher control and co-ordination which formerly vested in a Canning or a Curzon.'[19]

The Congress circles were indignant for they suspected that Jinnah, as usual, had tried to put them in a highly embarrassing position for Jinnah had gone a step further than the framers of the 'Quit India' Resolution in asking for an indigenous Governor General. He was accused of a breach of faith on the score that it had been agreed by both parties that for the transitional period Mountbatten should be Governor General of both Dominions. Jinnah denied these charges vehemently in his first press conference on 13 July 1947 after it had been announced on 10 July 1947 that he was to become Governor General of Pakistan. 'These reports are entirely devoid of any truth and I am surprised that even responsible men have been misrepresenting me and making false allegations against the League and myself.'[20]

In the same press conference he also put forward his own theory of Governor Generalship. Since the Governors General were nominated by the successor authorities, namely, the Congress and the League, 'the Governors General are the chosen of the people and not, as it is ordinarily understood, appointed by the King....'[21] Rather a startling statement from a constitutional purist like Jinnah! When he was asked whether it was not a fact that the Governor General held office during His Majesty's pleasure, Jinnah replied. 'It is purely a form, nothing but a form. The Governors General are the chosen of the people and that is the reason why I have accepted this honour.'[22]

League leaders were jubilant when it was announced that Jinnah would become the Governor General. Liaquat Ali Khan called it 'the natural consummation of our struggle for liberty under his leadership.'[23] Abdur Rab Nishtar, Communications Member, Interim Government, was of the view that 'it is in the fitness of things that the chief head of Pakistan—essentially a Muslim state—should be one who commands the implicit confidence of a hundred million Muslims. It is important that the Centre should have the guidance of such a personality always

[19] Editorial, 'Indian Independence', *The Times,* London, 11 July 1947, p. 5.
[20] *Dawn,* Delhi, 15 July 1947, pp. 1 and 3.
[21] Ibid.
[22] Ibid.
[23] Ibid., 14 July 1947, p. 1.

available. Mr Jinnah is the architect of the state and the best possible man to look after it. *Now everything will be all right.*' [author's italics][24] *Dawn* compared Jinnah's position with that of a dictator like Kemal Ataturk:

> Kemal, too, founded for his people a new virile state—but out of the already existing remains of a crumbled Empire, and by different means—and he too had to take upon himself the task of building it up. The Quaid-i-Azam's strategy, unique and unparalleled, has enabled him to carve out Pakistan for his own nation and his task henceforth as head of the state will be largely like that of the 'Father of Turks'. *Whatever the constitutional powers of the Governor General of a Dominion may nominally be, in Quaid-i-Azam's case no legal or formal limitations can apply* [author's italics]. His people will not be content to have him as merely the titular head of the government, they would wish him to be their friend, philosopher, guide and ruler, irrespective of what the constitution of a Dominion of the British Commonwealth may contain.[25]

Again, soon after the dawn of independence, *Dawn* wrote:

> The fact that Quaid-i-Azam will be at the head and personally direct the operations of civil administrations is ample guarantee that even out of the limited resources available an edifice will be reared which will put to shame those who had attempted to prevent its smooth and ordered creation.[26]

Thus, there was a striking contrast between opinions expressed by constitutional pundits in England and those held by League leaders and *Dawn*. The constitutional pundits were alarmed that such a powerful and autocratic politician had nominated himself as Governor General. In the opinion of the author, Pakistan at that time needed its founder as its Governor General. It was not correct to compare Jinnah's position and his powers with those of his contemporary Governors General in other Dominions. Apart from other differences, it was not possible that responsible government in Pakistan would start from the same stage that it had already reached in Canada or Australia by 1947. These Dominions also had the good fortune of having powerful Governors General in their formative period. Lord Elgin (1847–1854)

---

[24] Ibid., 12 July 1947, p. 1

[25] Editorial, 'From Founder to Builder', *Dawn*, Delhi, 13 July 1947, p. 4.

[26] Editorial, 'Freedom and After', *Dawn*, Delhi, 18 August 1947, p. 4.

1854) in Canada is an obvious example. Lord Dufferin as late as 1872–8 enjoyed considerable powers. In seconding the address of farewell to Lord Dufferin in the House of Commons, Sir John A. Macdonald declared:

> Like the hon. the First Minister, I would say that the office of Governor General is not a mere formal office. It is one of great power. It is one of great dignity. It is one of the greatest responsibility, and the Governor General is a person elevated, like the Sovereign, far above the shifting party politics of the day. He is at the helm of State. He guides, advises, warns and counsels, and he—while others absorbed in party politics, may forget for the moment the interests of the country—has only one object before him, and that is the common interests of all.[27]

---

[27] *Debates House of Commons, Dominion of Canada,* Session 1878, Vol. II; p. 1875.

8 CONSTITUTIONAL AND POLITICAL POWERS OF THE GOVERNOR GENERAL

I. CONSTITUTIONAL POWERS OF THE GOVERNOR GENERAL

Section II of Mohammad Ali Jinnah's Commission defined his powers as Governor General of Pakistan as follows:

> And We do hereby authorize, empower and command you to exercise and perform all and singular the powers and duties conferred and imposed upon Our Governor General of Pakistan by and under provisions of the Act passed in this the tenth and eleventh year of Our Reign intituled the Indian Independence Act 1947.[1]

As the Commission said that the powers of the Governor General of Pakistan were to be exercised according to the provisions of the Indian Independence Act, 1947, one must look for the powers of the Governor General in that Act. Section 9 of the Indian Independence Act, 1947, dealt with the powers of the Governor General. Thus, Clause (c) of Sub-Section (1) of Section 9 laid it down clearly that the Governor General was authorized to make such provisions as appeared to him to be necessary or expedient 'for making omissions from, additions to, and adaptations and modifications of, the Government of India Act, 1935, and the Orders-in-Council, rules and other instruments made thereunder, in their application to the separate new Dominions.' Lord Mountbatten, the Governor General of undivided India, exercised these powers of adapting the Government of India Act, 1935, before 'the appointed day', that is, 15 August 1947. But after that date, the Governor General of Pakistan was empowered to exercise these powers until 31 March 1948 according to Sub-Section (5) of Section 9. The latter date was extended by a year by Section 2 of the Indian Independence (Amendment) Act, 1947.

Sub-Section (2) of Section 8 of the Indian Independence Act

---

[1] Jinnah's Commission is included in Appendix II.

1947, stated clearly that each of the new Dominions and all Provinces and other parts thereof would be governed by the Government of India Act, 1935, as adapted in each Dominion by its respective Governor General. Sub-Section (3) of Section 8 stated that the Government of India Act, 1935, as adapted, could limit the power of the Legislature unless a law made by the Constituent Assembly of that Dominion set aside such provisions of the adapted Act which limited the powers of the Legislature. Section 8 also limited the powers of the Governor General and the Governor of a Province in the sense that these two authorities could no longer act in their discretion or exercise their individual judgment regarding any matter after the appointed day.[2]

Thus, in the second-reading debate on the Indian Independence Bill on 10 July 1947 Attlee pointed out that, unlike the Government of India Act, 1935, which granted discretionary executive powers to the Governor General and the Governors, the proviso in Section 8 of the new Bill placed these executive authorities in the same position as Dominion Governors General, that is to say, they would act only on the advice of their Ministers.[3] But since the Governors General were empowered to adapt the Government of India Act, 1935, as they deemed necessary or expedient, according to Section 9 of the Indian Independence Bill, Attlee in the same debate had to admit that the powers given to the Governors General to bring the Act into operation were extremely wide.[4]

This meant that the powers of the Governor General would depend upon the manner in which the Government of India Act, 1935, was adapted. It was clear that the Governor General of Pakistan had already lost those powers of the Governor General which he exercised 'in his discretion' or in his 'individual judgment', according to the Government of India Act, 1935. Thus, any adaptation order made under Section 9 of the Independence Act had to take account of these limitations. Jinnah's authority as Governor General came into being on 15 August 1947. It was considered desirable that adaptations of the Government of India Act, 1935, should be made before 15 August 1947, so that Jinnah might have a constitution ready soon after he assumed

---

[2] According to Clause (c) of Sub-Section (2) of Section 8 of the Indian Independence Act, 1947 (10 & 11 Geo. 6, ch. 30).

[3] *Hansard (Commons)*, Vol. 439, Cols. 2448–50.

[4] Ibid., Cols. 2455–6.

office. The only person who could make such adaptations before 14 August 1947 was Mountbatten. The order which Mountbatten issued on 14 August 1947 and which dealt with the powers of the Governor General of Pakistan was the Governor General's Order No. 22 called the Pakistan (Provisional Constitution) Order, 1947. This was drafted on the advice of the Provisional Government of Pakistan. Presumably, Jinnah had a decisive voice in the sort of advice that the Provisional Government tendered to the Governor General. Soon after the formation of the Pakistan Provisional Cabinet, *Dawn* started issuing a sort of court circular every day which invariably said that Quaid-i-Azam presided over a meeting of the Pakistan Provisional Cabinet.[5]

1. *The Powers of the Governor General Vis-a-Vis the Central Government*

Sub-Section (2) of Section 3 of the Pakistan (Provisional Constitution) Order, 1947, stated that all expressions, 'in his discretion', 'acting in his discretion', and 'exercising his individual judgment', should be omitted wherever they occurred.

Under the Government of India Act, 1935, the Governor General 'in his discretion' was empowered to choose and appoint his Council of Ministers and he could dismiss them also acting under his discretion. Similarly, the functions of the Governor General with respect to Defence, Ecclesiastical, and External Affairs, and those in relation to the Tribal Areas were to be exercised under his discretion. Those functions and powers which the Governor General was to 'exercise under his individual judgment' were defined by the Act as his special responsibilities. The latitude allowed under this Section included the following:

1. The maintenance of law and order in India.
2. The safeguarding of the financial stability and credit of the federal government.
3. The safeguarding of the rights and interests of minorities.
4. The prevention of commercial discrimination and action which would subject goods of United Kingdom or Burmese origin imported into India to discriminatory or penal treatment.
5. The protection of the rights of Indian states, etc.

---

[5] See *Dawn*, Delhi, 25 July 1947 to 6 August 1947.

In respect of matters in which he had special responsibility and in which he exercised his individual judgment, his Ministers would advise but the decision rested with him. Matters over which he exercised his discretion were placed outside the purview of Ministerial advice. In the same meticulous fashion it was expressly provided that it rested with the Governor General in every case to decide whether or not he was required to act in his discretion or to exercise his individual judgment.

Under the new dispensation all these inordinate powers listed in Sections 9 to 17 of the Government of India Act, 1935, were deleted. In addition to this, the Schedule of the Pakistan (Provisional Constitution) Order, 1947, omitted the Ninth Schedule of the Government of India Act, 1935. It was under the Ninth Schedule that the Governor General of undivided India had been exercising his powers. Part II of the Government of India Act, 1935, had not been used, as the Federation of India had not come into being. The Ninth Schedule gave even greater powers to the Governor General than those available in Part II of the Act. For example, under Section 67(b), if the Legislature failed to pass a Bill in the form recommended by the Governor General, the Governor General might certify that the passage of a Bill was essential for the safety, tranquillity, or interests of British India, or any part thereof.

Strangely enough, Campbell-Johnson in his book, *Mission With Mountbatten*, states quite categorically that one of Jinnah's first acts after putting his name forward as Governor General 'was to apply for powers under the 9th Schedule rather than Part II of the 1935 Act which gave him at once dictatorial powers unknown to any constitutional Governor General representing the King.'[6] Again, in another part of his book he states: 'As we have seen, Jinnah's concept of the proper functions of the Governor General were made plain enough when he at once invoked the special powers allowed under the Independence Act.'[7] It is difficult to see how Jinnah could have applied for powers under the Ninth Schedule when the Pakistan (Provisional Constitution) Order, 1947 removed all the discretionary powers of the Governor General and the Schedule of this Order omitted the Ninth

---

[6] Alan Campbell-Johnson, *Mission With Mountbatten*, London: Robert Hale, 1952, p. 156.

[7] Ibid., p. 230.

Schedule.[8] If he had applied for powers under the Ninth Schedule and if these powers had been granted, as Campbell-Johnson believes that they were, then the Pakistan (Provisional Constitution) Order should have been drafted in terms of the Ninth Schedule. It has been seen that this was not the case. Moreover, Mountbatten was expected to carry on 'the business of the Governor General in Council between the passing of this Act and the appointed day otherwise than in accordance with the provisions in that behalf of the Ninth Schedule to the Government of India Act, 1935.'[9] Thus, the Ninth Schedule made its exit on 19 July 1947 when two Provisional Governments were established. The author has looked up all the relevant documents and nowhere has he found any evidence to show that the Governor General of Pakistan had applied for and been granted his powers under the Ninth Schedule of the Government of India Act, 1935.

The powers of the Governor General with regard to his Council of Ministers were couched in terms which could be found in other Dominion Constitutions. Thus, Section 10 (1) said: 'The Governor General's ministers shall be chosen and summoned by him, shall be sworn as members of the council and shall hold office during his pleasure.'[10] Since the Governor General's powers exercisable in his discretion and under his individual judgment had been deleted, it could be said that he was expected to act only on the advice of his Ministers. But there was no specific provision which laid down that the Governor General was to act on advice. This was rather a striking omission. In the original Government of India Act, 1935, even though the Governor General had been empowered with wide discretionary authority yet in Paragraph 8 of his Instrument of Instructions he was clearly enjoined 'to bear constantly in mind the need for fostering a sense of joint responsibility among his

---

[8] *The Transitional Constitutions of India and Pakistan,* Calcutta: The Indian Law Review Office, 1947, p. 222. In this, the Schedule of Pakistan (Provisional Constitution) Order, 1947, is given. Ninth Schedule is omitted. See also *Unrepealed Constitutional Legislation,* Karachi: Government of Pakistan Press, 1951, p. 110.

[9] Section 9—(1) (e) of the Indian Independence Act, 1947 (10 & 11 Geo. 6, ch. 30).

[10] Corresponding provision in Canada is Section 11 of the British North America Act, 1867 (30–31 Victoria, Ch. 3).

ministers.'[11] In Paragraph 9 it was stated that the Governor General 'shall be studious so to exercise his powers as not to enable his ministers to rely upon his special responsibility in order to relieve themselves of responsibilities which are properly their own.'[12] In other Dominion Constitutions there are specific provisions which require that the Governor General should act on the advice of his Ministers. Thus, Section 13 of the British North America Act says: 'The Provisions of this Act referring to the Governor General in Council shall be construed as referring to the Governor General acting by and with the Advice of the Queen's Council for Canada.' Similarly, Section 63 of the Constitution Act of the Commonwealth of Australia lays down: 'The provisions of this Constitution referring to the Governor General in Council shall be construed as referring to the Governor General acting with the advice of the Federal Executive Council.' No such provision was incorporated in the Pakistan (Provisional Constitution) Order, 1947.

Section 17 of the adapted Government of India Act, 1935, empowered the Governor General to make rules for the more convenient transaction of the Federal Government, and for the allocation among Ministers of the said business.[13] It was also provided that the rules should include provisions requiring Ministers and Secretaries to Government to transmit to the Governor General all such information with respect to the business of the Federal Government as might be specified in the rules or any other information that the Governor General might require to be submitted to him. This Section gave a wide latitude of power to the Governor General in the matter of allocation of portfolios among his Ministers. This could mean that the Prime Minister's choice of his Ministers would either have to conform to that of the Governor General or the Governor General could himself

---

[11] J. P. Eddy and F. H. Lawton, *India's New Constitution*, London: Macmillan, 1935, Appendix I, p. 194.

[12] Ibid.

[13] Instead of quoting the particular Adaptation Order or Amendment Act of the Government of India Act, 1935, the author feels that it would be easier and clearer to simply refer to the Act as the adapted Government of India Act, 1935. The Ministry of Law of the Government of Pakistan has used the term 'Unrepealed Constitutional Legislation', which the author thinks is vague and not as clear as the term adapted Act.

select the Ministers for the Prime Minister and also allocate portfolios among them. By this Section it was also possible for the Governor General to allocate a subject to himself. Thus, a press note issued by the Government of Pakistan on 6 July 1948 stated: 'It has been decided to create a new Ministry with effect from 1 July 1948, to be known as the Ministry of States and Frontier Regions. This Ministry will deal with the affairs of the tribal territories of the N-W. Frontier, Baluchistan, the Baluchistan tribal areas adjoining Dera Ghazi Khan District of the West Punjab, the excluded areas and the Pakistan States. The affairs of the Ministry will be under the direct control of the Quaid-i-Azam and it will function under his guidance and direction.'[14] It may be pointed out that the Governor General was empowered to exercise his authority over Excluded Areas and Partially Excluded Areas by Section 92 of the adapted Act. Similarly, the Chief Commissioner's Province of Baluchistan was also placed under his jurisdiction by Sections 94 and 95 of the adapted Act. What was striking was that the Governor General had included the Tribal Areas within the purview of his own Ministry. Sections 11–15 of the original Government of India Act, 1935, which dealt with Tribal Areas, Defence, Ecclesiastical Affairs, External Affairs, etc. and the special responsibilities of the Governor General, had been omitted in the adapted Act. These subject came under the discretionary powers of the Governor General and therefore Sections 11–15 could not be retained in the adapted Act. But the Governor General was now bringing back Tribal Areas under his control and for this he used Section 17 of the adapted Government of India Act, 1935. This was also strange in the sense that separate Ministries had been created for Defence, External Affairs, etc., and a similar Ministry for Tribal Affairs and Frontier Regions could have been allocated to a Minister. The Governor General of Pakistan had created a unique precedent in the sense that besides being Governor General he had a Ministry under his control.

The emergency powers given to the Governor General in the original Government of India Act, 1935, were retained in the adapted Act. Under Section 102 of the adapted Government of India Act, 1935, the Governor General could declare by

---

[14] *Pakistan News*, 7–13 July 1948, Karachi: Press Information Department, Vol. 2, No. 28, p. 12.

proclamation that a grave emergency existed whereby the security or economic life of Pakistan or any part thereof was threatened by war or internal disturbance or circumstances arising out of any mass movement of population from or into Pakistan. By this proclamation the Governor General could make laws for a Province or any part thereof with respect to any of the matters enumerated in the Provincial Legislative List. Under clause 5 of this Section he could declare a proclamation of emergency even before the security or economic life of Pakistan was threatened by the actual occurrence of war or disturbance or other circumstances, if the Governor General was satisfied that an imminent danger existed. The Federal Legislature could make laws under this proclamation of emergency, but such laws should cease to have effect on the expiration of a period of six months after the proclamation had ceased to operate.

On 27 August 1948 the Governor General issued a proclamation under Section 102 of the Government of India Act, 1935, declaring that a 'grave emergency has arisen and exists in Pakistan'. The proclamation stated that 'whereas the economic life of Pakistan is threatened by circumstances arising out of the mass movement of population from and into Pakistan a State of Emergency is hereby declared'.[15] The reason why this emergency was declared was that the Central Government had so far failed to persuade the Provincial Governments in West Pakistan to absorb a surplus of 500,000 refugees. The West Punjab had settled 4.8 million refugees or one million more than the number of Hindu and Sikh refugees who had left the Province. Perhaps more could have been settled if tenancy reforms had been carried out and large landholdings abolished, but in the prevailing conditions a saturation point had been reached and a surplus of 500,000 had to be provided for elsewhere.

Various Provincial interests were retarding smooth settlement. Ministers of the Central Government, including the Prime Minister, had tried on many occasions to persuade the Provinces to absorb and resettle refugees more speedily. Since satisfactory cooperation was not forthcoming from the Provinces, recourse had to be made to the emergency powers of the Governor General. Thus, the Central Refugee Council, under a pro-clamation of emergency, directed Provinces and States to take up

---

[15] *The Times*, London, 28 August 1948.

the following number of refugees: Sind, 200,000; North-West Frontier Province, 100,000; Bahawalpur and Khairpur States and Baluchistan, 100,000. It was very difficult to tell who was advising whom, for the Governor General was, as will be seen later, probably as well informed as the Central Cabinet about the seriousness of the situation. Governors of these Provinces were writing letters fortnightly to the Governor General posting him with what was happening in their respective Provinces. Therefore, it was likely that the Governor General himself might have suggested that since the persuasive methods of the Central Cabinet had failed, they should seek his assistance and a State of Emergency should be declared.

2. *Powers of the Governor General with regard to Provinces, including the Chief Commissioner's Province of Baluchistan*

(a) *Governors as Agents of the Governor General*

It might have seemed strange and surprising to some of the ardent Muslim League nationalists that the Quaid-i-Azam had appointed British officers as Governors in three of the four Provinces in Pakistan. Sir George Cunningham was appointed Governor of the North-West Frontier Province; Sir Francis Mudie and Mr Ghulam Hussain Hidayatullah were assigned to West Punjab and Sind, respectively; and to East Bengal went Sir Frederick Bourne. Obviously Jinnah wanted experienced and strong Governors. He was fully conversant with the rifts, rivalries and intrigues in these various Provinces.

However, the fact remains that since the Quaid-i-Azam had made his choice it had to be accepted by all concerned. Sir Frederick Bourne, the Governor of East Bengal, was later to write, '...I was made to feel that I was welcome and that if the Quaid-i-Azam, as Mr Jinnah was by then always styled, thought I would do, all concerned in East Bengal would act on the assumption that he was right, a very generous attitude in the circumstances.'[16] However, Khan Abdul Ghaffar Khan, criticizing the policy of appointing British Governors, said:

---

[16] Sir Frederick Bourne, 'Constitutional Governors Before and After the Transfer of Power', *Asiatic Review*, October 1950, Vol. XLVI, No. 168, p. 1115.

I am very sorry to say that our Hindu brethren have appointed Indian Governors in their Provinces and not even men but a woman also can become a Governor there. Were there no Musalmans in Bengal or the Punjab who could become our Governors? I have to say, that to our misfortune, the British whom we had turned out have again been brought in and placed at our heads. Is this Islamic Fraternity? Would we call it a brotherhood? This is Islamic Pakistan![17]

Liaquat Ali Khan's reply to this criticism was equally significant:

We needed experienced men and therefore we employed a few Englishmen on temporary basis. But under the present Constitution, the man who has been vested with all powers is the Governor General. *He can do whatever he likes* [author's italics].[18]

From the evidence that the author has gathered, it seems clear that Sir George Cunningham presided over Cabinet meetings in the N-W. F. P. The Chief Minister himself seemed to prefer this arrangement. Similarly, the Rules of Business were also framed by the Governor of the N-W. F. P. *The Times* also wrote of 'the Governors of the N-W. F. and West Punjab provinces, Sir George Cunningham and Sir Francis Mudie, who because of the difficult conditions which have prevailed since August have been forced to play an executive role beyond their constitutional duties...'[19] *Dawn* of 23 August 1947 said that Sir Francies Mudie presided over a meeting of the Punjab Cabinet which was also attended by General Sir Frank Messervy, Commander-in-Chief of the Pakistan Army.[20] Sir Frederick Bourne has pointed out:

I did not attend Cabinet Meetings, though I received reports of all Cabinet proceedings; but I saw the Ministers on fixed days once a week, when I or they were not on tour, an arrangement which the Prime Minister himself desired. He was anxious that I should keep an eye on them and jog their memories when necessary.[21]

As will be seen later, in Sind the Governor, Ghulam Hussain Hidayatullah, was so powerful that he could go to the extent

---

[17] *Constituent Assembly (Legislature) of Pakistan Debates,* 5 March 1948. Vol. I, No. 8, p. 239.
[18] Ibid., 6 March 1948, Vol. I, No. 8, p. 279.
[19] *The Times,* London, 5 January 1948.
[20] *Dawn,* Delhi, 23 August 1947.
[21] Sir Frederick Bourne, op. cit., p. 1116.

of re-allocating the portfolios against the wishes of his Chief Minister.

These close contacts with their Ministers were necessary because the Governors had to write fortnightly letters to the Governor General. This system of fortnightly letters from Governors was started by Lord Linlithgow, continued by Lord Wavell and adopted in 1947 by Jinnah. One of these letters, written by Sir Francis Mudie to the Quaid-i-Azam and dated 5 September 1947, was obtained by K. L. Gauba. It has been published in his book, *Inside Pakistan*. This letter gives an amazingly clear and complete picture of what was happening in West Punjab around that time. The following extract shows how useful such letters were and how it enabled the Governor General and the Central Government to keep a close watch over Provincial administration:

> From various sources I hear that the political situation is deteriorating. Yesterday there was a minor refugee demonstration with shouts of 'Pakistan Murdabad'. I am told that Shaukat is afraid to show his face in the Muslim Refugee Camp here. I warned my Ministry about a week ago that this sort of thing was inevitable, that when things go wrong on a large scale it is always the Government that gets the blame. At first they were inclined to attribute any unpopularity they may have sensed to the machinations of Firoz, Khaksars, etc. This was mere self-delusion and very dangerous. This feeling of resentment against things in general and against the Government in particular is bound to grow. The ways in which, as far as I can see, it can be countered are (1) propaganda reiterating what Government is doing for the refugees and (2) efficient administration.[22]

---

[22] K. L. Gauba, *Inside Pakistan*, Delhi: Rajkamal Publications, 1948, Appendix A, pp. 301–3. The author feels that the letter of Sir Francis Mudie, as reproduced in this book, is fairly authentic, although the book is extremely anti-Pakistani. There is considerable corroboration between some of the facts mentioned in the letter and those included in a report on the same situation published in *The Times* of 5 September 1947. Thus, Sir Francis Mudie's letter states: 'Efficiency with my present staff is out of the question. We have one Financial Commissioner instead of a normal two or three and our present one, Akhtar Hussain, though loyal and a good technical revenue officer, is certainly not capable of doing two men's work. Out of three Commissioners of Divisions, we have only one and he is, from all accounts, hardly up to the job. Out of five D.I.G. Police, we have only three and two are recently joined outsiders, one from U. P. and one from C.P. Finally, to crown all, we have no Chief Secretary—the Finance Secretary, a mediocre officer, is supposed to be doing both jobs. I called on

Sir George Cunningham, Governor of the North-West Frontier Province, also wrote fortnightly letters in which he gave detailed reports of the administration of the Province. 'These reports', as he wrote in his first letter dated 8 September 1947, 'will be seen by nobody except my own Secretary.' All these letters have been seen by the author and they give an amazingly penetrating insight into the working of the Frontier administration. Many of the early letters gave a detailed account of the problem of law and order arising from communal riots in the Province. Later, one finds Sir George engrossed in problems like the propaganda of Abdul Ghaffar Khan in favour of Pathanistan, the dangers posed by the hostility of the Faqir of Ipi to Pakistan, and the support that his Government was likely to get in the Assembly during the Budget Session. The Governor reported to the Quaid-i-Azam that Abdul Ghaffar Khan and other 'Red Shirt' leaders were busy making speeches and hoisting the Pathanistan flag in public meetings. 'But the meetings always seem to fall pretty flat, and I think it is much better not to give them advertisement by prosecution, even if their doings were actionable (which is doubtful).' In the next letter, the Governor wrote: 'I am in the meantime warning Abdul Qayum, as you advised, not to risk a clash with the Red Shirts at this juncture without very good reason.' Abdul Ghaffar Khan, however, persevered in his propaganda and also attacked the Government of Pakistan for not being based on real

---

Liaquat and Mohammed Ali and had a joint meeting with them and my Ministers. Largely by Liaquat's help I got the Ministers to agree to our trying to get back a number of ex-Punjab and ex-U. P. British I.C.S. officers and to the retention of the Lahore Division. Shaukat was a bit difficult, I don't quite know why.'

The Times of 5 September 1947 described the situation as follows: 'In West Punjab the need for trained officers is desperate, as the province faces the worst crisis in its history, and very few Muslims of adequate training and experience exist. Six months ago there were nearly 100 British officials in the Punjab Government. Today in West Punjab there are about six. Many key posts are not filled, either by Muslims or British. For example, there is only one instead of three Divisional Commissioners, one instead of two Financial Commissioners, two instead of five Deputy Inspectors General of Police. Nearly all the District Officers are untried men who have never administered a District before. The only hope of restoring an efficient administration lies in the early enlistment of British Officers. Such a move would be opposed in some extreme nationalist quarters, but it has the full approval of the highest Government leaders, although the latter are unwilling to jeopardize their position by stating their needs publicly.

Islam and not free of foreign interference and control. One of the letters dated 31 December 1947 expressed some concern over the frequent demands that were being made at public meetings and tribal *jirgas* for the substitution of *Shariat* for the ordinary law. Another problem which Sir George tackled was that of building up friendly relations between the Government of Pakistan and the Frontier tribes and States. The Governor was not quite certain whether the Utmanzai Wazirs of North Waziristan would react favourably to his suggestion that the tribes should enter into friendly relations with the Government of Pakistan. He himself was pleasantly surprised when he found the tribes 'really all right at heart' in spite of the persistent propaganda of the Faqir of Ipi against Pakistan. In another letter the Governor reported with great pride the withdrawal of regular troops from Waziristan and. described the withdrawal from Razmak as 'far the most peaceful withdrawal of troops that I have ever known on the North-West Frontier in the last thirty-five years.'

Sir George also kept the Quaid-i-Azam fully informed of how his Ministry was functioning and particularly the prospects of it retaining a majority in the House. As the Budget Session approached, there was some doubt whether the seven Congress members who had joined the League Party would continue to support the Ministry. The Governor did not share the apprehension that these seven converts would betray the Muslim League Party. The Governor was in touch with the Members of the Assembly and particularly the Muslim League Party and kept the Quaid-i-Azam fully informed of the various developments and disagreements in the Muslim League Party.

In the event of a Governor withholding his assent to a Bill passed by the Provincial Legislative Assembly, the Governor was required to reserve the Bill for the consideration of the Governor General by Section 75 of the adapted Act. Whereupon the Governor General could either declare that he assented to the Bill or that he withheld his assent to the Bill. The Governor General could also direct the Governor to return the Bill to the Provincial Legislative Assembly for their reconsideration. Jinnah, as in other matters, took his powers of giving his assent to or withholding his assent from Provincial Bills very seriously. The evidence is provided by Jinnah's Private Secretary, S. M. Yusuf, who has recorded: 'A Provincial Government once wanted the

Quaid-i-Azam's assent to the promulgation of an Ordinance a few days before its Legislature was due to meet. Assent was refused, for by-passing the Legislature was not to be countenanced.'[23]

(b) Dismissals of Provincial Ministries

The first Ministry to be dismissed after the formation of Pakistan was that of Khan Sahib in the North-West Frontier Province. The Ministry was dismissed by the Governor on 22 August 1947. In a statement at a press conference in Peshawar on Monday 7 July 1947, before the results of the Frontier referendum were declared, Khan Sahib announced that if the Pathans voted to join Pakistan he would resign.[24] However, on 17 July he changed his mind and said, 'It is for my party to decide whether to resign or not. Last time I gave purely my personal opinion, subject to the condition that the Referendum will be honest, free and fair, but it is just the opposite.'[25] Soon after the results of the referendum were declared in which the N-W. F. P. had decided to join Pakistan, demands were made by League circles, specially by *Dawn*, for the dismissal of the Congress Ministry in the Frontier.[26] On 22 August 1947 the Ministry was dismissed. It has been reported that the Ministry was dismissed because Khan Sahib, the Chief Minister, had refused to take the new oath of loyalty to Pakistan. Thus, Lord Birdwood has written: 'For a while Dr Khan Sahib clung to his responsibilities. But on the establishment of Pakistan and his refusal to take the new oath Mr Jinnah removed him.'[27] *Dawn* alleged that Congress Ministers in the Frontier showed disrespect 'to the sovereign flag of the State by declining to attend its hoisting ceremony.'[28] From the evidence that the author has gathered, it is quite clear that neither of these versions is accurate. The dismissal of Khan Sahib's Ministry is also discussed later. Khan Sahib was dismissed by the Governor on clear instructions from Jinnah. Jinnah made it clear to his Governor in the Frontier that Khan Sahib's

---

[23] S. M. Yusuf, 'Quaid-i-Azam as Governor General', *Dawn* (Quaid-i-Azam Supplement), Karachi, 11 September 1949.

[24] *Dawn*, Delhi, 9 July 1947.

[25] Ibid., 20 July 1947.

[26] Editorial, 'Dismiss the Ministry', *Dawn*, Delhi, 23 July 1947.

[27] Lord Birdwood, *A Continent Decides*, London: Robert Hale, 1953. p. 35.

[28] Editorial, 'Dismissed', *Dawn*, Delhi, 27 August 1947.

Ministry should be dismissed under Sub-Section (5) of Section 51 of the adapted Act. Section 51 (5) clearly laid down:

> In the exercise of his functions under this section with respect to the choosing and summoning and the dismissal of ministers the Governor shall be under the general control of, and comply with such particular directions, if any, as may from time to time, be given to him by the Governor General.

It seemed Mountbatten had promised Jinnah that he would dismiss the Congress Ministry in the N-W. F. P., but was overruled by His Majesty's Government on the ground that such an action would not be proper as it would mean dismissal without any choice of dissolution when the Ministry still had a majority in the Assembly. In addition to this, dismissal of Khan Sahib would not have been liked by Nehru and other Congress leaders. However, Section 51 (5) gave enough powers to the Governor General of Pakistan to set aside constitutional conventions and dismiss the Ministry.

Another case of dismissal was that of M. A. Khuhro on 26 April 1948 when he was dismissed by the Governor under directions from the Governor General. The press communiqué issued from the Sind Governor's Secretariat on 26 April 1948 stated:

> Under directions from His Excellency, the Governor General, His Excellency, the Governor of Sind, has dismissed Mr Muhammad Ayyub Khuhro from his office of Premier of Sind under Section 51 (5) of the Government of India Act, 1935, as amended by the Pakistan (Provisional Constitution) Order, 1947, as *prima facie* case has been made out against him for charges of maladministration, gross misconduct and corruption in the discharge of his duty and responsibility.
>
> His Excellency, the Governor, is making arrangements immediately to appoint a Judicial Tribunal to enquire into the charges and allegations that have been made against Mr Khuhro and the fullest opportunity will be afforded to him to vindicate his position.[29]

Before Khuhro was dismissed it was also reported that serious differences had arisen between him and the Sind Governor, Sheikh Ghulam Hussain Hidayatullah, who had reallocated the

---

[29] *Pakistan News*, 21–27 April 1948, Karachi: Press Information Dept., Vol. 2, No. 17, p. 6.

Cabinet portfolios over the Chief Minister's head on the grounds that it would lead to more harmonious working and a more expeditious dispatch of business.[30] The Governor was within his rights to reallocate portfolios provided he was acting under the directions of the Governor General according to Section 51(5) of the adapted Act. However, Khuhro was dismissed on charges of maladministration and gross misconduct.

At the time when Khuhro was dismissed, other Provinces by no means presented a much better picture. On 25 April 1948, a day before Khuhro was dismissed, Jinnah was holding discussions with the West Punjab Premier, the Khan of Mamdot and two Ministers, Mian Mumtaz Daultana and Sardar Shaukat Hyat Khan. The talks concerned alleged West Punjab non-cooperation with Pakistan Special Police Officers appointed by the Central Government for dealing with corruption and the difficulties met in the expansion of the Cabinet.[31] In the North-West Frontier Province Khan Abdul Ghaffar Khan, on the charge that he had been in touch with the Faqir of Ipi, was arrested and promptly sentenced to three years' imprisonment under the Frontier Crimes Regulation. It was under these circumstances that the Governor General brought back a modified form of the old section 93 in the form of Section 92A in the adapted Act.

A notification issued on 16 July 1948 said: 'In exercise of the powers conferred by Section 9 of the Indian Independence Act, 1947, and of all other powers enabling him in that behalf, the Governor General of Pakistan has made the Pakistan Provisional Constitution (Third Amendment) Order, 1948.'[32] Under Section 93 of the Government of India Act, 1935, the Provincial Governor in his discretion, but with the 'concurrence of the Governor General in his discretion' could proclaim a State of Emergency within a Province. Under Section 92A the initiative was given to the Governor General, that is, it was the Governor General and not the Governor, who, when satisfied that the Government of a Province could not be carried on in accordance with the provisions of the adapted Act, might by proclamation, direct the Governor of a Province to assume on behalf of the Governor General all or any of the powers vested in or exercisable

---

[30] *The Times,* London, 26 April 1948.

[31] Ibid.

[32] *Pakistan News,* 13–20 July 1948, Karachi: Press Information Department, Vol. 2, No. 29, p. 8.

by any Provincial body or authority. Thus, under Section 92A the Governor functioned on behalf of the Governor General and interpreted not his own orders but those of the Central Government.

Khwaja Shahabuddin, Minister of Interior, while replying to a question regarding Section 92A in a press conference on 24 June 1948 said:

> I personally think that it is a question of confidence. If your elected head enjoys your confidence, I personally do not think that I shall hesitate to arm him with all the power that is necessary to meet certain contingency for the good of the public. I do not think that it creates an autocratic Government like what you had during the time of foreign domination here. A situation may arise when such powers may have to be exercised. It is the Governor General who will exercise these powers. It is still under consideration. Nobody knows what the final shape of things will be.[33]

(c) *Powers with regard to the Chief Commissioner's Province of Baluchistan*

Powers of the Governor General with regard to a Chief Commissioner's Province, like that of Baluchistan, are defined in Sections 94 and 95 of the adapted Act. Section 94(3) said:

> A Chief Commissioner's Province shall be administered by the Governor General acting, to such extent as he thinks fit, through a Chief Commissioner to be appointed by him.

Section 95(2) and (3) laid down:

> 2. The executive authority of the Federation extends to Baluchistan, but, notwithstanding anything in this Act, no Act of the Federal Legislature shall apply to Baluchistan unless the Governor General by public notification so directs, and the Governor General in giving such a direction with respect to any Act may direct that the Act shall in its application to the Province, or to any specified part thereof, have effect subject to such exceptions or modifications as he thinks fit.
>
> 3. The Governor General may make regulations for the peace and good government of Baluchistan, and any regulations so made may repeal or amend any Act of the Federal Legislature or any existing law which is for the time being applicable to the Province and, when promulgated by the Governor General, shall have the

---

[33] Ibid., 23–29 June 1948, Vol. 2, No. 26, pp. 6–7.

same force and effect as an Act of the Federal Legislature which applies to the Province.

It is again noteworthy that the words 'in his discretion' had been removed from the text of these Sections, but the Quaid-i-Azam in his Sibi Durbar Speech on 14 February 1948, while drawing attention of the audience to these constitutional provisions, included the word 'in his discretion' in the text that he quoted while making this speech.[34]

In the same speech the Quaid-i-Azam also said:

...I have come to the conclusion that our immediate object can best be achieved by making the governance and administration of Baluchistan more directly the concern of the Governor General himself acting in close collaboration with the acknowledged representatives of the people. For this purpose I have decided to constitute a Governor General's Advisory Council, a body which will enable the people to play their full part in the administration and governance of their province....[35]

Though the members of the Advisory Council would be nominated by the Governor General, yet it would have the power to advise the Governor General on any matter which in its opinion was connected with the good of the Province. The Budget of the Province, for instance, would be checked and scrutinized, first, by the Advisory Council, and it would be free to submit its recommendations to the Governor General. The Quaid-i-Azam went on to argue:

Thus, Gentlemen, in some ways you will be better off than the other provinces of Pakistan. Here you will have in fact a Governor General's province and you will become my special responsibility and care and let me assure you that in this sphere of activities, the Governor General will adopt such measures as may be necessary, in consultation with his Advisory Council from time to time.[36]

In the press conference that he held on 15 February 1948 the Quaid-i-Azam was asked whether he was in favour of a dictatorial form of government, rather than a democratic one, since in his Sibi

[34] *Pakistan News*, 11–17 February 1948, Karachi: Press Information Department, Vol. 2, No. 7, pp. 9–14. See also *Quaid-e-Azam Speaks*, Karachi: Pak Publicity, n.d., pp. 74–75.
[35] *Quaid-e-Azam Speaks*, op. cit., pp. 73–74.
[36] Ibid., pp. 76–77.

Durbar Speech he has said that Baluchistan would be better off than the other Provinces because it would be the Governor General's special responsibility. The Quaid-i-Azam replied that this would be a wrong assumption. 'I was thinking of provisional measures which would help in getting things done, rather than lengthy processes involved in full-fledged parliamentary discussions.' He pointed out that this did not mean that he was in favour of dictatorship. Baluchistan was a backward Province as compared with others which had gone through constitutional changes in 1910, 1921, and 1930 and 1935. Baluchistan, on the other hand, had not gone through these various stages of parliamentary form of government.[37] It is again interesting to see how closely similar are the ideas of the Quaid-i-Azam as regards progressive realization of responsible government to those of his predecessors, namely, the British Governors and Viceroys.

Thus, it is clear that the Quaid-i-Azam had inordinate constitutional powers. Even though his discretionary powers with regard to the Central Cabinet in Sections 10–17 had been deleted in the adapted Act and he was expected to act on advice, it has been seen that through Section 17 he had recovered most of these powers. Under this Section he could make rules for the more convenient transaction of the business of the Federal Government and also for the allocation of work among the Ministers of the Government. Through these rules the Governor General could establish his control over the entire mechanism of Cabinet Government. It was he who had picked the Central Cabinet and distributed the portfolios among the Ministers. He had also created a Ministry for himself. It will be seen later that he sometimes presided over the Cabinet Meetings, and the Cabinet accepted his decisions.

In the Provincial sphere, he had Sections 51 and 92A in his armoury. Here again no Ministry could advise him. As Liaquat Ali Khan said, 'He can do whatever he likes.'

Thus, here was a Governor General who was not only more powerful than his other contemporary Governors General, but also more powerful than his predecessors, the Viceroys of India. In the original Government of India Act, 1935, the Governor General, with all the paraphernalia of powers conferred on him

---

[37] *Pakistan News*, 11 17 February 1948, Karachi: Press Information Department, Vol. 2, No. 7, pp. 18–20.

in the Act and in his Instrument of Instructions, was still answerable to the British Parliament through the Secretary of State for India. If he were in error, relief could be obtained by an appeal, as in the classical case in 1892 in New Zealand when Ministers remained in office on the refusal of the Governor to add Members to the Upper Chamber until the Governor was advised by the Colonial Secretary to accept their advice.[38] But who was Jinnah answerable or responsible to? From the evidence that the author has collected it is clear that Jinnah, when he was Governor General of Pakistan, did not write personal reports to the King as other Governors General did. Nor would the Constituent Assembly or the Legislature think of questioning his powers. The nation was always in a mood of thankfulness to its father and creator. Perhaps it would have liked to crown him if he had agreed. As *Dawn* wrote, 'His people will not be content to have him merely the titular Head of the Government, they would wish him to be their friend, philosopher, guide and ruler, irrespective of what the Constitution of a Dominion of the British Commonwealth may contain.'[39]

II. POLITICAL POWERS OF THE GOVERNOR GENERAL

It has been seen that even though the Governor General had been endowed with enormous powers in the Indian Independence Act, 1947, yet Section 8 of the Act made it clear that he could exercise these powers only with the consent of the Constituent Assembly. The question, therefore, arises as to whether the Constituent Assembly of Pakistan could curtail or challenge the powers of the Quaid-a-Azam. In this section it will be seen that there was no likelihood of this happening as the Quaid-i-Azam, in addition to being Governor General, was also elected as President of both the Constituent Assembly and the Legislature.

On 11 August 1947 Jinnah was elected as President of the Constituent Assembly. This was the highest honour that any Assembly could confer on its Member. But Liaquat Ali Khan, the Prime Minister and Leader of the majority Muslim League Party, and other Members thought that Quaid-i-Azam was bestowing an honour on the Constituent Assembly by agreeing to

---

[38] Arthur Berriedale Keith, *Responsible Government in the Dominions*, Vol. I, Oxford: Clarendon Press, 1928, p. 219.

[39] Editorial, 'From Founder to Builder', *Dawn*, Delhi, 13 July 1947.

become its President. Liaquat Ali Khan said, 'Sir, you have been rightly described as the architect of Pakistan and what greater fortune could we have than to have you as the President of this sovereign body, to build the state which we have got through your devotion, untiring zeal, selfless service and unshakeable determination.'[40] Abul Kasem Khan (East Bengal Muslim) said, '...You have condescended today to accept the office of the President of this Assembly, though it is no honour to you. You have shown us, the members of this House, a great honour by accepting the office.'[41] Begum Jahan Ara Shah Nawaz (West Punjab Muslim) said, '...Our nation is lucky in having you as the one who is guiding our destinies, the like of which I have not seen anywhere in the world.'[42] During the first few meetings that Jinnah attended as President of the Assembly no one was allowed to waste the time of the House by making irrelevant remarks. Even Tamizuddin Khan was pulled up a few times and told to redraft his resolutions when the Report of the Committee on Rules of Procedure, etc. was being discussed. Later on, when Jinnah was either too weary or ill to attend the meetings of the Assembly and when the Assembly had elected a Deputy President to relieve the President of his work, it is reported that Jinnah was not willing to sign any badly drafted Bill.[43]

Jinnah in his capacity as President of the Constituent Assembly signed the various Bills passed by the Constituent Assembly. But according to the strict law, namely, Section 6(3) of the Indian Independence Act, 1947, he had to give his assent in His Majesty's name to any law passed by the Constituent Assembly or the Federal Legislature. In 1948 the Law Ministry did advise that formal assent of the Governor General was required. This

---

[40] *Constituent Assembly of Pakistan Debates*, 11 August 1947, Vol. I, No. 2, p. 12.

[41] Ibid., p. 16.

[42] Ibid., p. 17.

[43] Hector Bolitho writes: 'His Secretary at this time has said, 'His seriousness was contagious: there was no lightness or humour in our work. When Bills arrived for him to sign, he would go through them sentence by sentence: "Clumsy and badly worded," he would complain.... He would say, "Split it up into more clauses!" "This should go back and be rewritten!" When I pleaded, "You will be holding up a useful piece of legislation," he would relent. But his vigilance did not weaken. "They can't hustle me," he would say. "I won't do it."' Hector Bolitho, *Jinnah: Creator of Pakistan*, London: John Murray, 1954, pp. 214–15.

opinion was overruled. Since a Bill passed by the Constituent Assembly had to be signed and thus authenticated by the Quaid-i-Azam in his capacity as President of the Constituent Assembly before it became a constitutional Act, the Constituent Assembly was not likely to pass a Bill which would be against the wishes of the Quaid-i-Azam. The Quaid-i-Azam did assent to Bills passed by the Federal Legislature, but he disliked assenting to Bills 'in His Majesty's name' and struck out that phrase whenever he assented to Bills passed by the Federal Legislature.[43a]

On 11 August 1947 Jinnah made his famous speech in the Assembly. Although it was supposed to be merely a President's Address, yet it turned out to be an important policy-making speech. He himself appeared to be quite casual about it '…I shall say a few things as they occur to me.'[44] He laid stress on three things: firstly, maintenance of law and order; secondly, rooting out of bribery and corruption; and, thirdly, equal rights of all citizens, be they Hindu, Muslim or Christian. As regards the evil of nepotism and jobbery, speaking like the Head of the State and not merely as President of the Constituent Assembly, he said, 'This evil must be crushed relentlessly. I want to make it quite clear that I shall never tolerate any kind of jobbery, nepotism or any influence directly or indirectly brought to bear upon me. Wherever I find that such a practice is in vogue or is continuing anywhere, low or high, I shall certainly not countenance it.' As regards the equal rights of Hindus and Muslims, his pronouncement was as follows: '…You will find that in course of time Hindus would cease to be Hindus and Muslims would cease to be Muslims, not in the religious sense, because that is the personal faith of each individual, but in the political sense as citizens of the State.'[45] The latter pronouncement must have caused some stir, specially among the rigid and uncompromising advocates of an Islamic State. G. M. Sayed, who had voted against Pakistan in the Sind Assembly, came out with the statement that Jinnah's speech bespoke a 'chastened mood' and

---

[43a] Sir Ivor Jennings, *Constitutional Problems in Pakistan,* London: Cambridge, 1957, p. 25.

[44] Hector Bolitho thinks that Jinnah worked for many hours on the Presidential Address he was to give to the Constituent Assembly of Pakistan on 11 August 1947. Hector Bolitho, op. cit., p. 197.

[45] *Constituent Assembly of Pakistan Debates,* 11 August 1947, Vol. I, No. 2, pp. 18–20.

amounted to an abandonment of those fundamental principles on which the Muslim League had based its programme and carried on its struggle for Pakistan.[46] *Dawn* tried to correct this 'misinterpretation' of Jinnah's speech. It pointed out that when Jinnah declared that in course of time 'Hindus would cease to be Hindus and Muslims would cease to be Muslims, not in the religious sense…but in the political sense,' he merely meant that 'a Hindu or any other person not professing the Muslim faith will not be debarred from participating in the administration of Pakistan, nor will he be discriminated against by its laws, nor will he suffer economically.'[47]

Jinnah's pronouncement as regards purifying the administration of Pakistan by rooting out corruption, nepotism and jobbery was also important. The Central Government promulgated on 13 February 1948 two measures, a Government of India Act Amendment Order and an Ordinance 'to enable them to set up an efficient machinery for rooting out the evil of corruption in Pakistan.' The Amendment Order conferred on the Central Government the necessary legal power to create a Special Central Police Force with jurisdiction, both in the Central and Provincial spheres, and the Ordinance created the Police Force.[48]

What one notices in Jinnah's Presidential Address was that he was not merely speaking as President of the Constituent Assembly, nor was he making a Speech from the Throne. Obviously this speech was not written by his Prime Minister, nor is there any evidence to show that he had formulated his thoughts after consulting his Prime Minister.

On 12 August 1947 Liaquat Ali Khan moved 'that this Assembly resolves that Mr Mohammad Ali Jinnah, President of Constituent Assembly of Pakistan and Governor General designate of Pakistan be addressed as 'Quaid-i-Azam Mohammad Ali Jinnah, Governor General of Pakistan' in all official Acts, documents, letters and correspondence from 15 August 1947.'[49] Replying to the Debate on this Motion, Liaquat Ali Khan said:

---

[46] Editorial, 'Perverse Propaganda', *Dawn*, Delhi, 26 August 1947.

[47] Ibid.

[48] *Pakistan News*, 11–17 February 1948, Karachi: Press Information Department, Vol. 2, No.7, pp. 7–8.

[49] *Constituent Assembly of Pakistan Debates*, 12 August 1947, Vol. 1, No. 3, pp. 36–37.

Do not Honourable Members know that when Mustafa Kamal Pasha was always called in all official documents as 'Atta Turk' it meant the 'Father of the Turkish Nation'?.... Some people had been addressing Quaid-i-Azam as Shah-in-Shah (Emperor) of Pakistan. Some others had been addressing him a different way. Now he is not only the President of the Constituent Assembly and the Head of the State but he is also Governor General. That means he is also the legal Head of the State. Therefore it has been considered necessary and essential that there should be, as far as official correspondence is concerned, uniformity in the form of address for Quaid-i-Azam Mohammad Ali Jinnah.[50]

It was also announced on 23 August 1947 that the Governor General, Quaid-i-Azam Mohammad Ali Jinnah, who was the President of the Assembly and an expert on constitutional law, would also act as Legal Guide to the Assembly in drafting the Constitution.[51] On Friday, 22 August 1947 Quaid-i-Azam Mohammad Ali Jinnah's name was read in Khutba at the Pakistan Colony Mosque. Pir Illahi Bukhsh, Education Minister, Sind Government, who led the prayer, in his statement said:

It is customary among the Musalmans to recite the name of the Caliph or King, if any, of the Muslim country in Khutbas after the Juma and Id prayers. Since Pakistan is now an independent country, it is but fair that the name of Quaid-i-Azam, the Head of a Muslim country, be included in Khutbas throughout Pakistan. I appeal to Muslims to start this in all mosques throughout Pakistan as this is an indication of an independent Muslim state. Quaid-i-Azam is the real Head of the independent State—Pakistan. The name of Quaid-i-Azam was read as Amirul-Milat Quaid-i-Azam Mohammad Ali Jinnah.[52]

Campbell-Johnson, writing about Jinnah's powers under the Ninth Schedule of the Government of India Act, 1935, has said: 'Here indeed is Pakistan's King Emperor, Archbishop of Canterbury, Speaker and Prime Minister concentrated into one formidable Quaid-i-Azam.'[53] This is not an exaggerated description of Jinnah's powers, though based on wrong premises. The author has already pointed out earlier in this chapter that Jinnah did not derive his powers from the Ninth Schedule of the Government of India Act, 1935. Even though powers of the

---

[50] Ibid., pp. 46–47.   [51] Dawn, Delhi, 25 August 1947.
[52] Ibid.   [53] Campbell-Johnson, op. cit., p. 156.

Governor General exercisable 'in his discretion' and 'individual judgment' had disappeared, yet the all-powerful Quaid-i-Azam was still there, and if he wanted, he could exercise most of those powers which were now available to him in slightly different forms. The new forms of power were those of Quaid-i-Azam, the Governor General, Quaid-i-Azam, the President of the Constituent Assembly, Quaid-i-Azam, the President of the Federal Legislature and Quaid-i-Azam, the Legal Guide to the Assembly.

9 THE CENTRE AND THE PROVINCES, 1947–8

In the earlier chapters an impression may have been created that Quaid-i-Azam Mohammad Ali Jinnah had more than his full share of what Hobbes regarded as the central weakness of human nature, a quest or desire for power after power. But as pointed out earlier, the Quaid-i-Azam did not have to acquire these powers. Most of them were given to him by Section 9 of the Indian Independence Act, 1947, whereby he could make 'omissions from, additions to, and adaptations and modifications of, the Government of India Act, 1935' until 31 March 1948. On 2 March 1948 this power was further extended by the Constituent Assembly to 31 March 1949. In addition to all this, inherent in the adapted Government of India Act, 1935, were the powers to issue a proclamation declaring that a grave emergency had arisen or existed in Pakistan under Section 102 and to exercise overall control over the Provincial Governors with respect to the choosing and summoning and the dismissal of Ministers under Section 51(5). On 16 July 1948, by the Pakistan Provisional Constitution (Third Amendment) Order, 1948, the Quaid-i-Azam inserted Section 92A in the Government of India Act, 1935. By this the Governor General could direct the Governor of a Province to suspend the normal constitutional machinery in that Province on the plea that a grave emergency existed which meant the Government of that Province could not be carried on in accordance with the provisions of the Act. All these instruments of Central control had been there in the armoury of the British Government of India. Pakistan, as a successor Government, was carrying on these traditions. Pakistan's neighbour, India, was also working on the same model.

Thus, Pakistan was not unique in possessing and exercising such powers. What was extraordinary was the location of these powers. In other countries, these powers were exercised by the

Central Cabinet which was responsible to the Parliament. But in Pakistan, neither were the circumstances normal nor could its Governor General be described as a constitutional figurehead. He was not only the successor of the powerful Viceroy but also the Quaid-i-Azam of Pakistan. The author has been told that the Cabinet by a resolution had authorized him to exercise all these powers on its behalf. He could overrule the Cabinet. He had, again by a Cabinet resolution, direct access to all the Secretaries and all the files.

Could it be said that here were all the essential features of a constitutional dictatorship? Frederick M. Watkins in his essay, 'The Problem of Constitutional Dictatorship', lists three basic criteria to distinguish constitutional dictatorship from the various other forms of absolutism. 'In periods of temporary emergency,' he argues, 'the problem is to find an absolute regime (1) which will be just sufficiently absolute to safeguard the interests of an established constitutional order, (2) which will continue in existence only so long as those interests are actually in danger, and (3) which will then be followed by an integral return to the previous constitutional system.'[1] It could be said that the 'established constitutional order' of Pakistan was in danger and Pakistan could not tackle some of the abnormal problems it was faced with through the normal constitutional and parliamentary processes. What was debatable, however, was whether the democratic processes, once suspended, would be restored, and also whether the Central Government was eager and hasty in setting aside parliamentary processes on the pretext that the latter were totally unsuitable to cope with the problems that had arisen.

Pakistan had not only inherited the powers of the British Government of India but also its administrative machinery. Herein lay a great danger. Powers have a habit of falling into desuetude when the emergency for which they are created is over. But it is very difficult to dismantle the machinery that is created to translate these powers into action. Once administrators taste power, the appetite for it grows by what it is fed on. The machinery that was carried over from the British days largely rested on the Governor and the Central civil servants placed in the Provinces. This machinery was not related so much to the Prime Minister as

---

[1] Friedrich and Mason, eds., *Public Policy*, Vol. I, Cambridge: Harvard University Press, 1940, p. 329.

it was to the *primum mobile* of the Pakistan constitution at that time, the Quaid-i-Azam. It was to him the Governors wrote fortnightly letters, a practice initiated during the days of Lord Linlithgow. These letters, as stated earlier, gave detailed reports of Provincial administration ranging from purely administrative matters to political problems like intrigues in the ruling party or the Cabinet or the inability of certain Ministers to take decisions at the risk of popular disapproval. The Governors, with the exception of the Governor of East Bengal, presided over their Cabinet meetings. There was no doubt that this machinery served a highly useful purpose, considering the nature of the problems and the quality of Pakistan's political leaders. But the unfortunate result was that the administrative machinery was kept in full gear even after the emergency was over on the plea that the Central Government could not afford to dismantle it because of the irresponsibility and immaturity of political leaders. What was never realized was that political leaders could not become mature and responsible as long as this machinery was retained in its full vigour and power.

I. REFUGEES AND THEIR REHABILITATION

Pakistan had inherited inadequate physical apparatus and very few trained civil servants to run the State. Many economists had prophesied its doom. Many Indian leaders thought that Muslims would soon come to their senses and rejoin the Indian Federation. Pakistanis, in their turn, believed that the Indian Government had a deliberate policy of pushing every Muslim out of India into Pakistan with the idea of choking the latter. Nehru told General Sir Frank Messervy in 1945 that 'his deliberate plan would be to allow Jinnah to have his Pakistan, and gradually make things so impossible economically and otherwise for Pakistan that they would have to come on their bended knees and ask to be allowed back into India.'[2] On the other hand, it could be said that India was faced with a serious refugee problem as well. But at that time mutual suspicion was so great that Indian and Pakistani leaders had lost all sense of objectivity and were in no mood to appreciate each other's difficulties. However, it was clear that Pakistan started with vastly more difficult

---

[2] Sir George Cunningham's Diary, 1947–8, entry dated 21 September 1947, p. 12.

problems than India. India had inherited a fully-fledged Central Government with all its elaborate apparatus. Pakistan, on the other hand, had neither proper equipment nor trained personnel. It was reported that some of its Ministers had wooden boxes as their tables and practically no filing system. The special trains carrying essential files and records from Delhi to Karachi had either been burnt or derailed. The delivery of military equipment assigned to Pakistan was deliberately delayed and some of it never reached Pakistan. And now it looked as if to hasten its predicted disintegration, the communal war broke out in all its barbaric fury in the Punjab.

> More Indian people have been killed during the short space of the past month than in all the civil broils of the past fifty years. Millions have been rendered homeless. A transfer of populations has been enforced on two administrations reluctant and ill-fitted to cope with it that already dwarfs in scale anything caused by war in Europe.... Men on both sides of the new boundaries talk of the opposite community with a venom and anger that the British rarely expressed towards the Germans or even the Japanese in the worst days of the war.[3]

Another report said: 'Lahore and Amritsar, the two chief cities on either side of the border, have the crumbling, burnt-over look of blitzed London or Rotterdam.... The latest authoritative estimates give more than 50,000 dead in the last six months, most of them Muslims of Eastern Punjab.'[4]

As the refugees poured in, carrying their lurid accounts of the brutalities that were committed on their kith and kin in East Punjab, the temptation to equal the Sikhs in mass killing must have been very great indeed. Thus, the special correspondent of *The Times* of 5 September 1947 wrote: 'The slaughter in East Punjab was worse than in the West because the Sikhs were better armed and better organized, but there have been massacres in West Punjab, like that at Sheikhpura, which were as bad as anything in East Punjab and the brutalities have been just as bad on both sides.'[5]

It is very difficult to see how any Government, however popular it might be, could have persuaded the Muslims to refrain

[3] 'Indian Communal War', *The Times*, London, 18 September 1947.
[4] 'On the Sikh-Moslem Frontier', *The Nation*, 20 September 1947.
[5] *The Times*, London, 5 September 1947.

from retaliation. The Government of West Punjab consisted of mostly inexperienced Ministers and civil servants. Sir Francis Mudie, the Governor of West Punjab, in his letter to Jinnah dated 5 September 1947 wrote:

> From various sources I hear that the political situation is deteriorating. Yesterday there was a minor refugee demonstration with shouts of 'Pakistan Murdabad'. I am told that Shaukat is afraid to show his face in the Muslim refugee camp here. I warned my Ministry about a week ago that this sort of thing was inevitable, that when things go wrong on a large scale it is always the Government that gets the blame.[6]

It was at this time, when it was widely expected that the Muslims in West Punjab would indulge in the fearful 'competition in retaliation' and when both the Central and Provincial Governments in West Punjab were finding it extremely difficult to cope with the situation, that the Quaid-i-Azam stepped in to exercise his steadying influence. In a speech on 30 October 1947 the Quaid-i-Azam, addressing a huge open air meeting in Lahore, reminded the Muslims of West Punjab:

> Remember that the scrupulous maintenance and enforcement of law and order are the prerequisites of all progress. The tenets of Islam enjoin on every Mussalman to give protection to his neighbours and to the minorities regardless of caste and creed. Despite the treatment which is being meted out to the Muslim minorities in India, we must make it a matter of our prestige and honour to safeguard the lives of the minority communities and to create a sense of security among them. I would like to impress upon every Mussalman, who has at heart the welfare and the prosperiry [sic] of Pakistan, to avoid retaliation and to exercise restraint, because retaliation and violation of law and order will ultimately result in weekening [sic] the very foundations of the edifice you have cherished all these years to erect.[7]

It was too much to expect that in a situation surcharged with intense emotion and bitterness that much heed would be paid to the words of even the Quaid-i-Azam. As reported earlier, at

---

[6] Letter from Sir Francis Mudie to His Excellency Quaid-e-Azam Mohammad Ali Jinnah, Governor General of Pakistan. Reproduced in K.L. Gauba, *Inside Pakistan*, Delhi: Rajkamal Publications, 1948, Appendix A, pp. 301–3.

[7] *Quaid-e-Azam Speaks*, Karachi: Pak Publicity, n.d., pp. 42 and 43.

Sheikhpura in West Punjab Muslims in a spirit of retaliation followed the Sikh example. Obviously the West Punjab Government was finding it extremely difficult to prevent the Muslims from attacking the Sikhs. Mudie wrote to Jinnah: 'I am telling everyone that I don't care how the Sikhs get across the border; the great thing is to get rid of them as soon as possible.'[8]

In addition to the problems of maintaining law and order and preventing Muslims from attacking the minority community, the West Punjab Government was soon saddled with an equally difficult task of rehabilitating refugees who had already started pouring in their thousands into West Punjab. *The Times* of 4 September 1947 reported that a column of Muslim refugees 20 miles long and estimated to number 200,000, most of them on foot, had been straggling into the border town of Kasur, some thirty-five miles south of Lahore, since early morning of 3 September 1947.[9] It was not merely a problem of absorbing or settling the refugees on lands left by Hindus or Sikhs but also one of feeding thousands of them and rendering medical aid to those who arrived in a pitiful condition. In an appeal for Christian nurses and missionaries to go to Kasur, Diwan Bahadur S.P. Singha, the Punjab Indian Christian leader, said, 'I cannot get the sight of the maimed, fiendishly wounded and acid burnt people from my mind.'[10] Mudie, in a letter which he wrote to *The Times* appealing for funds for refugees, wrote:

> Thousands, perhaps tens of thousand, will never reach the border. They will die on the road of starvation and disease. How many have already died no one knows, No one will ever know. Of one convoy that recently arrived over one thousand who had struggled on till they reached the frontier post just laid down and died. They could go no farther. The road was littered with corpses for miles.[11]

By 8 October 1947 some 1,628,000 refugees had already been exchanged between East and West Punjab, 450,000 were on their way, and 2 million in West Punjab were awaiting evacuation to India. According to figures given by the Director of Public Relations, West Punjab, the mass evacuation of Muslims from East Punjab was completed in less than three and a half months,

[8] Letter from Sir Francis Mudie, in K.L. Gauba, op. cit., pp. 301–3.
[9] *The Times*, London, 4 September 1947.
[10] Ibid.   [11] Ibid., 17 October 1947.

leaving only the clearance of pockets to be carried out. A total number of about 5.5 million Muslims had crossed the border during this period and about 3.5 million Hindus and Sikhs had left West Punjab for India. The Director's Report observed that 'a job unprecedented in the history of the world in its magnitude was thus accomplished within record time.'[12]

As it has been pointed out in the previous paragraph, the administrative system of Pakistan did not have an adequate number of experienced Secretariat and District officers to cope with problems which would have overtaxed the resources and personnel of even a much better organized administrative system.[13] However, it may be noted that the Governor of West Punjab being a former ICS officer and all senior officers being drawn from the same service, were not willing to recruit young officers on an *ad hoc* basis to fill the positions that had been created as a result of Hindu and British officers leaving the Province or seeking early retirement. They were so set in their ways and thinking that to them the only way to cope with the new problems was to ask the senior officers to look after more than one job or employ retired British officers.

When the two Provincial authorities of East Punjab and West Punjab started rehabilitating the refugees, it soon became clear that both Provinces had acquired masses of unemployable people who could not perform some of the tasks essential for the life of their respective communities. The overwhelming majority of Muslim refugees who had fled from East Punjab were poor peasants. The Hindus who left West Punjab were mostly shopkeepers, clerical officials and middlemen. The result was that West Punjab suffered from a serious dislocation of its economic life. Banks, telegraph offices, factories, irrigation services could not function properly because nearly all the subordinate Hindu staffs had left in panic.

There was no doubt that East Punjab suffered as well. West Punjab inherited most of the physical apparatus of the old Provincial Government. It also had some of the rich, canal lands left by Hindus and Sikhs. East Punjab started with none of

---

[12] 'West Punjab's One Year of Struggle', *Pakistan News*, 11–17 August 1948, Karachi Press Information Department, Vol. 2, No. 33, pp. 2–6.

[13] Letter from Sir Francis Mudie, in K. L. Gauba, op. cit., pp. 301–3. For extracts from Sir Francis Mudie's letter see pp. 243, above.

these advantages. Its first Cabinet meetings were held in fields and by the roadside. 'And even now the Seat of Government consists of tents pitched around a vacated Muslim school at Jallundur....'[14] Nevertheless, the handicaps with which the administration in West Punjab started were greater. First of all, it was relatively more difficult for West Punjab to train administrators and technical personnel than it was for East Punjab to improvise offices and communications. Similarly, West Punjab had received 5.5 million refugees as compared with East Punjab's 3.5 million. One-sixth of the entire population of West Pakistan consisted of refugees. West Punjab formed a much more important part of Pakistan than East Punjab did of India. Thus, the Report of the Director of Public Relations, West Punjab Government, said:

> Imagine a person with his vital limbs suddenly paralysed, who is asked not only to run but also to carry on his back a load which would be heavy enough for him even if he were in the best of health. It will be a miracle if instead of collapsing, he performs simultaneously the dual feat of healing his paralysed limbs and running a race against time. The history of the province of the West Punjab during the past one year is a story of just such a miracle.[15]

1. *Rehabilitation of Refugees*

West Punjab had inherited the great canal colonies of Montgomery, Lyallpur and Shahpur, a large part of which had been vacated by Sikhs. Here, each refugee cultivator who was settled with his dependents, was granted between five and eight acres. Large tracts of the northern districts of the Province, however, and particularly in Rawalpindi and Attock, consisted of poor, rocky land already over-populated, many of whose inhabitants earned their living in the army or on merchant ships. In the western districts, Dera Ghazi Khan, Muzaffargarh and Mianwali, was found the greatest poverty of all. The refugee cultivator, who was settled outside the canal colonies, received more land, up to twelve and a half acres, but there was little doubt that in spite of high food, grain, and cotton prices, refugee cultivators

---

[14] Homeless Masses in Punjab', *The Times*, London, 20 January 1948.
[15] *Pakistan News*, 11–17 August 1948, Karachi: Press Information Department, Vol. 2, No. 33, pp. 2–6.

found it extremely difficult to wring their means of existence from the soil.

Mian Iftikharuddin, Minister for Rehabilitation of Refugees in the West Punjab Government, came out with the revolutionary proposal that the only proper way of rehabilitating the refugees was through land reforms. He suggested breaking up the large estates in West Punjab with a view to 'distributing land among the refugees. This was turned down by the Provincial Government which was dominated by landlords like Iftikhar Husain Khan of Mamdot, Chief Minister, Mian Mumtaz Muhammad Khan Daultana, Finance Minister, and Sardar Shaukat Hyat Khan, Minister for Revenue. Mian Iftikharuddin had also excited the jealousy of some of his Cabinet Ministers because of his energetic administration. He resigned when he found that the Provincial Ministry was not willing to take speedy measures to rehabilitate the refugees. He also complained that the Central Government could have intervened on his behalf to pressure the Provincial Government to undertake land reforms.

The Provincial Government, in its turn, felt that it had done everything it could to absorb the refugees. The Finance Minister, Daultana, claimed that the Provincial Government was spending as much as fifty to seventy million rupees a year for the mere feeding of refugees. The Punjab Provincial Government suggested that it was now the turn of Provinces like Sind and the Frontier to resettle refugees in their areas.

Sindhi landlords could not be moved by any considerations of Islamic brotherhood or simple humanitarianism. Ghulam Mohammed, the Central Finance Minister, pointing his accusing finger at M. A. Khuhro, who had been dismissed as Chief Minister of Sind in April 1948, on charges of corruption and maladministration, said in the Constituent Assembly:

He bamboozled the administration and inflamed the Sindhi and the non-Sindhi question. The people who had money, the Zamindars, were so much poisoned against the refugees that in some places not only were they turned out but they were attacked. The refugees had no place to live, whereas houses were lying vacant and they were kept for their favourites, for Sindhis and none else.[16]

---

[16] *Constituent Assembly (Legislature) of Pakistan Debates,* 20 May 1948, Vol. I, No. 20, p. 719.

It was obvious that the Provinces were not cooperating fully with the policy of the Central Government as regards the resettlement of refugees. The Central Government, realizing the gravity of the situation, had created their own Ministry of Refugees and Rehabilitation. The actual task of evacuating, feeding and settling refugees was mostly in the hands of two officers of the Central Government. Both these officers were Englishmen, E. de V. Moss, Chief Pakistan Refugee Commissioner, and Brigadier F. F. Stevens, who directed all movement of refugees by the Pakistan Army. Liaquat Ali Khan, the Prime Minister, was more or less permanently stationed in Lahore and exerted his maximum influence on the Punjab Provincial Ministry to tackle the problem of resettlement of refugees speedily and efficiently. Without his intervention, it would not have been possible for the Provincial Governor to persuade his Ministers to employ a number of ex-Punjab and ex-U. P. British I.C.S. officers. Similarly, Liaquat was also appealing to the people in general to help the refugees.

All this was not of much avail. Under the original Section 102 of the Government of India Act, 1935, the Central Government could make laws for a Province with respect to any of the matters enumerated in the Provincial Legislative List in the event of a grave emergency when the security of the country was threatened by war or internal disturbance. A new amendment was introduced which further widened this power by inserting phrases like 'economic life of Pakistan' or 'circumstances arising out of any mass movement of population from or into Pakistan'. Thus, under the Government of India (Second Amendment) Act, 1948, Quaid-i-Azam Mohammad Ali Jinnah, the Governor General of Pakistan, issued a proclamation on 27 August 1948, declaring that a 'grave emergency has arisen and exists in Pakistan'. The Proclamation stated that, 'Whereas the economic life of Pakistan is threatened by circumstances arising out of a mass movement of population from and into Pakistan, a State of Emergency is hereby declared.'[17]

Under these emergency powers the Central Refugee Council directed Provinces and States to take up the following number of refugees: Sind, 200,000; N-W. F. P., 100,000; Bahawalpur and Khairpur States and Baluchistan, 100,000.[18] It was expected that

---

[17] *The Times*, London, 28 August 1948.   [18] Ibid., 3 September 1948.

this decision would solve, at least for the time being, the problem of excessive concentration of refugees in West Punjab.

2. *Feuding Ministers and the Quaid-i-Azam*

The Central Government and the Provincial Governor, Sir Francis Mudie, were both dissatisfied with the way the administration of West Punjab was being conducted by the Ministry of the Nawab of Mamdot. Mamdot had been the largest landowner in Punjab before Partition. But the award of the Boundary Commission was such that all his lands lay in East Punjab. He was very bitter and derived his principal support from the refugees. The Governor and the officials wanted to deal with all those who disturbed communal peace or embezzled evacuee property with even-handed justice. The Provincial Premier could not agree wholeheartedly with the Governor because of his political difficulties. In addition, he had never had any experience in administration. He was not very hard working and disciplined in his habits. Nor did he have political finesse and a determination to succeed in his job. In committee meetings, he often said very little and when decisions went against him, he was given to blaming the Governor or his colleagues. Daultana, the Finance Minister, on the other hand, was brilliant, extremely ambitious, and intriguing, but lacked the most essential quality of political leadership, namely, courage. Thus, after the exit of Mian Iftikharuddin, the Muslim League Parliamentary Party was divided into two factions consisting of the followers of Mamdot and Daultana with Mamdot still commanding a majority. When Jinnah came to know of these feuds, he summoned the Governor along with Mamdot and Daultana to Karachi in April 1948. At this meeting, according to evidence disclosed to the author, the Governor General said that 'he found Mamdot totally unfit to be Prime Minister of the Punjab, however great his services to the League had been. He had therefore decided that Mamdot must resign and that Daultana should take his place.' Daultana, faced with such an order from the Governor General suggested that it would be better if he were to get himself elected to that post by the party. The Governor General was angry and surprised that Daultana had suggested such a course of action when the correct procedure should have been for Daultana to accept the Governor General's 'commission' and then ask the party to support him. After this episode, Jinnah lost interest in the matter and probably wanted to wait until the situation deteriorated so much that he would be forced to take action. The Governor who had been asked by Jinnah to bring the resignations of his two Ministers with him to the meeting, was advised to return them. The Ministers were delighted to have their resignations back but were puzzled and alarmed as to what further course of action their Quaid-i-Azam was likely to take.

Another controversy that the Quaid-i-Azam was called upon to decide was that relating to the opposition of Sindhi leaders to the contemplated move of the Central Government to make Karachi the capital of Pakistan. The Sind Assembly unanimously passed on 2 February 1948 a resolution opposing the 'contemplated move of the Pakistan Government to remove the city of Karachi from the control of Sind administration and place it under its own immediate jurisdiction as a centrally administered area.' This controversy brought to light the conflict and tension that was brewing between the Punjabi and Sindhi interests in Karachi. Sindhis felt that being much less advanced and sophisticated than the Punjabis they, as the hosts, were being gradually elbowed out by their guests. A typical comment was that of M. H. Gazder: '...But one defect in the Punjabi's character is that wherever a Punjabi goes, he establishes a Punjabi colony, Punjabi administration, employs Punjabis, he would invite all his relatives and he will use all his powers for appointment of all his relatives and friends.'[19] Even though the Constituent Assembly in May 1948, decided by a resolution that Karachi should be made the capital of Pakistan, the Muslim League Party in the Sind Assembly did not accept the decision of the Constituent Assembly and sent a deputation to Ziarat where the Quaid-i-Azam was lying ill to seek his advice on the matter. It is interesting to note that a communique from the Governor General's house said: 'The deputation submitted that they were anxious to know his views not so much as Governor General but as Quaid-i-Azam.' The communique said that 'the Quaid-i-Azam's advice and counsel to them finally was that they willingly accept the proposal of the Central Government which had been adopted by

---

[19] Quoted by M. H. Gazder in his Constituent Assembly Speech. *Constituent Assembly of Pakistan Debates,* 22 May 1948, Vol. III, No. 3, pp. 79–80.

the Constituent Assembly, the highest and supreme body in Pakistan....'[20] Karachi was declared the capital of Pakistan by the Governor General's Order called the Pakistan (Establishment of the Federal Capital) Order, 1948, issued on 23 July 1948.

How was it that when Pakistan was faced with such formidable problems as the rehabilitation of millions of refugees, the establishment of an administrative system almost from scratch in several parts of the country, and external dangers like the Kashmir conflict that its political leaders were feuding with each other? The answer lay in the way the Muslim League had been organized. Most of the League leaders had merely been used to carrying out orders of the Central Muslim League or the Quaid-i-Azam. Now for the first time they were being called upon to function as a team and tackle a number of serious administrative problems. They had no experience of so much authority being delegated to their hands. The Quaid-i-Azam was too weary, old and overwhelmed by other problems to give his directives on every detail. Intellectually as well the League leaders were mostly second-raters and it was too much to expect from them that they would rise to the occasion and meet the new challenges. It was obvious that in such a set-up the power and influence of the Central Government would increase and Provincial autonomy be reduced to a farce. Similarly, the Governor and his officials would occupy the vacuum created by the feuding Ministers. And the idea was gaining rapid currency among the officials that politicians could only make a mess of things. Not many people could foresee that the breakdown of the parliamentary system in the Provinces would ultimately result in its erosion at the Centre as well.

II. The N-W. F. P. Ministry

On 8 August 1947 Lord Mountbatten sent a telegram to the India Office saying that the Pakistan Provisional Government had officially advised him that he should either direct the Governor of the North-West Frontier Province to dismiss the Congress Ministry of Khan Sahib and form a Muslim League Ministry in its place or impose Section 93 in the Province, appoint Muslim League leaders as advisers and then install a Muslim

---

[20] *Pakistan News*, 23–29 June 1948, Karachi: Press Information Department, Vol. 2, No. 26, p. 4.

League Ministry by 14 August at the latest. The Viceroy proposed that the latter alternative should be adopted. He also added that according to the information furnished to him by Liaquat Ali Khan, Khan Sahib had intentions of proclaiming an independent Pathanistan in the Frontier on 15 August. The India Office disagreed with the Viceroy's suggestion and pointed out that since the Congress Ministry still had a majority in the House, the Ministry could not be dismissed. If the Governor were satisfied that Khan Sahib and his Ministry had lost the confidence of the people, the Assembly should be dissolved and fresh elections held. As regards Section 93, the India Office said that it could not be invoked because there was no clear indication that the constitutional machinery of the Province had broken down under the Congress Ministry. Similarly, they doubted whether Liaquat's information as regards the proclamation of Pathanistan was correct. Therefore, the India Office took the position that the Congress Ministry should not be removed before 15 August because His Majesty's Government would be held responsible for this action for which they could offer no justification.

It seems that the Quaid-i-Azam was angry with Mountbatten because he had originally promised to get the Ministry removed before 15 August and had failed to carry out his promise. The Quaid was not being quite fair to Mountbatten because the Viceroy did advise the Secretary of State to agree to the dismissal of the Congress Ministry in the Frontier but was overruled. Perhaps the Quaid did not relish the idea of himself dismissing Khan Sahib and thereby giving the impression of being arbitrary. On 22 August Sir George Cunningham, Governor of the N-W. F. P., was directed by the Governor General to dismiss the Ministry of Khan Sahib.

One can understand why Jinnah was reluctant to use the extraordinary powers available to him under the Government of India Act, 1935, to dismiss a Provincial Ministry. The dismissal of Khan Sahib's Ministry created a precedent and the later Central Governments also resorted to their reserve powers in dismissing Provincial Ministries. The Governor knew the Frontier and its leaders intimately. Khan Sahib, though under the influence of Khan Abdul Ghaffar Khan, was not an irresponsible person. He had given clear assurances to the Governor that as long as he was Chief Minister, he would do nothing injurious to the Pakistan Constitution, and that he had no intention of declaring an independent Pathanistan. Even if the League circles doubted the sincerity of Khan Sahib's professions of loyalty, they could have asked the Frontier Provincial League leader, Qaiyum Khan, to produce a majority in the Assembly and move a motion of no-confidence against Khan Sahib's Ministry. Such a course of action would have clearly saved the Central Government from resorting to its reserve powers and thereby creating a precedent. It may be noted that Qaiyum Khan did succeed in winning seven Congressmen to his side in January 1948. If this were not possible at an early stage, it was surely open to the Central Government to direct the Governor to dissolve the Provincial Assembly and hold fresh elections. The precedent of dismissing a Ministry which had a majority and then commissioning another man to form a Ministry in the hope that the latter would soon be in a position to produce a majority was bound to lead to political instability in the Provinces.

Abdul Qaiyum Khan was invited to form a Ministry on 22 August 1947. According to Jinnah's instructions given under Section 51(5) to the Governor, the Ministry was to consist of only two persons, including the Chief Minister. It may be pointed out that Section 51(5), which said that in the matters of 'the choosing and summoning and the dismissal of ministers', the Governor would have to comply with such particular directions as might be issued to him by the Governor General, was inserted in the Government of India Act, 1935, by Lord Mountbatten on the advice of Jinnah. This provision was reminiscent of Resolution No. 2 of the Muslim League Working Committee passed in October 1939. According to this resolution, the President was empowered to 'advise, guide and issue instructions to Muslim League parties in the various Provincial Legislatures in the event of some sudden emergency arising.' It has been seen in Chapter VI that Jinnah did make use of these powers. Thus, when Qaiyum pressed the Governor that he should have a third Minister in his Cabinet, the Governor wrote to Jinnah asking for his instructions in this matter.

Abdul Qaiyum Khan, as Deputy Leader of the Congress Party in the Central Legislative Assembly, had thundered ineffectively for a long time from the Congress benches. Power had come to him after a long time and now that it was within his grasp, he wanted to make full use of it. There was no doubt that he was a man of tremendous energy and knew how to get things done efficiently and promptly. There was one thing that he could not tolerate and that was opposition. He was not liked by some of the Muslim League leaders themselves, most notable among them being the Pir of Manki Sharif, mainly because of his autocratic and ruthless methods and also because he was not a Pathan, being a Kashmiri by origin. But more important than this discontent in the Muslim League ranks was the fact that Qaiyum for nearly two and a half months after he assumed office did not have a majority in the House. The Muslim League Party had about 15 members as compared to 21 members of the Congress Party. The Chief Minister was quite concerned about his position in the House as the Budget Session which was to be held in March 1948, was approaching. Furthermore, he was being pestered by his party men for all kinds of favours. Qaiyum suggested to the Governor that an ideal arrangement for the Province would be to remove the Legislature altogether and have a referendum every three years in which a leader would be chosen who would be allowed to select three or four colleagues to run the whole administration. The Governor also thought that perhaps a system like that was more suitable to conditions in the subcontinent than a parliamentary form of government. Jinnah, on the other hand, was thinking of dissolving the Assembly *sine die*. However, neither of the schemes came to fruition because the Muslim League was successful in persuading seven Congressmen to join their party in January 1948.

After Qaiyum Khan stabilized his position as Chief Minister, he turned towards his opponents and wanted to crush them on the plea that they were enemies of Pakistan. He was intent on arresting Khan Abdul Ghaffar Khan on one pretext or another. This was an extremely shortsighted policy so far as the larger interests of Pakistan were concerned. There was a dearth of talent and leadership in the Frontier. Qaiyum's policy should have been to work with moderate sections among the Congress led by Khan Sahib. By arresting a leader like Abdul Ghaffar Khan he made him not only a martyr in the eyes of the general public but also antagonized the moderates in the Congress. Abdul Ghaffar Khan before Partition had captured the imagination of the

Pathans for his defiance of the British Raj. He was popularly known as the Frontier Gandhi. Qaiyum was making the same mistake that the former British Home Secretaries had made. They also had taken the line that the best way of dealing with the Congress in the Frontier was to crush it. Perhaps a more important factor which influenced Qaiyum Khan's policy towards the Congress was his fear that if some sort of compromise or settlement were to be arrived at between the Pakistan Government and the Khan brothers, he might cease to occupy the most prominent place in the Frontier. There is clear evidence to show that Khan Abdul Ghaffar Khan, who had already met Jinnah in Karachi, was making overtures to the Muslim League leaders and assuring them that he would be loyal to Pakistan.

The Governor in a note submitted to Jinnah said that Pathanistan at that time was not mooted by anyone in the Frontier as a serious demand and that none of the Congress leaders harboured any feelings of disloyalty towards Pakistan. Khan Abdul Ghaffar Khan could be a source of serious trouble in the future if he were unnecessarily antagonized or not handled skilfully. 'The only sense in which the "Pathanistan" movement has any reality seems to be that there is a definite disinclination of the people (officials and public) to be linked with the Punjab. I think they fear that the Punjab might "swamp" them.' What the Governor had been striving for since a long time was to bring about a confluence between right-wing members of the old Congress Party and those elements like the Khans, professional men, villagers, etc. who were united under the Muslim League. But nobody took much heed of this sound advice and warning. However, it was clear that most of the seeds of future conflict were there during Jinnah's time itself.

III. First Signs of Discontent in East Bengal

As compared to the holocaust in the Punjab, there was comparative calm in Bengal. The problem of refugees and their rehabilitation was not very serious in East Bengal. But in the matter of setting up an administrative machinery, difficulties in East Bengal were much more formidable. Hindus had held more than their share on a population basis in the administrative services. Many of the most competent Registrars and Assistant Secretaries had been Hindus. The Secretaries in the Provincial Government after Partition were mostly Muslims who were either from the Punjab or from the U. P. In the entire Indian Civil Service of undivided India, there had been only one Muslim officer from East Bengal. He had risen from the ranks of the Provincial Civil Service and had been superseded many times before Partition. Thus, there was a serious shortage of competent officers in East Bengal. 'There was a time when over fifty per cent of the Civil and Criminal Courts could not function owing to the shortage of judicial and executive officers.'[21] Similarly, the economic life of the new Province was more or less paralysed when the exodus of Hindu businessmen and accountants took place.

Just as there was resentment against Punjabi officers in Sind, so was there a similar grievance against the Punjabi and U. P. officials in East Bengal. In the first flush of patriotic fervour, the differences in culture and language between East Bengalis and their superior officers did not seem serious. But soon the Bengalis became aware of the fact that the non-Bengali officials would not care to learn the local language and expected the people in Bengal to learn Urdu or English. They found it difficult to fill out their money order forms or understand the value of the money written on stamps, etc. because Bengali was nowhere to be found on any of these documents.[22] East Bengal also felt isolated from West Pakistan and therefore it was suggested that some of the sessions of the Assembly should also be held in Dacca. Supporting this suggestion, Begum Shaista Suhrawardy Ikramullah said, 'A feeling is growing among the Eastern Pakistanis that Eastern Pakistan is being neglected and treated merely as a 'colony' of Western Pakistan.'[23]

Thus, the tension and ill-feeling between the Punjabi and U. P. officers and their East Bengali subordinates and clerks increased slowly but steadily. Similarly, the relationship between some of the East Bengali politicians and their West Pakistani opposite numbers was far from cordial. There was a widespread belief in Karachi and Lahore that East Bengalis regarded themselves as

---

[21] Khwaja Nazimuddin's Address as the Governor General, *Constituent Assembly (Legislature) of Pakistan Debates*, 16 December 1948, Vol. II, No. 2, p. 4.

[22] *Constituent Assembly of Pakistan Debates*, 25 February 1948, Vol. II, No. 2, p. 16.

[23] Ibid., 24 February 1948, Vol. II, No. 1, pp. 6–7.

Bengalis first and Pakistanis second. A demand for the recognition of Bengali as a separate state language equal to Urdu had also sprung into being.

The Governor General visited East Bengal in March, 1948. His speeches clearly indicated that the grievances of East Bengalis with regard to their language, their economic and administrative backwardness, and the alleged supercilious or haughty attitude of the Punjabi and Urdu-speaking Muslim officers could not be brushed aside lightly. For each malady the Quaid-i-Azam prescribed a sovereign remedy. As regards the growing feeling of provincialism, the Quaid-i-Azam had this to say, 'Islam has taught us this, and I think you will agree with me that whatever else you may be and whatever you are, you are a Muslim. You belong to a nation now; you have now carved out a territory, a vast territory, it is all yours; it does not belong to a Punjabi or a Sindhi or a Pathan, or a Bengali, it is yours.'[24] But presumably the growing middle-class in East Bengal felt that in addition to Islam, they should be bound to the Centre by tangible means like better living conditions and better employment opportunities in their Province. As the father of the nation, Jinnah could soothe their tempers. He could advise them to be patient. And they knew he was impartial. He himself was neither a Punjabi, nor a Sindhi. They could not associate him with any Province. Thus:

> Please do not think that I do not appreciate the position. Very often it becomes a vicious circle. When you speak to a Bengali he says: 'Yes, you are right, but the Punjabi is so arrogant'; when you speak to the Punjabi or non-Bengali, he says, 'Yes, but these people do not want us here, they want to get us out'. Now this is vicious circle and I do not think anybody can solve this Chinese puzzle. The question is, who is going to be more sensible, more practical, more statesmanlike, and will be rendering the greatest service to Pakistan? So make up your mind and from today put an end to this sectionalism.[25]

In Muslim countries an aged person is regarded with great respect. The Quaid-i-Azam had not only won Pakistan, but also grown considerably old in winning it. Thus, many people were prepared to listen to him even if they were not sure that he was right. Thus, he could get away by declaring quite clearly that the

---

[24] *Quaid-e-Azam Speaks,* Karachi: Pak Publicity, n.d., p. 129.
[25] Ibid., pp. 131–2.

state language of Pakistan was going to be Urdu and no other language. 'Anyone who tries to mislead you is really the enemy of Pakistan. Without one State Language, no Nation can remain tied up solidly together and function.'[26]

The Governor General also knew that an agitation had been organized by the followers of Suhrawardy against the Provincial Government on the language issue. This agitation had also the support of a number of Muslim Leaguers who had been former supporters of Suhrawardy in undivided Bengal. Muhammad Ali (Bogra) and Tafazzal Ali were leading figures in the agitation. The Quaid's technique was to weaken the agitation by depriving it of some of its leaders. Muhammad Ali (Bogra), who later became Prime Minister of Pakistan, was sent to Burma as the Ambassador of Pakistan. Tafazzal Ali was offered a post in the Provincial Ministry. It may be noted that when in 1952 Khwaja Nazimuddin, as Prime Minister, advised the Bengalis that they should accept Urdu as the national language of Pakistan and reminded them that the Quaid-i-Azam had also expressed a similar desire, he raised a hornets' nest. There was so much commotion that it finally led to riots and political unrest and the defeat of the Muslim League in the elections of spring, 1954.

The Government of India Act, 1935 with all its shortcomings was a great improvement on the Government of India Act, 1919. Its most distinct contribution to the advance of responsible government in India lay in the considerable degree of autonomy that was granted to the Provinces. At first the Congress Ministers in 1937 refused to accept office unless and until they were assured that the Governors would not use their reserve powers in day-to-day administration. The Congress was assured that the reserve powers were to be used for special or rare occasions and that the Governors had no intention of seeking recourse to them in normal circumstances. According to the Muslim League, the British Governors went so far in appeasing the Congress appetite for power that they did not protect the minorities whose interests they had been called upon to safeguard both in the Act and in their Instrument of Instructions. In those days Nationalists used to be great champions of Provincial autonomy, particularly because it was an effective weapon to use against the Governors who were agents of a foreign power. In Pakistan the foreign

---

[26] Ibid., p. 133.

power had disappeared and the office of the Viceroy and the Quaid-i-Azam was combined in one person. In addition, the powers of the Central Government in the adapted Government of India Act, 1935, had actually expanded instead of contracting. This meant that it was not easy for the Provinces to defy either the Central Government or the Quaid-i-Azam, the Governor General.

In justification, the Government of Pakistan could argue that circumstances were such that Pakistan could not afford the luxury of a full-fledged federal system. The Provincial politicians instead of helping the Central Government to resettle the refugees had acted in a short-sighted and selfish manner. In fact, one could argue that the Central Government had not used their powers of control and regulation over the Provinces effectively and wisely. They could have used these powers, for example, to pressure the Provinces into introducing land reforms. Nobody knew better than the Governor General how powerful the landlords of Sind and the Punjab were for he had dealt with them in the political field before Partition. By introducing land reforms, the Government could have acquired land to resettle the refugees and at the same time broken the political power of the landlords.

10 THE VICEREGAL SYSTEM AND THE MUSLIM NATIONALIST MOVEMENT

In the political system of the British Empire in India, all power in the final analysis rested in the hands of the Viceroy or the Governor General in Council. The Governor General was under the overall control of the Secretary of State for India and the British Parliament. But it was well known that the Secretary of State for India did not interfere in day to day matters, and even in broad policy matters the directives that the Secretary of State issued to the Governor General were largely influenced by the kind of information and advice that the Governor General furnished to the Secretary of State. The Central Executive in India was the Governor General in Council. It was true that after the Provincial elections in 1937, when the Government of India Act, 1935 was applied to the Provinces, there took place a marked relaxation in the Governor General's control over the Provincial Governments. But in the Centre, where the Act of 1935 was not implemented, the authority of the Governor General in Council continued relatively intact. The transitional Central Government, which lasted from 1937 to 1947, derived its powers from the Government of India Act, 1919, as modified by certain amendments.

In this system, all matters pertaining to the Central Government were under the control of the Governor General in Council. The will of the legislature as expressed by a majority could be overruled by the Governor General. The Legislative Assembly rejected the budget for six successive years from 1934 onwards and each time the budget had to be 'certified'.[1] It was only when the Congress or the Muslim League Members were absent that the Government was able to get its budget approved by a majority. The Governor General chose his own Ministers,

---

[1] R. Coupland, *The Indian Problem*, New York, Oxford University Press, 1944, Part II, p. 232.

and Indian Ministers chosen until 1946 (when an Interim Government representing the Congress and the Muslim League was formed) were more or less loyal supporters of British rule in India. It was reported by some of the Indian Members of the Executive Council that they had never been overruled by the Viceroy.[2] The secret of this smooth functioning of the Executive Council lay in the fact that both in matters of policy formulation and implementation, the Governor General in Council depended heavily upon the Central Secretariat. In addition to seeing the Members of his Council, the Governor General could see directly the Secretaries of various departments. This dominant influence of the Civil Service was not confined merely to the Central Government; indeed, the main foundation of this system of bureaucratic dominance was the district administration which was under the control of the Deputy Commissioner or the District Magistrate. It was true that at the Provincial level from 1937 onwards, i.e. after the Provincial elections were held under the Government of India Act, 1935, this political system became a mixed political system in the sense that at the Provincial level the bureaucratic domination was modified by the presence of the Congress or Muslim League representatives or representatives of other political groups in the Government.

The British Empire in India was basically held together by the Central civil services, the most important of which was the Indian Civil Service. Members of this service not only controlled the district administration but also the Provincial and Central Secretariats. Some of the important portfolios in the Governor General's Council were also held by members of the Indian Civil Service. It may also be noted that Governorships of some of the Provinces, and particularly those which constituted West Pakistan later, were held by the members of this service. The basic characteristic of this system was that a central unitary structure was imposed on a heterogeneous base consisting of regions, castes, tribes, etc. The bureaucracy was impersonal and recruited by and large on a merit basis, but it also performed certain political functions: the District Magistrate or the Deputy Commissioner not only represented the Central and Provincial Governments in the district, but also gave voice to the interests of his particular district, maintaining law and order and collecting

---

[2] Ibid., pp. 227–8.

land revenue. In performing these functions, he had to employ political skills. He arbitrated in local disputes and while doing this he maintained a balance between various castes and tribes in the district, and he tried to make sure that his district by and large was law-abiding and loyal to the British Government. His political and administrative skills consisted of a judicious combination of force and persuasion, and force was used only in extreme cases. Even when coercion became necessary, a skilful Deputy Commissioner or District Magistrate was expected first to employ threats rather than the actual use of force. These political and administrative skills have been characterized as *hikmat-i-amali* (judicious management).[3]

The role of the Deputy Commissioner was like that of a French Prefect: he not only maintained law and order but also controlled or supervised a host of economic and social activities in the district. Departments like Public Health, Education, Agriculture, and Irrigation all worked under his supervision. In matters like remission of land revenue, granting of agricultural loans, or building of schools, the people in the countryside depended almost entirely upon the goodwill and leadership of the Deputy Commissioner. This seriously undermined the role of the politician for he could neither put forward vigorously the interests of his constituents, nor was much patronage available to him at the district level. In no other Provinces of British India did this system strike such deep roots as it did in the Provinces of the Punjab and the North-West Frontier, which became parts of West Pakistan. These Provinces inherited the administrative system of what were called the Non-Regulation Provinces. The British found that the over-legalistic administrative system of Bengal, Madras, and Bombay (known as Regulation Provinces), with its careful definition of rights and obligations of the citizens and officers, had not produced an equitable system of justice. In the Regulation Provinces, the district officers could not use their discretionary authority to help the illiterate and poor peasants against the exploitation of the landlords and the moneylenders. However, the administrative system of the Regulation Provinces with its careful definition of the rights of the citizenry and the restrictions it placed on the authority of the district

---

[3] Philip Woodruff, *The Men Who Ruled India: The Guardians*, London: Jonathan Cape, 1954, pp. 179–80, 249.

officer enabled the growth of political consciousness in these Provinces.

In the Non-Regulation Provinces like the Punjab and the North-West Frontier, all powers—executive, magisterial, and judicial—were concentrated in the hands of the Deputy Commissioner. These Provinces, which were acquired after sustained military activity, were governed by a mixed cadre of Deputy Commissioners, drawn from both the Indian Civil Service and the Indian Political Service. A large number of the officers of the Indian Political Service were drawn from the Indian Army. It has been reported that when these areas were first acquired, directions given to officers were no more than these: 'Settle the country, make the people happy, and take care there are no rows.'[4] In other words, the British in the Non-Regulation Provinces had restored the old Moghal administrative system in which enormous executive power was concentrated in the hands of the local representative of the Government. The system in the Non-Regulation Provinces was clearly paternal and authoritarian rather than legal or democratic. In order that the peasantry in these areas might remain contented, the administration of justice was to be simple and quick. The Deputy Commissioner thought that the people placed in his charge were to be protected both from money-lenders and wily urban politicians. Above all, in these areas British interests had to be protected so that the influence of anti-British elements might be undermined and that of the conservative elements promoted. Sir George Cunningham, Governor of the North-West Frontier Province (1937–45 and 1947–8), wrote to Jinnah:

> What I have been striving for, for some years past, is to get the good right-wing members of the old Congress party to join up with all those elements—Khans, professional men, villagers, etc.—who used to oppose Congress and are now united under the Muslim League.[5]

This partly explains why political consciousness in West Pakistan, which has inherited the system of Non-Regulation

---

[4] Cited in Lieut. Col. R. North, *The Literature of the North-West Frontier of India: A Select Bibliography,* North-West Frontier Province: Government Stationery and Printing Office, 1946, p. 12.

[5] Cunningham Papers. Note on the N.-W. Frontier Province. Sent to Jinnah on 8 May 1948, p. 2.

Provinces, has seldom been as high as that in East Pakistan, which has inherited the system of Regulation Provinces. In order to evaluate the total impact of the colonial system in terms of social change among Muslims in India, the colonial system may be regarded as an independent variable, and the traditional system consisting of its types of authority structure and values as an intervening variable. What emerges is the dependent variable, namely the emergent political system and political culture. One can see the impact of Western rationalism or liberalism on Islam in the writings of Sir Sayyid Ahmad Khan, Ameer Ali, and Sir Muhammad Iqbal. However, it may be noted that profound as this impact was, Islam continued to exercise a moderating or conservative influence. First of all, Muslim liberal thinkers sought Islamic sanctions for propagating and accepting modern ideas of democracy, Western systems of education, equal rights for women, and so on. Secondly, the impact of the colonial system on the traditional types of authority structure, particularly in parts which became West Pakistan later, was very little. One could go so far as to say that even the egalitarian ideas of Islam had hardly exercised any influence on the traditional hold of the landlord, the *mullah*, and the *pir* over the peasants. So far as the British were concerned, it could be said that under their regime a symbiotic relationship had developed between the Deputy Commissioner and the feudal interests represented by the landlord and the *pir*. The British wanted a contented peasantry because the Punjab and the N.-W. F. P. formed a major strategic area for the defence of their Indian Empire against any external attack, for example from Russia. They freed the peasants from the rapacity of the Hindu money-lender through the Punjab Alienation of Land Act, 1900, but the domination of the traditional interests was left relatively undisturbed because the landlord, the *mullah* and the *pir* formed important links in the system of indirect rule. This system enabled the British to maintain political tranquillity in the usually turbulent tribal areas of the Frontier; indeed, one could argue that if the tribes had erupted in 1947 in support of Khan Abdul Ghaffar Khan, the establishment of Pakistan would have been delayed and perhaps seriously jeopardized. This calm on the Frontier had been achieved after years of skilful propaganda by such British officials as Parsons and Cunning-ham since the early part of 1939. This was largely done through the *mullahs*, and the object was to keep the tribes on the British side in the war.[6]

The Viceregal system performed the governmental functions extremely well. The enormous and relatively accurate data that was communicated to the Governor General and the Governor from the district administration and the Secretariat enabled the British system to perform its rule-making and rule-implementation functions. The legislature played a muted role in rule-making or legislation because it was more or less under the autocratic power of the Governor General. The goals of the British rule were clear and the art of *hikmat-i-amali* (judicious management) was so skilfully practised that a proper balance could be maintained between what the British considered the right and necessary amount of political freedom and that degree of coercion necessary to maintain British rule.

The capabilities of the British Viceregal system in terms of extraction, regulation, and distribution were of a high order.[7] Problems like inflation, the Bengal famine and the 'Quit India' movement of the Congress neither disrupted seriously the war effort nor the foundations of British rule during the Second World War. During the Second World War, the Indian Army expanded from 189,000 men with 1,115 Indian officers to an Army of 2.5 million people with 15,740 Indian officers. Impressive as the Governmental functions and the capabilities of the Viceregal system were, it found itself increasingly inadequate in its political functions and capabilities. The Deputy Commissioner could maintain the rural areas in relative political quiescence, but there was political and social restlessness in the urban areas, generated by Western education and nascent industrialization and urbanization, and above all by the activities of political groups like the Indian National Congress.

After the famous declaration of the British Government of 1917 regarding progressive realization of responsible government as the goal of British policy, it was clear that the British were prepared to set up representative institutions in India. But it was

---

[6] Memorandum in Cunningham Papers, C., November 1939 to May 1943, pp. 17, 22.

[7] For an analysis of the capabilities of political systems, see Gabriel A. Almond and G. Bingham Powell, Jr., *Comparative Politics: A Developmental Approach*, Boston: Little, Brown, 1966, pp. 190–212.

also obvious from the very beginning that the kind of trust and understanding between the British and the Indians that were needed to facilitate the growth of parliamentary institutions and an orderly transfer of power were lacking in India. We have already seen earlier that in 1942 Mahatma Gandhi confessed to the Viceroy, Lord Linlithgow, that had he read the Government of India Act, 1935 when it was passed, the course of Indian history might have been different. In other words, Congress leaders had rejected the Act without reading it. Considerable bitterness was injected into the British-Indian dialogue as a result of hasty and indiscreet pronouncements of British leaders like Churchill. It is well known that Churchill denounced the Government of India Act, 1935. The author has also gathered that Churchill refused to follow the then Viceroy Lord Irwin's suggestion that he should bring himself up to date on the Indian situation by meeting some of the Indian leaders who were visiting Britain to attend the Round Table Conference. Churchill wrote to the Viceroy: 'I have got a point of view with which I am thoroughly well satisfied and I'm damned if I will have any bloody Indian upsetting it.'[8]

Prior to the emergence of Gandhi as the Nationalist leader and the launching of the Khilafat movement of the early twenties, Indian leaders like Gokhale and Jinnah were constitutionalists who believed in a gradual and orderly evolution of representative government in India. The terrorist movements unleashed by Tilak in Maharashtra and other Hindu leaders in Bengal were mostly of a sporadic nature. Jinnah was not only a constitutionalist in the narrow sense of the term but a political craftsman who regarded politics as the art of the possible. During the twenties and early thirties one sees him as a mediator and a compromiser trying to bridge the gulf between Gandhi and the British or engaged in the difficult pursuit of keeping the rival Muslim factions led by liberals and conservatives within the Muslim League.[9] It is noteworthy that he was not only opposed to

[8] This quotation from Winston Churchill's letter to Lord Irwin has been furnished to the author by Sir George Cunningham, who was Private Secretary to the Viceroy, Lord Irwin.

[9] For Jinnah's attempts to mediate between the Congress and the British, see *The Indian Annual Register 1922*, Calcutta, 1923, Vol. I, p. 277. For his success in keeping the rival Muslim factions within the Muslim League, see *The Indian Annual Register 1934*, Calcutta, Vol. I, p. 318.

the non-cooperation or civil disobedience movements launched from time to time by Gandhi, but also was against the Khilafat movement in which Hindus and Muslims cooperated under the leadership of Maulana Muhammad Ali and Mahatma Gandhi. Jinnah felt that if the broad masses of people were admitted into a political organization, it would be difficult to control that political movement. It is said that he once suggested that only matriculates should be admitted to the membership of the Congress organization. Gandhi, on the other hand, was of the opinion that power could not be wrested from British hands without a mass movement.

Tilak was the first leader who tried to broadbase the Nationalist movement by appealing to Hindu religious sentiments. This was also a shrewd move on his part because he thought that under the cloak of religion he could carry on his anti-British activities and it would be difficult for the British Government to ban religious meetings as easily as they could suppress political meetings. This was not merely a matter of political tactics, but also indicated how ambivalent leaders like Tilak were: they wanted to organize mass movements by using Hindu religious symbols and slogans, and at the same time they wanted to build Indian nationalism on the basis of Hindu-Muslim understanding. They did not seem to realize that if they achieved the first objective of building a mass movement through religious methods, the attainment of Hindu-Muslim accord would become well-nigh impossible. This was because both Hindu and Muslim urban leaders often lived in two different worlds. In the world of universities, law courts and bar associations they talked about constitutional liberties and could cooperate with leaders of other communities. But when confronted with the world of village and families, leaders like Tilak seemed to be under the spell of traditional Hindu mores, customs, and ideas.

It was left to the genius of Gandhi to bring together under one organization the liberals and constitutionalists like Motilal Nehru and C. R. Das and the more conservative followers of Tilak and other leaders like Malaviya. He also supported the Khilafat movement because such an opportunity, he said, would not 'recur for another hundred years.' To Jinnah, all this and particularly the non-violent non-cooperation movement was an extreme programme which for the moment might excite the imagination of the inexperienced youth and the ignorant and the illiterate masses, but would eventually lead to disorganization and chaos. It is well known that the Khilafat movement not only resulted in frustration but increased Hindu-Muslim tension. However, Gandhi's hold over the masses increased steadily. He appealed to Hindu sentiments through Hindu ideas and symbols, and when he succeeded in building a mass organization the Congress was no longer a political party but a nationalist movement. Its high command was very much like the Viceroy's Government, with final power in the hands of Gandhi, and a Working Committee to deal with day to day matters of organization and discipline. Like the British Government, the Congress organization was also heavily centralized, with hardly any autonomy available to the Congress organizations at the Provincial level. Even when the Congress formed Provincial Governments during 1937–9, the power of the central high command could not be defied by the Provincial Governments. Gandhi declared: 'When we march as an army, we are no longer a democracy. As soldiers we have got to take orders from the general and obey him implicitly. His word must be law. I am your general.'

In such a movement there was no careful aggregation of interests. Most of the opposition could be silenced. Even a duly elected President like Subhas Chandra Bose had to resign because Gandhi had opposed his election. Socialist groups and even Nehru often expressed their opposition to some of Gandhi's doctrines, but they were helpless because of the tremendous mass appeal that Gandhi possessed. They knew that in order to make the movement increasingly broadbased, a leader like Gandhi had to address his appeals in symbols and forms which would move the great majority of his Hindu followers. The term *Vidya Mandirs* (Temples of Learning) used in the Congress educational scheme might appear highly distasteful to Muslims, but a great majority of Congressmen who were Hindus thought it 'a source of inspiration to ninety-nine per cent of the village population.'[10] Another factor which widened the gulf between the leaders of the two communities was that the Congress movement with its grassroot support produced new kinds of leaders whose cultural roots were closer to the broad Hindu masses rather than to highly Westernized leaders like Jinnah, or even to other

[10] R. Coupland, op. cit., Part II, p. 191.

Muslim leaders who were much less Westernized but Muslim in their culture and outlook.

Thus, a nationalist movement is not a carefully constructed aggregation of interests. It is led by charismatic leaders whose political skills do not lie in the art of compromise but in the capacity with which they can galvanize the dull docile masses into fierce fighters of the battles of freedom. A grand passion for freedom and social justice and not pragmatism becomes the life blood of such a movement. However, the British policy of progressive transfer of power and the extension of the franchise to thirty million voters under the Government of India Act, 1935 made the Congress and the League movements realize that they needed elaborate organizations if their representative claims were to be successfully tested through elections. This injected a sense of pragmatic realism into what otherwise would have been purely politics of the grand design. The Indian National Congress was much more successful than the All-India Muslim League in evolving within its organization appropriate mechanisms to resolve disputes between rival and regional factions.

To trace the development of Jinnah's political ideas from the first decade of this century onwards is to identify the links and clues that explain the growth of the Muslim nationalist movement leading to the establishment of Pakistan. To Hindus and the Indian National Congress, the changes that took place in Jinnah's ideas during the thirties and forties constitute a great tragedy which tore asunder the sacred unity of India. To Muslims, such changes symbolize the triumph of Muslim nationalism. During the first two decades of this century, one sees Jinnah as an ardent and tireless nationalist who believed that the foundations of the future Indian state should rest on the bedrock of Hindu-Muslim unity. In 1910, at the twenty-fifth session of the Indian National Congress, he introduced a resolution deprecating the extension of separate electorates to local bodies.[11] But Jinnah was always a hard-headed political realist. He knew that the great majority of influential Muslims wanted separate electorates, and the Lucknow Pact of 1916, of which he was one of the great architects, conceded separate electorates to Muslims. In 1919,

---

[11] Annie Besant, *How India Wrought for Freedom: The Story of the National Congress Told from Official Records,* Madras: Theosophical Publishing House, 1915, p. 518.

before the Joint Select Committee on the Government of India Bill, he declared: 'Nothing will please me more than when that day comes' when all distinctions between Hindus and Muslims would have disappeared.[12] He pointed out that within the next decade or so Muslims would cease to demand separate electorates, but leaders like himself, who believed in joint electorates, constituted a minority at that time.[13] Jinnah once said that it was his ambition to become the Muslim Gokhale, and Gokhale's own estimate about Jinnah was: 'He has true stuff in him and that freedom from all sectarian prejudice which will make him the best ambassador of the Hindu-Muslim unity.'[14]

In spite of his liberalism and modern outlook and his great skill in playing the role of a mediator between Hindus and Muslims, the realities of Indian politics were such that he found himself moving closer to the Muslim League than to the Congress. His increasing association with the Muslim League enabled him to understand that it was not so much their suspicion or communalism that explained the Muslim adherence to separate electorates as their genuine fears of being dominated by the more advanced Hindus even in Muslim-majority Provinces like Bengal and Punjab. Thus, in 1925, while explaining the details of the Lucknow Pact of 1916, Jinnah pointed out that even in the Muslim-majority Provinces of Punjab and Bengal, Muslims feared that under joint electorates they would 'never get even ten or fifteen per cent of the seats.'[15] The explanation was that numerically Muslims were in a majority in these Provinces, but as voters they were in a minority because of poverty and backwardness.

However, until the late twenties, Jinnah's basic approach to Indian political problems was more or less that of a detached or dispassionate expert who was expected to bring to bear his knowledge and skill to solving given problems. During this time

---

[12] *Joint Select Committee on the Government of India Bill Vol. II: Minutes of Evidence*, London: H.M. Stationery Office, 1919, p. 225.

[13] Ibid., p. 229.

[14] *Mohamed Ali Jinnah: An Ambassador of Unity: His Speeches and Writings 1912–1917. With a Biographical Appreciation by Sarojini Naidu*, Madras: Ganesh & Co., n.d., p. 1.

[15] *The Indian Quarterly Register 1925*, Calcutta: The Annual Register Office, n.d., Vol. I, pp. 68–69. See also his testimony before the Joint Select Committee on the Government of India Bill, *Joint Select Committee on the Government of India Bill*, op. cit., p. 225.

he did not identify himself with any particular group or community. Addressing the All-Parties Conference in 1925, he said: 'I have not come to say what Mussalmans want.... Let us put our heads together not as Hindus or Mahomedans but as Indians.'[16] Even though Jinnah had worked closely with the Congress, the League, and other party leaders, he was not only personally aloof but put forward a point of view which was often different from that of most of his colleagues. Even during the days when the Congress and the League followed their constitutional courses of action, his views were at variance with those held either by the League or the Congress or even the Home Rule League. Giving evidence before the Joint Select Committee of the Government of India Bill in 1919, Jinnah said: 'I told you that my position is this, that I have openly disagreed with the Congress, I have openly disagreed with the Moslem League, and there are some views which the Home Rule League holds with regard to these reforms which I do not.'[17] Later, when Gandhi established his ascendancy in the Congress, Jinnah's political loneliness became even more pronounced. Jinnah found during the late twenties that his constitutional compromises and formulae were being swept aside by the tide of the Congress nationalist movement that Gandhi had organized; similarly, he found that his own community, the Muslims, were somewhat distrustful of his liberal views. There is considerable evidence to show how politically lonely and helpless he was during this time. Commenting on Jinnah's role during the Round Table Conference, Lord Templewood has written:

> It is true that he intermittently took a prominent part in the debates, but many of us could never follow the movements of his volatile mind. He never seemed to wish to work with anyone. Was he in favour of All-India Federation? We could not tell for certain, though it is worth remembering that he never then suggested the division of India and the creation of Pakistan. Was he in favour of provincial autonomy without change in the Centre? Sometimes he gave us the impression that he did not wish to go beyond provincial autonomy, and at other times, that he demanded responsible government both in the Centre and in the Provinces. It was this elusiveness that

---

[16] *The Indian Quarterly Register 1925*, Vol. I, op. cit., p. 67.
[17] *Joint Select Committee on the Government of India Bill*, op. cit., p. 219.

made it difficult for us to cooperate with him, or for him to give any clear lead to his Muslim colleagues.[18]

In a speech that Jinnah made in February 1936, in Lahore, he said that during the Round Table Conference his views could not be identified with those of any delegate belonging to any political party:

Muslims were unhappy with me because of my views regarding joint electorates. My Hindu friends were angry with me because of the fourteen points that I advocated. Rulers of Indian states were indignant because I had opposed their secret negotiations and activities during the Conference. The British Parliamentarians were also resentful because I had characterized the Round Table Conference itself as a fraud.[19]

Similarly, one cannot do better than to quote Jinnah himself to show his sense of political frustration and helplessness:

At that time, there was no pride in me and I used to beg from the Congress.... I began to feel that neither could I help India, nor change the Hindu mentality, nor could I make the Musalmans realize their precarious position. I felt so disappointed and so depressed that I decided to settle down in London. Not that I did not love India; but I felt utterly helpless. I kept in touch with India. At the end of four years I found that the Musalmans were in the greatest danger. I made up my mind to come back to India, as I could not do any good from London. Having no sanction behind me I was in the position of a beggar and received the treatment that a beggar deserved.[20]

In February 1929, Jinnah suffered a personal loss when his wife, who was by origin a Parsi and younger than him by over twenty years, died. His marriage had failed in the sense that he had been separated from his wife when she died. Kanji Dwarkadas, who was a close friend of Jinnah and his wife, has recorded that Jinnah took her death 'as a failure and personal

---

[18] Viscount Templewood (The Rt. Hon. Sir Samuel Hoare), *Nine Troubled Years*, London: Collins, 1954, p. 52.

[19] Ashiq Husain Batalwi, 'Iqbal awr Tahrik-i-Pakistan (I)', Lectures in Memory of Iqbal, Panjab University, *Nawa-i-Waqt*, 14 March 1967. Extracts from Jinnah's speech given in Urdu in this lecture have been translated by the author.

[20] Jamil-ud-Din Ahmad, ed., *Speeches and Writings of Mr. Jinnah*,, Lahore: Ashraf, 1960, Vol. I, pp. 38–39.

defeat in his life.... He never recovered from this loneliness, and this loneliness added to the bitterness of his life; and I must add that this bitterness, born out of this personal loss and disappointment travelled into his political life.'[21]

Psychological explanations of why and how great men strive for power have recently gained considerable currency and intellectual respectability. Nathan Leites and Harold D. Lasswell have pioneered these studies. Lasswell has pointed out: 'Our key hypothesis about the power seeker is that he pursues power as a means of compensation against deprivation. Power is expected to overcome low estimates of the self, by changing either the traits of the self or the environment in which it functions.'[22] Following this line of thinking, Alexander L. George and Juliette L. George wrote their famous book *Woodrow Wilson and Colonel House: A Personality Study*. They tried to show how Wilson was so completely dominated by his father during his childhood that he sought compensation from this deprivation through his ceaseless struggle for the acquisition of political power. 'Throughout his life his relationships with others seemed shaped by an inner command never again to bend his will to another man's.'[23] Jinnah is also reported to have said that you could break him but never bend him. Like Jinnah, Wilson also had a 'single-track mind'. But there is no evidence to suggest that Jinnah's deprivation arose as a result of his personality being suppressed and dominated by his father. However, as we have seen, the deprivation that Jinnah suffered was the traumatic experience arising out of the failure of his marriage and the death of his young wife. Lasswell has cited cases 'in which a severe deprivation relatively late in life has led to furious concentration upon power.' The untimely death of his beloved wife and above all the shock that his wife had not loved him transferred Joseph II of Austria into the grim figure of his later days. Another case is that of John Bright, whom Jinnah admired and often quoted his famous prophecy regarding the disintegration of the Indian

[21] Kanji Dwarkadas, *Ruttie Jinnah: The Story of a Great Friendship*, Bombay: Kanji Dwarkadas, n.d., pp. 57, 58.

[22] Harold D. Lasswell, *Power and Personality*, New York: The Viking Press, 1962, p. 39.

[23] Alexander L. George and Juliette L. George, *Woodrow Wilson and Colonel House: A Personality Study*, New York: Dover Publications, 1964, p. 11.

empire into several states, who was so grief-stricken by the death of his first wife that he was persuaded by Richard Cobden to immerse himself completely in the struggle for the repeal of the Corn Laws.[24]

It may be suggested that there was a congruence between the personal needs and ambitions of a leader like Jinnah and the needs of the Muslim community. He had a domineering personality and nearly always had a point of view different from that of other Indian leaders. Since he could not get along with others, he needed an organization which he could dominate and through which he could put forward his point of view. It must have also become apparent to him that politics in India had undergone a remarkable change as a result of the growing strength of a mass organization like the Indian National Congress under the leadership of Gandhi. Under such conditions, power would gravitate towards leaders with a mass following. And if Jinnah were to confine his role to that of a skilful mediator, he could be neither powerful nor effective. After the Provincial elections of 1937, how Jinnah became increasingly and acutely aware of the power of a mass organization is indicated by the following extracts from his speeches:

> It does not require political wisdom to realize that all safeguards and settlements would be a scrap of paper, unless they are backed up by power. Politics means power and not relying only on cries of justice or fair-play or goodwill.[25]

> What is the difference between the Hindus and the Muslims? If Wardha makes any decision and issues orders tomorrow, millions of Hindus will follow and obey. I ask you, suppose the Muslim League were to issue any order, what will happen to it? We are not sufficiently equipped and trained, and therefore it will be difficult to produce lakhs of Muslims to carry out orders. The British Government is always thinking of what the Congress is doing, what is going to be the repercussion of the British policy in the Congress camp. But will the British Government think of you? No; because you are not an organized power. Therefore develop your power and establish your solidarity.[26]

In addition to all this, Jinnah had suffered a deep personal tragedy. In the dominant role that he played in the Muslim

---

[24] Harold D. Lasswell, *Power and Personality*, op. cit., p. 51.

[25] Jamil-ud-Din Ahmad, op. cit., Vol. I, p. 30. [26] Ibid., Vol. I, p. 44.

League movement after 1937, he found an outlet for the political talents and leadership qualities that he possessed. In the warmth and affection that Muslims displayed towards him, he could overcome his loneliness and personal tragedy; Muslims turned to him as a great saviour, for after the death of Maulana Muhammad Ali there was no political leader of sufficient stature to lead them.

Several volumes have appeared on Jinnah's life, and year after year Pakistani newspapers and journals publish articles on his achievements. The author is still unaware of any book or article which has analyzed carefully and convincingly the political strategy that Jinnah followed in building almost from scratch the Muslim League movement which helped him in achieving the state of Pakistan. When one looks through the ground that has been covered by other authors, several questions still remain unanswered. How did Jinnah succeed in establishing his mesmeric hold over the Muslim masses when he was not familiar with languages like Urdu or Bengali? How was it that through the Muslim League organization he obtained maximum support in Provinces where the Hindus were in a considerable majority, and above all during the time when Congress Governments were in power? How did Jinnah revitalize the Muslim League in Provinces like Bengal and the Punjab, where in the elections of 1937 the Muslim League had emerged as an extremely weak political party?

The secret of Jinnah's mesmeric hold over the Muslim masses lay in the fact that through Pakistan he was answering one of the deepest urges of the Muslim community, namely, the fulfilment of the promise of political power that the Qur'an offers to Muslims. Another explanation was that Jinnah, in hurling defiance at the great Hindu majority community, was doing something which a Muslim urban dweller or a student or a civil servant wanted very much to do in retaliation for the alleged slights and defeats that he suffered in competing with members of the Hindu community.

As regards Jinnah's success in building and popularizing the Muslim League in Provinces where the Congress Governments were in power during the years 1937 to 1939 and obviously had considerable patronage at their disposal, it may be suggested that part of the secret of his success was that he quickly made capital of the alleged injustices and persecutions that the Muslims were subjected to at the hands of Congress Governments in these Provinces. In a Province like the United Provinces, the Muslim League was helped by the fact that Muslims held important posts in the Police and Revenue administration, and their sympathies obviously were with the Muslim League rather than with the Congress. Another factor was the cry of Islam in danger raised by Muslim religious leaders. It may also be noted that the Congress Governments resigned their offices after the outbreak of the war in 1939, thus leaving the political field wide open for Jinnah to strengthen his political organization under the relatively impartial regimes of British Governors.

The task of organizing the Muslim League in Muslim majority Provinces and particularly in a Province like Punjab was extremely difficult. As suggested earlier, some of these Provinces in North-Western India were so dominated by Deputy Commissioners and landlords that it was a formidable undertaking for any political party to build grassroot support in the districts. When Jinnah tried to set up an independent Muslim League organization in the Punjab, he was bluntly told by the Unionist Party Chief, Sir Fazl-i-Husain, not to interfere in Punjab politics. This meant that Jinnah had to proceed warily. On all such occasions Jinnah's political shrewdness was at its best, and he often snatched victory from the jaws of defeat. During the elections of 1937, undaunted by the poor performance of the Muslim League in the Punjab when it obtained one out of eighty-six Muslim seats, he entered into a pact with the Unionist Party whereby the Muslim members of that party were admitted to the Muslim League Party. The Muslim poet, Iqbal, was against such a pact with Unionists, who in his eyes were either opportunists or reactionaries. Jinnah asked him to be patient for he wanted 'to pull them [the Muslims] up step by step and before making them run I want to be sure that they are capable of standing on their own legs.'[27]

This was precisely the strategy that Jinnah followed during the thirties and particularly during 1936–7. He knew that the Muslim League was no more than a forum for Muslim leaders for expressing their views and passing resolutions on all-Indian matters. Most of these Muslim leaders had their political bases in

---

[27] *Dawn*, Karachi, 25 December 1955. Also cited earlier on p. 93.

their respective Provinces. When Jinnah was empowered by the All-India Muslim League in April 1936, to set up the Central Election Board, it was well known that the Central Muslim League had no political base of its own and that Jinnah had to work in cooperation with Provincial leaders and their organizations. In Bengal, Fazl-ul-Huq had his Proja Party; in Punjab, Sir Fazl-i-Husain had organized the Unionist Party; in the United Provinces, Nawab Saheb Chathari and Sir Muhammad Yousuf had formed the National Agricultural Party. In Provinces like Sind, the Frontier, Bihar, and Assam, Muslim leaders had their respective political parties. It may also be noted that when Jinnah announced the formation of the Central Election Board in May 1936, consisting of fifty-six members, he included eleven representatives from the Punjab. These representatives from the Punjab were not drawn from the Muslim League alone, but representatives from parties like the Majlis Ittehad-i-Millat (Conference for National Unity), Ahrar, and the Congress were also included.[28] Later, when in the elections Congress emerged as the largest party in eight Provinces and refused to recognize the separate existence of the Muslim League as the representative of Muslims, Jinnah was able to persuade some of these leaders to join the Muslim League. Jinnah's next move was to establish or revitalize the Muslim League organization in the various Provinces. After the Pakistan resolution was passed in 1940, Jinnah's popularity and power increased with gathering momentum. The Muslim League constantly reminded the Muslims of their religious duty to support its programme and its goal of a Pakistan State which it claimed would be established on Islamic foundations. With such slogans and symbols, the Muslim League under Jinnah was able to overwhelm the opposition of both the Deputy Commissioner and the landlords in the Punjab. It also became apparent to the politicians that they could not gain any political office without the approval and support of Jinnah.

As we have suggested earlier, there is a marked difference between the structure and functions of a political party and a nationalist movement. The function of a political party is to aggregate the various interests in such a way that these group interests or demands may be converted into general policy alter-

---

[28] Ashiq Husain Batalwi, op. cit. See Lectures (2) and (6), *Nawa-i-Waqt,* 15 and 20 March 1967.

natives. Gabriel Almond has pointed out that interest aggregation
involves considerable political skill. A party has to juggle, bargain,
compromise, and coalesce conflicting interests into some form of
policy statement which accommodates all the major interests.[29]
The main purpose which motivates a political party is the capture
of power and running the government of the country. A nationalist
movement like the Muslim League, the supreme objective of
which was the achievement of Pakistan, needed different skills.
The Muslim League leaders knew that the British would soon
have to transfer substantial power to Indian representatives. They
had to rally quickly the different regional, tribal, and linguistic
Muslim groups behind the Muslim League movement. The most
potent symbol available to produce this unity was Islam. Thus, a
movement like the Muslim League sought to achieve its purpose
by reinforcing and capitalizing upon the existing and dominant
political beliefs and attitudes of the Muslims in India. We have
also seen that Gandhi, in his eagerness to mobilize maximum
political support among the masses, had to rely on Hindu symbols
and ideas. But the Congress organization had a much longer
history and experience, and had also been able to evolve a
machinery to resolve disputes or adjust differences between rival
factions. The Muslim League, on the other hand, had not been
able to devise such a machinery, and relied more or less completely
upon Jinnah to arbitrate the disputes that emerged.

Jinnah's main technique was to exhort the various regional
groups and other factions to overcome their differences and rival
claims so that the Muslim League could concentrate all its energies
towards the achievement of Pakistan.

> We shall have time to quarrel ourselves and we shall have time when
> these differences will have to be settled, when wrongs and injuries will
> have to be remedied. We shall have time for domestic programme
> and politics, but first get the Government. This is a nation without
> any territory or any government.[30]

But neither these exhortations nor his charismatic authority were
able to eliminate the deep-seated differences that existed among

---

[29] Almond and Powell, op. cit., p. 98.

[30] Jamil-ud-Din Ahmad, op. cit., Vol. II (1964), p. 199. Also cited earlier on
p. 181.

various groups, particularly in parts which became West Pakistan later. The normal political process was one in which rival landlords and *pirs* constantly feuded against each other. Sir Francis Mudie, Governor of Sind (1945–7), in one of his letters to Lord Wavell wrote:

> I don't know what will happen when our assembly meets at the end of this month or in July. There are the usual stories that Khuhro, in league with Sayed, will try to upset Sir Ghulam. On the other hand, Khuhro is afraid that Sir Ghulam will intrigue with Sayed and the Hindus of his party to oust him. It is possible, too, that Bandeh Ali will try some more of his tricks as he is dissatisfied at not being Home Minister.[31]

This indicates that certain cleavages existed in the horizontal coalition of regional and economic interests that Jinnah had hastily put together. There was neither fundamental agreement among the landlords of the same Province nor did there exist any clear understanding based on a political programme between the rural and the urban interests of a Province. When the refugees poured into Pakistan they brought with them another source of future conflict between themselves and the local landlords. All this meant that Islam was enough to unify the Muslims against the Hindus, but as a mere symbol it could not act as a cementing force among conflicting interests after the establishment of Pakistan. The Muslim League had also been unable to achieve much vertical integration in its organization. The social structure in the villages and the districts was semi-feudal or traditional, and virtually under the control of the Deputy Commissioner and the landlords. Muslim League party workers, most of whom were from urban areas, did succeed in arousing the political consciousness and support of the rural people, but they had not been able to build a viable political organization or change the power structure in the countryside. They needed an economic and social programme designed to mobilize both the support of the landowners and the peasants. The Muslim League had neither a programme nor an adequate mechanism within its organization to resolve or adjust the conflict of interests and views that existed between different social and economic classes.

---

[31] Sir Francis Mudie's letter to Lord Wavell, DO No. 298/FR, dated 11 June 1946.

After Pakistan was established and even during Jinnah's lifetime, the Governments of Sind and West Punjab were riddled with intrigues and feuds between rival factions led by landlord politicians. In addition, Pakistan was faced with a host of difficulties: communal carnage and killing along the Punjab frontier, the inflow of over six million refugees into West Pakistan, the Kashmir conflict with India, and the precarious financial and administrative position of the Government as a result of the withholding of payments and supplies by the Indian Government appeared as almost insurmountable difficulties to the newly established and inexperienced Government of Pakistan. There is no doubt that it was the inspiring leadership of Jinnah and the dedicated efforts of the civil servants which enabled Pakistan to succeed in this struggle for survival. It was felt that Pakistan could not overcome these difficulties by relying on the ability and skills of politicians. Jinnah had to rely heavily on the traditions of the Viceregal system that Pakistan had inherited from British India; as Governor General, he called upon the Governors and civil servants to keep a close watch over the Cabinet meetings and other activities of the politicians. In the case of Sind, he went so far as to instruct the Governor of Sind to dismiss the Provincial Ministry of M. A. Khuhro.

As we have seen, the main components of the Viceregal system were a powerful Viceroy, otherwise known as the Governor General, an Executive Council chosen by the Governor General, a Central Assembly with limited powers, subordinate Provincial Governments, and, above all, a powerful bureaucracy placed in strategic positions in the Centre, in the Provinces, and in the districts. The army in this system provided the coercive cover and was called into action only in extreme cases. All these characteristics of the Viceregal system have been in operation in Pakistan ever since its establishment. During the first two decades of its existence Pakistan has had several constitutional systems, but the basic political system with some variations has more or less been the Viceregal system. However, it would not be fair to characterize the role of the bureaucracy only in negative terms. Its positive role as a centralized institution that held the heterogeneous and physically separate parts of the country together should be recognized. Similarly, the increasingly influential role that the army has acquired in Pakistan's political system may be explained by the fact that Pakistan's leaders have felt that the security of their country has been under constant threat as a result of the Kashmir dispute and other causes of conflict with India. It is only when one takes into account factors like national unity and the security of the country that one begins to appreciate why Pakistan has not been able to dismantle the Viceregal system that it has inherited from the British.

It is often said that bureaucracy has been the most powerful and stable element in the decision-making process in Pakistan. But it must be noted that without a powerful Viceroy or Head of the State like a Jinnah or an Ayub to provide the necessary leadership and directional thrust, Pakistan's bureaucracy has not been able to function efficiently or independently. However, Jinnah's position as the founder of the state was unique. He was the first and the only Governor General who derived his ultimate authority neither from the power of the army nor the support of the bureaucracy nor from any constitutional prerogatives, but from the political support that his people gave him in an abundant measure.

APPENDIX I

MUSLIMS IN THE CIVIL AND MILITARY SERVICES OF THE GOVERNMENT OF INDIA, 1946–7

I. MUSLIMS IN THE SECRETARIAT OF THE GOVERNMENT OF INDIA, 1946–7[1]

1. Secretariat of the Governor General

Personal Secretary—British
Secretary (Public)—Reforms Commissioner—Hindu
No Muslim in the Secretariat

2. Cabinet Secretariat

Secretary—British
Joint Secretary—Hindu
Establishment Officer—British
Deputy Secretary (Military)—British
Deputy Secretary (Civil)—Muslim
Under Secretary (Civil)—Muslim
Rest—all British

3. Department of Education

Secretary—British
Deputy Secretary—Hindu
Deputy Educational Advisers—three, one of whom a Muslim
Assistant Educational Advisers—two, both Muslims

4. Department of Health

Secretary—British
Deputy Secretaries—two, both Hindus
Assistant Secretaries—two, one of whom a Muslim

5. Department of Agriculture

Secretary—Hindu
Joint Secretaries—two, both Hindus
Deputy Secretaries—two, one of whom a Muslim

---

[1] This information has been gathered from *The Indian Year Book 1946–47*, Vol. XXXIII, Bombay and Calcutta: Bennett Coleman.

Under Secretaries—two, one of whom a Muslim
Out of nearly fifty technical officers, only seven Muslims.

6. *Labour Department*

Secretary—Hindu
Joint Secretary—Hindu
Deputy Secretaries—Hindus
Only one Muslim officer—Officer on Special Duty

A. *Directorate General of Resettlement and Employment*

Director General and ex-officio Joint Secretary—Muslim
Deputy Secretaries—two, one of whom a Muslim
Assistant Secretaries—three Hindus
A number of offices in the Department of Labour called
Directorates of Training, Employment Exchanges, Re-
settlement and Employment, etc.—only one Muslim
Director

7. *Department of Works, Mines and Power*

Secretary—Hindu
Joint Secretary—Hindu
Deputy Secretaries—Hindus
Under Secretaries—Hindus
Assistant Secretaries—Hindus
No Muslim except an officer called 'Attache'

8. *Finance Department*

Principal Secretaries—two, one British, one Hindu
Joint Secretaries—four, no Muslim
Deputy Secretaries—eight, no Muslim
Under Secretaries—six, only one Muslim

A. *Communications Division*

Financial Adviser—Hindu
Deputy Financial Advisers—two, one of whom a Muslim

B. *Joint Financial Adviser Food*

All Hindu officers

C. *Financial Department Revenue Division, Central Board of
Revenue*

Additional Secretary—British
Joint Secretaries—three, all British
Deputy Secretary—Hindu
No Muslim

In the Inspectorate of Customs and Central Excise and Income Tax—no Muslim except a minor inspecting officer in Customs and Central Excise

9. *War Department*
   Secretary—British
   Officiating Secretary—Hindu
   Joint Secretaries—three, two British, one Muslim
   Deputy Secretaries—no Muslim
   Under Secretaries—eleven, only one Muslim
   In the Pensions Branch, only two Muslims

   A. *Military Finance Department*
      Financial Adviser—Muslim
      Additional Financial Advisers—two, both British
      Joint Financial Adviser—British
      Deputy Financial Advisers—nine, only one Muslim

10. *Home Department*
    Secretary—British
    Joint Secretary—British
    Deputy Secretaries—six, one Muslim

11. *Information and Broadcasting Department*
    Secretary—British
    Deputy Secretary—Muslim
    Under Secretary—British
    In the Publications Division of the Ministry, special officers dealing with Persian and Arabic publications were Muslims
    In the Press Information Bureau, mostly Hindus and British, only one Assistant Principal Information Officer—Muslim

12. *Indian Council of Agricultural Research*
    No Muslim

13. *Central Agricultural Marketing Department and Indian Central Sugar Cane Committee*
    Twenty-one officers—only three Muslims.

14. *External Affairs Department*
    Secretary—British
    Joint Secretaries—British
    Under Secretaries—mostly British, one Hindu and no Muslim

15. *Commonwealth Relations Department*
    Secretary—Hindu

Deputy Secretaries—all Hindus, except one Additional Deputy
Secretary—Muslim
Hajj Officer—Muslim

16. Political Department
All British officers

17. Department of Commerce
Secretaries—two, both Hindus
Joint Secretaries—three, two Hindus, one Muslim
Deputy Secretaries—three, all Hindus
Under Secretaries—three, all Hindus
Chief Controller of Exports—Muslim

18. Department of Industries and Supplies
Secretary—British
Officiating Secretary—British
Joint Secretaries—two, one Hindu, one British
Deputy Secretaries—six, three of whom Muslim

19. Department of War Transport
Secretary—British
Joint Secretary—British
Deputy Secretaries—two, one British, one Hindu
A number of other officers like Chief Controller, Railroad Priorities;
Chief Controller, Motor Transport, were mostly either British or
Hindu
Civil Aviation Directorate was entirely in the hands of British and
Hindu officers

20. Railway Department
Mostly Hindu or British

21. Legislative Department
Secretary—British
Additional Secretary—British
Joint Secretary—Hindu
Deputy Secretary—Hindu
No Muslim in the Department except Assistant Solicitor to the
Government of India (Supply)

II. MUSLIM OFFICERS IN THE ARMY, 1946-7[2]

	Muslims	Non-Muslims	Total
Field-Marshals	0	0	3
Generals	0	0	3
Lt. Generals	0	0	4
Maj. Generals	0	0	20
Colonels	1 (Acting Colonel)	Not Known	126
Lt. Colonels	3	5	890
Majors	16	32	577
Captains	80	173	1,033

---

[2] These figures have been taken from *Indian Army List, October, 1946, I.* In the above figures, officers who had military rank but were holding non-military posts and were in the Supernumerary List, have not been included. It is obvious from the figures that an overwhelming majority of the officers in the Indian Army were British. These figures do not include officers who were on Emergency Commissions.

APPENDIX II

DOCUMENTS RELATING TO THE OFFICE OF GOVERNOR GENERAL OF PAKISTAN[1]

I. COMMISSION OF MUHAMMAD ALL JINNAH

GEORGE THE SIXTH by the Grace of God of Great Britain, Ireland and the British Dominions beyond the Seas, King Defender of the Faith.

To Our Right Trusty and Well-Beloved Muhammad Ali Jinnah.

GREETING

I. We do by this Our Commission under Our Sign Manual, appoint you, the said Muhammad Ali Jinnah, to be, during Our pleasure, Governor General of Pakistan with all the powers, rights, privileges, and advantages to said office belonging or appertaining.

II. And we do hereby authorize, empower and command you to exercise and perform all and singular the powers and duties conferred and imposed upon Our Governor General of Pakistan by and under provisions of the Act passed in this the tenth and eleventh year of Our Reign intituled the Indian Independence Act 1947.

III. And that they and We do hereby authorize and empower you in Our name and on Our behalf to grant any offender convicted in exercise of its Criminal Jurisdiction by any Courts of Justice within Our territories in Pakistan a pardon either free or subject to such lawful conditions as to you may seem fit.

IV. And We do hereby further authorize and direct you to cause this Our Commission to be read and published in the presence of the Chief Justice or other Judge of the Federal Court or in the presence of the Chief Justice or other Judge of the High Court of any of the Provinces in Our Dominion of Pakistan.

V. And We do hereby further authorize and direct you to take the Oath of Allegiance and the Oath for the due execution of the Office of Our Governor General of Pakistan in the form hereto appended which Oaths the said Chief Justice of the Federal Court or other

---

[1] Texts of these Commissions have been supplied to the author by the Cabinet Secretariat, Government of Pakistan, Karachi.

Judge of the said Court or Chief Justice or other Judge of the High Court of any of the Provinces in Our said Dominion shall and is hereby required to tender and administer unto you.

VI. And We do hereby further authorize and require you by yourself or by any other person to be appointed by you in that behalf to administer to every person appointed by you to hold office as a Minister and to every person appointed by you to be a Chief Commissioner the Oaths of Allegiance and Office and of Secrecy hereto appended.

VII. And We do hereby direct that every person who under this Commission shall be required to take an Oath may make an affirmation in place of an Oath if he has any objection to making an Oath.

GIVEN at Our Court at Balmoral this fourteenth day of August in the year of Our Lord 1947 and in the eleventh year of Our Reign.

BY HIS MAJESTY'S COMMAND.

Listowel.

I, Muhammad Ali Jinnah, do solemnly affirm true faith and allegiance to the Constitution of Pakistan as by law established, and that I will be faithful to His Majesty King George the Sixth, His Heirs and Successors, in the Office of Governor General of Pakistan.

SELECT BIBLIOGRAPHY

I. BOOKS (Titles of Urdu books are not included)

Afzal, M. Rafique, ed., *Selected Speeches and Statements of the Quaid-i-Azam Mohammad Ali Jinnah (1911–34 and 1947–48)*, Lahore: Research Society of Pakistan, University of the Punjab, 1966.

Ahmad, Aziz, *Studies in Islamic Culture in the Indian Environment*, Oxford: Clarendon Press, 1964.

Ahmad, Jamil-ud-Din, ed., *Speeches and Writings of Mr. Jinnah,*, two vols. Lahore: Ashraf, Vol. I, 5th ed., 1952; Vol. II, 2nd ed., 1952.

Albiruni, A.H., *Makers of Pakistan and Modern Muslim India*, Lahore: Ashraf, 1950.

Alexander, Horace, *India Since Cripps*, London: Penguin, 1944.

Ali, Maulavi Saiyid Amir, *The Mohammedans of India*, London: Association in Aid of Social Progress in India, 1872.

Ali, Syed Ameer, *The Spirit of Islam*, London: Christophers, 1922.

Alva, Joachim, *Leaders of India*, Bombay: Thacker, 1943.

Ambedkar, B.R., *Pakistan or the Partition of India*, 3rd ed., Bombay: Thacker, 1946.

Ashraf, Mohammad, ed., *Cabinet Mission and After*, Lahore: Ashraf, 1946.

Azad, Maulana Abul Kalam, *India Wins Freedom*, Calcutta: Orient Longmans, 1959.

Baljon, J. M. S., *The Reforms and Religious Ideas of Sir Sayyid Ahmad Khan*, Leiden: Brill, 1949.

Besant, Annie, *How India Wrought for Freedom: The Story of the National Congress Told from Official Records.* Madras: Theosophical Publishing House, 1915.

Bevan, Edwyn, *Indian Nationalism*, London: Macmillan, 1913.

Blunt, Sir Edward, *The I.C.S.: The Indian Civil Service*, London: Faber, 1937.

Blunt, W. S., *India Under Ripon: A Private Diary*, London: T. Fisher Unwin, 1909.

Bolitho, Hector, *Jinnah: Creator of Pakistan*, London: John Murray, 1954.

Brailsford, H. N., *Subject India*, London: Victor Gollancz, 1943.

Brecher, Michael, *Nehru: A Political Biography*, London: Oxford University Press, 1959.

Campbell-Johnson, Alan, *Mission With Mountbatten*, London: Robert Hale, 1952.

Caroe, Olaf, *The Pathans*, London: Macmillan, 1958.

Carstairs, R., *The Little World of an Indian District Officer*, London: Macmillan, 1912.

Casey, R.G., *An Australian in India*, London: Hollis and Carter, 1947.

Chatterjee, Bankim Chandra, *Anandamath*, Translated by Chandra Sen-Gupta, Calcutta: Padmini Mohan Neogi, n.d.

Chaudhuri, Nirad C., *The Autobiography of an Unknown Indian*, New York: Macmillan, 1951.

Chirol, Valentine, *Indian Unrest*, London: Macmillan, 1910.

Coatman, J., *Years of Destiny: India 1926–1932*, London: Jonathan Cape, 1932.

Coupland, R., *India: A Re-Statement*, London: Oxford University Press, 1945.

————, *The Indian Problem. Report on the Constitutional Problem in India*, three parts, New York: Oxford University Press, 1944.

Cumming, John, ed., *Political India 1832–1932: A Co-operative Survey of a Century*, London: Oxford University Press, 1932.

Dar, Bashir Ahmad, *Religious Thought of Sayyid Ahmad Khan*, Lahore: Institute of Islamic Culture, 1957.

Darling, Malcolm Lyall, *Apprentice to Power: India 1904–1908*, London: Hogarth, 1966.

————, *At Freedom's Door*, London: Oxford University Press, 1949.

————, *The Punjab Peasant in Prosperity and Debt*, London: Oxford University Press, 1932.

————, *Rusticus Loquitur: The Old Light and the New in the Punjab Village*, London: Oxford University Press, 1930.

Dodwell, H.H., ed., *The Cambridge History of the British Empire*, Vols. I-VI, London: Cambridge University Press, 1932.

Dumont, Louis, ed., *Contributions to Indian Sociology*, Vol. VII, The Hague: Mouton, 1964.

Dutt, R. Palme, *India Today and Tomorrow*, London: Lawrence and Wishart, 1955.

————, *Modern India*, London: Communist Party of Great Britain, 1927.

Fuller, Sir Bampfylde, *Some Personal Experiences,* London: John Murray, 1930.

Gandhi, M. K., *Communal Unity,* Ahmedabad: Navajivan Publishing House, 1949.

Garratt, G. T., *An Indian Commentary,* London: Jonathan Cape, 1928.

Gopal, Ram., *Indian Muslims: A Political History (1858–1947),* Bombay: Asia Publishing House, 1959.

Gopal, S., *The Viceroyalty of Lord Irwin 1926–1931,* Oxford: Clarendon Press, 1957.

Griffin, Sir Lepel H., *Chiefs and Families of Note in the Panjab: A Revised Edition of the Panjab Chiefs,* two vols., and Appendix vol., Lahore: Superintendent, Government Printing, Punjab, 1940.

Griffiths, Sir Percival, *The British Impact on India,* London: Macdonald, 1952.

Gwyer, Sir Maurice and Appadorai, A., eds., *Speeches and Documents in the Indian Constitution 1921–47,* two vols., London: Oxford University Press, 1957.

Gwynn, J. T., *Indian Politics: A Survey,* London: Nisbet, 1924.

Halifax, The Earl of, *Fulness of Days,* London: Collins, 1957.

El Hamza, *Pakistan: A Nation,* Lahore: Ashraf, 1946.

The Historic Trial of the Ali Brothers, Dr Kitchlew, Shri Shankaracharya. Maulana Hussain Ahmed, Pir Ghulam Mujaddid and Maulana Nisar Ahmed. Part I. Proceedings in the Lower Court, Karachi: New Times Office, n.d.

Horne, E. A., *The Political System of British India: With Special Reference to the Recent Constitutional Changes,* Oxford: Clarendon Press, 1922.

Howell, Evelyn, *Mizh: A Monograph on Government's Relations With the Mahsud Tribe,* Simla: Government of India, 1931.

Hunter, W. W. *The Indian Mussalmans,* Lahore: Premier Book House, 1964. Reprinted from 1st ed. of 1871.

Husain, Azim, *Fazl-i-Husain: A Political Biography,* Bombay: Longmans, 1946.

Husain, Mahmud, et al, eds., *A History of the Freedom Movement,* three vols., Karachi: Pakistan Historical Society.

Ibbetson, Sir Denzil, *Punjab Castes,* Lahore: Government Printing, Punjab, 1916.

Ilbert, Sir Courtenay and Meston, Rt. Hon. Lord., *The New Constitution of India,* London: University of London, 1923.

Indian Nation Builders, three parts, Madras: Ganesh, n.d.

Iqbal, Afzal, ed., *My Life: A Fragment: An Autobiographical Sketch of Maulana Mohamed Ali*, Lahore: Ashraf, 1946.

———, *Select Writings and Speeches of Maulana Mohamed Ali*, 2nd ed., two vols., Lahore: Ashraf, 1944.

Iqbal, Dr Sir Muhammad, *The Reconstruction of Religious Thought in Islam*, Lahore: Javid Iqbal, 1960.

Ispahani, M. A. H., *Qaid-e-Azam Jinnah As I Knew Him*, Karachi: Forward Publications Trust, 1966.

Jack, J. C., *The Economic Life of a Bengal District*, Oxford: Clarendon Press, 1916.

Khaliquzzaman, Choudhry, *Pathway to Pakistan*, Lahore: Longmans, 1961.

Lateef, S. Abdul., *The Great Leader*, Lahore: Lion Press, 1947.

MacMunn, Lieut. General Sir George, *The Martial Races of India*, London: Sampson Law, n.d.

Majumdar, P. C., *A Defence of the Congress League Scheme: A Study in Comparative Politics*, Calcutta: Sahitya Prochar Samiti, 1918.

Malik, Hafeez, *Moslem Nationalism in India and Pakistan*, Washington, D.C.: Public Affairs Press, 1963.

Mallick, Azizur Rahman, *British Policy and the Muslims in Bengal 1757–1856*, Dacca: Asiatic Society of Pakistan, 1961.

Manshardt, Clifford, *The Hindu-Muslim Problem in India*, London: Allen & Unwin, 1936.

Mehta, Asoka and Patwardhan, Achyut, *The Communal Triangle in India*, Allahabad: Kitabistan, 1942.

Mehtar, M. A., *Whys of the Great Indian Conflict*, Lahore: Ashraf, 1947.

Menon, V. P., *The Transfer of Power in India*, Calcutta: Orient Longmans, 1957.

Meston, Lord, *Nationhood for India*, London: Oxford University Press, 1931.

Mohomed Ali Jinnah: An Ambassador of Unity: His Speeches & Writings 1912–1917: With a Biographical Appreciation by Sarojini Naidu, Madras: Ganesh, n.d.

Montagu, Edwin S. *An Indian Diary*, London: William Heinemann, 1930.

Moon, Penderel, *Divide and Quit*, Berkeley and Los Angeles: University of California, 1962.

———, *The Future of India*, London: Pilot Press, 1945.

———, *Strangers in India*, New York: Reynal & Hitchcock, 1945.

Morley, Viscount, *Indian Speeches (1907–1909)*, London: Macmillan, 1909.

Mukherjee, Haridas and Uma, *'Bande Mataram' and Indian Nationalism* (*1906–1908*), Calcutta: Firma K. L. Mukhopadhyay, 1957.

———, *The Growth of Nationalism in India (1857–1905)*, Calcutta: Presidency Library, 1957.

———, *India's Fight for Freedom or The Swadeshi Movement (1905–1906)*, Calcutta: Firma K. L. Mukhopadhyay, 1958.

Murphy, Gardner, *In the Minds of Men*, New York: Basic Books, 1955.

Nazir Yar Jung, Nawab Dr, *The Pakistan Issue*, Lahore: Ashraf, 1943.

Nehru, Jawaharlal, *An Autobiography*, London: The Bodley Head, 1958.

———, *A Bunch of Old Letters*, Bombay: Asia Publishing House, 1958.

———, *The Discovery of India*, London: Meridian Books, 1956.

Nichols, Beverley, *The Verdict on India*, Bombay: Thacker, 1944.

Noman, Mohammed, ed., *Our Struggle 1857–1947*, Karachi: Pakistan Publications, n.d.

O'Dwyer, Sir Michael, *India As I Knew It 1885–1925*, London: Constable, 1925.

O'Malley, L. S. S., *The Indian Civil Service 1601–1930*, London: Oxford University Press, 1931.

Panikkar, K. M., and Pershad, A., eds., *The Voice of Freedom. Selected Speeches of Pandit Motilal Nehru*, Bombay: Asia Publishing House, 1961.

Panjabi, K. L., *The Indomitable Sardar*, Bombay: Bharatiya Vidya Bhavan, 1962.

Pirzada, Syed Sharifuddin, *Evolution of Pakistan*, Lahore: All-Pakistan Legal Decisions, 1963.

———, ed., *Quaid-e-Azam Jinnah's Correspondence*, Karachi: Guild Publishing House, 1966.

Prasad, Rajendra, *India Divided*, Bombay: Hind Kitabs, 1947.

Pyarelal, *Mahatma Gandhi: The Last Phase*, two vols., Ahmedabad: Navajivan Publishing House, 1958.

———, *A Pilgrimage for Peace. Gandhi and Frontier Gandhi Among N.W.F. Pathans*, Ahmedabad: Navajivan Publishing House, 1950.

Qureshi, Ishtiaq Husain, *The Muslim Community of the Indo-Pakistan Subcontinent, 610–1947. A Brief Historical Analysis*, Gravenhage: Mouton, 1962.

Rai, Lajput, *Young India: An Interpretation and a History of the*

Nationalist Movement From Within, London: Home Rule for India League, n.d.

Rajput, A. B., *Muslim League Yesterday and Today*, Lahore: Ashraf, 1948.

Rawlinson, H. G., *The British Achievement in India*, London: William Hodge, 1948.

Reed, Sir Stanley, *The India I Knew 1897–1947*, London: Odhams, 1952.

Ronaldshay, Lord, *The Life of Lord Curzon*, three vols., London: Ernest Benn, 1928.

Roy, Sir Bijoy Prasad Singh, *Parliamentary Government in India*, Calcutta: Thacker, 1943.

Saiyid, Matlubul Hasan, *Mohammad Ali Jinnah (A Political Study)*, Lahore: Ashraf, 1953.

Sayed, G. M., *Struggle for New Sind*, Karachi: 1949.

Sayeed, Khalid B., *The Political System of Pakistan*, Boston: Houghton Mifflin, 1967.

Schuster, Sir George and Wint, Guy, *India and Democracy*, London: Macmillan, 1941.

Sen, Dr Sachin, *Birth of Pakistan*, Calcutta: General Printers & Publishers, 1955.

Shafi, Alhaj Mian Ahmad, *Haji Sir Abdoola Haroon: A Biography*, Karachi: Begum Daulat Anwar Hidayatullah, n.d.

Shafi, Sir Mian Muhammad, *Some Important Indian Problems*, Lahore: 1930.

'Shamloo', ed., *Speeches and Statements of Iqbal*, 2nd ed., Lahore: Al-Manar Academy, 1948.

Singh, Khushwant, *The Sikhs*, London: Allen & Unwin, 1953.

Singh, Tara, *Why We Must Avoid The Civil War In India*, Lahore: S. Harkishan Singh, 1946.

Sitaramayya, B. Pattabhi, *The History of the Indian National Congress*, two vols., Bombay: Padma Publications, Vol. I, 1946; Vol. II, 1947.

Smith, Vincent A., *The Oxford History of India*, Oxford: Clarendon Press, 1958.

Smith, Wilfred Cantwell, *Modern Islam in India*, Lahore: Ripon Press, 1954.

Spear, Percival, *India, Pakistan and the West*, 3rd ed., London: Oxford University Press, 1958.

Speeches by Quaid-i-Azam Mohamed Ali Jinnah Governor General of Pakistan: 3rd June 1947 to 14th August 1948, Karachi: n.d.

Suleri, Zia-ud-Din Ahmad, *My Leader*, 3rd ed., Lahore: Lion Press, 1946.

Tahmankar, D.V. *Lokamanya Tilak*, London: John Murray, 1956.

Thompson, Edward, *Enlist India for Freedom!* London: Victor Gollancz, 1940.

———, *The Reconstruction of India*, London: Faber & Faber, 1930.

———, and Garratt, G.T., *Rise and Fulfilment of British Rule in India*, Allahabad: Central Book Depot, 1958.

Thorburn, S. S., *Asiatic Neighbours*, Edinburgh and London: William Blackwood, 1894.

———, *Musalmans and Moneylenders*, Edinburgh and London: William Blackwood, 1886.

Tinker, Hugh, *Experiment With Freedom: India and Pakistan 1947*, London: Oxford University Press, 1967.

———, *South Asia: A Short History*, New York: Praeger, 1966.

Topa, Ishwar Nath, *The Growth and Development of National Thought in India*, Hamburg: Friederichsen, de Gruyter, 1930.

Trevaskis, Hugh Kennedy, *The Punjab of To-Day*, two vols., Lahore: Civil & Military Press, 1931.

Tuker, Lieut. General Sir Francis, *While Memory Serves*, London: Cassell, 1950.

Tyabji, Husain B. *Badruddin Tyabji: A Biography*, Bombay: Thacker, 1952.

Vairanapillai, M. S., *Are We Two Nations? Nationalities in Indian Politics: A Scientific and Non-Partisan Approach*, Lahore: Madras, 1946.

Waheed-uz-Zaman, *Towards Pakistan*, Lahore: Publishers United, 1964.

Wasti, Syed Razi, *Lord Minto and the Indian Nationalist Movement 1905–1910*, Oxford: Clarendon Press, 1964.

Wedderburn, Sir William, *Allan Octavian Hume*, London: T. Fisher Unwin, 1913.

Woodruff, Philip, *The Men Who Ruled India: The Guardians*, London: Jonathan Cape, 1954.

Yeats-Brown, F. *Martial India*, London: Eyre & Spottiswoode, 1945.

Yunus, Mohammad, *Frontier Speaks*, Bombay: Hind Kitabs, 1947.

II. GOVERNMENT PUBLICATIONS

Annual *Administration Reports* of the Provinces of Bengal, Punjab, the North-West Frontier Province, and Sind.

Baluchistan District Gazetteers.

Bengal District Gazetteers.

Constituent Assembly (Legislature) of Pakistan Debates (1948–1954).

Constituent Assembly of Pakistan Debates (1947–54).

Final Report on the Survey and Settlement Operations (of the various districts of Bengal).

Gazetteer of the Bombay Presidency, Vol. IX, Part II, Gujarat Population Musalmans and Parsis. Bombay: 1899. (For Muslim merchant classes.)

Gazetteer of the Province of Sind.

Government of India Act, 1935, 26 Geo. 5 Ch. 2. London: H.M. Stationery Office.

Hunter, Sir William Wilson, *The Imperial Gazetteer of India,* 2nd ed., fourteen vols., London: Trubner, 1885–7.

Imperial Gazetteer of India Provincial Series, Calcutta: 1908.

Indian Independence Act, 1947, 10 & 11 Geo. 6. Ch. 30, London: H.M. Stationery Office.

Joint Select Committee on the Government of India Bill, Vol. II. Minutes of Evidence, London: H.M. Stationery Office, 1919.

N.-W. F. Province Gazetteers.

Orders of the Governor General 1947–1950, Karachi: Manager, Governor General's Press and Publications, 1951.

Proceedings of the Round Table Conference, Cmd. 3778; Cmd. 3997; Cmd. 4238, three Sessions, 1931–2.

Punjab District Gazetters.

Report on Indian Constitutional Reforms. (Montagu-Chelmsford Report.) Cmd. 9109, Calcutta: Superintendent, Government Printing, 1918.

Report of the Indian Statutory Commission. (Simon Commission.) Cmd. 3568–9, two vols., London: H.M. Stationery Office, 1930.

The Report of the Sind Special Court of Enquiry.

The Transitional Constitutions of India and Pakistan, Calcutta: The Indian Law Review Office, 1947.

Unrepealed Constitutional Legislation. (As modified up to 26th April 1951.) Karachi: Manager, Government of Pakistan Press and Publications, 1951.

III. ALL-INDIA MUSLIM LEAGUE PUBLICATIONS AND OTHERS

All Parties Conference, 1928. Report of the Committee Appointed by the Conference to Determine the Principles of the Constitu-

tion for India. (Nehru Report.) Allahabad: All-India Congress Committee.

The Constitution and Rules of the All-India Muslim League. (Constitutions for the years 1928, 1940, 1941, 1942, 1944, and 1946.) Delhi: All-India Muslim League.

Constitutional Proposals of the Sapru Committee, Moradabad: Sapru Committee, 1945.

The Indian Annual Register. (For the years 1919–1947.) Calcutta: The Annual Register Office.

It Shall Never Happen Again, Delhi: All-India Muslim League, 1946.

List of the Members of the Council of the All-India Muslim League. (Lists for the years 1940, 1941, and 1942.) Delhi: All-India Muslim League.

The Report of the Inquiry Committee Appointed by the Council of the All-India Muslim League to Inquire into Muslim Grievances in Congress Provinces. (Pirpur Report.) Delhi: All-India Muslim League, 1938.

Rules and Regulations of the All-India Muslim League, Aligarh: The Institute Press, 1909.

SELECT LIST OF PERSONS INTERVIEWED

Sir George Abell. Private Secretary to Viceroy, 1945–7.

Aziz Ahmad. I.C.S. officer of the Bengal cadre. Chief Secretary of the Government of East Bengal, 1947–52. Secretary General, 1958–9.

Jamil-ud-Din Ahmad. Member, Council of the All-India Muslim League.

Amjad Ali. Finance Minister, 1955–8.

Chaudhri Mohamad Ali. Financial Adviser, Military Finance Department. Government of India, 1946–7. Secretary General, 1947–51. Prime Minister, 1955–6.

Nurul Amin. Chief Minister, East Pakistan, 1948–54.

Zafar Ahmed Ansari. Joint Secretary, All-India Muslim League.

Lord Attlee. Prime Minister of Britain during the time of Partition.

Field-Marshal Sir Claude Auchinleck. Commander-in-Chief, Indian Army, 1943–7.

M. Ayub. During 1946 and 1947 held the positions successively of Deputy Secretary, Department of Industries and Supplies, and Private Secretary to the Minister of Commerce, Government of India.

Sir Frederick Bourne. I.C.S. officer of the Punjab cadre. Governor of East Pakistan, 1947–50.

Sir Olaf Caroe. Governor of the N.-W. F. P., 1945–7.

Hamidul Haq Chowdhury. Minister, Commerce and Industries, East Pakistan, 1947–9. Foreign Minister, 1955–6.

I.I. Chundrigar. Member, Working Committee of the All-India Muslims League. Prime Minister, 1957.

Sir Eric Coates. I.C.S. officer of the Bengal cadre who rose to be Finance Member, Government of India.

Sir George Cunningham. I.C.S. officer who served mostly in the Frontier. Private Secretary to Viceroy, Lord Irwin, 1926–31. Governor of the N.-W. F. P., 1937–45 and 1947–8.

Sir Malcolm Darling. I.C.S. officer of the Punjab cadre and author of several books on the cooperative movement and the Punjab peasantry.

Mian Mumtaz Muhammad Khan Daultana. Minister of Finance, Government of West Punjab, 1947–9. Chief Minister, West Pakistan, 1951–3.

Arbab Abdul Ghafoor. Frontier leader and a follower of Khan Abdul Ghaffar Khan.

Sir Douglas Gracey. Commander-in-Chief, Pakistan Army, 1947–1950.

Mushtaq Ahmad Gurmani. Governor, West Pakistan, 1955–6.

Lord Hailey. Governor of Punjab, 1924–8. Governor of the United Provinces, 1928–30.

Shamsul Hasan. Assistant Secretary, All-India Muslim League.

Mahmud Husain. Central Minister, 1949–53.

Abul Hashim. Secretary, Bengal Provincial Muslim League, 1945–1946.

Muhammad Ikramullah. Secretary, Ministry of Foreign Affairs and Commonwealth Relations, 1947–51.

Husain Imam. Member, Working Committee of the All-India Muslim League.

Lord Ismay. Chief of Staff to the Viceroy of India, 1947.

M.H. Ispahani. Member, Working Committee of the All-India Muslim League.

Sir Evan Jenkins. I.C.S. officer of the Punjab cadre who rose to be Governor of Punjab, 1946–7.

Sir Ivor Jennings. Former constitutional adviser to the Government of Pakistan.

Miss Fatima Jinnah.

Choudhry Khaliquazzaman. Member, Working Committee of the All-India Muslim League.

Abdul Qaiyum Khan. Chief Minister, N.-W. F. P., 1947–53. President, Pakistan Muslim League, 1958.

Ghazanfar Ali Khan. Muslim League leader from Punjab and Central Minister, both in the Interim Government, 1946–7, and in the Government of Pakistan.

Liaquat Ali Khan. Secretary, All-India Muslim League. Prime Minister of Pakistan, 1947–51.

Malik Lal Khan. Influential Muslim League leader from Punjab.

Maulana Akram Khan. Member, Working Committee of the All-India Muslim League. President, Bengal Muslim League (pre-Partition).

Sir Muhammad Zafrulla Khan. Foreign Minister, 1947–54.

Tamizuddin Khan. President, Constituent Assembly, 1948–54.

Muhammad Ayub Khuhro. Chief Minister, Sind, several times. Central Minister, Defence, 1958.

Iftikhar Husain Khan Mamdot. Chief Minister, West Punjab, 1947–9.

Philip Mason. I.C.S. officer of the U.P. cadre. Well-known author.

Lieutenant General Sir Frank Messervy. First Commander-in-Chief of the Pakistan Army, 1947.

Iskander Mirza. President of Pakistan, 1956–8.

Lord Mountbatten. Viceroy of India, 1947. Governor General of India, 1947–8.

Sir Francis Mudie. Governor of Sind, 1946–7. Governor of West Punjab, 1947–9.

Khwaja Nazimuddin. Governor General, 1948–51. Prime Minister, 1951–3.

Pandit Jawaharlal Nehru. Prime Minister of India, 1947–64.

Hamid Nizami. Editor, *Nawa-i-Waqt.*

Lord Pethick-Lawrence. Secretary of State for India, 1945–7.

Syed Sharifuddin Pirzada. Worked on Jinnah's staff. Has edited Jinnah's correspondence.

Dr Ishtiaq Husain Qureshi. Central Minister, 1949–54.

Habib Ibrahim Rahimtoola. Former High Commissioner in the U.K. and Muslim League leader.

Fazlur Rahman. Central Minister, 1947–53.

Muhammad Amir Ahmad, Raja of Mahmoodabad. Member, Working Committee of the All-India Muslim League.

C. Rajagopalachari. Congress Premier of Madras and later Governor General of India.

Abdur Razzak. Lecturer, Political Science, University of Dacca.

Abdul Sattar Sait. Member, Working Committee of the All-India Muslim League.

Abdus Salam. Editor, *The Pakistan Observer.*

Abu Husain Sarkar. Chief Minister, East Pakistan, 1955–6.

G. M. Sayed. Muslim League leader from Sind (pre-Partition). Later organizer of the National Awami Party.

Sir Harold Shoobert. I.C.S. officer who later became Secretary of Food, Agriculture, and Health, Government of Pakistan, 1948–51.

Huseyn Shaheed Suhrawardy. Chief Minister, Bengal, 1946–7. Prime Minister, 1956–7.

Khizr Hyat Khan Tiwana. Chief Minister of the Punjab, 1943–7.

Sir Victor Turner. I.C.S. officer of the U.P. cadre who later became Secretary, Minister of Finance, Government of Pakistan, 1947–1950.

Lady Wavell.

INDEX

Abdali: *see* Ahmad Shah Abdali

Abd-ul-Aziz, Shah, 14, 61

Abdul Hamid, Sultan of Turkey, 15

Abd-ul-Majid, 59

Abell, Sir George, 170, 172

Adamjees, the, 95

Administration, posts in: *see* Government services

Afghanistan, 42, 51; suggested Afghan invasion of India, 4, 53

Afzal Khan, 23

Aga Khan, The, 28, 33, 38, 69, 71, 77, 79, 111, 177

Age of Consent Act (1891), 23

Agriculture, 94, 95; Departments, 281, 301, 303

Ahmad, Maulana Husain, 199

Ahmad, Mian Bashir, 188

Ahmad, Nazir, 33

Ahmad, Sir Sultan, 184

Ahmad Shah Abdali, King of Afghanistan, 4

Ahmedabad, 26, 81, 95

Ahrars, 180, 296

Akali Sikhs, 135

Akbar Allahabadi, 11

Alexander, A.V., 136, 151

Al-Hilal (newspaper), 38, 43–44, 62

Ali, Ameer, 283

Ali, Bandeh: *see* Talpur

Ali, Begum Muhammad, 188

Ali, Chaudhri Mohamad, 160–1

Ali, Choudhry Rahmat, 105–6, 108

Ali, Malik Barkat, 93, 188–9

Ali, Maulana Muhammad, 28, 38–39, 49, 56–57, 61–63, 73, 76, 103;
personality, 35, 184, 294; imprisoned, 39, 45, 51, 56; and Afghan invasion, 53; *Comrade* started by, 38, 43–44; Khilafat leader, 7, 11, 56, 59, 63, 96, 286; and Muslim League, 30, 66

Ali, Muhammad (of Bogra), 277

Ali, Shaukat, 39, 45, 49, 51, 56–57, 69

Ali, Tafazzal, 277

Aligarh, 43, 90; Muslim University (earlier College), 16, 28–29, 32, 34, 61, 110, 200

Al-Jamiat (newspaper), 201

All-India Commission, proposed, 137

All-India Federation: *see* Federation

All-India Muslim Conference (1929), 71, 76

All-India Muslim League, established (1906), 30; *see* Muslim League

All-Parties, Conference, (1925) 290, (1928), 64, 68–70, 75; National Convention (1928), 70–72

Allahabad, 47, 103, 176, 195

Almond, Gabriel, 297

Ambala Division, 104, 117

Ambedkar, Dr B.R., 49, 77–79

American goods, Chinese boycott, 26

Americans, and Islam, 52

Amery, L.S., 129

Amritsar, 261; tragedy (1919), 42, 46–48

Anglo-Oriental College, 16 (*later* Aligarh University, *q.v.*)

Angora, 52–53, 56

Anjam (newspaper), 201

Ansari, Dr, 38, 64, 74

Arabia, Arabs, 21, 45, 54, 59, 104–5

Archbold, W.A.J., 28–29

Armed forces and equipment, division, 167, 172–3, 227, 261

Army, British-Indian, 6, 46, 282, 299; Muslims and, 39, 44, 52, 160, 219, 305; communal politics in, 155; strength, 284

Arya Samaj, 22

Asre-Jadid (newspaper), 201

Assam, constitutional proposals, 106, 109, 111–12, 114, 117–18, 138–9, 141, 143–6, 162–3; incorporated in Eastern Bengal and Assam (1905–1912) (*q.v.*) 25; ministry, 135; Muslims, 78, 87, 189, 207, 213, 296; and Partition, 124, 136, 168, 171, 205; Premier, 87, 183–4, 207, 213; Sylhet: *see that title*

Ataturk, Kemal (Mustafa Kemal Pasha), 52, 59, 231, 256

Attlee, C.R. (*later* Lord Attlee), 164–5, 234

Attock, 265

Auchinleck, Field-Marshal Sir Claude, 173, 226–7

Aurangzeb, Emperor, 3, 227

Australia, 100, 231, 238

Austro-Hungarian dual monarchy, 226

Azad (newspaper), 201–2

Azad, Maulana Abul Kalam, 49, 61–63, 67–68, 74, 85–86, 120, 135, 155, 169; interned, 39; *Al-Hilal* started by, 38, 43–44; and Executive Council, 129–30; and Hindu-Muslim unity, 35, 42–44, 62, 133; Khilafat leader, 11, 56, 59, 63; on language question, 91–92; and migration idea, 51; Nehru and, 85–86, 161; attitude to Partition, 9, 138, 145–7, 166–7, 174; religious views, 61–63

Aziz, Syed Abdul, 108

Azizul Huque, Muhammad, 70

Babur, 227

Bahawalpur, 109, 241, 267

Balkanization, dangers of, 171

Balkans, 38

Baluchistan, as Chief Commissioner's province, 239, 249–52; Constituent Assembly, 173–4; constitutional proposals, 103, 109, 112, 117; Governor General's Advisory Council, 250; Hindu minority, 65, 68, 71; Muslim League, 188, 192; and Partition, 117, 124, 136, 138, 172; reforms proposed, 65, 73; refugees, 241, 267

Bande Mataram (national song), 23, 88, 91, 97, 99

Bande Mataram (newspaper), 27

Banerjee, Sir Surendranath, 19

Bang-i-Islam, 106

Banks, 7

Baqrid (Muslim festival), 50

Benares, 18; Hindu University, 61

Bengal:
administration, 13–14, 96, 281

British, and, 20, 21, 26, 216

communal clashes, 57, 155–6, 285

constitutional proposals, 106, 109–118, 138, 143–6

elections, 83, 135, 213

famine, 214–15, 284

Faraiziyah Movement, 11, 14, 24

Hindus, 19, 23, 94, 96, 213–16, 285, 289

Legislative Assembly, 31, 121, 212–13, 215

ministry, 132, 135, 159, 213–16

Muslim League, 189, 207–9, 213–216, 219, 294

Muslims, 5, 7, 20, 24–25, 31, 67–72, 77–78, 87, 93–94, 101, 118, 178, 201–11

Partition, First (1905): *see* Eastern Bengal and Assam

Partition plans, 124, 136, 141, 168–74

Partition, Second (1947), 114 (*see* East Bengal)
police, 154
Premier, 183, 213–16
Proja Party, 94, 213, 296
separate electorates, 41, 65
Bengali language, 26, 201–2, 210, 275–6, 294
Bengalis, 181, 216, 275–7
Bentinck, Lord William, 13
Berar, 110, 112
Besant, Annie, 47
Bhagavad Gita, the, 23
Bhopal, Nawab of, 158
Bihar, constitutional proposals, 112, 117, 142; ministry, 135; Muslim League, 188; Muslims, 20, 78, 109, 296; relief fund, 208; riots, 154, 156
Bijnor, 201
Bikaner, 112
Bills, on communal issues: see Communal issues; Governor General's powers, 236; provincial governors and, 245–6; Jinnah and, 253–4
Birdwood, Lord, 246
Birkenhead, Lord, 64, 66, 68
Birla, G.D., 67, 96
Birlas, the, 95
Blunt, Wilfrid Scawen, 20, 31–32, 102–3
Boers, 101
Bohras, 185, 208
Bombay City, 39–40, 45, 76, 82, 103, 124, 146; commercial communities, 7, 81, 95, 177, 185, 207–8, university, 21
Bombay province, British and, 21, constitutional proposals, 112, 142; district administration, 281; elections, 135; Governor, 127, 183; ministry, 135; Muslim League, 187–8, 191, 196, 207; Muslims, 78; and Partition, 73
Bose, Subhas Chandra, 56, 73, 90, 287

Boundary Commissions, 172–4, 268
Bourne, Sir Frederick, 241–2
Boycotts (*see also under* subjects), of British goods, 26; under non-cooperation campaign, 48–50, 60, 62; of Simon Commission, 64, 66, 75; policy, 66; of elections, 76
Brahmins, 8, 23
Bright, John, 102, 292
Britain, British (*see also* subject headings throughout the index):
Bengali boycott of British goods, 26
Congress, and, 29, 285
'divide and rule' policy, 3, 6–8, 23–24
Hindus, and, 5–7, 20–23, 26–27, 31, 35, 46, 54–55, 216
Muslims, policy towards, 7–8, 13–17, 20, 29–35, 39, 45–46, 66, 107, 187; and loyalty to British rule, 6, 15–16, 30, 32, 34, 37, 43, 50
Pakistan and, 223, 228, 258–9; British as governors of provinces, 241–2; as officials, 244, 267
Persia, and, 42–43
rule in India, 3–8, 13, 42, 49, 65, 96, 103, 129, 148, 285 (*see also* Viceregal system)
trade agreement (1935), 80
transfer of power and withdrawal from India, plans for, 7, 13, 164–6, 168–74
Turkey, relations with, 7, 44–45, 47, 53, 56
unifying influences, 6
War: *see* War
British North America Act, 237–8
Buddhism 22
Budgets, 80, 161, 244–5, 279
Bukhsh, Allah, 218
Bukhsh, Pir Illahi, 256
Bukhsh, Moula, 193

Bureaucracy, Pakistan and, 280, 299–300

Burma, 277

Cabinet, Indian (Central), representation in, 71, 73, 86, 98; system, 120–1, 127; Budget meeting, 161; Interim Government as, 161–2; Coordination committee, 160–1; secretariat, 301

Cabinet, Pakistan, provisional, 235, 237–239, 241, 251; powers, 259

Cabinet Mission Plan (1946), 11, 112, 136–60, 162–8, 172, 187

Cabinets, provincial: *see under* Provinces

Calcutta, 70, 83, 101–2, 213; cloth shortage, 215; commercial communities, 7, 207–8; Congress session at, 47, 49–50; Muslim League session at, 64; Muslim share of Corporation services, 67; newspapers, 26, 201; and Partition, 24, 115; riots, 154–6, 216; separate electorates, 211; university, 21

Caliphate, Islamic: *see* Khalifa

Campbell-Johnson, Alan, 223, 229, 236–7, 256

Canada, 70, 100, 231–2, 237–8

Canal colonies, 265

Canarese language, 9

Canning, George, 230

Capital city of Pakistan, Karachi declared, 269–70

Carnatic, 110

Casey, R.G., 186, 215

Caste system, 8, 22

Central government, Indian, and provinces, 78, 258–78; choosing of Ministers by Governor General, 279–80 (*see also* Cabinet)

Central government, Pakistan, Governor General's powers, 232–252, 258–9

Central Provinces, constitutional proposals, 112, 142; education, 97; elections, 135; ministry, 135; Muslims, 78, 188; separate electorates, 41

Centre, the, 279; Nehru Report proposals, 69; powers, 78; 1935 Act and, 80, 279; recommendations in schemes, 109, 112–14, 163, 168; Jinnah and, 136–7; Congress and, 137–8, 154; Union Centre, 137, 141–3, 147

Chathari, Nawab Saheb, 296

Chatterjee, Bankim Chandra, *Anandamath*, 4–5, 22–23, 91

Chauri-Chaura, 58

Chief Commissioner of Province, 249–52

China, boycott of American goods, 26

Chitpavan dynasty, 23

Chittagong, 24

Chowdhry, Abdul Matin, 108, 189

Christianity, Christians, 14–16, 21–22, 130, 149, 254

Chundrigar, I.I., 159, 187–8

Churchill, Lord Randolph, 20

Churchill, Sir Winston, 106, 285

Civil disobedience, 53, 76, 151, 217–218, 286

Civil servants: *see* Government services, posts in

Civil Service, British, 88

Civil Service, Indian, 6, 36, 244, 267, 275, 280, 282

Cloth, shortage in Calcutta, 215

Coalitions, 86, 99, 127, 213

Colonial self-government, 37

Colonial system, impact of, 283

Colville, Sir John, 127

Commerce and commercial communities, 6–7, 95, 177, 184–185, 207–8, 210; Department, 304

Commonwealth, British, 119 (*see also* Dominion status)

Commonwealth Relations Department, 303

Communal award (1932), 77–80

Communal issues, taking of decisions on, 65, 72–73, 99, 140–2, 149, 159
Communal riots and disorders, 5, 54–55, 57–58, 154–6, 169, 172, 201, 216, 218, 226, 261–3
Communalism, 6, 9, 28, 98
Communists, 102, 182, 208, 215
Comrade (newspaper), 38, 43–44
Congress, Indian National (*see also* subject headings throughout the index):
All-India Congress Committee, 122, 146, 163, 174–5
annual sessions, 39, 40, 47, 49–50
British and, 29, 285
Cabinet Mission proposals, and, 11, 136–41, 144–8, 150–2, 155–158, 162–4, 168
civil disobedience, and, 53
constitution, and, 66
Dominion status, and, 75–76
educational scheme, 97, 287
elections, (1934), 79; (1937), 83–84, 88; (1945), 135
factions, 'Pro-Changers' and 'No-Changers', 66, 73
flag, 99
Gandhi and, 61, 182, 287, 290, 293
Government of India Act (1935), and, 106, 288
Governor Generalship, and, 223
Hindus and, 67, 97, 287
Interim Government, and, 149–153, 159–60, 164, 166
Jinnah resigns from, 50; his relations with, 187, 285–6, 290
leaders in jail, 181
Moplahs and, 54–55
Muslim League, pact with (1916), 32, 38–42, 75, 82, 97, 288–9; relations with, 92, 187
Muslims, and, 17–19, 23, 36–37, 39–40, 66, 80, 84–86, 88–90, 92, 295; alleged persecutions, 97, 178–9, 197, 201–2, 295
newspapers, 201
non-cooperation, and, 47–49, 63, 66
Pakistan, and, 8–11, 85
Parliamentary government, and, 86, 98
political activities, 284
President, 36, 39, 146; first Muslim, 18–19
programme, 36–37
provincial governments, 6–7, 23, 84, 86–88, 97–99, 107, 135, 178, 287, 295, 296; called on to resign, 99
publicity machinery, 81
'Quit India' campaign, 122, 152, 230, 284
Round Table Conference, and, 75–76
separate electorates, and, 5, 288
Simon Commission, and, 64, 75
structure and organization, 182, 287–8, 297
Subjects Committee, 55
unity, lack of, 73
war, and, 8, 98–99, 295
Working Committee, 55, 64, 76, 91, 98–99, 119–20, 132, 144, 146–7, 149–50, 174–5, 287; members in jail, 124, 127
Connell, Joh, 226
Conservative Government, British, 65, 134
Constantinople, 58, 103
Constituent Assembly, Cabinet Mission's proposals (1946), 139–41, 146–7, 157, 162–3; Muslim League members absent, 164; effect of Partition, 173–4
Constituent Assembly, Pakistan, Governor General and, 252, 258; legal guide, 256–7; President, 252–7
Constitution, safeguards, 8–9; reforms, 39, 41–42; Jinnah as constitutional-

ist, 64, 285; provision for changes, 73; problems, 101, 190; (*see also* All-Parties Conferences; Nehru Report; Simon Commission, etc.)

Constitution, Pakistan, Governor General's powers, 233–5, 258–259; Provisional Order, 234–8, 258; drafting, 256

Converts, 55–58

Coorg, 112

Corruption, charges, 247, 266; measures against, 254–5

Cotton Bill, 95

Council of Ministers: *see* Cabinet

Courts, boycott, 48, 60, 62

Cow sacrifice, 18, 19, 50, 56, 91

Criminal Law Amendment Bill, 80

Cripps, Sir Stafford, mission to India (1942), 118–22, 126, 195; member of Cabinet Mission (1946), 134, 136

Crusades, the, 16

Cultural zones scheme, 109

Cunningham, Sir George, 169, 225, 241–2, 244–5, 271–2, 282–3, 285

Curzon, Lord, 6, 24–25, 58–59, 230

Cutch, 185

Dacca, 24–25, 30, 275

Dacca, Nawab of, 209

Dalmias, the, 95

Darjeeling, 117

Darling, Sir Malcolm, 202

Dar-ul-harb, 14, 50, 55

Das, C.R., 48–49, 58, 66–67, 286

Daultana, Mian Mumtaz Muhammad Khan, 177, 207, 248, 266, 268–9

Dawn (newspaper), started (1942), 188, 201; quoted, 132, 155, 224, 227, 231, 235, 242, 246, 252, 255

Dayanand Saraswati, 22

Deccan, 109, 111, 199

Defence, responsibility, 120–1, 129, 160; Pakistan Governor General and, 235, 239

Defence Council, National, 183–4, 200, 213

Defence of India Act, 39

Delhi, 13, 166, 188, 207, 224–5, 227, 261; Congress session at, 66; constitutional proposals, 109–110; Durbar (1911), 31; Khilafat conference at, 47, 50; Muslim League sessions at, 108, 118, 174, 177, 197–8, 223; newspapers, 201

Deliverance Day, 99–100

Depressed classes, 66, 77–78

Dera Ghazi Khan District, 239, 265

Desai, Bhulabhai, 80, 126–7

Desai-Liaquat Pact (1944), 126–8

Devnagri script, 18, 91

Dictatorship, Jinnah's views on, 250–1; constitutional, 259

Direct Action, 148, 151–4, 164, 192

Disraeli, Benjamin, 35

District administration, 28, 36, 264, 280–4, 295–6, 299

'Divide and rule' policy, 3, 6–8, 23–24

Dobden, Richard, 293

Dominion status, 64, 74, 171–3, 229, 231; British declarations (1929), 75; (1939), 98

Drinking, 53

Dufferin, Lord, 20–21, 29, 232

Durand Line, 44

Dwarkadas, Kanji, 291–2

Dyarchy, 80

Dyer, General R., 46

East Bengal (province of Pakistan), administration short of officers, 274–6; Assembly, 173; Dacca meetings suggested, 275; Governor, 241–2, 260; Hindus, 274–275; Jinnah's visit (March 1948), 276–7; language issue, 277; refugees, 274

East Pakistan, Assembly scenes (1958), 215; Chief Minister, 211; political consciousness, 283; attitude to West Pakistan, 275–6

East Punjab, 174, 261–5; civil war: *see under* Punjab
Eastern Bengal and Assam (province, 1905–1912), 6, 24–28, 30–32, 35, 37–38
Ecclesiastical affairs, 235, 239
Economist, The, 229
Educated classes, Muslim, 179–80
Education, Congress scheme, 97, 287; Departments, 281, 301; English, 6, 15, 17, 32–33, 35, 42; expenditure on, 36; Muslim, 16–17, 21, 32–33, 73; non-cooperation and, 48, 50, 60, 62; Western systems, 283–4
Egypt, 70
Elections in India, boycott, 76; (1923), 66–67; (1926), 67; (1934), 79; (1937), 81–84, 87–88, 177, 213, 279–80, 293–5; (1945–6), 7, 11, 134–5, 178, 197, 200, 208, 217
Electorates, Depressed Class, 77–78; Joint, 5, 65, 71–72, 189, 291; Separate, 4–6, 28–31, 36–37, 41, 65, 69, 71–72, 77, 82, 100, 144, 148, 211, 288–9, (table), 78
Elgin, Lord, 231
Elite, Muslim, 35, 92, 176
Ellenborough, Lord, 20
Emergency powers, Governor General's, 239–41, 248, 258, 267
English language, 6, 15, 21, 275
Excluded Areas, 239
Executive, composite, 109–10
Executive Council, Viceroy's, 177, 299; inclusion of representatives of Indian political parties, 99, 129–32, 136, 159, 184, 280; suggested Cabinet system, 120–121; reconstituted as Interim Government (*q.v.*), 161–2
External Affairs, 235, 239; Department, 303

Famine, 214–15, 284
Faraiziyah Movement, 11, 14, 24
Fascism, 182

Fatwa, 14, 50, 199
Fazl-i-Husain, Sir, 50, 106–7, 177, 182, 216, 295–6
Fazl-ul-Huq, 41, 45, 87, 94, 180, 183–4, 213–14, 296; expelled from Muslim League, 213–14
Federal Legislature, Pakistan, 249–250, 252–4, 257
Federation, schemes, 71–72, 88, 108–15, 125; All-India Federation, 80, 107, 112, 190, 236; cultural zones scheme, 109; Muslim attitude to, 71–72, 80, 82, 88, 101, 107, 111, 114–15; Pakistan Federation, 106, 110, 140; three-tier, 137–9; two-tier, 111–12
Finance, Muslims and, 160; Department, 302
Firoz, 243
Flag, Congress, 99
Food distribution, 214–15
Foreign goods, boycott, 48, 50
France, 59
Franchise, extension, 288
Fraser, Sir Andrew, 25
Fuller, Sir Bampfylde, 25, 27

Gallipoli, 44
Gandhi, Mahatma, 156–7, 181, 228, 285–7; arrested and imprisoned (1922), 58; withdraws from political activities, 58, 73
British, relations with, 46, 285–6
civil disobedience Movement, 76
Congress, and, 61, 182, 287, 290, 293
Cripps Mission, and, 120
Desai-Liaquat Pact, support for, 127
fasts over Communal award (1932), 77
Government of India Act (1935), read for first time in 1942, 106, 285
Hindu-Muslim conflict, 3, 42, 49, 56, 57, 128

Hindus, and, 56, 61, 73, 76, 96, 287, 297

Jinnah, and, 76, 158; correspondence with, 90; talks with (1944), 122–6, 172

Khilafat Movement, and, 47–49, 54, 56, 60–61, 286–7

leader, as, 184, 285

minority representation, and, 77

Muslim League, formula on, 158

Muslims, and, 9, 60, 75–6, 81, 96, 97

non-cooperative Movement, 47–49, 58, 63, 66, 286

Partition, and, 167, 175

politics, on, 1

Round Table Conference, and, 76

separate electorates, and, 71

Gauba, K. L., 243

Gazder, M. H., 194, 269

George VI, King, 165

George, A. L. and Juliette L., 292

Germany, war declared, 98

Ghose, Aurobindo, 27

Gladstone, W. E., 35

Gokhale, G. K., 61, 285, 289

Government of India Act (1919), 41–42, 79–80, 103, 161, 277, 279, 289–90

Government of India Act (1935), 78–81, 84, 88, 106–8, 127, 129, 172, 277, 279–80, 288; read for first time by Gandhi in 1942, 106, 285; denounced by Churchill, 285; adaptations and amendments for new Dominions, 233–40, 245, 247–9, 251–2, 256, 258, 267, 271–2, 278

Government of India (Second Amendment) Act (1948), 267

Government services, posts in (including civil servants), Hindus in, 7, 13–14, 96, 213; Indians (non-Muslim) in, 73, 81; Muslims in, 7, 13–14, 36, 73, 95–96, 154, 160, 213, 275, 295, 301–5; shortage of

trained civil servants in Pakistan, 219, 243–4, 260–2, 264, 267, 270, 275, 299; British as Governors of provinces, 241–2; suggested enlistment of British officials, 244, 267

Governor General, Joint or Supreme, suggested, 172, 223–8, 230

Governor General of India (see also Viceroy), 279, 284, 299; control over provinces, 279; Council, 18, 279; powers, 78, 106, 127

Governor General of Pakistan, Jinnah's appointment as, 223–33; Commissions (text), 306–7; powers, 233–52, 256; Ministry under his control, 239, 251; emergency powers, 239–41, 248, 258, 267; powers with regard to provinces, 241–52; political powers, 252–7; constitutional powers, 258–9

Greece, 52, 59

Griffin, Lepel H., 216

Gujarat, 185

Gujaratis, 46, 185, 201, 207–8

Gujamwalla, 46

Gwalior, 112

Habsburgs, 226

Haig, Sir Harry, 85

Hali, Altaf Hussain, 4–5, 11, 18

Hamdam (newspaper), 201

Hamdard (newspaper), 44

Haroon, Sir Abdoola, 108, 111, 207

Hasan, Professor Syed Zafarul, 110, 117

Hashim, Abul, 116, 209–10

Health Department, 281, 301

Hidayatullah, Sir Ghulam Hussain, 132, 193–4, 209, 218, 241–3, 247–8, 298

Hijrat: see Migrations

Hikmat-i-amali, 281, 284

Hindu language, 18, 82, 91–92

Hindu Mahasabha: see Mahasabha

Hindu-Muslim conflict, 3–14, 17–18, 21–32, 107, 125, 133, 148, 168,

201, 214, 254–5, 286–9; cooperation, 32; attempts at unity, 34–101
Hindus (see also subject headings
    throughout the index):
    British and, 5–7, 20–23, 26–27, 31,
        35, 46, 54–55, 216
    Caste, 8, 131, 148, 213
    converted by force, 55–56; recon-
        verts, 57
    cultural zones, 109
    Depressed Classes: see that title
    Gandhi and, 56, 61, 73, 76, 96,
        287, 297
    Ghose on, 27
    idolatrous practices, 11, 14, 22, 24
    Moplahs rising against, 54–55
    Muslims, and: see Hindu-Muslim
        conflict
    nationalism, 5
    power, growth of, 3–5
    non-violence, and, 53
    religion, 9–10, 23–24, 42, 286
    Revivalist Movement, 21–24, 42,
        201
Hindustan, 110, 117, 168, 205
Hindustani, 63, 91
Hoare, Sir Samuel: see Templewood,
    Lord
Hobbes, Thomas, 258
Holy Places, suzerainty over, 51–52,
    58–59
Home Department, 303
Home Rule League, 290
Hoti, Nawab of, 44–45
Howrah, 117
Hume, A.O., 29
Hunter, Sir William, 13, 14, 20
Hunter Committee (1920), 46
Hussain, Akhtar, 243, 264
Hyderabad, 106, 108–12, 199

Ibbetson, Sir Denzil, 10
Iftikharuddin, Mian, 181, 266, 268
Ikramullah, Begum Shaista
    Suhrawardy, 275
Imam, Sir Ali, 65

Imam, Hussain, 131, 159, 187–8
Imperialism, 93, 99
Independence and self-government (see
    also Swaraj), British pledge (1917),
    46, 284–5; Congress-League policy,
    32, 37–38, 43, 74, 76, 81–82, 88,
    103–4, 126, 133; Cripps on, 134–5;
    Khilafat Conference and, 53, 56;
    policy for British transfer of power
    and withdrawal from India, 13,
    164–6, 168–74, 288; Act: see Indian
    Independence Act (1947)
Independence Day (26 January 1930),
    celebrated, 76
India: see subject headings throughout
    the index
India Office, 270–1
Indian Civil Service: see Civil Service,
    Indian
Indian Councils Act (1909), 30–31
Indian Independence Act (1947), 233,
    236, 248, 252–3, 258
Indian Mutiny (1857), 13–14, 24, 216;
    Muslim role, 13, 18
Indian National Congress: see Con-
    gress
Indian Political Service, 282
Indian Union, 119, 122, 137–48, 170
Indus, 10, 110
Industries, 6, 7
Industries and Supplies, Department
    of, 304
Inflation, 284
Information and Broadcasting Depart-
    ment, 303
Inqilab (newspaper), 201
Intelligentsia, 6, 184, 208
Interim Government, pre-Partition,
    proposed, 126–34, 137, 146, 148;
    formation, 149–62, 192, 280; Con-
    gress-League tension in, 156–66,
    172–3; Vice-Presidency, 159–62
Ipi, Faqir of, 244–5, 248
Iqbal, Sir Muhammad, 1, 11, 93–94,
    103–6, 108, 117, 176, 283, 295
Iran, Iranians (Persia), 37, 42–43, 59

Iraq, 45, 59
Irrigation Departments, 281
Irwin, Lord, 66, 75–76, 285
Isa, Qazi Muhammad, 188, 192
Islam (*see also* Muslims), 3–4, 9–11, 16, 24, 33, 49–52, 60–63, 276, 283, 295, 297; caliphate, 43; in India, 24, 45, 60; 'Islam has saved Muslims', 1; law and traditions, 198–9, 203, 262; Pakistan and, 211, 242, 244–5; state, 11, 104–5, 180–1, 254
Ismay, Lord, 167–8, 170, 172
Ispahani, M. A. H., 189
Ispahani Company, 214
Ispahanis, the, 95
Italy, 38

Jaisalmer, 112
Jalandhari, Hafiz, 176–7
Jalianwala Bagh: *see* Amritsar
Jallunder, 265
Jama'at-i-Islami, 199
Jamiyat al Ulama-i-Hind, 50, 58, 84, 199
Jamiyat al Ulama-i-Islam, 153
Jan Mahomed, 51
Japan, war against, 128
Jats (Hindu), 45
Jayakar, M. R., 70, 136
Jazirat-ul-Arab, 45, 51–52
Jenkins, Sir Evan, 170
Jews, 15
Jihad, 14, 43–44, 54
Jinnah, Mohammad Ali, Quaid-i-Azam, death of his wife (1929), 291–2; self-imposed exile in Britain (1931), 81, 178; returns to India (1934), 81, 178, 291
    brutal bluntness, instances of, 162
    Cabinet Mission proposals, and, 136–8, 140, 143–5, 147–8, 157–158, 168
    commercial communities' support, 7, 95, 177, 184–5, 207–8, 210

Congress, resigns from, 50; his relations with, 187, 285–6, 290
    Constituent Assembly, President, 252–5; address, 254–5
    Constitutionalist, as, 64, 285
    Councils and Dominion status, resolution on, 64
    'Deliverance Day', and, 99–100
    denunciations of, 87, 199–200, 203
    dictatorship, on, 250–1
    'Direct Action', and, 148, 152, 154
    doctrine, 181
    dress, 198
    East Bengal visit (1948), 276–7
    'Emperor of Pakistan', 227–8, 256
    federation, and, 80, 113, 115
    Fourteen Points, 70–74, 91, 205, 291
    Gandhi and, 76, 158; correspondence with, 90; talks with (1944), 122–6, 172
    Governor General of Pakistan, as, 223–36, 241–52, 256–9, 262, 267–72, 274–8, 299; Commissions (text), 306–7
    health, 199, 224
    Hindu-Muslim unity, efforts for, 64, 75, 79–83, 97, 99–101, 121–126, 214, 254–5
    Interim Government, and, 127–132, 149, 151, 153, 156–62
    Khilafat Movement, and, 63, 286
    leader, as, 8–9, 50, 63, 65, 86–87, 183–9, 193–9, 252, 294–5, 299–300
    London Conference (1946), attends, 163
    Lucknow Pact, and, 40–41, 75, 97
    minorities, on, 262
    Mountbatten, and, 171, 173, 225–226
    Muslim League, enrolled in, 37; leader of left wing, 37, 39, 79–80; his reorganization of, 81,

87, 90, 92–95, 97–101, 176–83, 186, 190, 212; President, 177

Nehru, J., and, 63, 86, 90–92, 98, 100, 158

non-cooperation Movement, and, 48–49, 63–64, 285–6

Pakistan, and creation of, 9, 11, 19, 60, 94, 98, 102, 161, 182, 198–9, 209, 219, 290; origin of word, 118

Partition, and, 170, 174

Patel, and, 162

personality and character, 35, 87, 90, 161–2, 285–6

political ideas, development of, 288–97

'politics mean't power…', 87, 92

position and prestige, 227–8, 230–231

powers, 258–9

Punjab, and, 106–7, 177, 217

Quaid-i-Azam title, 94, 255–7

Sibi Durbar speech, 250–1

Simla Conference, and, 127–32

Simon Commission, and, 64

tributes to, 221

Urdu, not familiar with, 11, 199, 294

wife's death (1929), 291–2

Joseph II of Austria, 292

Jowett, Benjamin, 32

Judiciary, 6, 36, 282

Jung (newspaper), 201

Jung, Nawab Bahadur Yar, 199–201, 208

Justice, administration of, 281–2

Kaffirs, 54

Kali (goddess), 26, 27

Karachi, 101, 185, 224, 261, 268; Resolutions (1921), 51–53, 56; declared capital of Pakistan, 269–70

Karnal District, 188

Kashmir, 111–12, 115, 225; conflict, 225, 270, 299, 300

Kasur, 263

Kasuri, Abdul Kadir, 74

Kathiawar, 185

Kesari (newspaper), 23

Khairpur, 109, 241, 267

Khaksars, 180, 243

Khalifa (*see also* Khilafat Movement), 43, 59, 61

Khaliquzzaman, Choudhry, 85, 114–115, 159, 179, 187–8

Khan, Abdul Qaiyum, 244, 272–4

Khan, Abul Kasem, 253

Khan, Khan Abdul Ghaffar, 201, 241, 244, 248, 271, 273–4, 283; 'Frontier Gandhi', 274

Khan, Liaquat Ali, 108, 131, 167, 173, 192, 251–3, 271; biographical, 187–8; pact with Desai (1944), 126–8; Finance Minister in Interim Government, 159–62, 164; attends London Conference (1946), 163; Secretary of Muslim League, 187, 189; 207; Prime Minister of Pakistan, 224, 252, 267; on Jinnah, 221, 230, 253, 255–6; and appointments for British officers, 242–4

Khan, Malik Zaman Mehdi, 93

Khan, Maulana Akram, 189

Khan, Maulana Zafar Ali, 44, 88, 200

Khan, Nawab Ismail, 85, 108, 159, 187–8, 192, 207

Khan, Nawab Sir Muhammad Shah Nawaz, 110, 130

Khan, Raja Ghazanfar Ali, 84, 159–160

Khan, Sardar Aurangzeb, 108, 188, 219

Khan, Sardar Shaukat Hyat, 203, 218, 243–4, 248, 262, 266

Khan, Sir Sikander Hyat, 87, 93–95, 108, 111–15, 177, 183, 217

Khan, Tamizuddin, 253

Khan brothers, 135, 169, 274 (*see also* Khan, Khan Abdul Ghaffar; *and* Khan Sahib)

Khan Sahib, Dr, 219, 246–7, 270–4

Khan Tiwana, Malik Khizr Hyat, 130–1, 135, 169, 207, 216–18

Khilafat Movement, 7, 11, 42–64, 87, 96, 126, 180, 285–7; Karachi Resolutions (1921), 51–53, 56; consequences to Muslims, 60–63, 287

Khojas, 7, 181, 185, 208

Khuhro, Muhammad Ayub, 188, 194, 247–8, 266, 298–9

Khutbas, 256

Khyber Pass, 51

Kurds, 59

Labour, 68; Department, 302

Labour Government, British, 134, 151–2, 158, 226

Lahore, 40, 261–3, 267, 291; Congress session at, 76; Muslim League session at, 64; newspapers, 44, 201

Lahore Resolution on Pakistan (1940), 9–10, 101, 104, 113–18, 124–5, 131, 179, 197, 211, 213, 296

Land reforms, proposed, 266, 278

Land revenue, 281

Landlords, 202, 206–7, 209–10, 213, 216, 281, 283, 295–9

Landowners, 13, 36–37, 44, 206–7, 209

Language question, 13, 18, 91–92; National language of India, 82, 91; State language of Pakistan, 277

Lari, Z. H., 189

Lasswell, Harold D., 292

Latif, Dr Syed Abdul, 108–10

Latifi, Danyal, 181, 209

Lausanne, 59

Lawrence, Sir Henry, 216

Lawyers, 207, 213

Layton, Lord, 229

League of Nations, 59, 226

Leghari, 207

Legislation affecting Muslims, decisions on: see Communal issues

Legislative Councils and Assemblies (provinces), 17, 31, 48–49, 64, 66–67, 72, 77–78, 191

Legislative Department, 304

Legislature, Central, 65, 69–72, 76–77, 79–80, 135, 191, 207, 279, 284

Leites, Nathan, 292

Liaquat Ali Khan: see Khan

Liberals, 39, 68, 136, 286

Linlithgow, Lord, 78, 98, 106, 118, 181, 243, 260, 285

Linlithgow Committee, 78–80, 86

Liquor traffic, 53

Lloyd George, David, 45

London Conference (1946), 163, 165

Lucknow, 69, 201; Congress annual session at, 40; Muslim cultural zone, 109; Muslim League sessions at, 40, 64, 87–88, 90, 92, 182–3, 210, 213; newspaper, 201

Lucknow Pact, Congress-Muslim League (1916), 32, 38–42, 75, 82, 97, 288–9

Lyallpur, 265

MacDonald, James Ramsay, 77

Macdonald, Sir John A., 232

Madina, 204

Madina (newspaper), 201

Madras city, 116, 195; university, 21

Madras province, 21, 55, 122, 142; constitutional proposals, 112, 142; district administration, 281; elections, 135; ministry, 135; Muslim League, 188, 192; Muslims, 78

Madras States, 112

Maharashtra, 23, 285

Mahasabha, Hindu, 78, 70, 73, 76, 79, 136, 214

Mahmoodabad, Raja of, 177, 188

Majlis Ittehad-i-Millat, 296

Malabar, 54, 55, 110

Malaviya, Pandit, 48, 53, 57, 67, 96, 286

Malir, 224

Malkhana Rajputs, 57

Mamdot, Nawab Iftikhar Husain Khan of, 188, 192, 203, 207, 216, 218, 248, 266, 268–9

Manchester Guardian, 100
Mandal, Jogendranath, 159
Manki Sharif, Pir Sahib of, 198, 203, 205, 273
Manshoor (newspaper), 201
Marathas, 3, 4, 23
Marriage, intermarriage, 12
Martial Law, after Amritsar (1919), 46–47; (1921), 55
Marx, Karl, 208
Masha'ikh, 203
Maudoodi, Maulana, 105, 199
Maulanas, 205
Mazhar-ul-Huq, 30, 39
Mecca, 204
Meerut, 108
Melechas (unclean), 8, 23, 60
Memons, the, 7, 185, 208
Menon, Krishna, 171
Menon, V.P., 131, 154, 166, 171–172
Merchants and industrialists, 207–210, 213
Mesopotamia, 48, 52
Messervy, General Sir Frank, 225, 242, 260
Mianwali, 265
Middle classes, Indian, 7
Middle East, 6, 42, 45
Midnapore, 117
Migrations, 51, 62, 109–11, 170; following Partition, 240–1, 263–4 (*see also* Refugees)
Military expenditure, 36
Minorities, inclusion of members in ministries, 86, 120; and Interim Government, 127, 149, 151; Jinnah on, 262; and Partition, 170, 263; representation (*see also* Electorates), 69, 71–72, 77–78, 87, 144; rights and interests, 84, 110, 119, 134, 235, 277
Minto Lord, 26, 28–32, 77
Minto, Mary, Countess of, 33
Moghuls, 3, 14, 17, 21, 105, 227, 282
Mohammed, Ghulam, 266

Mohammedan National Association of Calcutta, 20
Mohani, Maulana Hasrat, 55, 189, 195
Money-lenders, 94, 104, 202, 217, 281–2
Montagu, Edwin S., 58, 86
Montagu-Chelmsford Report, 46
Montgomery District, 265
Mookerjee, Dr Shyama Prasad, 214
Moplah rising (1921), 54–55, 57
Morley, Lord, 26, 30
Moss E. de V., 267
Mosul, 59
Mountbatten, Admiral Lord, appointed Viceroy (February 1947), 164; predilections towards Partition, 166–7; views on Cabinet Mission Plan, 167; hastening of transfer of power, 168–9; his plan of Partition, 169–73, 195; suggested as joint or supreme Governor General, 223–8, 230; suspected pro-Indian leanings, 225; exercises powers as Governor General of undivided India, 233, 235, 237; on area of Pakistan, 117–18; and Interim Government, 157; and Kashmir, 225, 228; and North-West Frontier Province ministry, 247, 270–2
Mudie, Sir Francis, 130, 241–3, 262–263, 268, 298
Muhajirin Relief Fund, 53
Muhammad, prophet, 16
Muharram festival, 57
Mullahs, 206, 209, 283–4
Multan, 57
Multan, Makhdum Raza Shah of, 203
Municipal and District Board elections, 36
Murders, political, 23, 26
Muslim League (*see also* subject headings throughout the index):

annual sessions, 1915, 39; 1916, 40; 1918, 45; 1923, 64; 1930, 103; 1931, 177; 1935, 177, 182; 1937, 87–88, 90, 92, 182–3, 210, 213; 1938, 107; 1941, 116, 195; 1943, 190, 197; held in private houses, 177
Cabinet Mission proposals, and, 136–41, 143–5, 147–8, 152, 156–8, 162–4, 168
Central Election Board, 296
Central Parliamentary Board, 84, 93–94, 177, 188, 192–3, 196
Committee of Action, 188, 190–3, 196, 207
Congress, pact with (1916), 32, 38–42; relations with, 92, 187
Constitution for India, committee appointed to confer on drafting, 64–66, 101 (see Nehru Report)
Constitutions and Rules, 185–6
Council, 185–6, 189, 195–6, 206–7
criticism, of, 36–37
Cripps proposals, and, 121
denunciations of, 199, 203–4
'Direct Action' call to achieve Pakistan, 148, 151–4, 164, 192
District Leagues, 196
election results, (1934), 79; (1937), 83–84, 87, 177; (1945–6), 7, 11, 135, 178, 197, 208, 217
expulsions from, 184, 189, 213–14
funds, commercial communities' support, 7, 177, 208
Gandhi's formula, 158
Governor Generalship, and, 223
groups and factions, 206–11, 288
growing strength, 86–101
Interim Government, and, 9, 126–133, 149–62, 164, 166, 192
Jinnah and, 293–4, 297; enrolment, 37; leader of left wing, 37, 39–40, 79–80; reorganization of League: see under Jinnah

Lahore Resolution: see that title
leadership, 36–37
left wing (led by Jinnah), 37, 39–40, 79–80
Masha'ikh Committee, 203
membership, 176, 178
Mountbatten, and, 225–6
newspapers, 188, 197, 201
organization and role, 9, 81, 87, 90, 92–95, 97–101, 176–219, 294–8
Pakistan, objective for achievement of: see under Pakistan
Parliamentary government, and, 211–19
Partition, and, 10–11, 115, 121, 125, 167
popularity, 169
President, 38–40, 45, 70, 177–8, 183, 185–6, 189–90, 192–6, 206
Primary Leagues, 196
programme, 36, 37
propaganda method and machinery, 196–202
Provincial Leagues, 182–3, 185–6, 189–96, 207, 270, 272, 297
Secretary, 187–9, 206–7
self-government, and, 32
Subjects Committee, 116, 197
subscription rate, 180
Working Committee, 108, 110, 113–15, 121, 128, 131, 138, 149, 153, 156–7, 164, 207, 213, 272; powers of functions, 185–7, 190–4, 196; members (1945–7), 188–9, 206
Muslims:
anti-League organizations, 180
British policy towards: see under Britain
Congress and: see under Congress
culture, 73; cultural zones, 109
Deliverance Day, 99–100
education, 16–17, 21, 32–33, 73
Hindu-Muslim conflict: see that title

Khilafat Movement, effects of, 60–63, 287
leaders, 288, 295–6
League: *see* Muslim League
merchants and industrialists, 95
Mosques desecrated, 201
nationalists, 135, 156–7, 174
persecutions, alleged (1937–9), 97, 178–9, 197, 201–2, 295
population in India, 204
Powers, decline, 37
refugees: *see* Refugees
religion, 9–10, 15–16, 21, 24, 33, 35, 50–53
'Saved by Islam', 1
separatism: *see that title*
separate electorates: *see under* Electorates
Separate State idea: *see* Pakistan
social change among, 283
Western Powers' hostility to, 38, 42–43
Westernized, 50
Mustafa Kemal Pasha, Ghazi: *see* Ataturk, Kemal
Mutiny (1857): *see* Indian Mutiny
Muzaffargarh, 265
Mymensingh District, 202
Mysore, 111–12

Nagpur, 49, 54, 63
Nagri script, 18, 91
Naidu, Mrs Sarojini, 37
National Agricultural Party, 84, 296
National Defence Council: *see* Defence
Nationalism and Nationalists, 4, 12, 24, 26, 29, 66, 79, 286–8, 290, 296–7; newspapers, 201; song: *see* Bande Mataram
Nationality, common, 5, 35, 37; based on religion, 12
Nationalization, 209
'Nawabs' and 'Nawabzadas', 187, 203, 207
Nawa-i-Waqt (newspaper), 201

Nawaz, Begum Jahan Ara Shah, 184, 253
Nazimuddin, Sir Khwaja, 108, 156, 159, 186, 189, 203, 209, 214–15, 277
Nehru, Jawaharlal, 9, 35, 73–74, 85–86, 120, 157, 161–2, 169, 182, 247
Bande Mataram, on, 91
Benares University, and, 61
Cabinet Mission Plan, and, 146–7
'Direct Action', on, 148, 153
Gandhi, and, 96, 287
Jinnah, and, 3, 86, 90–92, 98, 100, 158
language question, on, 91
London Conference, attends (1946), 163
Mountbatten, and, 170–1, 224
Muslim League, on, 207
Muslims and, 9, 81–83, 92
Pakistan, attitude to, 260
Partition, and, 166–7
Nehru, Motilal, 9, 47, 58, 66–67, 73–74, 96, 286 (*see also* Nehru Report)
Nehru Report (1928), 66–74, 76, 86, 103, 205
New Delhi: *see* Delhi
New Zealand, 252
Newspapers, 44, 188, 197, 201
Niazi, Maulana Abdul Sattar Khan, 205
Nichols, Beverley, 102
Nicholson, General John, 216
Nilambur, 54
Nishtar, Abdur Rab, 159, 188, 230
Noakhali, 154, 156, 216
'No-Changers', 66, 73
Non-Brahmins, 68
Non-cooperation Movement, 47–50, 53, 55, 58, 61–66, 286
Non-violence, 50, 53–54, 58
Noon, Malik Feroz Khan, 203
North-West Frontier, 14, 20, 50–51, 216

North-West Frontier Province:
  Congress in, 132, 135, 145, 159, 270–4, 282
  Constituent Assembly, 173
  constitutional proposals, 65, 68–69, 71–73, 103, 109, 112, 117, 121, 142, 146
  district administration, 281–3
  elections, 83–84, 135, 141, 170, 172, 197, 204–5, 219
  Frontier Crimes Regulation, arrest under, 248
  Governor, 169, 241–2, 244–7, 271–272, 282
  Hindus, 65
  ministry, 132, 135, 145, 218–19; dismissed, 246–7, 270–2; formed by Qaiyum Khan, 272–4
  minorities, 65, 69, 71
  Muslim League, 188, 197, 219, 228
  Muslims, 72, 78, 101, 136, 138, 270–4, 282, 296
  Pakistan, and, 124, 135–6, 239; referendum decides to join, 246
  referendum, 174, 246
  refugees, 241, 266–7
  tribes, 245

Orissa, 112, 135, 142
Osmani, Maulana Shabbir Ahmad, 153, 203–5
Osmani, Maulana Zafar Ahmad, 204–5
Osmanli Turks, 59
Oudh, 13

Paisa Akhbar (newspaper), 201
Pakisan (word), 102, 105, 118
Pakistan, Dominion of (*see also* subject headings throughout the index):
  Congress and, 8–11, 85
  'Direct Action' call to achieve, 148, 151–4, 164, 192
  East Pakistan: *see that title*
  emergence of, 102–33, 134–75
  establishment of (1947), 219, 288, 299–300
  federation scheme, 106, 110, 140
  India, relations with, 226–7, 260, 299–300
  Jinnah as supreme founder of: *see under* Jinnah
  Lahore, Resolution demanding (1940): *see* Lahore Resolution
  Muslim League's objective for achievement of, 179–82, 190, 195, 197, 203–4, 206, 208–9, 211, 217, 296–7
  origin of idea, 3–12, 102–6
  propaganda to popularize idea, 197–9
  provinces: *see* Provinces; *and under* their names
  two states visualized, 113–17
  West Pakistan: *see that title*
Palestine, 45, 59
Pall, B.C., 48
Pant, Pandit, 174
Paramountcy, 142
Parliamentary government, 29–30, 34–35, 100, 109, 185, 251, 270, 285; Congress and, 86, 98; Muslim League and, 211–19
Parliamentary Select Committees (1919), 74; (1934), 78–80, 86
Parsis, 149
Parsons, Sir Arthur, 283
Parties, political, 36, 98
Partition of Bengal (1905): *see* Eastern Bengal and Assam
Partition of India and Pakistan (*see also* Pakistan), history of idea, 9, 67, 102–33, 134–75; Mountbatten plan (1947), 169–73, 195; 'Heads of Agreement', 172–3
Patel, Sardar Vallabhbhai, 9, 160, 162, 164, 166–7, 171–2, 174, 182
Pathanistan, 244, 271–2, 274
Pathans, 44, 199, 205, 246, 274, 276

Patiala, 109
Patna, 92, 107
Peasants, 213, 216, 281–3
Persia: see Iran
Persian language and script, 13, 18, 21, 92
Peshawar, 169, 246
Pethick-Lawrence, Lord, 136, 145, 151
Physical exercises, popularizing, 57
Pripur Report, 97–98, 201
Pirs, 53, 202–3, 206, 209–10, 283, 298
Plague, 23
Police, Muslims in, 154, 160, 295; communal hostility in, 155; Pakistan force, 255
Politics, 35–36; Gandhi quoted, 1; religion and, 42, 62
Poona, 23
Poona Pact, 77–78
Population, exchanges of: see Migrations
Power seekers, 292–3
Prasad, Rajendra, 28, 57
Press Act, 39
Prime Minister, position of, 161–2
Princes, Indian, 80, 98, 106, 148 (see also States)
'Pro-Changers', 66, 73
Progressive Coalition Party, 213
Proja Party, Bengal, 94, 213, 296
Property, expropriation of, 82
Provinces (see also under their names):
autonomy, 77, 80–82, 112–13, 137–8, 146, 182, 270, 277, 287, 290
Cabinet Mission grouping plan, 139–40, 142–8, 151, 156–7, 162–164
Cabinets, 71, 73–75, 86, 98, 178, 182, 242–3, 260
central government and, 78, 258–278
Chief Commissioner, 249–52

Congress governments: see under Congress
elections, 69, 71–73; (1937), 81–84, 87–88, 177, 213, 279–80, 293–5
feuding ministers, 268–70
Governor General's powers regarding, 241–52, 279
Governors, 86, 88, 280; powers, 106, 234, 277–8; fortnightly letters to Governor General, 243–5, 260; Governor General and, 258–60, 278
Legislative Councils and Assemblies: see that title
ministries, 84, 86–88, 97–99, 101, 127, 132, 135, 212–13; dismissal of ministries and ministers, 246–9, 258, 270–2
Regulation and Non-Regulation, 281–3
secretariat, 280, 299
Provisional Government in India (see also Interim Government), 120, 126; in Pakistan, 235, 237, 270
Punjab:
civil war, 169, 226, 261–3, 274
constitutional proposals, 103, 109, 112, 115, 117–18, 142–5
district administration, 281–3, 295
East: see East Punjab
elections, 83–94, 135, 204, 208, 217, 294
Hindus, 10, 67–69, 94–95, 170–1, 217, 289
Jats, 45
Legislature, 31, 121, 138, 212, 216
ministry, 135, 169, 217–18
Muslim League, 87, 90, 93–95, 106–7, 130–2, 135, 169, 178, 183, 188–9, 192, 197–200, 207–212, 216–19, 294–6
Muslims, 31, 41, 44, 65, 68–72, 77–78, 130–2, 159–60, 177, 212, 289

Partition, and, 115, 124, 136, 138,
    141, 168–74
peasants, 202
police, Muslims in, 154
Premier, 183
refugees, 170, 261–5
Sikhs, 14, 71, 77, 135, 164, 170,
    216–17, 261, 263, 265
Unionists, 84, 93, 130, 132, 177,
    200, 213, 216–17, 295–6
West: *see* West Punjab
Punjabi language, 276
Punjabis, 181, 216, 269, 275–6
Purnia, 117
Pushtu, 200

Qadri, Dr Mohammad Afzal Husain,
    110, 117
Qizilbash, Nawab Muzaffar Ali Khan,
    216
Quaid-i-Azam (title), 94, 255–7 (*see*
    Jinnah)
'Quit India' campaign, 122, 152, 230,
    284
Qur'an, The, 10, 16, 54–55, 61–63,
    198, 294
Qureshi, Muhammad Hayat, 203

Rahim, Sir Abdur, 12
Rahman, Professor F., 59
Rahman, Latifur, 188
Rai, Lala Lajpat, 49, 67, 96
Railway Department, 304
Rajagopalachari, C., 9, 122, 124, 126,
    171
Rajistan, 111
Rajputana, 11–12
Rajputs, 57
Ram, Jagjivan, 149
Ram Mohan Roy, Raja, 21
Ram Raj, 96
Rasool, Ghulam, 93
Rawalpindi, 225, 265
Razmak, 245
Reading, Lord, 57–58
Red Crescent Mission, 38

'Red Shirts', 244
Refugees, 240–1, 243, 260–8, 274,
    278, 298–9; rehabilitation, 263–
    268, 270, 274
Religion, 10, 16–17, 24, 35, 179–180;
    nationality based on, 12; and poli-
    tics, 42, 62; religious freedom, 65,
    72
Religious leaders, 14, 33
Republic, threat, 53, 56
Reservation of seats, 65, 69, 71
'Resumptions', 13
Rizwanullah, Syed M., 189
Round Table, The, 228
Round Table Conferences (1930–
    1932), 3, 7, 63, 75–78, 285, 290–
    1
Rowlatt Report and Act, 46
Russia, 42–43

Saadullah, Sir Muhammad, 87, 183–
    4, 189, 207
Saharanpur, 103
Sait, Abdul Sattar, 188, 192
Salimullah, Nawab, 30
Sangathan Movement, 57
Sannaiyat, 44
Sapru, Sir Tej Bahadur, 9, 47, 79,
    90–91, 136
Sarkar, Abu Husain, 211
Sarkar, Sir Jadunath, 3
Sayed, G.M.: *see* Syed
Sayyid Ahmad Barelawi, 14, 24, 61
Sayyid Ahmad Khan, Sir, 14–19, 28,
    31–35, 63, 283; and Muslim edu-
    cation, 14–17, 32–33; policy of
    loyalty to British, 15–16, 34, 37,
    50; and Congress, 17–19
Scheduled Castes, 127, 130, 144, 149,
    151, 159, 213
Science, Western, 15, 33; Vedas and,
    22
Scotsman, The, 151
Secretariat, Central (India), 280, 284,
    299; Muslims in, 301–4
Secretary of State for India, 279

Self-government: *see* Independence
Separatism, Muslim, 4, 7–11, 13
Sevres, Treaty of, 58
Shafi, Sir Muhammad, 37, 50, 64–66, 68, 75, 77
Shah, Pir Jama't Ali, 203
Shah, Syed Abdur Rauf, 188
Shahabuddin, Khwaja, 214, 249
Shahpur, 265
Shariat, 198–200, 245
Sheikhpura, 261, 263
Sherwood, Miss (missionary), 46
Shibli Nomani, Maulana, 35–37, 42
Shivaji, 3, 23
Shradhanand, Swami, 40, 50, 53–54, 57; murder (1926), 57
Shuddhi Movement, 57
Sibi, 250–1
Sikander Hyat Khan: *see* Khan
Sikhs, 3, 68, 136, 155, 163, 168, 216; Akali, 135; representation in interim Government, 127, 130, 149, 151 (*see also under* Punjab; *and* Refugees)
Sikkim 112
Simla, 28, 77, 170
Simla Conference (1945), 129–34, 187
Simon Commission, 64, 66, 68, 75; no Indian members, 64, 68
Sind:
constitutional proposals, 65, 68, 71, 73, 103, 109, 112, 117, 143, 205
elections, 83, 135
Governor, 241–3, 247–8
Hindus, 65
Karachi as capital of Pakistan, 269–70
landlords, 209, 218, 278, 299
Legislative Assembly, 121, 173
migration from, 51
ministry, 132, 135, 192–3, 218, 298; ministry dismissed, 247–8, 266, 299

Muslim League, 107, 135, 187–8, 192–4, 204, 209, 218–19, 228
Muslims, 51, 68, 78, 178, 296
Pakistan, and, 115–17, 124, 136, 138, 172–3, 254, 299
police, Muslims in, 154
Premier, 183
refugees, 241, 266–7
Singh, Baldev, 163
Singha, Diwan Bahadur S.P., 263
Sinha, Lord, 39
Sleeman, W.H., 17
Smith, Professor W.C., 19, 59
Smyrna, 52–53, 58
Social amenities, expenditure on, 36
Social change, among Muslims, 283
Socialism, 181, 209, 287
South Africa, 100–1
Stalin, Joseph, 102
Star of India (newspaper), 81, 201
States, Indian, 112, 129, 139, 142–3, 235; Princely States, 171; successor States, 102, 170–1
States and Frontier Regions, Ministry of (1948), 239
Statesman, The, 155
Stephens, Ian, 225
Stevens, Brigadier F.F., 267
Students and propaganda campaign, Muslim, 197, 200
Sudras (low castes), 199
Sufi, 3
Suhrawardy, H.S., 154–5, 188, 214–216, 277
Sunday Times, 224
Sunni Muslims, 181
Swadeshi Movement, 26
Swaraj (*see also* Independence), 46, 48, 50, 56, 76, 96
Swaraj Party, 58, 66–67
Switzerland, 98
Syed (Sayed), G.M., 116, 187, 189, 192–4, 209–10, 254–5, 298
Sylhet Division, 117, 138, 170, 172–174, 204–5
Syria, 45, 59

Tabligh Movement, 58
Tairsee, Mr, 49
Talpur, Bandeh Ali Khan, 218, 298
Talpurs, 207
Tandon, Purshottamdas, 174
Tanzim Movement, 58
Tariffs, 95
Taxation, 76, 139, 161, 209
Technical education, 36
Templewood, Lord (*earlier* Sir Samuel Hoare), 99, 290
Thrace, 52, 58
Tilak, B.G., 23, 61 285–6
Times, The, 38, 221, 229–30, 242–4, 261, 263
Tirur, 55
Tiruvangadi, 54
Tiwana: *see* Khan Tiwana
Trade agreement (Britain-India) rejected, 80
Travancore, 112
Tribal areas, 44, 235, 239, 283
Tripoli Wars, 38
Tuker, Lieutenant General Sir Francis, 155
Turkey, Turks, British policy towards, 7, 44–45, 47, 53, 56, war against, 32, 39, 44–45; Muslim medical mission to, 38; decline as Muslim power, 37, 42, 45; Khilafat Movement and, 51–53, 56; revision of treaty, 58; Khalifa (*q.v.*) abolished, 59; Lausanne negotiations, 59
Two-nation theory, 9–10, 19, 113–117; 166
Tyabji, Badruddin, 18–19

Ulama, 16, 52, 62, 181, 197, 202–6
Unionists, Punjab, 84, 93, 130, 132, 177, 200, 213, 216–17, 295–6
Unitarians, 16
United Provinces:
    Congress, 88–89, 135
    constitutional proposals, 109, 112, 142
    elections, 84, 135

Hindus, 57, 67, 85, 88, 96
land reforms, 85
Legislative Council, 31
ministry, 75, 84–86, 135
Muslim League, 84–85, 89–90, 96, 188–9, 192, 207
Muslims, 28, 31, 78, 88–89, 95–96, 109
National Agricultural Party, 84, 296
police, Muslims, in, 154, 160, 295
University education, 21, 36
Urdu language and script, 18, 40, 50, 97, 109, 275–7; Jinnah not familiar with, 11, 199, 294; campaign for substitution, 18, 91–92; protection of, 36, 82, 91–92, 97; newspapers in, 201; proposed as official language, 210–11
Usmanistan, 106
Utmanzai Wazirs, 245
Vedas, 21–22
Viceregal system, 279–300; as Pakistan's basic political system, 299–300
Viceroys, 251–2, 259, 279, 280, 284, 299
Viceroy's Executive Council: *see* Executive Council
Vidya Mandirs, 97, 287
Viqar-ul-Mulk, Nawab, 30, 34–35
Vivekananda, Swami, 21–22

Wahhabis, 14, 21
Waliullah, Shah, 3–4, 14, 21
Waqfs, Muslim, 36
War, First World, 32, 38–39, 44–46
War, Second World, 8, 98–99, 120–122, 126, 128–9, 181, 183, 284, 295
War Department, 303
War Transport, Department of, 304
Watkins, Frederick M., 259
Wavell, Lord, 9, 127–32, 135–6, 145, 147–62, 164–5, 243, 298
Waziristan, 245

Wellington, Lord, 20

West Bengal, 174

West Pakistan, 114, 298; and East Pakistan, 275–6; Islamic culture, 10; politics in, 216, 282–3; provinces, 280–1

West Punjab (province of Pakistan), administration, 239, 243–4, 248, 262, 264–6, 268–9; Assembly, 173; civil war: *see under* Punjab; civil servant shortage, 243–244, 260–2, 264, 267; communal war, 261–3; Governor, 241–3, 262, 268–9; land reforms, 266, 278; ministry, 218, 262, 268; politics in, 228, 262, 268, 299; refugees, 240, 261–8

Western culture and sciences, 14–17, 33, 35, 42, 74, 180, 283

Western powers, hostility to Muslims, 38, 42–43

Women, age of consent, 23; equal rights, 283

Woodhead Commission, 214–15

Works, Mines and Power, Department of, 302

Yar, Ahmad, 177

Yousuf, Sir Muhammad, 296

Yugantar (newspaper), 26

Yusuf, S. M., 245–6

Yusuf Ali, A., 17

Zamindar (newspaper), 44, 201

Zamindars, 53–55, 93–95, 210, 266

Zetland, Lord, 114

Ziarat, 269

Zinkin, Maurice, 161